Laos
a country study

Federal Research Division
Library of Congress
Edited by
Andrea Matles Savada
Research Completed
July 1994

959.4
L 298
1995

On the cover: Boats tied up on the Mekong River, at the foot of wide steps leading to Wat Xieng Thong in Louangphrabang

Third Edition, First Printing, 1995.

Library of Congress Cataloging-in-Publication Data

Laos: a country study / Federal Research Division, Library of Congress ; edited by Andrea Matles Savada.—3rd ed.
    p. cm. — (Area handbook series, ISSN 1057–5294) (DA Pam ; 550–58)
    "Supersedes the 1971 edition of Area Handbook for Laos.
    "Research completed July 1994."
    Includes bibliographical references (pp. 313–338) and index.
    ISBN 0–8444–0832–8
    1. Laos. I. Savada, Andrea Matles, 1950– . II. Library of Congress. Federal Research Division. III. Series. IV. Series: DA Pam ; 550–58
DS555.3.L34 1995   95–17235
951.93—dc20   CIP

Headquarters, Department of the Army
DA Pam 550–58

For sale by the Superintendent of Documents, U.S. Government Printing Office
Washington, D.C. 20402

Foreword

This volume is one in a continuing series of books prepared by the Federal Research Division of the Library of Congress under the Country Studies/Area Handbook Program sponsored by the Department of the Army. The last two pages of this book list the other published studies.

Most books in the series deal with a particular foreign country, describing and analyzing its political, economic, social, and national security systems and institutions, and examining the interrelationships of those systems and the ways they are shaped by cultural factors. Each study is written by a multidisciplinary team of social scientists. The authors seek to provide a basic understanding of the observed society, striving for a dynamic rather than a static portrayal. Particular attention is devoted to the people who make up the society, their origins, dominant beliefs and values, their common interests and the issues on which they are divided, the nature and extent of their involvement with national institutions, and their attitudes toward each other and toward their social system and political order.

The books represent the analysis of the authors and should not be construed as an expression of an official United States government position, policy, or decision. The authors have sought to adhere to accepted standards of scholarly objectivity. Corrections, additions, and suggestions for changes from readers will be welcomed for use in future editions.

Louis R. Mortimer
Chief
Federal Research Division
Library of Congress
Washington, DC 20540–5220

Acknowledgments

This edition supersedes the *Area Handbook for Laos*, published in 1971. Various members of the staff of the Federal Research Division of the Library of Congress assisted in the preparation of the book. Sandra W. Meditz made helpful suggestions during her review of all parts of the book. Robert L. Worden also reviewed parts of the book and made numerous suggestions and points of clarification. Tim L. Merrill checked the contents of all the maps and reviewed the sections on geography and telecommunications. Thomas D. Hall also assisted with some of the maps. Thanks also go to David P. Cabitto, who managed graphics production; Marilyn L. Majeska, who managed editing and production and edited portions of the manuscript; Andrea T. Merrill, who provided invaluable assistance with regard to tables and figures; and Barbara Edgerton, Alberta Jones King, and Izella Watson, who did the word processing.

The authors also are grateful to individuals in various United States government agencies who gave their time and special knowledge to provide information and perspective. These individuals include Ralph K. Benesch, who oversees the Country Studies/Area Handbook Program for the Department of the Army, and the staff of the Embassy of the Lao People's Democratic Republic to the United States.

Others who contributed were Joel Halpern, who reviewed the text and also offered many valuable suggestions and points of clarification; Ly Burnham, who reviewed the portions of the text on demography; Harriett R. Blood, who prepared the topography and drainage map; Maryland Mapping and Graphics, which prepared maps and charts; Teresa Kemp, who designed the cover and chapter art; Juliet Bruce, who edited chapters; Sheila L. Ross, who performed the final prepublication editorial review; Joan C. Cook, who compiled the index; and Stephen C. Cranton, David P. Cabitto, and Janie L. Gilchrist, who prepared the camera-ready copy. The inclusion of photographs was made possible by the generosity of individuals and the Embassy of the Lao People's Democratic Republic.

Contents

List of figures

Preface

This edition of *Laos: A Country Study* replaces the previous edition, published in 1971, prior to the establishment of the Lao People's Democratic Republic, which came into being in December 1975. Like its predecessor, this study attempts to review the history and treat in a concise manner the dominant social, political, economic, and military aspects of contemporary Laos.

Sources of information included books, scholarly journals, foreign and domestic newspapers, official reports of governments and international organizations, and numerous periodicals on Asian affairs. A word of caution is necessary, however. The government of a closed communist society such as Laos controls information for internal and external consumption, limiting both the scope of coverage and its dissemination. And, data from and on Laos are, on the whole, limited, and often contradictory.

Chapter bibliographies appear at the end of the book, and brief comments on some of the more valuable sources recommended for further reading appear at the end of each chapter. A glossary and chronology (see Table A) also are included.

• A word must also be offered on the use of the terms *Lao* and *Laotian.* The term *Lao* refers to people who are ethnic Lao; it is not used to refer to those living in Laos who are members of other ethnic groups, for example, Vietnamese, Chinese, or Hmong. The term *Laotian* is used to refer to all the people living in Laos, regardless of ethnic identity.

Spellings of place-names used in the book are in most cases those approved by the United States Board on Geographic Names. However, as internal divisions have been drawn and redrawn, place-names within Laos have also changed. Insofar as possible, the present volume reflects these changes.

Measurements are given in the metric system. A conversion table is provided to assist readers unfamiliar with metric measurements (see table 1, Appendix).

The body of the text reflects information available as of July 1, 1994. Certain other portions of the text, however, have been updated. The Introduction discusses significant events that have occurred since the completion of research, the Country Profile includes updated information as available, and the Bibliography lists recently published sources thought to be particularly helpful to the reader.

Table A. Chronology of Important Events

Period	Description
ca. 2,000 B.C.–A.D. 500	Early pottery and bronze culture, middle Mekong Valley.
First century B.C.–fifth century A.D.	Early *mandala* (see Glossary) formed in middle Mekong Valley.
Mid-sixth century	Zhenla established, centered on Champasak.
Early eighth century	Zhenla divided into "Water Zhenla" and "Land Zhenla."
717	First tributary mission from Land Zhenla to Tang China.
Eighth–twelfth centuries	Mon *mandala* of central Mekong region fall under Khmer domination; Theravada Buddhism spread by Mon monks.
Tenth–twelfth centuries	Muang Sua (Louangphrabang), renamed Xieng Dong Xieng Tong; *mandala* infiltrated by Lao descending the Nam Ou.
Twelfth century	Candapuri *mandala* in Vientiane region absorbed within Khmer Empire.
1271–72	Panya Lang rules Xieng Dong Xieng Thong.
1279	Tai *mandala* of Sukhotai founded by King Ramkhamhaeng; Xieng Dong Xieng Thong and Muang Vieng Chan Vieng Kham (Vientiane) briefly incorporated into Sukhotai *mandala*.
1353–73	Reign of Fa Ngum, king of Lan Xang; beginning of recorded Laotian history.
1373–1547	Successors of Fa Ngum continue to organize Lan Xang; Phetsarath (r. 1520–47) involves Lan Xang in battles against Burma and Siam lasting two centuries.
1574–78	Lan Xang reduced by Burma to vassal state.
1603	Lan Xang renounces tributary ties to Burma.
1621–1713	Succession struggles for throne of Lan Xang result in accession of King Souligna Vongsa (r. 1633–90); his death engenders succession struggle among his nephews, culminating in division of Lan Xang into kingdoms of Louangphrabang and Vientiane; south further divides into Kingdom of Champasak in 1713.
Eighteenth century	Lao states of Louangphrabang, Vientiane, and Champasak try to maintain independence from Burma and Siam but eventually come under Siamese control.
1772	Suryavong seizes throne of Louangphrabang.
1778	Beginning of Siamese domination of Champasak, Vientiane, and Louangphrabang.
1867–87	Mekong expedition of Doudart de Lagrée and Francis Garnier arrives in Louangphrabang, 1867; Siam contends with France, which establishes protectorate over Vietnam, to extend influence in Indochina; France eventually installs Auguste Pavie in Louangphrabang as first vice consul, February 1887.
1890	French colonial rule begins, lasts until 1953.
May 1893	French military occupation of Lao territories east of the Mekong.
July 1893	"Paknam incident" gives France excuse to demand cession of east bank territories.

Table A. Chronology of Important Events

Period	Description
October 1893	Treaty concluded on October 3, 1893, between the Government of the French Republic and the Government of His Majesty the King of Siam formalizes Siamese acceptance of French seizure of east bank territories.
1895	Laos, as French protectorate, divided into Upper Laos and Lower Laos.
January 15, 1896	Anglo-French Convention defines British and French spheres of influence in mainland Southeast Asia.
April 19, 1899	Laos reorganized under *résident supérieur* in Vientiane.
1902–07	France pacifies unrest in Bolovens Plateau; Sisavang Vong becomes king (r. 1904–59); annexation of Laotian territories completed by treaties with Siam (1904, 1907), acquiring borders of contemporary Laos.
1925–26	Further treaties and agreements finalize border questions and establish permanent Franco-Siamese High Commission of the Mekong.
June 5, 1930	Laos designated French colony by French Legislative Council.
1931–32	Louangphrabang confirmed as protectorate of France.
1940–45	August 30, 1940, Matsuoka-Henry Pact ending Franco-Thai War gives all Lao territories west of the Mekong to Thailand; May 9, 1941, Peace Convention between France and Thailand; August 29, 1941, Treaty of Protectorate between France and the Kingdom of Louangphrabang; Laos occupied by Japan, March 9, 1945; Laos "independent"; after surrender of Japan, Sisavang Vong proclaims continuation of Laos as a French protectorate; Lao Issara (see Glossary) activists seize power in Vientiane, Savannakhét, and other Laotian towns, establish provisional government.
1946	Sisavang Vong deposed; French begin reoccupation of Laos, March; Sisavang Vong reinstated as king by Lao Issara government; French retake Vientiane, and Lao Issara government flees to Thailand; Franco-Lao modus vivendi establishes unity of Kingdom of Laos; Thailand returns former Laotian territories of Xaignabouri and Champasak to Laos.
1947	Constitution promulgated, making Laos a constitutional monarchy; elections held for National Assembly; Prince Souvannarath forms government of Kingdom of Laos.
1949	Kaysone Phomvihan forms Latsavong detachment, armed forces of Pathet Lao, the genesis of Lao People's Liberation Army (LPLA); Franco-Lao General Convention grants Laos limited self-government within French Union; Lao Issara government-in-exile dissolves, and members return to Laos or join newly formed Pathet Lao on Vietnam border.
February 1950	United States and Britain recognize Laos as an Associated State in French Union.
August 1950	Pathet Lao form "resistance government."
February 1951	Indochinese Communist Party dissolves; separate parties established in Laos, Cambodia, and Vietnam.

Table A. Chronology of Important Events

Period	Description
October 22, 1953	Franco-Lao Treaty of Amity and Association transfers remaining French powers to Royal Lao Government (RLG)—while retaining control of military affairs—and completes independence of Laos.
May–July 1954	Laos participates in Geneva Conference on Indochina; under armistice agreements signed by French and Viet Minh on July 20, Viet Minh agree to withdraw from Laos, and Phôngsali and Houaphan provinces are designated regroupment areas for Pathet Lao; RLG pledges to integrate Pathet Lao fighters; International Control Commission established to implement agreements.
March 1955	Phak Pasason Lao (Lao People's Party—LPP) established; first congress held.
December 14, 1955	Laos admitted to the United Nations.
1956–57	Negotiations between RLG and Pathet Lao.
January 1956	Pathet Lao congress establishes Lao Patriotic Front (LPF).
September 1956	Constitution amended to allow formation of coalition government.
November 1957	First coalition government formed.
May 1958	LPF and allies win partial elections for National Assembly.
July 1958	Souvanna Phouma government resigns following cabinet crisis caused by rightists.
August 1958	Rightist government of Phoui Sananikone formed, excluding LPF.
July–August 1959	Fighting breaks out in northern Laos; UN subcommittee investigates charges of North Vietnam's involvement; LPF deputies arrested.
October 1959	King Sisavang Vong dies; Savang Vatthana succeeds to the throne, rules until 1975.
January 1960	Kou Abhay forms provisional government following coup attempt by army.
April 1960	Elections for National Assembly believed rigged.
August 9, 1960	Kong Le carries out successful Neutralist coup d'état against rightist government of Prince Somsanith; General Phoumi Nosavan forms countercoup committee in Savannakhét and declares martial law; Kong Le hands over power to Souvanna Phouma's third government.
December 1960	Phoumi Nosavan captures Vientiane; Soviet airlift begins to Kong Le and Pathet Lao troops.
January 1961	Souvanna Phouma government recognized by communist bloc; Prince Boun Oum's Vientiane government recognized by West; heavy fighting breaks out; North Vietnamese troops involved.
May 1961–June 1962	Second Geneva Conference on Laos; agreements among Neutralist, Pathet Lao, and rightist factions prepare way for second coalition government.
July 1962	Declaration on the Neutrality of Laos and its Protocol signed in Geneva.

Table A. Chronology of Important Events

Period	Description
1963–May 1964	Laos increasingly linked with developments in Vietnam; North Vietnamese troops fail to withdraw; Ho Chi Minh Trail expanded; second coalition government collapses; Pathet Lao offensive against Neutralists on Plain of Jars succeeds; International Control Commission proves ineffective; bombing by United States begins.
1968–74	Fighting escalates between Pathet Lao's LPLA and Royal Lao Army; Hmong under Vang Pao resist Pathet Lao-North Vietnamese advances; Second Party Congress held, 1972; LPP renamed Lao People's Revolutionary Party (LPRP); RLG and Pathet Lao begin negotiations for cease-fire in 1972, resulting in Vientiane Agreement signed in February 1973; cease-fire proclaimed, bombing by United States ends; protocol forming third coalition government signed September 1973; government takes office by royal decree April 1974 as Provisional Government of National Union.
August 1974–November 1975	Fighting resumes; Vang Pao flees to Thailand; senior rightist ministers and generals leave for Thailand; LPLA "liberates" provincial capitals; reeducation centers or "seminar camps" opened; "Revolutionary Administration" takes power in Vientiane; elections held for local people's councils.
December 1975	Provisional Government of National Union dissolved; King Savang Vatthana abdicates; Lao People's Democratic Republic (LPDR) proclaimed; Souphanouvong becomes first president (in power until 1991); Kaysone Phomvihan, first prime minister.
May 1976	LPRP Central Committee passes Third Resolution, guidelines for establishing the socialist revolution.
July 1977	Twenty-Five-Year Lao-Vietnamese Treaty of Friendship and Cooperation signed.
February 1979	Lao Front for National Construction established; replaces LPF.
January 1978	Interim three-year economic development plan begins.
January 1981	First Five-Year plan begins.
April 1982	Third LPRP Congress held.
May 1984	Constitution drafting committee named.
March 1985	First national population census taken.
January 1986	Second Five-Year Plan begins.
November 1986	Fourth LPRP Congress held; Kaysone Phomvihan general secretary LPRP; New Economic Mechanism formalizes reforms.
1988	First elections since 1975 held; at district level in June, provincial level in November.
1989	National elections held in March; delegates elected to first Supreme People's Assembly; opening session held May-June; last Vietnamese troops reportedly leave Laos.
April 1990	LPRP approves draft constitution for discussion.
March 1991	Fifth LPRP Congress held, Secretariat abolished; Kaysone Phomvihan chairman, LPRP; Souphanouvong retires.

Table A. Chronology of Important Events

Period	Description
August 1991	New constitution endorsed by Supreme People's Assembly and adopted; Kaysone Phomvihan becomes president of LPDR; Khamtai Siphandon, prime minister.
1992	Kaysone dies in November; replaced as president by Nouhak Phomsavan; Khamtai becomes chairman, LPRP, and prime minister, LPDR; elections to National Assembly (renamed Supreme People's Assembly) held in December.
1993	Nouhak and Khamtai reelected as president and prime minister in February; Council of Ministers reorganized.
1994	Phoumi Vongvichit, former acting president and high-ranking party figure, dies in January.

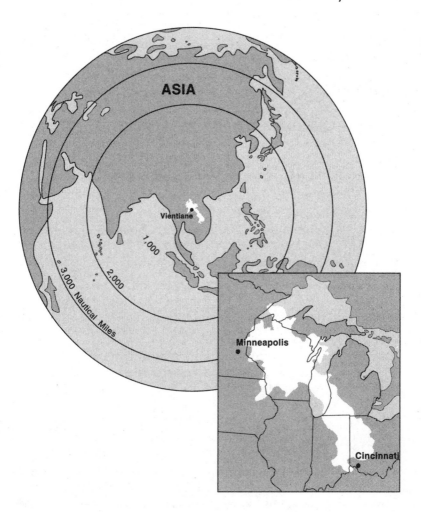

COUNTRY

Formal Name: Lao People's Democratic Republic (LPDR, or Laos).

Note—The country Profile contains updated information as available.

Short Form: Laos.

Term for Citizens: Laotian(s).

Capital: Vientiane.

Date of Independence: July 19, 1949, from France.

Geography

Location and Size: Landlocked nation of approximately 236,800 square kilometers in center of Southeast Asian peninsula, bordered by China to the north, Burma to the northwest, Thailand to the west, Vietnam to the east, and Cambodia to the south.

Land Boundaries: 5,083 kilometers total; Burma, 235 kilometers; Cambodia, 541 kilometers; China, 423 kilometers; Thailand, 1,754 kilometers; Vietnam, 2,130 kilometers. Most of western border demarcated by Mekong River.

Topography and Drainage: Largely mountainous, with elevations above 500 meters typically characterized by steep terrain and narrow river valleys. Only about 4 percent of total land area arable.

Climate: Tropical monsoon; rainy season from May through October, cool dry season from November through February, and hot dry season March and April.

Society

Population: Estimates vary; approximately 4.7 million in July 1994. Growth rate estimates range from 2.6 to 2.9 percent per year. More than 85 percent population rural, early 1990s. Approximately 9,000 Laotians—mostly Hmong—in refugee camps in Thailand according to United Nations Office of the High Commissioner for Refugees, January 1995; approximately 1,500 refugees in southern China, late 1994.

Ethnic Groups: Officially multiethnic nation with more than forty ethnic groups, classified into three general families: Lao Sung (upland Lao), 10 percent of population in 1993; Lao Theung (midland Lao), 24 percent; and Lao Loum (lowland Lao), 66 percent. The term *Laotian* is used for the national population; *Lao* for the ethnic group.

Language: Lao, official language; also French, English, various highland ethnic languages.

Religion: Provision for religious freedom in constitution; almost all Laotians Buddhist. Theravada Buddhism predominant among Lao Loum and some Lao Theung; animist beliefs widespread.

Education and Literacy: Universal, compulsory education after establishment of LPDR in 1975 but limited resources. Enrollments: estimated 603,000 primary school students, almost 130,000 secondary school students—including lower- and upper-secondary school—in 1992–93. Universal primary education goal for 2000. Nine-month school year includes five years primary school, three years lower-secondary school, and three years upper-secondary school. Those able to read and write estimated by United Nations at 84 percent (92 percent of men and 76 percent of women) ages fifteen to forty-five as of 1985; other figures cite only 45 percent total literacy; government acknowledges need for improved literacy.

Health: Health and health care poor. Chronic moderate vitamin and protein deficiencies common, especially among upland ethnic groups. Poor sanitation. Number of health care personnel increasing; concentrated in Vientiane area, where population per physician 1,400:1 versus national ratio of 10,000:2.6 in 1989. Birth rate 43.23 per 1,000; death rate 14.74 per 1,000 (1994 estimates). Life expectancy at birth 50.16 years male, 53.28 years female (1994 estimates).

Economy

General Character: Predominantly rural and agricultural; market-oriented economic liberalization measures beginning in 1986 stimulated economic growth. Policy reforms continue, including decentralizing and expanding private-sector economy; reversing agricultural collectivization policy and ending cooperatives; introducing foreign investment code; and restructuring banking system. Agriculture accounts for almost 56 percent gross domestic product (GDP) and approximately 85–90 percent of workforce (1993 estimate). Unemployment 21 percent (1989 estimate).

Gross Domestic Product (GDP): Estimates vary. US$989 million, US$295 per capita income (1993 estimate); from US$295 to US$335 per capita (1994 estimate); real growth rate from 4.5 percent to 5.9 percent. Composition of GDP:

agriculture and forestry, approximately 56 percent; industry including construction, approximately 17 percent; services, approximately 25 percent; and import duties, 2 percent (1993 estimate). GDP growth targeted at 7 percent for fiscal year (FY) 1993–94. US$4.1 billion purchasing power equivalent (1993 estimate).

Industry: Almost no industrial production outside Vientiane area.

Agriculture, Forestry, and Fishing: Rice main crop; corn, tobacco, coffee also grown.

Resources: Tin and gypsum most important mineral resources although exploitation on a small scale; electrical energy from hydroelectric power; electricity exported to Thailand.

Foreign Trade: Total exports US$133 million—free on board (f.o.b.) (1993 estimate); primarily to France, Germany, Japan, Russia, Thailand, Vietnam, and United States. Principal exports—timber and wood products, US$42 million; textiles and garments, US$27 million; assembled motorcycles and other items, US$20 million; electricity, US$16 million (1993 estimate). Total imports US$266 million—cost, insurance, and freight (c.i.f) (1992 estimate); primarily from China, France, Italy, Japan, Russia, Thailand, and Vietnam; increased by approximately 20.5 percent in 1993. Principal imports—petroleum, food, vehicles, machinery, consumer goods. US$353.2 million total (1993 estimate).

Balance of Payments: Record trade deficit of estimated US$150 million in 1993. Foreign debt US$1.1 billion (1992 estimate).

Foreign Aid: Approximately US$167 million in 1992. Almost totally dependent on foreign assistance for development and financing deficit on current account balance. Major foreign aid partners formerly communist countries, particularly Council for Mutual Economic Assistance (Comecon) members until 1990; since then, Australia, Japan, the Netherlands, Sweden, and multilateral agencies, primarily the World Bank and Asian Development Bank.

Currency and Exchange Rate: Kip (K). In 1992 exchange rate averaged US$1 = K705; in June 1994, estimated average US$1 =K721.

Fiscal Year: October 1 to September 30.

Transportation And Telecommunications

Roads, Railroads, and Ports: Landlocked; no ports, but some inland waterways, primarily on Mekong River and its tributaries. Poorly developed road system although greater infrastructure development, particularly as result of foreign aid; few reliable transportation routes because of mountainous topography and lack of development. No railroad system although memorandum signed with Thailand in November 1994 to conduct six-month survey on possibility of construction of railroad from middle of Friendship Bridge connecting Laos and Thailand to a station in Laos.

Civil Aviation: Lao Aviation, state airline. Wattai Airport, Vientiane, planned for upgrade to international standard. Louangprabang Airport targeted for refurbishment and expansion beginning May 1994. Lao People's Army building new airport in Oudômxai. Main international routes to Bangkok, Guangzhou, Hanoi, Ho Chi Minh City, Kunming, and Phnom Penh. Limited internal air service includes flights to Louangphrabang, Pakxé, Savannakhét, Vientiane, and Xiangkhoang.

Telecommunications: Limited domestic and international telecommunications links. Four government-owned television channels (1994); ten medium-wave AM radio stations, seven short-wave AM radio stations, and one FM radio station (1994). One ground satellite station linked to Intersputnik system (1994); all other international telecommunications go by antiquated high-frequency radio to Hong Kong and short-wave link to Bangkok (1987). Approximately 8,000 telephones, largely limited to government users in capital (1986).

Government And Politics

Government: Lao People's Democratic Republic proclaimed December 2, 1975, abolishing monarchy of Royal Lao Government. New constitution unanimously endorsed by unicameral eighty-five-member Supreme People's Assembly, August 14, 1991; renamed National Assembly (1992); exercises power according to principle of democratic centralism. National Assembly elected December 1992; inaugural session,

February 1993. As legislative organ, oversees judiciary and activities of administration. President head of state, elected by National Assembly for five-year term; also commander in chief of armed forces. Council of Ministers highest executive organ; chairman is prime minister; vice chairmen oversee work of ministers. Real power exercised by members of the ruling party, Lao People's Revolutionary Party (LPRP), particularly Political Bureau (Politburo) and Central Committee.

Politics: LPRP only legal party. Party conference held late November 1993 to include representatives of provincial party units, Central Committee members, secretaries of party committees in ministries, departments, factories, and schools. Speeches on neglect of party activities and quality of membership hint at concern with corruption and need to build party at grass-roots level.

Judiciary: Comprises Supreme People's Court, provincial and municipal courts, people's district courts, and military courts.

Administrative Divisions: Divided into sixteen provinces (*khoueng*): Attapu, Borikhan, Bokeo, Champasak, Houaphan, Khammouan, Louang Namtha, Louangphrabang, Oudômxai, Phôngsali, Saravan, Savannakhét, Xaignabouri, Xekong, Xiangkhoang, and Vientiane; one municipality (*kampheng nakhon*), Vientiane; two special zones, Xaisomboun in northeastern Vientiane Province (established June 1994), and Xianghon-Hôngsa, formerly two districts in Xaignabouri Province (established mid-1992); districts (*muang*); and villages (*ban*).

Foreign Affairs: "Special relationship"—twenty-five-year mutual security treaty signed 1977—with Vietnam continues, although intensity lessening. Relations with Thailand—primary economic partner, particularly in hydroelectricity—improved after period of distrust punctuated by border clashes. Increased intra-regional ties; observer status, Association of Southeast Asian Nations (ASEAN), since 1992. United States granted Laos national interest waiver in April 1994 for counternarcotics cooperation; determined necessary for continued cooperation on issue of unaccounted-for United States military personnel.

National Security

Armed Forces: Total strength approximately 37,000 in 1994:

33,000 Lao People's Army; 3,500 Lao People's Air Force; 500 Lao People's Navy. Approximately 49,000 reach military age annually (1994 estimate).

Internal Security Forces: Paramilitary self-defense force, or Irregular People's Army, acts as lightly armed local defense force organized at provincial level for territorial defense and at local levels. Most members retired military personnel; approximately 100,000 persons. Also acts as reserve for regular armed forces. Police force under jurisdiction of Ministry of Interior.

Major Equipment and Military Expenditures: End of military support from Russia and Vietnam combined with lack of domestic funding inhibits needed modernization of aging equipment, much of it from former Soviet Union and Vietnam. Military expenditures—including public security budget—approximately US$104.9 million (1993 estimate). Degenerating capabilities because of poor state of equipment and personnel skills.

Figure 1. Administrative Divisions of Laos, 1994

Introduction

A LANDLOCKED NATION in the center of the Southeast Asian peninsula, the country that is now the Lao People's Democratic Republic (LPDR, or Laos), is bordered by Cambodia, China, Burma, Thailand, and Vietnam (only Cambodia is smaller), neighbors which, to varying degrees, have influenced Laotian historical, cultural, and political development. Slightly smaller than the state of Oregon, Laos is largely mountainous and forested; only about 4 percent of its total land area is arable. The tropical monsoon climate is a major determining factor in agricultural productivity and transportation.

Laos was inhabited five or more millennia ago by Austroasiatic peoples. From the first century A.D., princely fiefdoms based on wet rice cultivation and associated with the pottery and bronze culture of Ban Chiang developed in the middle Mekong Valley. Various other kingdoms reflecting the cultures of Cham and Mon peoples existed in the region; the fiefdoms were subject to the influence of *mandala* (see Glossary) in the central Mekong region. Migrations in the seventh century continued to expand both the various influences and the cultural mix of the region. By the eighth century, the Mon *mandala* were under Khmer domination.

Beginning in the thirteenth century, Mongols exercised a decisive political influence in the middle Mekong Valley; dynastic conflicts associated with their intervention led to the founding of the Kingdom of Lan Xang (Kingdom of the Million Elephants). At that time, the beginnings of a multiethnic state—in the configuration of small confederative communities—were evident. The recorded history of Laos began in the fourteenth century with Fa Ngum (r. 1354–73), the first king of Lan Xang. Under Fa Ngum, the territory of Lan Xang was extended; it remained in these approximate borders for another 300 years.

The reign of King Souligna Vongsa (r. 1633–90)—a time when the kingdom was united and ruled by its own king—has been referred to as the golden age of Laos. With the death of Souligna Vongsa, however, succession struggles led to the division of Lan Xang. Conflicts with Burma, Siam, Vietnam, and the Khmer kingdom continued in the eighteenth century, culminating in Siamese domination.

Early in the nineteenth century, Siam held hegemony over much of the territory of contemporary Laos, which then consisted of the principalities of Louangphrabang, Vientiane, and Champasak. Siam faced contention from France—which had established a protectorate over Vietnam—and sought to extend its influence in Indochina. By the end of the nineteenth century, France had supplanted Siam as the dominant power. Laos was integrated into the French colonial empire of Indochina as a group of directly ruled provinces, except for Louangphrabang, which was ruled as a protectorate.

Laos remained under French administration from about 1890 until World War II, when Japan occupied French Indochina. Japanese military authorities induced King Sisavong Vong of Louangphrabang to declare the independence of his kingdom from France in April 1945, prior to Japan's surrender in the war. In September 1945, an "independent" government under the Lao Issara (Free Laos—see Glossary) defied the king and declared the union of Vientiane and Champasak with Louangphrabang. The following year, French troops reoccupied the country, conferring limited autonomy on the unified Kingdom of Laos within the French Union. A constitution was promulgated in 1947, and elections were held for a National Assembly. The independence of Laos was formally recognized within the French Union in 1949; Laos remained a member of the union until 1953.

The 1954 Geneva Conference on Indochina provided for the cessation of hostilities in Cambodia, Laos, and Vietnam—the first Indochina War—the struggle for independence against French colonial forces, and the withdrawal of foreign forces. The Royal Lao Government (RLG—see Glossary) agreed to include the Pathet Lao (Lao Nation—see Glossary; Pathet Lao became the generally accepted term for the communist-led guerrilla movement) in the government coalition. Phôngsali and Houaphan (Sam Neua) provinces were designated areas of regroupment for Pathet Lao forces, "pending a political settlement."

Negotiations between the RLG and the Pathet Lao continued from 1955 to 1957. The Neo Lao Hak Xat (Lao Patriotic Front—LPF; superseded by the Lao Front for National Construction in 1979), established in 1956, served as a political front for the Pathet Lao and was secretly guided by the Lao People's Party, which was established in 1955 as part of the Indochinese Communist Party. In 1972 the Lao People's Party changed its name to the Lao People's Revolutionary Party (LPRP). Since 1975 it has been the ruling party.

A coalition government, including some Pathet Lao personalities, was formed by Prince Souvanna Phouma in 1957. It collapsed the following year, and rightist politicians took over. United States aid increased greatly. The communist insurgency resumed in northern Laos in 1959.

In 1960 Kong Le, a young Royalist paratroop captain, led a coup d'état to install a Neutralist government under Souvanna Phouma—neither rightist nor Pathet Lao—which would end the fratricidal fighting. But within a year, rightist forces under General Phoumi Nosavan drove Souvanna Phouma's government from Vientiane. The Neutralists then naively allied themselves with the Pathet Lao and received airlift support from the Soviet Union. North Vietnamese troops intervened in Laos in regular units for the first time, inflicting heavy losses on the rightists receiving military and economic aid from the United States.

A Second Geneva Conference on Laos was held in 1961–62. Agreements provided for the independence and neutrality of Laos—something realized only on paper. A second coalition government formed in July 1962 proved to be equally short-lived. The civil war quickly resumed and continued into the 1970s, with each side—backed either by the United States or Vietnam (supported by the Soviet Union)—trading accusations of violating the agreements. Souvanna Phouma, prime minister in the first coalition government in 1957, again following Kong Le's coup in 1960, and again in July 1962 following that year's Geneva agreements, became prime minister of a third coalition government, or Provisional Government of National Union, with the participation of the LPF in 1974. (He resigned upon the establishment of the LPDR in 1975.)

The collapse of South Vietnam and Cambodia in mid-1975 played into the hands of the LPF and hastened the decline of the third coalition government. The LPRP, the mastermind behind the Lao Patriotic Front, dismissed the Provisional Government of National Union and persuaded King Savang Vatthana to abdicate.

The Lao People's Democratic Republic was proclaimed on December 2, 1975, ending the era of a conservative monarchy dominated by a few powerful families. Souphanouvong became the first president of the LPDR. A half-brother of Souvanna Phouma, cousin of Savang Vatthana, one of the original founders of the Neo Lao Hak Xat, and the titular head of the LPF, Souphanouvong was known as the "red prince" because of his royal lineage and communist associations. The LPDR has been a single-party communist government since its proclamation.

Ethnically diverse, Laos has more than forty ethnic groups. *Lao* is the distinction for some of the ethnic groups; *Laotian* is the term used to refer to all people of Laos, or the national population. The Lao, descendants of the Tai peoples who began migrating from China in the first millennium A.D., constitute approximately half the people of Laos. Although government rhetoric celebrates the multiethnic nature of the nation and asserts that it wishes to reduce the favoritism historically extended toward the "lowland" Lao Loum (see Glossary) and the discrimination against the "midland" Lao Theung (see Glossary) and "upland" Lao Sung (see Glossary), the ethnic minorities are underrepresented in the LPRP Central Committee, the National Assembly, and in government offices. (Some of the ethnic minorities have populations of only a few hundred persons.)

Although the different ethnic groups have different residential patterns, agricultural practices, and religious beliefs, for all groups the village community has a kinship nexus, which may also differ in form. The mountainous topography, which has inhibited roadbuilding and limited exchanges among villages and ethnic groups, has contributed to maintaining distinctions among ethnic groups.

Buddhism was the state religion of the Kingdom of Laos; the present constitution formally proclaims religious freedom. Although many communist nations do not look favorably upon the practice of religion—constitutional stipulations notwithstanding—this is not necessarily the case in Laos, where approximately 85 percent of citizens are Buddhist. Theravada Buddhism is predominant among the Lao Loum and some Lao Theung groups; animist beliefs are widespread among the entire population. The *wat*, the Buddhist temple or monastery complex, is a central fixture of village life, and the site of major religious festivals, which occur several times a year. Since the LPDR's establishment in 1975, the government has attempted to manipulate Buddhism to support its political goals, although without provoking a schism in the *sangha*, or clergy.

The population as of mid-1994 was estimated at approximately 4.7 million people. The population growth rate is relatively high—estimated at approximately 2.9 percent per year. But, child and infant mortality rates are also high, and life expectancy averages less than fifty-two years. Laos has a relatively low population density; more than 85 percent of the population is rural, living in small villages of typically fewer than 1,000 people. Rural life is tied to the changing agricultural seasons. Of the "urban" areas, most people live in the Mekong River valley towns and those of its tributaries. Vientiane, the capital and largest city, is also the center of a very limited industrial sector. The reach of recent economic reforms—and the change and opportunity they offer—has not extended much beyond the Vientiane plain.

Education and social services are rudimentary, although some improvements have been made. The LPDR has made a commitment to five years of universal primary education, but limited financial resources and a lack of trained teachers and teaching materials have restricted educational opportunities. Enrollments have increased, however. Western health care is largely confined to the more "urban" areas, dictated in part by the difficulties of transportation. Similarly, improvements in health care are constrained by finances and the limited numbers of trained health care workers.

Presenting a clear quantitative economic profile of Laos is complicated by the lack of recent (or other) statistics, as well as by reliability, as there are internal contradictions in many statistics. Nonetheless, Laos is clearly one of the poorest countries in the world, with per capita GNP estimates ranging from US$295 to US$350 per annum. A rural, subsistence, agricultural economy heavily influenced by weather—that is, conditions of drought or flood—Laos still has not met self-sufficiency in food production. LPDR officials frequently note that Laos remains "underdeveloped," has a largely unskilled work force, and needs infrastructure development. Such advancements are recognized as particularly important in such fields as agro-forestry and hydropower, two areas with potentially high foreign exchange earnings. Imports far outpace exports. Even primary exports—hydroelectricity, timber, and coffee—are limited. The potential for the exportation of mineral resources, particularly tin and gypsum, has not yet been realized.

Centralized economic measures of a command economy were instituted when the LPDR was proclaimed in 1975. Beginning with the New Economic Mechanism in 1986, however, and with various other reform measures since then, Laos has opened up to market forces. The government has also encouraged both foreign and domestic investment—especially for the private sector. Reforms have abolished agricultural cooperatives, privatized most state enterprises while encouraging private-sector initiatives, and revised the taxation system. Although still dominated by the agricultural sector, the economy has been stimulated and the availability of goods has increased. However, Laos remains dependent on continued foreign aid and concessional loans.

As it came to power in late 1975 on the coattails of communist victories in Vietnam and Cambodia, the LPDR naturally turned to the communist bloc for economic support and received aid from both the Soviet bloc countries and China. Since the collapse of the Soviet Union, however, Soviet bloc aid has halted and Vietnamese patronage has diminished, necessitating a search for other investors and aid donors.

The situation with regard to economic assistance from Russia has begun to change. During 1994 Laos and Russia signed two cooperation agreements. In March the Lao National Council of Trade and Industry and the Russian Council of Trade and Industry signed documents on scientific and technical cooperation. Laos will receive technical assistance from Russia and funds from third countries, the International Monetary Fund (IMF—see Glossary), and interested businessmen for programs to protect the environment, conserve and restore forests, raise harvest efficiency, eradicate crop pests, and increase mining and exploration efforts. In August, Laos signed a trade protocol with Russia for economic and trade cooperation. According to its terms, Laos will buy construction materials, electric appliances, spare parts for aircraft, and other items; Russia will purchase tin, coffee, tropical wood products, and clothing from Laos.

In the early 1990s, Laos received increased aid from Japan and from Western nations—including Australia, France, and Sweden—as well as increased support from international and regional organizations. Foreign assistance in 1993–94 was estimated at US$211.7 million, of which US$141.4 million was gratis aid and US$70.3 million was in the form of loans bearing low interest rates.

Assistance from the World Bank (see Glossary), the IMF, and the Asian Development Bank has both guided and been predicated upon reform measures. Their programs, however, have tended to be concentrated in Vientiane and the Mekong Valley centers, with improvements in infrastructure thus benefitting only the urban areas; rural areas have lagged behind on the developmental scale.

The LPDR's Socio-economic Development Plan 1993–2000 emphasizes the production of foodstuffs, commercial products, rural development, human resources development, and the exploitation of natural resources in conjunction with concerted efforts to protect the environment. It also calls for an expansion of economic relations and cooperation with the outside world. The importance of infrastructure development is also recognized. Roadbuilding is seen as strategically important for socioeconomic development—especially with regard to programs for public health and education—particularly for rural areas and areas inhabited by ethnic minorities. The Public Investment Programme (PIP), a part of the plan, is to be supported by donors for as much as US$1.4 billion. PIP targets include irrigating unused land, planting forests, and moving away from subsistence production and slash-and-burn agriculture toward sedentary market agriculture and a more diversified economy.

As elsewhere, foreign and economic relations are linked; for Laos, this is particularly true with regard to Thailand, its primary trading and investment partner. Laos and Thailand must constantly negotiate a variety of political and economic issues, including the status of Lao refugees and refugee camps in Thailand as well as LPDR claims that Thailand is sheltering Lao insurgents. Laos has pressed for additional border crossing points and clearer border demarcation; free and fair competition in providing transport services for cross-border trade; cooperation in various economic and technical projects and joint trade and investment enterprises; and cooperation between banks and customs services. Thailand is the primary purchaser of timber and hydroelectricity from the LPDR; the export of hydroelectric power is paradoxical given the low level of electrification in Laotian villages.

Notwithstanding several border incidents in the late 1980s, relations between Laos and Thailand have improved over the past decade. More recently, the April 1994 opening of the Friendship Bridge linking the two countries has provided for greater commercial potential—increased trade, tourism, and transit. And, in July 1994, a joint venture agreement was signed to allow a Thai company to build and develop a special economic zone—with nine projects—in Vientiane Municipality.

The two countries have also agreed in principle to establish consular missions outside each others' capitals. Insurgent raids in rural areas, primarily from the Hmong, but also from smaller Lao resistance groups based in Thailand, complicate Lao-Thai relations and are an annoyance, but not a threat, to the stability of Laos.

The improved investment climate in Laos has also raised the possibility of building a rail line; currently there is none. In November 1994, Thailand was granted permission to conduct a six-month feasibility study on a railway line between Vientiane and Nong Khai, Thailand, via the Friendship Bridge. Forty-two percent of the cost of the survey will be paid by the British government, the remainder by a Thai company. If it is found economically feasible to develop a railway, and the Thai company decides to invest in its construction, the National Railway Company, Limited, of Laos will be established. The LPDR will hold 25 percent of the railroad company, the Thai company the remaining 75 percent.

As noted, the LPDR was established following communist party victories in Vietnam and Cambodia. Similarities with other one-party communist states exist. The party dominates the government and still operates under relative secrecy. High-ranking party members occupy high-level posts in the government, military, and mass organizations, and there is a distinct overlap of military personnel. In fact, the ministers of interior, agriculture and forestry, and national defense are army generals, as is the prime minister. At the third congress of the Lao People's Revolutionary Youth Union held in May 1994, 214 of 247 delegates were LPRP members.

Even though the party's role and powers are scarcely mentioned in the constitution, the LPRP determines national policies through its nine-member Political Bureau (Politburo) and fifty-two-member Central Committee. A constitution was not adopted until 1991—sixteen years after the LPDR's founding. The executive branch retains the authority to issue binding decrees, but the party retains the power to make critical decisions.

The legislative branch is by constitutional provision the highest organ of state. Elections are held by secret ballot. The first elections to the Supreme People's Assembly were held in March 1989, almost fourteen years after the LPDR's proclamation; the opening session was in May–June. Elections to the National Assembly (the renamed Supreme People's Assembly) for five-year terms were held in December 1992; the first session did not convene until February 1993. Although more than 150 candidates vied for eighty-five seats in the assembly, most candidates belong to the LPRP—as it is the only legal party—and most are approved by the LPRP prior to the elections. Although the National Assembly seemed to be playing a larger role in the passage of legislation in the early 1990s, in reality the assembly merely "discusses and endorses" all laws in controlled policy debates during the twice-yearly plenary sessions.

The LPRP grew from approximately 25,000 members at its inception in 1975 to approximately 60,000 members at the time of the Fifth Party Congress in March 1991. (By contrast, in 1993 there were more than 70,000 Lao Federation of Trade Union members.) During the Fifth Party Congress, the LPRP removed several elder statesmen from the Politburo and elected some slightly younger cadres to a new Central Committee. The party is not immune to internal criticism and has acknowledged official corruption (and nepotism) as a serious and continuing problem.

Formal avenues of information and communication have been limited by lack of funds since French colonial rule and are now tightly controlled. Dissemination of information is sporadic and further restricted by controls on the distribution of printing materials. Radio and television services are also monopolized by the party. Broadcasts from Thailand, however, have a large audience in Laos.

Broad security measures limit freedoms as under other communist regimes; freedoms may be guaranteed in the constitution, but in reality they are quite restricted. After the communist victory in 1975, many members of the previous Royal Lao Government and military who had remained in the country instead of fleeing were placed in reeducation centers or "seminar camps." "Social deviants" as well as political opponents were held in these centers; these camps have been closed and most "political prisoners" have since been released. However, Amnesty International continues to press for the release of persons still in detention.

After the LPRP seized power, and during its consolidation of the government, some 350,000 persons—of whom many were Hmong belonging to Vang Pao's United States-funded irregulars—fled the country. Many persons remained in refugee camps in Thailand; some departed from there to third countries; still others resided in southern China. The refugee situation has recently changed significantly.

Although there are variations in the numbers of refugees repatriated and/or remaining in the camps according to the sources reporting, it can be said that a significantly larger number of refugees have been repatriated or resettled in a third country compared with those who remain in Thailand. The United Nations Office of the High Commissioner for Refugees (UNHCR—see Glossary) began a voluntary repatriation program in 1980. Ten years later, fewer than 6,000 refugees had been repatriated under UNHCR supervision. Approximately 15,000 refugees had returned to Laos independently, and the vast majority—approximately 300,000—had resettled abroad. In 1989 there were an estimated 90,000 Lao refugees in Thailand; as of June 1991, an estimated 60,000 refugees remained. This number was further reduced by half at the end of 1993. As of January 1995, UNHCR estimates were that only 9,000 refugees, mainly Hmong, remained in Thai camps. Vientiane estimated that the more than 8,000 refugees remaining in Thailand at the end of 1994 would be repatriated by the end of 1995. Laos, Thailand, and the UNHCR have agreed to resettle or repatriate all remaining Lao refugees by the end of 1995.

The foreign relations of Laos have in large part been determined by the country's physical location and its desire to maintain national security. During the communist revolutionary struggle in Indochina, Laos had close ties with Vietnam—a "special relationship"—which was formalized by a twenty-five-year treaty of friendship and cooperation signed in 1977. More recently, Laos has sought to improve relations with China, an ally during the Indochina Wars, but with whom relations deteriorated following the 1979 China-Vietnam conflict. Trade between the two countries has increased, and Laos has received some economic and military aid. In May 1994, a high-level LPDR military delegation paid an official visit to China to promote relations of friendship and "all-around solidarity between the two armies."

The end of the Cold War, concomitant with the limited ability of the former Soviet bloc and Vietnam to offer economic assistance, has influenced the LPDR to become more flexible in its foreign policy in the 1990s. Since 1992 Laos has held observer status with the Association of Southeast Asian Nations (ASEAN—see Glossary); this has been viewed as a likely precursor to membership in that organization. And, despite various cooperation projects with the Democratic People's Republic of Korea (North Korea) during the 1980s, in January 1994 Laos contracted with a Republic of Korea (South Korea) construction company to build a hydropower dam on the Ho River in Champasak Province. Laos resumed diplomatic relations with Israel in December 1993. The LPDR minister of foreign affairs visited Israel in August 1994; and Israel has agreed to provide training grants to LPDR officials. In September 1994, Laos established diplomatic relations with South Africa and Lithuania.

Diplomatic relations between the United States and Laos were maintained upon the proclamation of the LPDR in 1975, and the two countries have seen a slow, but steady, improvement in relations since 1982. Two key—and intertwining—components have dominated the United States relationship with Laos: accounting for those Americans classified as prisoners of war (POW) or missing in action (MIA) at the end of the Indochina Wars, and controlling the growth of, and trafficking in, narcotics. Cooperation in one area begets cooperation in the other.

As a measure of sincerity for improving relations, the United States has sought greater LPDR cooperation in providing information on the fate of POW/MIAs and in searching for their remains. As of September 1994, thirty-three joint missions of field searches and excavations of crash sites had been conducted. In August 1994, the two sides agreed to carry out six joint field activities in the future, and the United States was permitted to increase the number of personnel on its teams. In counternarcotics cooperation, Laos agreed to step up its efforts to combat the cultivation, production, and transshipment of opium, heroin, and marijuana. Crop substitution programs in conjunction with the United States and the United Nations Development Programme, as well as narcotics training programs and improved law enforcement measures, have been instituted. In 1994, after four years of United States certification (with explanation) for counternarcotics cooperation, Laos was granted a national interest waiver in lieu of full certification because of poor counternarcotics performance. (Certification is dependent on counternarcotics cooperation either with the United States or with the LPDR taking steps on its own to achieve full compliance with the goals and objectives of the 1988 United Nations Convention on Illicit Traffic in Narcotic Drugs and Psychotropic Substances). In 1995 Laos was again certified as cooperating fully. If the United States were to deny certification, continued efforts in counternarcotics cooperation and cooperation in POW/MIA accounting would be jeopardized. Counternarcotics efforts have made limited progress, constrained in part by limited training, management and administrative skills, and law enforcement, as well as by LPDR finances and higher priorities. A decline in opium production in the 1993–94 growing season was a result of adverse weather rather than decreased areas under cultivation.

The LPDR is poorly equipped in the national security arena, and the need for modernization is evident. Constrained by its economic limitations and foreign assistance geared toward economic (primarily infrastructure) improvements, the Lao People's Army has been unable either to modernize its outdated equipment or to elevate the level of training.

The primary mission of the armed forces has been to maintain national defense and public security, political stability, and social order. However, national defense objectives and the security environment have changed. The armed forces are no longer fighting a war of national liberation, although their wartime exploits are still extolled in the official media. Domestic opposition is contained by the police and a system of party control. External opposition, in particular resistance elements based in Thailand, is limited. Each of these factors has contributed to a reduction in the size of the armed forces in the 1990s. In 1991 there were approximately 55,000 persons in the armed forces; by 1994 armed forces personnel reportedly totaled 37,000.

The armed forces now have the additional assignment of contributing to socioeconomic and rural development, with the aim of achieving greater self-sufficiency. Thus, the military is ordered to check and boost crop cultivation and monitor livestock transport; grow vegetables for daily meals; and create favorable conditions for promoting poultry and fish breeding. In 1989 the Corporation for Agro-Forestry Development and Service was established. Connected to the Ministry of National Defense, the corporation is responsible for improving and building the agricultural base and engaging in public security activities in three southern districts of Xaignabouri Province. In the five years since its establishment, the corporation has repaired and paved roads and built irrigation systems. In another venue, the Lao People's Army began a joint venture in 1994 with the Chinese People's Liberation Army to produce pharmaceuticals for the Lao People's Army as well as for domestic and foreign markets.

The military relationship with Vietnam has also evolved. In July 1994, it was noted that the Political and Military Institute of the People's Army of Vietnam had accepted more than 400 students from the LPDR since 1978. Nonetheless, Laos cannot rely on Vietnam for military assistance and equipment to the extent it had previously.

Since its inception in December 1975, the LPDR has been notable for its remarkable stability and continuity. For almost twenty years, the same few men have been in power. The leadership core, an elite group of founding members of the LPRP, hold key positions in the party, government, and military organs. The majority of the members of the Politburo and the Central Committee are people who participated in the revolutionary struggle.

In the early 1990s, the deaths of high-ranking leaders—a natural consequence of an aging leadership—have meant a reshuffling of positions. Of note is the fact that no power struggles were in evidence. Rather, leaders simply moved up in rank. The death in November 1992 of Kaysone Phomvihan, who had been active since the 1940s in the resistance forces, then proclaimed the LPDR's first prime minister, and finally elected president in 1991, left no gap in the leadership. Nouhak Phomsavan was elected to the largely ceremonial position of president. A close comrade of Kaysone, and similarly a veteran of the revolution, Nouhak was a former minister of finance and a deputy prime minister. Nouhak will be eighty-one years old in April 1995. Khamtai Siphandon, another leader in the early resistance efforts, and a former minister of national defense (1975–91) and deputy prime minister, moved up to the prime minister's post in 1991. Supposedly ten years younger than Nouhak, Khamtai's "youth" was seen by some as the reason for his appointment to the more active role of prime minister.

Other elder statesmen also died in the early 1990s. Former Politburo member Phoumi Vongvichit, acting president of the LPDR from the retirement of Souphanouvong in 1986—until his own retirement in 1991—died in January 1994. Among other Politburo members who have died are deputy prime minister Phoun Sipraseut, who was also chief of the Foreign Relations Committee, LPRP Central Committee, and "official in charge of guiding foreign affairs" (and former minister of foreign affairs), who died in December 1994; Somlat Chanthamat, who died in 1993; Sisomphon Lovansai, who died in 1993; and Sali Vongkhamsao, who died in 1991. Some of these leaders had already retired and held largely ceremonial posts at the time of their death.

Coming full circle, with a royalist heritage but communist sympathies, was Prince Souphanouvong. President from the founding of the LPDR until he withdrew for health reasons in 1986, his position was not officially relinquished until March 1991 at the Fifth Party Congress, when he was also removed from the Politburo. His death in January 1995 ended the last direct link between the monarchy established in the mid-fourteenth century by Fa Ngum and the single-party communist regime, that is the LPDR. (Two of Souphanouvong's sons, however, are active in the government, one in the Ministry of Finance, the other in the Social Science Commission.)

Almost twenty years after the LPDR's founding, Laos is, once again, as during many prior kingdoms, dominated by a small and powerful elite marked by nepotism. The country will have to deal with several significant issues in the years ahead even as the remaining aging leaders continued to govern in early 1995 as a cohesive group without active opposition. These issues include: How effectively will the LPDR use the assistance proffered by various international banks, friendly aid donors, and foreign investors? How will Laos deal with its considerable economic potential but also considerable educational deficits? When will students begin to seek greater opportunities for advancement outside the single-party system? Will the party remain in full control and will there be a regularized political succession? These are but some of the issues regarding the future direction of Laos as the nation responds to the challenges presented by economic reform and progress.

March 1, 1995

*   *   *

Since the Introduction was written, the work of the party and government have continued as usual. The sixth ordinary session of the National Assembly closed and the tenth plenary session of the LPRP's Fifth Central Committee was held. The National Assembly endorsed a ministerial reshuffle involving lateral personnel changes. Meetings between the foreign ministers of Laos and Thailand discussed the need to resolve the still unsettled 1987 border dispute.

Of economic significance, was the April 5 signing of the Agreement on Cooperation for the Sustainable Development of the Mekong River Basin. The agreement, supported by the United Nations Development Programme, replaces a 1957 pact among Laos, Cambodia, Thailand, and Vietnam, and took two years to negotiate. The agreement establishes the Mekong River Commission as an institutional body and legal framework with which to promote basin-wide studies and joint development projects in the lower Mekong River basin; China and Burma are expected to join the commission at some point. Five areas of cooperation have been delineated: hydropower generation, irrigation, fisheries, navigation, and tourism. Plans for a series of dams on the Mekong, however, have been contested by various environmental groups although the agreement purportedly takes environmental protection into account.

April 26, 1995

*   *   *

On May 12, 1995, the United States removed Laos from its list of countries prohibited from receiving foreign assistance funds for reasons of national interest, making development aid an option.

June 22, 1995   Andrea Matles Savada

Chapter 1. Historical Setting

Detail from a door of Wat Ba Khe in Louangphrabang shows courtier blowing conch shell.

HISTORICAL RESEARCH SHOWS that the rudimentary structures of a multiethnic state existed before the founding of the Kingdom of Lan Xang in the thirteenth century. These pre-thirteenth-century structures consisted of small confederative communities in river valleys and among the mountain peoples, who found security away from the well-traveled rivers and overland tracks where the institutions and customs of the Laotian people were gradually forged in contact with other peoples of the region. During these centuries, the stirring of migrations as well as religious conflict and syncretism went on more or less continuously. Laos's short-lived vassalage to foreign empires such as the Cham, Khmer, and Sukhothai did nothing to discourage this process of cultural identification and, in fact, favored its shaping.

In the thirteenth century—an historically important watershed—the rulers of Louangphrabang (Luang Prabang) constituted a large indigenous kingdom with a hierarchical administration. Even then, migratory and religious crosscurrents never really ceased. The durability of the kingdom itself is attested to by the fact that it lasted within its original borders for almost four centuries. Today, the Lao People's Democratic Republic (LPDR, or Laos) covers only a small portion of the territory of that former kingdom.

Internecine power struggles caused the splitting up of Lan Xang after 1690, and the Lao and the mountain peoples of the middle Mekong Valley came perilously close to absorption by powerful neighboring rivals, namely Vietnam and Siam (present-day Thailand); China never posed a territorial threat. Only the arrival of the French in the second half of the nineteenth century prevented Laos's political disintegration. In a "conquest of the hearts" (in the words of the explorer and colonist Auguste Pavie)—a singular event in the annals of colonialism in that it did not entail the loss of a single Lao life—France ensured by its actions in 1893 that Laos's separate identity would be preserved into modern times. During the colonial interlude, a few French officials administered what their early cartographers labeled, for want of a better name, "le pays des Laos" (the land of the Lao, hence the name Laos), preserving intact local administrations and the royal house of Louang-phrabang.

Laos's incorporation into French Indochina beginning in 1893 resulted, however, in Vietnamese immigration, which was officially encouraged by the French to staff the middle levels of the civil services and militia. During the few months in 1945 when France's power was momentarily eclipsed, the consequences of this Vietnamese presence nearly proved fatal for the fledgling Lao Issara (Free Laos—see Glossary) government. The issue of Vietnamese dominance over Indochina remained alive into the postindependence period with the armed rebellion of the Pathet Lao (Lao Nation—see Glossary), who proclaimed themselves part of an Indochina-wide revolutionary movement. The Royal Lao Government (RLG—see Glossary) grappled with this problem for ten years but never quite succeeded in integrating the Pathet Lao rebels peacefully into the national fabric.

By the 1960s, outside powers had come to dominate events in Laos, further weakening the Vientiane government's attempts to maintain neutrality in the Cold War. For one thing, the Democratic Republic of Vietnam (North Vietnam), the most powerful entity left in Indochina by the 1954 Geneva armistice and the exit of France, cast a large shadow over the mountains to the west. Also, the United States, which had exerted strong pressure on France on behalf of the independence of Laos, became involved in a new war against what it regarded as the proxies of the Soviet Union and China. Even then, however, high-level United States officials seemed ambivalent about Laos's claim to national sovereignty, and Laos became the country where the so-called "secret war" was fought.

In late 1975, months after the fall of Cambodia and the Republic of Vietnam (South Vietnam) to the communists, the Pathet Lao came to power in Laos, proclaiming that Laos's territorial integrity, as well as its independence, sovereignty, and solidarity with other new regimes of Indochina, would be defended (see fig. 1). In a demonstration of this determination, Laos fought a border war with Thailand in 1988, and protracted negotiations were necessary to demarcate the border between the two countries. Internally, the regime proved ruthless in stamping out political and armed opposition. Only since the introduction of the New Economic Mechanism in 1986 has the government made some headway in the long and difficult process of bettering the lives of its citizens.

Early History

The original inhabitants of Laos were Austroasiatic peoples, who lived by hunting and gathering before the advent of agriculture. Skilled at river navigation using canoes, Laotian traders used routes through the mountains, especially rivers, from earliest times. The most important river route was the Mekong because its many tributaries allowed traders to penetrate deep into the hinterland, where they bought products such as cardamom, gum benzoin, sticklac, and many foods.

Power Centers in the Middle Mekong Valley

A number of princely fiefdoms based on wet rice cultivation and associated with the pottery and bronze culture of Ban Chiang developed in the middle Mekong Valley from the first century A.D. These fiefdoms exercised power over their neighbors, in circumstances of generally sparse populations, through expanding and contracting spheres of influence best described by the term *mandala* (see Glossary). Commerce, marriage contracts, and warfare served to expand the *mandala*.

Thus, a plurality of power centers occupied the middle Mekong Valley in early times. Sikhôttabong was a *mandala* whose capital was located on the left bank of the Mekong at the mouth of the Xé Bangfai and then moved westward as a result of the expansion of Champa, an Indianized state on the coast of Vietnam founded in A.D. 192. Cham, descendants of Champa, were present at Champasak (Bassac) in the fifth century. The Mon kingdom of Candapuri, the earliest name of present-day Vientiane (Viangchan), was another *mandala*. The social structure of Sikhôttabong and Candapuri appears to have been strongly hierarchical, with an aristocracy, a commoner class, and a slave class. The fact that some kings came from the commoner class appears to indicate the presence of some sort of consensus in effecting royal succession. At its peak, another important regional power, Funan, had its *mandala* incorporate parts of central Laos. The smaller, but also important, Mon kingdom of Dvaravati (through which Theravada Buddhism—see Glossary—reached Laos in the seventh and eighth centuries) was centered in the lower Menam Valley beginning in the fifth century (see Buddhism, ch. 2).

In the seventh century, a northwesterly migration of Thais from their region of origin in northwestern Tonkin brought to the Ta-li region (in what is present-day Yunnan, China) a successor state to the Ai Lao kingdom. This new kingdom, Nan-chao, expanded its power by controlling major trading routes, notably the southern Silk Road. Culturally, this polyethnic, hierarchical, and militarized state was to have a great influence on later societies in Indochina, transmitting the Tantric Buddhism of Bengal to Laos, Thailand, the Shan state, and possibly Cambodia, as well as the political ideology of the *maharaja* (protector of Buddhism). Nan-chao was organized administratively into ten prefectures called *kien*. This term seems to be the origin of place-names *keng* (for example, Kengtung), *chiang* (for example, Chiang Mai), and *xiang* (for example, Xiangkhoang). Moreover, the population and army of Nan-chao were organized in units of 100, 1,000, and 10,000, a form later found in Indochina. Also, the title *chao* (prince) appears to have been of Nan-chao origin. Another branch of this same migration began at the headwaters of the Nam Ou and followed it downstream to Louangphrabang, continuing on through Xaignabouri to Chiang Mai.

As a result of the expansion and contraction of *mandala*, places of importance were known by more than one name. Muang Sua was the name of Louangphrabang following its conquest in A.D. 698 by a Thai prince, Khun Lo, who seized his opportunity when Nan-chao was engaged elsewhere. Khun Lo had been awarded the town by his father, Khun Borom, who is associated with the Lao legend of the creation of the world, which the Lao share with the Shan and other peoples of the region. Khun Lo established a dynasty whose fifteen rulers reigned over an independent Muang Sua for the better part of a century.

In the second half of the eighth century, Nan-chao intervened frequently in the affairs of the principalities of the middle Mekong Valley, resulting in the occupation of Muang Sua in 709. Nan-chao princes or administrators replaced the aristocracy of Thai overlords. Dates of the occupation are not known, but it probably ended well before the northward expansion of the Khmer Empire under Indravarman I (r. 877–89) and extended as far as the territories of Sipsong Panna (see Glossary) on the upper Mekong.

In the meantime, the Khmers founded an outpost at Xay Fong near Vientiane, and Champa expanded again in southern Laos, maintaining its presence on the banks of the Mekong until 1070. Canthaphanit, the local ruler of Xay Fong, moved north to Muang Sua and was accepted peacefully as ruler after the departure of the Nan-chao administrators. Canthaphanit and his son had long reigns, during which the town became known by the Thai name Xieng Dong Xieng Thong. The dynasty eventually became involved in the squabbles of a number of principalities. Khun Cuang, a warlike ruler who may have been a Kammu (alternate spellings include Khamu and Khmu) tribesman, extended his territory as a result of the warring of these principalities and probably ruled from 1128 to 1169. Under Khun Cuang, a single family ruled over a far-flung territory and reinstituted the Siamese administrative system of the seventh century. Muang Sua next became the Kingdom of Sri Sattanak, a name connected with the legend of the *naga* (mythical snake or water dragon) who was said to have dug the Mekong riverbed. At this time, Theravada Buddhism was subsumed by Mahayana Buddhism.

Muang Sua experienced a brief period of Khmer suzerainty under Jayavarman VII from 1185 to 1191. By 1180 the Sipsong Panna had regained their independence from the Khmers, however, and in 1238 an internal uprising in the Khmer outpost of Sukhodaya expelled the Khmer overlords.

Mongol Influence

Recent historical research has shown that the Mongols, who destroyed Nan-chao in 1253 and made the area a province of their empire—naming it Yunnan—exercised a decisive political influence in the middle Mekong Valley for the better part of a century. In 1271 Panya Lang, founder of a new dynasty headed by rulers bearing the title *panya*, began his rule over a fully sovereign Muang Sua. In 1286 Panya Lang's son, Panya Khamphong, was involved in a coup d'état that was probably instigated by the Mongols and resulted in the exile of his father. Upon his father's death in 1316, Panya Khamphong assumed the throne.

Ramkhamhaeng, an early ruler of the new Thai dynasty in Sukhothai, made himself the agent of Mongol interests, and from 1282 to 1284 eliminated the vestiges of Khmer and Cham power in central Laos. Ramkhamhaeng obtained the allegiance of Muang Sua and the mountainous country to the northeast. Between 1286 and 1297, Panya Khamphong's lieutenants, acting for Ramkhamhaeng and the Mongols, pacified vast territories. From 1297 to 1301, Lao troops under Mongol command invaded Dai Viet but were repulsed by the Vietnamese. Troops from Muang Sua conquered Muang Phuan in 1292–97. In 1308 Panya Khamphong seized the ruler of Muang Phuan, and by 1312 this principality was a vassal state of Muang Sua.

Mongol overlordship was unpopular in Muang Sua. Internal conflicts among members of the new dynasty over Mongol intervention in their affairs resulted in continuing family upheavals. Panya Khamphong exiled his son Fa Phi Fa and most likely intended to leave the throne to his younger grandson, Fa Ngieo. Fa Ngieo, involved in various coups and coup attempts, in 1330 sent his two sons to a Buddhist monastery outside the Mongol realm for safety. The brothers were kidnapped in 1335 and taken to Angkor, where they were entrusted to King Jayavarman Paramesvara, whose kingdom had acknowledged Mongol suzerainty since 1285.

The Founding of Lan Xang

It was as a result of these family conflicts that the Kingdom of Lan Xang—the name still carries associations of cultural kinship among the Lao—was established. The younger brother, Fa Ngum, married one of the king's daughters and in 1349 set out from Angkor at the head of a 10,000-member Khmer army. His conquest of the territories to the north of Angkor over the next six years reopened Mongol communications with that place, which had been cut off. Fa Ngum organized the conquered principalities into provinces (*muang*—see Glossary), and reclaimed Muang Sua from his father and elder brother. Fa Ngum was crowned king of Lan Xang at Vientiane, the site of one of his victories, in June 1354. Lan Xang extended from the border of China to Sambor below the Mekong rapids at Khong Island and from the Vietnamese border to the western escarpment of the Khorat Plateau.

The first few years of Fa Ngum's rule from his capital Muang Sua were uneventful. The next six years (1362–68), however, were troubled by religious conflict between Fa Ngum's lamaistic Buddhism and the region's traditional Theravada Buddhism. He severely repressed popular agitation that had anti-Mongol overtones and had many pagodas torn down. In

1368 Fa Ngum's Khmer wife died. He subsequently married the ruler of Ayuthia's daughter, who seems to have had a pacifying influence. For example, she was instrumental in welcoming a religious and artistic mission that brought with it a statue of the Buddha, the *phrabang*, which became the palladium of the kingdom. Popular resentment continued to build, however, and in 1373 Fa Ngum withdrew to Muang Nan. His son, Oun Huan, who had been in exile in southern Yunnan, returned to assume the regency of the empire his father had created. Oun Huan ascended to the throne in 1393 when his father died, ending Mongol overlordship of the middle Mekong Valley.

The kingdom, made up of Lao, Thai, and hill tribes, lasted in its approximate borders for another 300 years and briefly reached an even greater extent in the northwest. Fa Ngum's descendants remained on the throne at Muang Sua, renamed Louangphrabang, for almost 600 years after his death, maintaining the independence of Lan Xang to the end of the seventeenth century through a complex network of vassal relations with lesser princes. At the same time, these rulers fought off invasions from Vietnam (1478–79), Siam (1536), and Burma (1571–1621).

The Division of Lan Xang

In 1690, however, Lan Xang fell prey to a series of rival pretenders to its throne, and, as a result of the ensuing struggles, split into three kingdoms—Louangphrabang, Vientiane, and Champasak. Muang Phuan enjoyed a semi-independent status as a result of having been annexed by a Vietnamese army in the fifteenth century, an action that set the precedent for a tributary relationship with the court of Annam at Hué.

Successive Burmese and Siamese interventions involved Vientiane and Louangphrabang in internecine struggles. In 1771 the king of Louangphrabang attacked Vientiane, determined to punish it for what he perceived to be its complicity in a Burmese attack on his capital in 1765. The Siamese captured Vientiane for the first time in 1778–79, when it became a vassal state to Siam. Vientiane was finally destroyed in 1827–28 following an imprudent attempt by its ruler, Chao Anou, to retaliate against perceived Siamese injustices toward the Lao.

The disappearance of the Vientiane kingdom and the weakened condition of Louangphrabang led to a period of direct Siamese rule on the left bank of the Mekong and to the virtual annexation of Xiangkhouang as well as part of Bolikhamxai by the Vietnamese. Moreover, the Siamese soon became more directly involved with the Kingdom of Louangphrabang, whose ruler, Manta Thourath (r. 1817–36), had sought to preserve neutrality in the conflict between Siam and Vientiane. The Siamese intervention was caused by an appeal by King Oun Kham (r. 1872–94) for help in clearing his northeastern territories of the Hô (Haw), bands of armed horsemen who had fled the bloody Manchu campaign to pacify Yunnan.

The last major migration into Laos in the nineteenth century was that of the Hmong (see Glossary). Accustomed to growing crops of dryland rice and maize at the highest elevations in mountainous southern China, where they had lived for centuries, the Hmong practiced a peaceful coexistence with their neighbors at lower elevations. Their major interaction with others occurred in selling their chief cash crop, opium.

Developments in the Nineteenth Century

The French, in their early forays into the interior of Indochina, had stuck mainly to the rivers, looking for access routes to China. An April 1867 expedition led by Ernest Doudart de Lagrée and Francis Garnier visited the ruins of Vientiane. In 1869 an expedition led by Rheinart and Mourin d'Arfeuille traveled up the Mekong without penetrating the mountains. Although another explorer, Jules Harmand, a French army physician, reached Attapu on the Xé Kong, these forays provided the French with only a superficial knowledge of the peoples of the interior. What these early French explorers and scientists did find, however, were the Siamese and the Vietnamese already contesting for suzerainty over the territory between the mountains and the Mekong.

The Hold of Siam

This conflict had a long history. At the time of Siam's retributive campaigns against Vientiane in 1827–28, relations between Vientiane and Annam were good. The Vietnamese called Vientiane Van Tuong (the Kingdom of Ten Thousand Elephants). But when Vientiane's ruler, Chao Anou, sought refuge in Hué following Siam's destruction of his capital, it caused serious embarrassment to the Vietnamese. King Rama III of Siam wrote to the Vietnamese emperor, Minh Mang, explaining that Chao Anou had refused obedience to him and had

Stone jars dating back to prehistoric times, Plain of Jars, Xiangkhoang Province Courtesy Embassy of the Lao People's Democratic Republic, Washington

started hostilities. Minh Mang, pursuing a consistently cautious policy toward Rama III, lent Chao Anou two companies of men to escort him back to Vientiane, instructing them to return immediately after accomplishing their mission. Siamese and Vietnamese sources—the Laotian primary sources having for the most part disappeared—give conflicting versions of what happened next. In any event, in mid-October 1828, Chao Anou found himself once again engaged in hostilities with a stronger Siamese force. He again fled to safety, this time to Muang Phuan because a Siamese force was encamped at Nakhon Phanom, blocking the Mekong downstream.

The arrival of Chao Anou on their doorstep with a Siamese army in pursuit confronted the leaders of Muang Phuan with a dilemma. When the Siamese commander issued an ultimatum to surrender Chao Anou under penalty of an attack on Xiangkhoang, the leaders of Muang Phuan quickly accepted. The Siamese took Chao Anou to Bangkok and kept him captive.

What followed was illustrative of the consequences of the constant meddling in each other's affairs that went on among the Laotian principalities. The reigning prince of Muang Phuan was Chao Noi, son of the ruling family. Vientiane had attempted to take advantage of Chao Noi's youth when his father died to install Chao Xan, the head of a rival family from Muang Kasi. The Phuan elders of Xiangkhoang refused to accept this candidate, so power was shared under a compromise arranged with help from Hué. Chao Xan, however, led a delegation to Hué, where he accused Chao Noi and his cousins of bringing dishonor to the emperor by surrendering a vassal prince to another king, of obstructing passage of a tribute mission from Louangphrabang across the territory of Muang Phuan to Hué, and of negotiating to acknowledge Siamese suzerainty.

Chao Noi was accordingly summoned to Hué to explain himself but sent his eldest son, Po. Angered by this flagrant disregard of a direct order, Minh Mang took no action, awaiting news of the fate of Chao Anou, who was the nominal suzerain and ordinarily would have dealt with the Phuan on behalf of Hué. Once word was received that Chao Anou had died, Minh Mang sent a Vietnamese detachment to Muang Phuan and arrested Chao Noi and most of his family. In May 1829, the prisoners were taken to Annam, where Chao Noi and his cousin were executed in January 1830. Chao Noi's young sons and their mothers were kept in exile in Nghe An. The Muang Phuan succession thus fell to Chao Xan. Minh Mang, however, posted a *quan phu* (commissioner), supported by a garrison of 500 soldiers who were rotated seasonally, to reside permanently at Chiang Kham (Khang Khay), at the headwaters of the Nam Ngum, as a precaution against a recurrence of conflict with the Siamese king.

Rama III sent a further letter to Minh Mang in early 1829 outlining his view of Chao Anou's treachery and thanking the emperor for his presents. But the king failed to provide an explanation for a serious incident at Nakhon Phanom in which three Vietnamese mandarins had been killed. In November 1829, Siamese envoys returned home with a letter from Hué reiterating earlier demands for punishment of those people responsible. When it became obvious that Rama III would not revert to the old arrangement of joint administration, Hué gave administrative control over the entire eastern half of the former kingdom of Vientiane to Vietnamese officials in Annam and Tonkin. The territory was virtually annexed by Hué in 1831 under the name Tran Ninh Phu Tam Vien. The Vietnamese presence at Khang Khay continued until the mid-1850s.

Chao Anou's wars with the Siamese had stirred massive disruptions of villages on the right bank. Terrified Lao fled every which way. When the Siamese arrived at Nakhon Phanom in 1827, they found the town deserted, the officials having fled across the river to Mahaxai. In the aftermath of the war, however, the Siamese established new towns—Chiang Khan, Nong Khai, Mukdahan, and Kemmarat—at key points on the Mekong to serve as administrative centers and as logistical bases for expeditionary forces operating across the river toward the mountains.

On the left bank, where the writ of Siam ran as far south as Stung Treng, the Siamese followed a policy of depopulating the country. This policy had actually been initiated as early as 1779; the first Phuan carried off by the Siamese arrived in Bangkok around 1792, where they were used as workers in the fields of the official classes. By removing people from the left bank, the Siamese deprived any invader from Annam of food supplies, transport, and recruits. Sporadic resistance, however, led for some time by the *latsavong* (first prince) of the old Vientiane kingdom, continued at Mahaxai until 1835, when the leading Lao official there agreed to become governor of Sakon Nakhon on the right bank, and the Siamese resettled there. From 1837 to 1847, the Siamese carried out depopulation raids annually during the dry season in Khamkeut and Khammouan and in the valley of the Xé Banghiang. Entire Lao villages were uprooted.

Meanwhile, the leaders of Houaphan principality, fearing that the example of Muang Phuan might be applied to them, submitted to the suzerainty of Bangkok through the intermediary of Louangphrabang. Events were not going well for the Siamese in Muang Phuan. After the Siamese removed Chao Xan and some of the elders to Bangkok in 1836, the Vietnamese in effect ruled the state directly, appointing local officials as administrators. The depopulation activities the Siamese carried out on the Plain of Jars and elsewhere in Xiangkhoang caused the remaining population to migrate eastward and southward, forming new villages in the upper reaches of the Nam Mat and around the northern extremities of the Nam Kading basin, around Muang Mo, Muang Mok, and Muang Ngan. This expansion of the Phuan state was encouraged by the Vietnamese in their administrative reorganization. Some of the Phuan, however, perhaps enticed by Lao governors acting for the Siamese, moved down the river valleys toward the Mekong.

There, new towns such as Bolikhamxai and Pakxan were founded and given satellite status by the Siamese in the 1870s.

Tu Duc, on his accession as Vietnamese emperor at Hué in 1847, allowed the sons of Chao Noi to return home with their families and to reestablish Xiangkhoang as the Phuan capital. They were given administrative responsibilities, and the eldest, Prince Po, at last was permitted to replace the commissioner. Meanwhile, King Tiantha Koumane of Louangphrabang (r. 1851–69), one of three sons of Manta Thourath who succeeded to the throne, while in Bangkok to receive the investiture, quickly arranged with the new Siamese king, Rama IV, to become once again the suzerain over the Phuan state. The Vietnamese had no objection to vassal relations of the Phuan with Louangphrabang. But Rama IV was deeply suspicious of the Phuan elders and set as a condition for accepting this arrangement that the Phuan send an annual tribute mission to Louangphrabang. Tiantha Koumane hence was able to reestablish his authority over Muang Phuan.

A new element—the Hô—entered the picture, further complicating the situation in northern Laos. The Hô first appeared in mid-1869 in the upper valley of the Nam Ou, where they made common cause with some Lu dissidents displaced from the Sipsong Panna during a civil war lasting twenty-five years. An army from Louangphrabang attacked these bands and withdrew, taking prisoners.

The Lao and Siamese were ill prepared to face up to the new danger of anarchy in their domains. Tiantha Koumane was dying of malaria, and the Siamese, preoccupied with preparations for the cremation of their own monarch, Rama IV, demanded that a tribute mission from Louangphrabang arrive in Bangkok in time for the ceremony. Many princes and senior officials had to absent themselves from Louangphrabang at this critical time and had to remain in Bangkok afterward for audiences with the new monarch. Oun Kham, who was already fifty-eight years old, did not receive his crown from the Siamese until 1872.

It was not until 1873 that the Siamese sent an army up the Nam Ou to attack the Hô and drive them out. Some Hô retreated into Houaphan, while others overran the Plain of Jars, where Chao Hung had succeeded his brother Chao Pho as ruler of the Phuan state, which became the main theater of conflict. The Hô camped at Chiang Kham and demanded "tax" payments from the local population, threatening to kill anyone who resisted. Chao Hung raised a small army and led it to assist the beleaguered governor of Chiang Kham in 1874, but a fatal bullet wound to Chao Hung prompted the withdrawal of his army. Chao Hung's son, Prince Khanti, appealed to Annam for aid. A joint attack was made on Chiang Kham but was also repulsed.

Early the following year, the Hô began plundering the lowlands along the Mekong as far upriver as Chiang Khan and as far south as Nakhon Phanom, directly threatening Siam's security. The teenage King Rama V was unable to mount an effective response. The governor of Khorat took a force of men across the flooded Mekong at the height of the monsoon and attacked the Hô encamped in the ruins of Vientiane, killing their warlord and forcing the others to retreat to Muang Phuan. A concerted campaign against the Hô in their stronghold was finally put in motion in 1876, but it resulted more in pillaging and looting the inhabitants than in stopping the Hô, who, with their horses, were more than a match for the Siamese and Lao foot soldiers. Rama V blamed the Phuan for having brought trouble on themselves by giving rice, silver, and horses to the Hô, which, in fact, they had done in a desperate effort to appease them. He rejected further appeals for aid on the grounds that the local leaders would prove incapable of dealing with the situation after the army withdrew.

Meanwhile, the troubles in the upper valley of the Nam Ou continued. Siamese commissioners had to assist Oun Kham in restoring order in 1876 and to prod him into reorganizing the towns under his rule. Affairs remained in a state of flux for the next six years, and when in late 1882 Oun Kham appealed again to Bangkok for help against the Hô, the Siamese sent a major military mission. Subsequently, the Siamese maintained a permanent garrison at Louangphrabang.

The Eviction of Siam

The French, meanwhile, had imposed a treaty of protectorate on Annam in 1884. This treaty implied a French interest going beyond exploratory involvement in the affairs of Laos. In June 1885, the French consul general in Bangkok notified the Siamese government that a vice consulate would be established in Louangphrabang under terms of a most-favored-nation clause contained in a Franco-Siamese treaty of 1856. A

Franco-Siamese convention of May 1886 acknowledged the role of Siamese officials in Laos for the conduct of administrative matters but avoided implying French recognition of Siamese claims to sovereignty there.

Auguste Pavie arrived at Louangphrabang in 1887 to assume his post as vice consul. Pavie played a key role in saving Oun Kham's life from raiders from Lai Chau, earning the king's gratitude and a promise that he would place his kingdom under France's protection. Incidents between Siamese and French officials on the left bank, where the French had made themselves advocates of Vietnamese claims to suzerainty, continued in 1887–93. Finally, in March 1893, the French government, acceding to a campaign by the colonialist lobby in Paris, decided to send three French commissioners, each with a small armed force, to evict the Siamese from outposts they had established in central and southern Laos. The commissioners had secret orders to avoid exchanges of fire if at all possible; ironically, the Siamese were under identical orders from their government.

The French government dispatched two warships to the Gulf of Siam, and, in what became known as the Paknam incident, forced passage of a fort at the mouth of the Menam River on July 12 and anchored in the river with their guns trained on the royal palace. On July 20, the French gave an ultimatum to the Siamese government to recognize the rights of Annam to the left-bank territories and to meet a list of other demands within forty-eight hours. The Siamese replied on July 22, accepting the first demand on central and southern Laos but rejecting the rest. The French declared a blockade of Bangkok, whereupon the Siamese accepted the rest of the French demands. By terms of the treaty concluded on October 3, 1893, between the Government of the French Republic and the Government of His Majesty the King of Siam, Siam renounced all claims to territories on the left bank and to islands in the river.

Laos under the French

The Kingdom of Louangphrabang became a protectorate and was initially placed under the governor general of Indochina in Hanoi. Pavie saw to the officialization in Hanoi of the titles of King Oun Kham, his eldest son who assumed the duties of king under the name Zakarine—also known as Kham Souk (r. 1894–1904)—and the viceroy, Boun Khong.

The French originally divided central Laos into two administrative districts. By April and May 1894, however, the initial organization was already being modified, and a new plan was put into effect a year later. In 1899 Upper Laos was integrated with Lower Laos under one administrator.

In 1904 and 1905, Laos was deprived of southern plateaus that were previously part of its territory (see fig. 2). Under the February 13, 1904, Convention Modifying the Treaty Concluded on October 3, 1893, Siam ceded to France control of the right-bank portion of Louangphrabang (present-day Xaignabouri Province) and part of the right-bank territory of Champasak. The French governor general, by a decree of March 28, 1905, fixed the border between Laos and Cambodia at the Tonle Repou River. Under the March 23, 1907, Treaty Between France and Siam, the French retroceded the territory of Dan Sai, southwest of the "elbow" of the Mekong, to Siam.

The French thus reestablished a political entity in the middle Mekong Valley extending from China to the Khong falls on the Cambodian border that owed allegiance to neither Vietnam nor Siam, thereby eluding Vietnamese claims to Laos, whose historical basis they had verified in the archives in Hué. Detachment of the administration of the left-bank territories from Annam was justified on grounds of budgetary necessity in the new French Indochina.

World War II and After

The French presence in Laos was sufficient to preserve internal peace and cope with sporadic localized revolts among some of the mountain tribes in the years 1900–40. These revolts owed their origin to resistance to paying taxes and supplying corvée labor or to outbreaks of messianic hysteria. However, the French military in Indochina was too ill-equipped to contemplate resisting Japan's movement to the south, which by 1940 had become the main focus of Japanese military strategists. On August 30, 1940, the French Vichy government signed the Matsuoka-Henry Pact granting Japan the right to station troops in Indochina and use bases there for movement of forces elsewhere in the region. The agreement, although recognizing Japan's preeminent role in Southeast Asia, preserved France's sovereignty over Indochina.

To the west, French forces in Indochina were confronted by a threat from Thailand (Siam adopted this name in June

1939), where Pibul Songkram's government was arousing public unrest with inflammatory speeches in Bangkok and radio broadcasts to those he called his brethren across the Mekong. The broadcasts called for an uprising against the French, an endeavor in which Pibul promised help—and for which he had secretly sought Japanese backing. After a series of increasingly serious incidents in the last months of 1940, Thai ground troops attacked French forces in Cambodia in January 1941. The May 9, 1941, Peace Convention Between France and Thailand, under mediation from Japan, was highly favorable to Thailand, which regained the right-bank territories that it had given up in 1904.

Laotian outrage was predictable. King Sisavang Vong of Louangphrabang (r. 1904–59) had only the promises made to his grandfather by Pavie as the basis for France's intentions to treat his kingdom as a protectorate. Worried in this regard, he had obtained in 1932 from Paul Raynaud, the French minister for colonies, written guarantees that France would continue to honor Pavie's promises. Therefore, the French were obliged to explain their giving away part of his kingdom or else offer the king suitable compensation. As a result, the French governor general, Admiral Jean Decoux, offered the king a treaty regularizing the protectorate and enlarging his domain. The Franco-Laotian Treaty of Protectorate between France and the Kingdom of Louangphrabang of August 29, 1941, attached the provinces of Vientiane, Xiangkhoang, and Louang Namtha to Louangphrabang, which already included Phôngsali and Houaphan.

The French Protectorate and Direct Administration

The territory of Laos thus consisted of the Kingdom of Louangphrabang, under French protection, and the provinces south of the Nam Kading, which were administered directly by a *résident supérieur* in Vientiane. The latter had direct authority over the provincial *résidents*, who were on an equal footing with the Lao *chao khoueng* (provincial governors). The *résident supérieur* also acted as the representative of the French state to the king of Louangphrabang and supervised the administration of the kingdom through provincial commissioners. The affairs of the kingdom were conducted by a four-member council headed by the viceroy. The *résident supérieur* also coordinated the activities of the public services of the Indochinese Federation, which operated in both the north and the south, and employed French, Vietnamese, and Lao civil servants.

The treaty also reinstituted the position of viceroy, which had been abolished by the French at the death of Boun Khong in 1920. Boun Khong's son, Prince Phetsarath, became one of the major figures of modern Laos. Among his accomplishments were the establishment of the system of ranks and titles of the civil service, promotion and pension plans, the organization of a Laotian consultative assembly consisting of district and province chiefs, the reorganization of the king's Advisory Council along functional lines, and the establishment of a school of law and administration. Phetsarath also reorganized the administrative system of the Buddhist community of monks and novices, the clergy (*sangha*), and established a system of schools for educating monks in which the language of instruction was Pali, the sacred language of Theravada Buddhism.

Nationalist Stirrings

Although French rule in Laos was punctuated by rebellions among tribal peoples that had to be suppressed by force, the Laotians by and large accepted the French presence. The need to counter the pan-Thai irredentism propagated by the Pibul regime in Bangkok nevertheless led the Decoux administration to foster Laotian nationalism through the Lao Renovation Movement (Lao Nhay). The goals of this movement were to "provide Laos with its own personality with respect to its neighbors and to inculcate the sense of *patrie*." The first Lao-language publications in the style of the modern press, for example, *Lao Nhay* (New Laos), and *Tin Lao* (News of Laos), both launched in 1941, resulted from this movement.

An activist group of teachers and students among the Lao nationalists, however, attempted to stage a coup d'état at the Collège Pavie in Vientiane in July 1940. When the coup failed, they fled across the river and founded a semisecret organization, Laos for the Lao (Lao Pen Lao). Founding members included the Pali teacher and historian Maha Sila Viravong, Tham Sayasithena, Thongdy Sounthonvichit, and Oudone Sananikone and his half-brother Oun.

Beginning in December 1944, with the upswing of Allied fortunes in Europe and the Pacific, General Charles de Gaulle's provisional government in Paris began airdropping French agents into Indochina with the aim of recruiting and training guerrilla forces to harass the Japanese and maintain a French presence. These agents readily found supporters in Laos, and soon Franco-Laotian guerrilla groups were operating from jungle camps scattered from Louang Namtha Province in the north to Champasak Province in the south. On March 9, 1945, however, the Japanese carried out a *coup de force* that overturned the 1940 political agreement and ended French administrative control throughout Indochina. Having the Indochinese rulers renounce their treaties of protectorate with France formed an integral part of Japanese plans, but no steps were taken to prepare the Laotians or others for "independence."

Events in 1945

Japanese troops moved into the towns and quickly imprisoned French officials and their families and confiscated their property. Prince Phetsarath, after ordering Laotian civil servants to continue their duties as usual, left Vientiane for Louangphrabang to be with the king.

After being delayed on the roads from Xiangkhoang and Vientiane by the Franco-Laotian guerrillas (of whom the Hmong were particularly effective), two battalions of Japanese troops finally arrived in Louangphrabang on April 7. They found the French gone. A Japanese representative suggested that the king proclaim Laos's independence and send someone to discuss the terms of Laotian-Japanese cooperation. Sisavang Vong replied that he would stay with his people and that his attitude toward the French would not change. Laos was too small to be independent, but if he was obliged to accept independence he would do so. At the same time, he reluctantly issued a proclamation on April 8 ending the French protectorate. The king secretly entrusted Prince Kindavong, a younger half-brother of Phetsarath, with the mission of representing him in the Allied councils abroad while he maintained clandestine contact with the Franco-Laotian guerrillas in Laos. He also sent Crown Prince Savang Vatthana to Japanese headquarters in Saigon, where he vigorously protested the Japanese actions.

Phetsarath no doubt saw some good coming from the turn of events. The Japanese had told him that they intended that the king's proclamation of independence apply to all of Laos. Interested in the unity of Laos, he gave the Japanese a proposal for unifying the Laotian civil service. Phetsarath also opened an account for the royal treasury with the Indochinese treasury in Hanoi, which gave the kingdom greater fiscal autonomy. Problems began to appear almost immediately, however. At the end of June, the coffers were empty in spite of an infusion of money brought back from Saigon by the crown prince. Japan, no longer able to provide for the salaries of the Laotian administration, allowed the civil service to languish.

Beyond this was the Vietnamese problem. In 1943 the six chief towns of Laos counted 30,300 Vietnamese inhabitants out of their total population of 51,150. Vietnamese occupied key positions in the federal civil service, public works, posts and telegraph, treasury, customs, and police. The political dangers to Laos of the Vietnamese presence were demonstrated on April 8 when Vietnamese residents of Khang Khay tried to detach Tran Ninh (Xiangkhoang), an integral part of the territory of the Kingdom of Louangphrabang, from Laos and attach it to Vietnam.

After their *coup de force*, the Japanese put prices on the heads of the Franco-Laotian guerrillas and anyone caught helping them. In spite of the danger, the guerrillas sought recruits in the countryside and stepped up their armed attacks against Japanese communications, virtually cutting off several towns. The guerrillas' message to Laotian civil servants: Disregard the Japanese-inspired proclamation of independence and carry on your regular duties without helping the Japanese. *Chao khoueng* (provincial governors) who joined the guerrillas and *chao muang* (district chiefs) faced the hard decision of leaving behind their colleagues and sometimes their families. Whereas many of the leading Lao and tribal figures supported the Franco-Laotian guerrillas, some families had divided loyalties.

After Japan's surrender, Phetsarath acted on the premise that the king's proclamation of independence was still in force. On August 28, 1945, he sent a telegram to all provincial governors notifying them that the Japanese surrender did not affect independence and warning them to resist any foreign intervention in their administration. Phetsarath also refused to recognize the authority of the French *résident supérieur* when he was released from prison. Three days earlier, however, Colonel Hans Imfeld, commissioner of the French Republic, had entered Louangphrabang with a party of Franco-Laotian guerrillas and had received assurances from the king that the protectorate was still in force. Japanese troops having withdrawn to the south, a party of Franco-Laotian guerrillas under the command of Major Fabre entered Vientiane peacefully on September 3 to await developments. French civilians released from internment were evacuated.

Vietnamese residents in Vientiane and other towns had already begun spreading anti-French propaganda and making preparations to resist the French. In these actions, they were guided by agents of the Indochinese Communist Party (ICP), a Marxist-Leninist party founded in 1930 by Ho Chi Minh. The ICP adhered to a Leninist strategy of seizing power by revolutionary action—national liberation followed by the transition to socialism. The ICP had established cells in Laos in the early 1930s made up entirely of Vietnamese.

The Vietnamese agitation came to a head with a large demonstration in Vientiane on August 23. Phetsarath favored taking advantage of the French difficulties. As head of government, however, he was restricted not only by the wishes of the king, but also by the 1941 arrangement with the French that had made the crown prince the chairman of the King's Council. The French design had, perhaps intentionally, created an ambiguity that made for conflict. On September 2, Phetsarath sent a message to the king requesting a royal proclamation of the unity of Laos.

While he was dealing with these matters, Phetsarath received an unsolicited message on September 3 from Prince Souphanouvong, another of his half-brothers. Souphanouvong had spent the previous sixteen years working as an engineer in Vietnam. Souphanouvong flew from Vinh to Hanoi in an aircraft provided by the United States Office of Strategic Services (OSS) to meet with Ho Chi Minh, who had just proclaimed the Democratic Republic of Vietnam in Hanoi in the name of the Viet Minh (see Glossary), an ICP front organization. (Although OSS personnel were not authorized to operate in Indochina, the OSS station in Kunming, China, took advantage of a mandate for OSS teams to perform prisoner of war (POW) recovery work to enter Indochina.) Prince Souphanouvong said he was in a position to represent the interests of Laos and asked for instructions. On September 5, he sent another message to Phetsarath saying that he had begun to negotiate with the Vietnamese for aid in the independence struggle and to form "an Indochinese bloc opposing the return of colonialism." Phetsarath rejected Souphanouvong's offer.

Wat Pa Huak, one of Louangphrabang's oldest Buddhist temples, has gilded and carved wood front doors, a mosaic facade depicting Buddha riding a three-headed elephant, and beautiful interior murals showing historical scenes along the Mekong River. Courtesy Gina Merris

The official United States position, communicated to France, was that there was no question concerning France's sovereignty over Indochina. At the end of August, President Harry S. Truman was personally assured by de Gaulle that Indochina would be granted independence once the status quo before the Japanese aggression had been restored. Meanwhile, United States recognition of French sovereignty was qualified by the proviso that the French claim of support by the Indochinese populations be borne out by future events. Apparently without the knowledge of Washington, however, an OSS team that reached Vientiane in September—escorted by members of the Lao Pen Lao newly returned from Thailand—assured Phetsarath that the French would not be allowed to return. The team advised Phetsarath to await the arrival of the Inter-Allied Commission that was to decide his country's future. This information misled Phetsarath into believing that the international community supported an independent Laos.

On September 7, however, Phetsarath was informed by the minister of interior that a royal proclamation had continued the French protectorate over the Kingdom of Louangphrabang. On September 15, with the Inter-Allied Commission nowhere in sight, Phetsarath issued a proclamation that unified the Kingdom of Louangphrabang with the four southern provinces of Khammouan, Savannakhét, Champasak, and Saravan (Salavan). Vientiane would be the capital, and the Congress of People's Representatives would soon meet to decide all political, economic, and social questions.

On September 21, Fabre demanded the dismissal of Xieng Mao (also known as Phaya Khammao, or Khammao Vilay), the provincial governor since 1941, for anti-French activities, and his replacement by Kou Voravong. The next day, an advance guard of the Chinese Nationalist troops responsible for receiving the surrender of the Japanese arrived by boat down the Mekong. They appeared more interested in buying up the opium crop (harvested from late December to early February) than in disarming the already departed Japanese.

The Lao Issara Government

On October 7, Souphanouvong and a Vietnamese escort arrived in Savannakhét to find that Oun and his partisans, who included Phoumi Nosavan, had crossed the river from Thailand, taken control of the town, and, in a loose alliance with the large Vietnamese population, armed themselves from looted armories of the local militia and with arms discarded by the withdrawing Japanese. As a result of negotiations, their forces merged. Souphanouvong became commander in chief and Oun second in command. Souphanouvong and his escort proceeded upriver, first to Thakhek and then to Vientiane, where a provisional revolutionary government had been proclaimed two weeks earlier, taking the name Lao Issara (Free Laos—see Glossary). Moreover, the Committee of Independence, strongly influenced by the Lao Pen Lao, controlled Vientiane. Upon his arrival, Souphanouvong was made minister of foreign affairs and commander in chief. At his urging, a military cooperation convention was signed with Ho Chi Minh's government.

Meanwhile, bolstered by renewed assurances of support from the French, Sisavang Vong had sent messages on October 10 to Vientiane accusing Phetsarath of exceeding his authority and stripping him of his position as prime minister and his title of viceroy. Phetsarath protested but accepted these decisions and, after thanking the Laotian civil servants for their support, immediately announced his withdrawal from public life. His decision was no doubt influenced by the fact that he was married to a sister of Sisavang.

The royal dismissal of Phetsarath turned Lao Issara leaders against the monarchy, which they saw as hopelessly compromised by the French. In an effort to give their government some semblance of legitimacy, Lao Issara leaders hastily named the People's Committee, consisting of thirty-four members, many of them Lao Pen Lao activists, but also including the governors of several provinces who were not even in Vientiane. Members of the Chamber of People's Representatives were elected—and simply notified after the fact—by the members of the People's Committee in accordance with a provisional constitution adopted on the morning of October 12.

At the news of the king's deposition and the report that the Lao Issara government had dispatched an armed contingent to Louangphrabang under Sing Ratanassamay's command, the agitation in the royal capital grew rapidly. With Imfeld and his men disarmed and held under house arrest by Chinese troops, the governor, Boungnavath, was free to act, and he had Royal Lao Government (RLG—see Glossary) supporters arrested. On November 10, hours before the arrival of Sing's force, a mob surrounded the royal palace, fired shots in the air, climbed over the walls, and forced entry. Sing and his men had an audience with the king that afternoon. The king declared himself to be a simple citizen, prepared to hand over the *phrabang* and to vacate the royal palace when the government thought it appropriate. Later that month, the government issued a formal decree that no government member would henceforth have any contact with the French.

A Confusing Situation

At the outset of its rule, the authority of the Lao Issara provisional government was extremely limited outside Vientiane. In the north, the towns of Louangphrabang, Phôngsali, and Louang Namtha were occupied by the Chinese. The Franco-Laotian guerrillas, with support from Touby Lyfoung's Hmong, had taken control of the main towns of Xiangkhoang Province at the beginning of September. Their hold on Houaphan was much less solid, in spite of efforts on the part of the provincial governor, Phoumi Vongvichit, to prevent the Chinese from entering the province. Here, because of its proximity to Vietnam, the revolutionary propaganda spread by the Viet Minh was strong but also pro-Viet Minh rather than pro-Lao Issara. Moreover, the main roads leading east were denied to the Franco-Laotian guerrillas by Viet Minh detachments coming from Vietnam. In the center and south, the Lao Issara government controlled the towns of Thakhek and Savannakhét. Most of the remainder of the provinces of Khammouan and Savannakhét was controlled by the Franco-Laotian guerrillas. The same was true for the southernmost provinces of Pakxé and Saravan, which fell largely in the British zone of operation decided upon at the Potsdam Conference. Here also, Prince Boun Oum of Champasak, sympathetic to the French, had 15,000 troops under his command.

The outlook became more favorable for the Lao Issara as the year ended. France, preoccupied with the situation in Vietnam, was unable to send reinforcements to the Franco-Laotian guerrillas. Fabre and his men were evacuated from Vientiane—eventually to Thailand—under an escort provided by the Chinese. Various events led the Franco-Laotian guerrillas to evacuate Xiangkhoang town and Louang Namtha. While Viet Minh propaganda exploited differences between the Lao and Phuan on the one hand and Touby's Hmong on the other, the Viet Minh were themselves putting together a Hmong guerrilla force under Faydang Lobliayao of the Lo clan. In Louangphrabang, Imfeld and his men had been subjected to all kinds of pressure, culminating in their evacuation across the river under Chinese escort on January 4.

In Vientiane, the Lao Issara government was confronted with a growing list of problems. The most serious was how to finance the government because the treasury was empty, and there were no funds to pay civil servants. An attempt to tax opium exports was unenforceable because the government did not control opium trade routes. The government even took steps to abolish the Indochinese *régie* (state monopoly) that regulated the opium trade and make it a Laos monopoly. In desperation, the government appealed to the Thai government for a press on which to print money. Foreign relations and the procurement of military equipment were also problems.

Beginning in January 1946, with the loss anew of Xiangkhoang, the fortunes of the Lao Issara government began to decline. The Franco-Laotian guerrillas were receiving reinforcements and supplies by air and road from French headquarters in Saigon, which made entry into the towns possible for the first time. Lao Issara appeals to the Viet Minh for assistance went largely unheeded, and the Franco-Laotian guerrillas once again were positioned along the main roads leading from Vietnam.

After long negotiations in Chongqing, China's wartime capital, the French government obtained China's commitment to withdraw its troops from Indochina. The withddrawal allowed the Franco-Laotian guerrillas to make their entry into Savannakhét against token resistance camouflaged by the Chinese withdrawal. At Thakhek, however, Souphanouvong and his largely Vietnamese force were determined to make the French pay. In a day-long battle on March 21, approximately 700 of the defenders and 300 civilians were killed.

With the French menacing Vientiane, the first move of the Lao Issara government was to attempt to regularize its relations with the monarchy. On March 23, Xieng Mao, having abandoned Vientiane for Louangphrabang, sent the king a letter asking him to resume his throne. But the king was in no hurry, and it was not until April 23 that the king signaled his acceptance of the constitution and reaffirmed the unity of Laos by a royal ordinance.

Meanwhile, a strong French column was making its way up the road from Vientiane to Louangphrabang. Simultaneously, Hmong guerrillas moved west to harass Chinese troops in the vicinity of the royal capital. The French column entered Louangphrabang, forcing Phetsarath and the Lao Issara ministers to flee Laos. The king welcomed the French by declaring null and void all acts that he had sanctioned under pressure from the Japanese, the Chinese, and the Lao Issara since April 4, 1945. He also promised a democratic constitution.

The Lao Issara government-in-exile set up its headquarters in Bangkok. Scattered groups of armed partisans mounted raids into Laos from bases along the Mekong and in southern Laos. One group was under the command of Thao O Anourack. After the Japanese takeover, Thao O had refused the Franco-Laotian guerrillas' appeal to join them. When the Lao Issara took over Savannakhét, the provincial governor appointed him commander of liberation forces in Xépôn. Thus, when the Franco-Laotians reoccupied Xépôn in March 1946, Thao O made his way east with some 200 to 300 men to the safety of Lao Bao just across the border of Vietnam. Eventually, he was forced to abandon Laos altogether and to make his way to Hanoi, where the Viet Minh put him in touch with Kaysone Phomvihan, a Vietnamese-Lao *métis* (person of mixed race) from Savannakhét who had been sent to direct Lao Issara radio broadcasts over Radio Hanoi, and Nouhak Phoumsavan, a Vietnamese from Mukdahan. Neither Kaysone Phomvihan nor Nouhak Phoumsavan had a significant role in the Lao Issara, but both had the confidence of Ho Chi Minh and saw in Ho's government the salvation of an independent Laos.

The Vietnamese proposed to Thao O—and he accepted—that he form a committee for the liberation of Laos. Nouhak became president of the committee. The enlistment of other small groups from Xiangkhoang and Houaphan brought the effective strength under Thao O's command to 500; he dispatched one company each to Xam Nua, Xiangkhoang, Muang Mo, Napé, and Muang Sen. Thao O soon received secret codes from Phetsarath and Souvanna Phouma in Bangkok that allowed him to communicate with his companies.

The Coming of Independence

At the urging of the United States, France took steps to normalize its relations with Laos. In June 1946, a joint Franco-Laotian commission was established in Vientiane to discuss future relationships. This commission produced a document confirming the existence of a unified Laos under the sovereignty of the king of Louangphrabang. Major political, military, and economic powers remained in French hands. Elections for a Constituent Assembly were to be held within a year. A modus vivendi was signed on August 27. A Franco-Siamese agreement signed in Washington on November 17, 1946, restored the right-bank provinces of Xaignabouri and Champasak to Laos. The multinational conciliation commission that examined Thailand's claims to these territories found in favor of Laos in its report of June 27, 1947.

The Kingdom of Laos

On December 15, 1946, in the face of guerrilla raids from across the Mekong, forty-four delegates to the Kingdom of Laos's first popularly elected Constituent Assembly were chosen. Under French supervision, the delegates worked on a constitution promulgated by Sisavang Vong on May 11, 1947. This constitution declared Laos an independent state within the French Union. On November 26, 1947, the thirty-three deputies to Laos's first National Assembly invested a government headed by Prince Souvannarath, another half-brother of Phetsarath. By the terms of a confidential protocol of February 25, 1948, Boun Oum was allowed to keep his title of Prince of Champasak but renounced his suzerain rights to this former kingdom. In return he was made inspector general of the kingdom, the third-ranking personage of Laos after the king and crown prince.

Under a successor government headed by Boun Oum, the Franco-Lao General Convention of July 19, 1949, gave Laos greater latitude in foreign affairs. Over the following months, France transferred its remaining powers. A Royal Lao Army was created, which by the end of 1952 comprised seventeen companies, in addition to a battalion entirely commanded by Laotian officers. On February 7, 1950, the United States and Britain recognized Laos. Later that year, the United States opened a legation in Vientiane.

Meanwhile, contacts had been made in Bangkok between the French and moderates in the Lao Issara government-in-exile. A coup d'état in Thailand ushered in a government much less sympathetic to the anti-French resistance in Laos than its predecessor and deprived the hardliners among the Lao Issara of precious support. A conflict developed between Phetsarath and Souphanouvong over the issue of the Lao Issara's ties to the Viet Minh. This conflict led to Souphanouvong's dismissal from the government-in-exile. When France offered an amnesty, the government decreed its own dissolution in October 1949 and returned to Vientiane in a French plane. Phetsarath was left in Thailand. Souphanouvong, vowing to continue to fight, headed for Vietnam. The Lao Issara was a spent force, although it lived on in legend.

The Pathet Lao

War had broken out in the meantime between the French and Ho Chi Minh's government at the end of 1946. Leaving Nouhak in charge of the resistance committee, Thao O set up his base at Con Cuong (Vietnam), from which his men could cross the border into Laos with relative impunity. In January 1949, Kaysone formed the first unit of a new resistance army, the Latsavong detachment, named after the *latsavong* of Vientiane, who had led resistance against the Siamese in the nineteenth century. To lend the resistance the appearance of authority it lacked in reality, a government headed by Souphanouvong was formed at a congress held in Vietnam in August

1950. This government included Kaysone, Nouhak, Tiao Souk Vongsak, and Phoumi Vongvichit.

The congress created the Neo Lao Issara (Free Laos Front—see Glossary). The basic stance of this front's propaganda was the united struggle against the French without reference to political parties or ideology. Illustrative of this stance was the use henceforth of the name Pathet Lao (Lao Nation—see Glossary). Indicative of the "single battlefield" theme repeated in Viet Minh propaganda were the increasing numbers of Viet Minh agents sent to Laos: 500 to 700 political and military agents at the end of 1946 and the beginning of 1947, approximately 5,000 to 7,000 agents at the end of 1950 and the beginning of 1951, and 17,000 agents in 1953.

In keeping with the united front against the French, Souphanouvong's Pathet Lao government included not only leaders who had developed close ties to the Viet Minh over the previous five years, but also members of the Lao aristocracy (such as Souphanouvong himself) and former officials of the RLG. Significantly, the Pathet Lao government also included two representatives of Laos's tribal groups who were made ministers without portfolio.

By 1950 both Kaysone and Nouhak had become members of the ICP. The party's strategy was to operate clandestinely behind broad national front organizations such as the Viet Minh and the Neo Lao Issara that were capable of mobilizing support from people for whom Marxism-Leninism held no appeal. This strategy applied particularly to Laos, where issues such as land reform and other aspects of class struggle, antithetical to the notion of Buddhist harmony, had almost no appeal. The overthrow of the monarchy, which had figured as a goal in the ICP program since 1932, was also not publicized.

Although the ICP had announced its dissolution in 1945, it continued to operate secretly. In February 1951, at its second congress, the ICP decided to split into separate parties for each of the three countries—Vietnam, Laos, and Cambodia—in accordance with the need to mobilize mass support for the anti-French war throughout Indochina. At this time, of 2,091 ICP members in Laos, only thirty-one were Laotians. The Laotian members of the ICP were "transferred" to a new party whose name reflected its Laotian constituency but that was still tied to the two other parties of the ICP in the new triad.

That Luang in Vientiane, the most important Laotian national monument, has a golden stupa believed to contain a relic of the Buddha.
Courtesy Gina Merris

The decision to form a new party led to considerable discussion among noncommunist Pathet Lao supporters unfamiliar with Leninist strategy. In the second half of 1954, an important meeting of Pathet Lao leaders was held near the Houaphan Province border, where the need to establish this new party to ensure success of the struggle in the postwar period was explained. Some participants supported this proposal; others did not. Proponents of the new party met in secret. The Phak Pasason Lao (Lao People's Party—LPP) was formally established on March 22, 1955. The very existence of the party was kept a secret from nonparty people.

By 1951 enough Pathet Lao troops had been recruited and trained to take part in Viet Minh military operations against French Union forces in Laos. In the spring of 1953, the Viet Minh overran almost all of Houaphan Province and portions of

Phôngsali, Xiangkhoang, and Louangphrabang provinces. Approximately 300 Pathet Lao accompanied the Viet Minh. On April 19, Souphanouvong formally established the Pathet Lao government in Houaphan Province. A "people's tribunal" presided over by Kaysone condemned the acting province chief to death for having helped organize guerrilla resistance to the invaders.

With Louangphrabang in danger of Viet Minh occupation, Crown Prince Savang Vatthana received a letter from the United States chargé d'affaires in Saigon, Robert McClintock, expressing concern for the king's safety and saying that withdrawal from the capital "would seem the course of wisdom." Savang said that the king intended to stay to bolster morale for the defense of his capital. At the end of 1953 and beginning of 1954, the Viet Minh again invaded Laos, pushing as far as Thakhek and creating considerable difficulties for the French Union defenders. Their appearance seemed timed to coincide with the sale of the opium crop in Houaphan and Xiangkhoang provinces.

In elections to the National Assembly held on August 26, 1951, the National Progressive Party (Phak Xat Kao Na) formed by the returned Lao Issara ministers, Xieng Mao, Souvanna Phouma, and Katay Don Sasorith, won fifteen of thirty-nine seats. The Democratic Party (Praxathipatay) of Kou Voravong and his brother-in-law, Major Phoumi Nosavan, won four seats; the National Lao Union (Lao Rouam Samphan) of Bong Souvannavong won three; and seventeen seats went to independents that included Phoui Sananikone and Leuam Insixiengmay. With Xieng Mao having failed to form a government, Prince Souvanna Phouma headed a government that was invested on November 21. The Franco-Lao Treaty of Amity and Association on October 22, 1953, removed the last strictures on independence.

Toward Neutrality: The First Coalition

It was thus as a fully sovereign country that Laos sent a delegation headed by its foreign minister, Phoui Sananikone, to the Geneva Conference on Indochina that put an end to the First Indochina War in July 1954. The armistice agreement for Laos, signed by a French general on behalf of French Union forces and a Viet Minh military official, provided for a cease-fire to take effect at 8:00 a.m. on August 6. Viet Minh forces were to be withdrawn from Laos to North Vietnam within 120 days. The Viet Minh delegation had brought Nouhak and another Pathet Lao member, Ma Khamphitay, with them to Geneva on Viet Minh passports, intending to have a Pathet Lao delegation seated, but they were not recognized by the conference. A provision in the armistice agreement for Laos was nevertheless inserted providing for the "fighting units of Pathet Lao" to be regrouped in Houaphan and Phôngsali provinces pending a political settlement. The RLG pledged to take steps to integrate all Laotian citizens into the political life of the kingdom.

The representatives of the other powers at Geneva signed no conference documents but instead subscribed to the Final Declaration taking note of the armistice agreements. United States Secretary of State John Foster Dulles lobbied hard to ensure that the Laotians made no unnecessary concessions to the communists. At the final session, the United States delegation declared that it would refrain from the threat or use of force to disturb the armistice agreements and that it would view any violations of them as a threat to peace and security. Chinese premier Zhou Enlai stressed the advisability of a coalition government to the Laotians, urging an early meeting between princes Souvanna Phouma and Souphanouvong. He seemed prepared to offer an exchange of diplomats, his main concern being that Laos be free of United States military bases.

Initial Difficulties

Implementation of the armistice agreement in Laos began on schedule. The Joint Commission, on which the RLG was represented by General Bounphone Maekthepharak, Colonel Sengsouvanh Souvannarath, and Colonel Boun Ma, and the Pathet Lao by Singkapo, Sisavath, and Ma Khamphitay, held a number of meetings at Khang Khay to deal with the details. The presence of the International Control Commission (ICC), made up of Canada, India, and Poland, also helped force the two sides to live up to their commitments. However, the insistence of the Pathet Lao that their regroupment areas cover the entire territory of the two provinces, along with a right to exclusive administration of those provinces, raised serious problems almost immediately. Another part of the armistice agreement that caused difficulties was, as noted in an ICC report, the ". . . glaring differences regarding the number and categories of prisoners of war and civil internees exchanged."

It became clear that higher-level negotiations were needed. Princes Souvanna Phouma and Souphanouvong met at Khang Khay on September 8. The assassination of the defense minister, Kou Voravong, in Vientiane on September 18, however, demonstrated the fragility of the Laotian political structure. The act seemed to be a settling of old scores, dating probably to Kou's energetic measures as interior minister to suppress banditry perpetrated from across the river. Thailand also seemed to be implicated, but the announcement by Thai police that they had arrested the assassin, who claimed to have been in league with Phoui, only poisoned relations between the Voravong and Sananikone families. Crown Prince Savang wondered aloud whether Phetsarath, with the help of foreigners, was trying to oust the monarchy.

The Pathet Lao and their North Vietnamese backers, meanwhile, took advantage of the cease-fire to launch a vast recruitment campaign. In the cases of numerous recruits who were later interviewed, the offer of schooling or more specialized training in North Vietnam proved decisive to their enlistment, and even those who were initially skeptical were ultimately won over by the attentions of their Vietnamese instructors and the persuasiveness of the political lessons they received. One major consequence of this campaign was that the Pathet Lao ranks were swelled by recruits from the many different hill tribes of Laos. These men were to constitute the initial Pathet Lao units. The immediate goal after regrouping in the two provinces was to form nine battalions, plus independent companies for propaganda missions.

Laos, a member of the United Nations (UN) since December 14, 1955, seemed an unlikely place for a resumption of hostilities. Peaceful coexistence was the dominant mood of the time. A new government under Katay was represented at the Asian-African Conference held in April 1955 in Bandung, Indonesia, where he and North Vietnamese prime minister Pham Van Dong spoke of peace and noninterference in each other's affairs. But an initial round of negotiations between the government and the Pathet Lao in Rangoon in October collapsed, dashing hopes of a rapid settlement of the Pathet Lao question. Armed clashes between the Royal Lao Army and the Pathet Lao continued sporadically in the two provinces.

The threat to the RLG posed by a combination of internal subversion and outside aggression preoccupied its leaders, none more so than Crown Prince Savang Vatthana. As early as summer 1954, fearing a French deal with the Viet Minh that might be injurious to Laotian sovereignty and territorial integrity, Savang had flown to Paris to make his own soundings of French intentions. He was also anxious to probe United States diplomats for reassurances as to the nature of the support Laos could expect in the event of an attack from its communist neighbors. He told Dulles that Laos was in a "life or death struggle" for survival and that the Laotian people were opposed to communist dictatorship. Dulles replied, "You can count upon our support—moral, political, and material—so long as that support goes to a government vigorously seeking to maintain its own independence."

Washington's immediate concern was that the Royal Lao Army was inadequately trained and equipped because all French troops, except for a small detachment at Xéno in the south, had departed. The Geneva armistice terms prohibited Laos from having foreign military bases and participating in any foreign military alliance, but allowed a small French training mission. Dissatisfied with the French mission and seeing a larger role for itself, the United States established a disguised military mission in Vientiane, the Programs Evaluation Office (PEO). This mission became operational on December 13, 1955, under the command of a general officer, who, like others on his staff, had been removed from Department of Defense rosters of active service personnel. The secrecy stemmed from the Department of State's concern that the PEO's existence might be construed as a violation of the Geneva Agreement of 1954, which United States policy continued to uphold.

The RLG held elections in December 1955 without the Pathet Lao. As a result, the Progressive Party again emerged as the leading party with eighteen seats; the newly formed Independent Party (Phak Seli) of Phoui Sananikone and Leuam secured nine seats, the Democratic Party secured four seats, and the National Union Party won two seats.

Renewed Negotiations

After the elections, Souvanna Phouma signaled a renewed effort at negotiations, when, presenting his new government to the National Assembly on March 20, 1956, he called the settlement of the Pathet Lao problem "the gravest and most urgent" question before the country. He opened negotiations in Vientiane in August; the Pathet Lao were represented by Soupha-nouvong. Two joint declarations issued shortly thereafter by the delegations pledged agreement on a foreign policy of peaceful coexistence, a new cease-fire in the two northern provinces, exercise of democratic freedoms, authorization for the Pathet Lao's political party to operate, procedures for the RLG's administration in the two provinces, integration of Pathet Lao units into the Royal Lao Army, the formation of two mixed commissions to work out the above-mentioned details, the holding of supplementary elections to an enlarged National Assembly, and the establishment of a coalition govern-ment. In preparation for engaging in the politics of the king-dom, the Pathet Lao had formed an organization to act as a front—the Neo Lao Hak Xat (Lao Patriotic Front—LPF; see Glossary) in January 1956, with an innocuous-sounding plat-form. Souphanouvong and the other Pathet Lao delegates took the oath of allegiance to the king in the presence of Souvanna Phouma and Kou Abhay, president of the King's Council. This round of negotiations concluded in a further series of agree-ments covering a cease-fire, implementation of a policy of peace and neutrality, and measures guaranteeing civic rights and nondiscrimination against Pathet Lao followers.

In late August, Souvanna Phouma visited Beijing and Hanoi, where he was warmly received. Far from committing Laos to the communist bloc as the United States Department of State feared, these visits formed part of Souvanna Phouma's strategy to neutralize the danger to Laotian independence posed by the Pathet Lao. It was obvious to him that communism held little appeal for the inhabitants of Laos. Although there were com-munists among the leaders of the Pathet Lao—and Souvanna Phouma refused to believe his half-brother was one of them—the communists depended on the exercise, or at least the threat, of armed force to carry out their "revolution." Sou-vanna Phouma's strategy was intended to separate the national-ists from the communists in the Pathet Lao. He warned the Pathet Lao's foreign backers that if they provided sanctuary to armed resistance groups—once the Pathet Lao had been rein-tegrated into the kingdom's political life—they would be going back on their pledges of noninterference.

At the same time, however, Souvanna Phouma's ideas for safeguarding Laotian independence differed radically from Dulles's. Dulles viewed the Pathet Lao as unacceptable coali-tion partners; in his view, they were all simply communists rather than a front comprising a number of nationalists. The United States ambassador in Vientiane, J. Graham Parsons, informed Souvanna Phouma that Washington was implacably opposed to a coalition government. The United States remained unmollified by a secret protocol attached to a November 2, 1956, agreement on a neutral foreign policy that proscribed the establishment of diplomatic relations with North Vietnam and China in the immediate future. On November 22, Parsons was instructed to inform the prime minister that the United States was unable to respond favorably to his appeal for support.

Negotiations with the Pathet Lao resumed in February 1957 but were interrupted when Souvanna Phouma resigned in May over an unfavorable vote in the National Assembly. In the interim, Phetsarath had been persuaded to return from Thailand. Unbowed by age, but no longer keen on a role for himself in politics, he returned in March and took up residence in Louangphrabang, where, in a gesture of royal reconciliation, he made his obeisance to the king and received back his old title of viceroy.

A Fragile Unity

Souvanna Phouma returned as prime minister in August 1957 following a cabinet crisis and was charged by the king with forming a new government. He reopened negotiations, and on October 22, a final agreement was reached. This agreement called for reestablishing RLG administration over the two provinces, forming a coalition government, and holding supplementary elections to the National Assembly. The government set elections for May 1958. On November 18, Souphanouvong symbolically returned to RLG authority, represented by Crown Prince Savang, the two provinces, together with all the troops, civil servants, and war matériel belonging to the Pathet Lao. A RLG governor was appointed in Houaphan and a Pathet Lao governor in Phôngsali, each with a deputy of the opposite camp. Mayoral and other provincial official positions were equally divided between the two parties. It was agreed that two Pathet Lao battalions, totaling 1,500 troops, would be integrated into the Royal Lao Army and the remainder would be demobilized and sent home. The National Assembly unanimously approved the coalition government. Souphanouvong became minister of planning, reconstruction, and urbanism, and Phoumi Vongvichit became minister of culture and fine arts.

Souvanna Phouma visited Washington in January 1958 hoping to persuade United States policy makers, who worried about his having accepted Pathet Lao participation in the government in advance of elections, that his strategy for dealing with the Pathet Lao was the best course. He left Washington, however, without gaining unqualified support for his strategy.

United States aid failed to blunt the effects of Pathet Lao propaganda and indoctrination in the villages. The Pathet Lao were masters of political persuasion, exploiting popular themes of nationalism, anticorruption, and "anti-big family." There were exceptions, however, to the general negative perception of United States aid. Tom Dooley, a physician from the United States, brought health care to the people who needed it most, those in remote villages. Another American—an Indiana farmer named Edgar "Pop" Buell—devoted the last years of his life to helping the Hmong, including training the first Hmong nurses and opening Hmong schools.

The 1958 Elections

The stunning success of the LPF and its allies in winning thirteen of the twenty-one seats contested in the May 4, 1958, elections to the National Assembly changed the political atmosphere in Vientiane. This success had less to do with the LPF's adroitness than with the ineptness of the old-line nationalists, who were more intent on advancing their personal interests than on meeting the challenge from the LPF. The two largest parties, the Progressive Party and the Independent Party, could not agree on a list of common candidates in spite of repeated prodding by the United States embassy and so split their votes among dozens of candidates. The LPF and the Peace (Santiphab) Party carefully worked out a strategy of mutual support, which succeeded in winning nearly two-thirds of the seats with barely one-third of the votes cast. Souphanouvong garnered the most votes and became chairman of the National Assembly. The Progressive Party and the Independent Party tardily merged to become the Rally of the Lao People (Lao Rouam Lao).

In the wake of the election fiasco, Washington concentrated on finding alternatives to Souvanna Phouma's strategy of winning over the Pathet Lao and on building up the Royal Lao

Viet Minh and Laotian officials on November 1, 1945, reviewing a parade of troops of the Chinese Nationalist 93d Division in Vientiane. Prince Souphanouvong, commander in chief, Lao Issara forces, is in uniform in the front row, next to his young son, Ariya. Courtesy Tran Van Dinh (former military adviser, intelligence and operations, to Prince Souphanouvong)

Army as the only cohesive nationalist force capable of dealing with the communists' united front tactics. On June 10, 1958, a new political grouping called the Committee for the Defense of the National Interests (CDNI) made its appearance. Formed mainly of a younger generation not tied to the big families and as yet untainted by corruption, it announced a program for revitalizing the economy, forming an anticommunist front that excluded the Pathet Lao, suppressing corruption, and creating a national mystique.

Washington, which was paying the entire salary cost of the Royal Lao Army, was enthusiastic about the "young turks" of the CDNI. This enthusiasm was not altogether shared by

United States ambassador Horace H. Smith, who asked what right a group untested by any election had to set its sights on cabinet appointments. Whereas Souvanna Phouma tried and failed to form a government, creating a drawn-out cabinet crisis, Phoui Sananikone eventually succeeded and included four CDNI members and Phoumi Nosavan in a subcabinet post.

North Vietnamese Invasion

In foreign and domestic affairs, the atmosphere changed in the summer of 1958. Souvanna Phouma announced that with the holding of elections the RLG had fulfilled the political obligations it had assumed at Geneva, and the ICC adjourned sine die. Phoui, less scrupulous about preserving Laos's neutrality than his predecessor, angered Beijing and Hanoi by admitting diplomats from Taipei and Saigon. China and North Vietnam, already upset by the departure of the ICC, which they had seen as a restraining influence, protested. The United States worked out an agreement with France that reduced the role of the French military mission and enlarged that of the PEO, which embarked on a major strengthening of its staff and functions.

The occupation by North Vietnamese security forces in December 1958 of several villages in Xépôn District near the Demilitarized Zone (DMZ) between North Vietnam and South Vietnam was an ominous development. The RLG immediately protested the flying of the North Vietnamese flag on Laotian territory. Hanoi claimed the villages had historically been part of Vietnam. With regard to precedent, this was a decidedly modest claim; nonetheless, it represented a unilateral reinterpretation of the French map used by the Truong Gia Armistice Commission in the summer of 1954 to draw the DMZ, and, backed by force of arms, it constituted nothing less than aggression. Phoui received extraordinary powers from the National Assembly to deal with the crisis. But the failure to regain their lost territory rankled the Laotian nationalists, who were hoping for a greater degree of United States support.

One of Washington's major preoccupations was the danger that the Royal Lao Army would integrate the Pathet Lao troops without the safeguard of "screening and reindoctrinating" them. The embassy was instructed to tell the government that it would be difficult to obtain congressional approval of aid to Laos with communists in the Royal Lao Army. Before the final integration of 1,500 Pathet Lao troops (two battalions) into the

Royal Lao Army could take place as planned in May 1959, the Pathet Lao used a quibble about officer ranks to delay the final ceremony. As monsoon rains swept over the Plain of Jars one night, one of the two battalions slipped away, followed soon after by the other, near Louangphrabang. The event signaled a resumption of hostilities. In July Phoui's government, after protracted cabinet deliberations, ordered the arrest of the LPF deputies in Vientiane—Souphanouvong, Nouhak, Phoumi Vongvichit, Phoun Sipaseut, Sithon Kommadan, Singkapo, and others. Tiao Souk Vongsak evaded arrest.

Fighting broke out all along the border with North Vietnam. North Vietnamese regular army units participated in attacks on July 28–31, 1959. These operations established a pattern of North Vietnamese forces leading the attack on a strong point, then falling back and letting the Pathet Lao remain in place once resistance to the advance had been broken. The tactic had the advantage of concealing from view the North Vietnamese presence. Rumors of North Vietnamese in the vicinity often had a terrifying effect, however. Among the men who heard such rumors in the mountains of Houaphan Province that summer was a young Royal Lao Army captain named Kong Le. Kong Le had two companies of the Second Paratroop Battalion out on patrol almost on the North Vietnamese border. When they returned to Xam Nua without encountering the enemy, they found that the garrison had decamped, leaving the town undefended.

Direct North Vietnamese involvement in Laos began taking another form wherein aggression was difficult to prove. Two months after the 1954 Geneva Conference on Indochina, the North Vietnamese established a small support group known as Group 100, on the Thanh Hoa-Houaphan border at Ban Namèo. This unit provided logistical and other support to Pathet Lao forces. In view of the reversion to a fighting strategy, the North Vietnamese and Lao parties decided to establish an upgraded unit. The new unit, known as Group 959, headquartered at Na Kai, just inside the Houaphan border, began operating in September 1959. Its establishment coincided with a major effort to expand the hitherto small Pathet Lao forces. According to an official history published after the war, its mission was "serving as specialists for the Military Commission and Supreme Command of the Lao People's Liberation Army, and organizing the supplying of Vietnamese matériel to the Laotian revolution and directly commanding the Vietnamese volunteer units operating in Xam Nua, Xiangkhoang, and Viangchan." These actions were in violation of the obligation Ho Chi Minh's government had assumed as a participant in the 1954 Geneva Conference to refrain from any interference in the internal affairs of Laos.

The Vietnamese party's strategy was by now decided with regard to South Vietnam. At the same time, the party outlined a role for the LPP that was supportive of North Vietnam, in addition to the LPP's role as leader of the revolution in Laos. Hanoi's southern strategy opened the first tracks through the extremely rugged terrain of Xépôn district in mid-1959 of what was to become the Ho Chi Minh Trail.

Phetsarath and Sisavang Vong, viceroy and king, died within two weeks of each other in October 1959. Sisavang Vong reigned over Laos for fifty-four turbulent years as a man of honor, and, after his death, his memory was so venerated that when the communists came to power in Vientiane they left his statue standing. His successor, Savang Vatthana, lacked both his father's hold on his people and Phetsarath's charisma. A deeply fatalistic man who foresaw he would be the last king of Laos, Savang Vatthana remained uncrowned for the rest of his reign because a propitious date for the coronation ceremony could not be found.

The Army Enters Politics

With the LPF's deputies in prison, the political scene became increasingly chaotic, even lawless. When Phoui's mandate ended in December 1959, Phoumi Nosavan and his CDNI supporters began their move to force the king to grant them power by announcing that the supreme command of the armed forces was "handling current affairs." Their move, however, was too bold and caused the Western ambassadors in Vientiane to present a united front to the king in support of constitutionality. An interim government headed by Kou Abhay was charged with preparing for new elections. Phoumi, temporarily rebuffed, bided his time as minister of defense. The army had entered politics but not quite in the manner Washington had hoped.

In the April 24, 1960, elections, Phoumi found his revenge. By exerting considerable pressure, he had changes made in the electoral law. With financial support from Marshal Sarit Thanarat of Thailand, Phoumi bought off strong or inconvenient candidates and enlisted civil servants as his campaign workers. Election balloting was fraudulent, and the results, giving rightist candidates large majorities, were totally unbelievable. A new government was formed on June 3, ostensibly headed by Somsanith but in fact controlled by Phoumi acting as minister of defense under the aegis of his new political party, the Social Party (Paxa Sangkhom). Souvanna Phouma, elected without fraud, became the president of the National Assembly. The imprisoned LPF deputies had not been allowed to run for the Assembly, but sent word to LPF supporters to vote for any LPF candidates who had dared run or else to vote for Peace Party candidates. However, on May 23, under darkness and with the cooperation of personnel at their prison, the LPF deputies escaped and disappeared into the countryside.

The Attempt to Restore Neutrality

On August 9, Captain Kong Le led the Second Paratroop Battalion in a virtually bloodless coup d'état that changed the history of modern Laos. In taking over Vientiane, the paratroopers had unwittingly chosen a moment when the entire cabinet was in Louangphrabang conferring with the king. They informed their compatriots and the outside world by broadcasting their communiqués on the radio. In a rally at the city football stadium on August 11, Kong Le expanded on his goals: end the fighting in Laos, stem corruption, and establish a policy of peace and neutrality. Recalling the experience of the first coalition when the country was temporarily at peace, Kong Le asked for the nomination of Souvanna Phouma as prime minister.

On August 11, General Ouan Ratikoun, as the cabinet's envoy, arrived in Vientiane from Louangphrabang. After negotiations with Kong Le and Souvanna Phouma as president of the National Assembly, Ouan returned to Louangphrabang with a document in which the coup leaders requested the cabinet to return. They agreed to withdraw their forces to specified points in the city and stipulated that these steps would lead to negotiations on the government's future. Two days later, however, when Ouan returned alone, it became evident that the cabinet was reluctant to return to Vientiane. Once this news spread, demonstrators gathered outside the Presidency of the Council of Ministers demanding Somsanith's immediate resignation; they next marched on the National Assembly, where

Souvanna Phouma met them and, startled by their vehemence, attempted to moderate their demands. Inside, the forty-one deputies present voted unanimously to censure the Somsanith government. On August 14, a delegation of the assembly carried the news of this vote to Louangphrabang and asked the king to name Souvanna Phouma to form a new government. Fearing violence in Vientiane, Somsanith resigned, and the king named Souvanna Phouma prime minister. The new government was invested by thirty-four deputies on August 16. The next day, Kong Le declared his coup d'état over and vacated the Presidency of the Council of Ministers.

On receiving word of the coup, Phoumi flew from Louangphrabang to Ubol, where he informed Thai and United States officials of his intention to "straighten things out" in Laos and from where he sent emissaries to Savannakhét and Pakxé. In Bangkok the following day, Phoumi met with Sarit, United States embassy counselor Leonard Unger, and the chief of the United States military mission in Thailand. He outlined plans for a parachute drop to recapture the Vientiane airport and ferry in additional forces by air to oust the rebels. He requested that Thailand and the United States provide air transport, fuel, salaries for his troops, and two radio broadcasting units. He also asked for a secure channel of communication between his new headquarters at Savannakhét and Bangkok.

These steps, taken in secrecy, received immediate approval in Washington. Orders went out to designate a senior PEO officer as liaison to Phoumi, and a PEO channel was established between Savannakhét and the United States military mission in Bangkok, bypassing the embassy in Vientiane. Aircraft of Civil Air Transport, a Central Intelligence Agency (CIA) front, were made available to Phoumi, and Laotian troops training at bases in Thailand were to be returned as soon as possible to Savannakhét.

Sarit, Pibul's minister of defense who had come to power in a coup in October 1958, had invested heavily in Phoumi and was not about to let him go. The United States Joint Chiefs of Staff, for their part, saw aid to Phoumi as preserving at least part of the anticommunist forces in Laos from the effects of the split in the royal army. But from this point on, much as United States officials tried to separate the two issues, aid to the anticommunists in Laos was inseparable from Sarit's personal commitment to Phoumi. The United States embassy in Bangkok was also alarmed by the possibility that inadequate support for Phoumi might lead Sarit to intervene unilaterally in Laos because he had already imposed a blockade on Vientiane.

A Deepening Split

Phoumi enlisted the support of the commanders of four of Laos's five military regions. He also began immediately broadcasting propaganda denouncing Kong Le as a communist and on August 15 proclaimed the establishment of a Counter Coup d'État Committee. He appealed to all military personnel to rally behind him, guaranteed their salaries, and proclaimed his intention to liberate Vientiane from communist hands. Forces loyal to Phoumi seized Pakxan.

The United States considered Souvanna Phouma's return to office bad news. A Department of State cable stated that the United States sought "to bring about an acceptable power balance of non-communist elements which would eliminate Kong Le and restore authority and stability."

Souvanna Phouma, wanting to avoid civil war, with Phoumi's concurrence convoked the National Assembly in Louangphrabang on August 29. A new government, with Souvanna Phouma as prime minister and Phoumi as deputy prime minister and minister of interior, was sworn in on August 31. Phoumi announced the dissolution of his Counter Coup d'État Committee. This might have defused the crisis, but the same day, Kong Le made a radio broadcast protesting the presence of Phoumi in the cabinet. Souvanna Phouma convinced him to change his mind, which he did "for the sake of peace and reconciliation" on September 1. Phoumi returned to Savannakhét and waited.

On September 10, Prince Boun Oum, speaking from Savannakhét in the name of the new Revolutionary Committee, announced that the constitution had been abolished, and he and Phoumi were assuming power. In mid-September, two companies of Kong Le's paratroopers routed the two battalions of Phoumi's advance guard from their position at Pakxan and installed a defensive line on the north bank of the Nam Kading. Phoumi made no move to organize his paratroop drop on Vientiane, in spite of the considerable means at his disposal. On the evening of September 21, Sarit made a speech in which he hinted at Thai armed intervention in Laos.

Kong Le's reputation as a giant slayer had by now spread from the capital to the far corners of the kingdom. On September 28, when he dropped a handful of paratroopers near Xam Nua in order to explain the situation to the 1,500-person garrison that in principle was loyal to Souvanna Phouma, rumors that the garrison's officers, some of whom had been in contact with Phoumi, might be cashiered created a panic. The garrison abandoned the town to the Pathet Lao, who were accompanied by their North Vietnamese advisers from Group 959. The withdrawing column surrendered its arms to the Pathet Lao near Muang Peun on October 2.

The Pathet Lao now claimed to be supporting Souvanna Phouma. The coup and Phoumi's resistance with foreign assistance, which the United States and Thailand had difficulty camouflaging, gave the still-secret LPP an unprecedented opportunity to burrow more deeply behind the nationalist mantle, and it lost no time in seizing the occasion. Many Laotians came to see the Pathet Lao as acting to defend the country against United States- and Thai-backed aggression. Even in Vientiane, there was growing resentment of the Thai blockade, which caused a shortage of consumer goods and rising prices. Foreseeing an opening for the Pathet Lao to negotiate with the new government, Radio Hanoi and Radio Beijing broadcast support for Souvanna Phouma.

Although Souvanna Phouma's government was accepted as the legal government of Laos by Britain, France, and the United States, this did not prevent the United States from broadening its support to Phoumi's forces on the grounds that they were fighting the Pathet Lao. In fact, there is no record of their taking any offensive action against the Pathet Lao. Phoumi had ordered the pullback from Xam Nua. Winthrop G. Brown, the new United States ambassador, reported instances where Phoumi refused help to engage the Pathet Lao because it was offered by Vientiane. The only offensive actions taken by Royal Lao Army troops against the Pathet Lao between August and December 1960 were those taken by troops loyal to Souvanna Phouma in Phôngsali and elsewhere.

The "compromise" worked out by the embassy with Souvanna Phouma, in which the prime minister would not object to direct United States military aid to Phoumi as long as this aid was not used against his government, was a sham. Whenever the embassy tried to persuade Phoumi to give up his plan and return to Vientiane, Phoumi pleaded fear for his safety and escalated his demands. In Louangphrabang, King Savang Vatthana temporized, hoping to bring the military leaders together at least in a united stand against the communists and putting off a political solution until later. Failing to achieve his aim, he retreated, saying he was disgusted with all concerned. Brown felt he was waiting for Phoumi's capture of Vientiane to get him off the hook and avoid the necessity of his taking any categoric action.

Brown cabled Washington on October 5 that, in the continued absence of an agreement between Phoumi and Souvanna Phouma, United States support of Phoumi would lead to "further disintegration" of the anticommunist forces and would involve the United States in actions that risked internationalizing the conflict in Laos.

At a meeting on October 11 with a visiting United States delegation made up of Parsons, Assistant Secretary of Defense John N. Irwin II, and Vice Admiral Herbert D. Riley, chief of staff to the commander in chief, Pacific, Souvanna Phouma gave an indictment of the provocative errors committed by his successors after formation of the first coalition. He warned that the only course for Laos was to implement the 1957 agreements before the Pathet Lao—with whom he was in touch and intended to resume negotiations—presented even more far-reaching demands. The first Soviet ambassador to Laos, Aleksandr N. Abramov, arrived as Parsons was leaving.

After conferring with the king, the Parsons-Irwin-Riley team proceeded to Bangkok. On October 17, Irwin and Riley met with Phoumi in Ubol. Although the Department of State at that point was under the impression that United States policy required that Phoumi dissolve the Revolutionary Committee, both as a gesture of good faith toward Souvanna Phouma in preserving the unity of anticommunist forces in Laos and, more practically, in order to avoid the growing impression abroad that the United States was illegally aiding a rebel movement, no mention of this point was made either in Parsons's instructions to his two colleagues or at the October 17 meeting.

Following the formal conversation, Riley took Phoumi aside and told him that the United States had completely lost confidence in Souvanna Phouma and was backing Phoumi to go back and clean up the situation. Irwin similarly told Phoumi that although the United States was only supporting him in building up his defenses for the moment, in the long run the United States was supporting him all the way. The message was not lost on Phoumi. The effect of these unauthorized remarks was to undercut both Souvanna Phouma's efforts to negotiate a compromise solution with Phoumi and Brown's bona fides with Souvanna Phouma, already strained by the continuing United States aid flowing into Savannakhét in the absence of any matching military action against the Pathet Lao. Phoumi's intransigence in turn led the Department of State to make ever-increasing demands on Souvanna Phouma in the interest of "compromise," beginning with the charge that the prime minister was not exercising sufficient control over Kong Le, the demand that he take appropriate precautions to prevent Kong Le from launching an attack on Savannakhét, and so forth.

Souvanna Phouma began negotiations with the Pathet Lao on October 18. However, his position was much weaker than in 1957 when he faced the same set of Pathet Lao demands. Although nothing substantive would come from these negotiations, they provided fuel for Phoumi's anticommunist propaganda and heightened nervousness in Washington and Bangkok.

Next, Phoumi forced the commander of the Louangphrabang garrison to declare for the Revolutionary Committee. This was an important move, for it placed the king within Phoumi's territory. In Bangkok, Sarit's first reaction on hearing the news was to ask the United States ambassador, U. Alexis Johnson, whether now would be a good time for the Revolutionary Committee to "establish itself as a government." General Ouan Ratikoun quickly defected to Savannakhét. Phoumi captured another general, Amkha Soukhavong, at Xiangkhoang and gained the support of General Sing Ratanassamay. Phoumi's troops had been paid without Brown's having been consulted. Ambassador Johnson, without consulting Brown, assured Sarit that the United States would pay Phoumi's troops, an action that Brown protested.

When Phoumi finally launched his offensive on the Nam Kading on November 21, Souvanna Phouma vainly attempted to contact him. With badly needed supplies to Vientiane, especially fuel, still cut off by the Thai blockade, Souvanna Phouma's forced acceptance of a Soviet offer of aid lent Phoumi's imminent attack "to drive out the communists" a semblance of legitimacy. On December 11, Phoumi led the forty National Assembly deputies who had gathered in Savannahkét over the preceding weeks to vote no confidence in Souvanna Phouma's government. The king accepted the vote as legal the next day when he signed Royal Ordinance No. 282, dismissing Souvanna Phouma's government and giving powers provisionally to the Revolutionary Committee. Royal Ordinance No. 283, approving a provisional government formed by Prince Boun Oum, who acted as front man for Phoumi—the king had scruples about naming a general to be prime minister—was signed on December 14. The Department of State notified its acceptance of the new regime and said it was acting to meet its requests for assistance "to restore peace to the country." At this time, neither the deputies nor the court were free agents—and Souvanna Phouma had not resigned.

The Battle of Vientiane

The capital braced for Phoumi's attack. A last-minute and temporary switch of sides by Colonel Kouprasith Abhay, commander of the Vientiane military region headquartered at Camp Chinaimo on the eastern outskirts, was quickly neutralized by Kong Le, but tension heightened. The Pathet Lao delegation hurriedly left town. More of Souvanna Phouma's ministers disappeared and reappeared. The situation was becoming ungovernable. Souvanna Phouma viewed battle as inevitable, and, accompanied by his ministers Boun Om (Boun Oum's nephew), Tiao Sisoumang Sisaleumsak, and Inpeng Suriyadhay, flew to Phnom Penh on December 9, having delegated his powers to the military. The following morning, Quinim Pholsena, the minister of information whom Souvanna Phouma had left behind, flew to Hanoi accompanied by Phoumi Vongvichit, the chief Pathet Lao negotiator, and Lieutenant Deuane Sunnalath, Kong Le's deputy, on a mission to seek Soviet and North Vietnamese military aid, which began arriving the following day on Soviet aircraft.

Phoumi began his attack on December 13. From his command post near the airport, Kong Le had positioned his men at key points on the outskirts, intending merely to fight a delaying action to allow the safe evacuation to the north of his men and their equipment. The regional command post of the Pathet Lao, situated at Na Khang, sixty kilometers north of the capital, disposed of three guerrilla groups but did not take part in the battle of Vientiane. A massive display of firepower by Phoumi's troops resulted in the deaths of 400 to 500 civilians in the town, mostly Vietnamese residents, and the wounding of another 1,000 to 1,500 civilians. Kong Le's troops only lost seventeen. Phoumi's armor rolled into town on December 16.

Kong Le retreated slowly northward toward Louangphrabang, while Soviet aircraft parachuted in badly needed supplies—rice, salt, sugar, blankets, light arms, ammunition, and radios. With new recruits, his ranks had swelled from 800 to 1,200 men. On December 23, at Phôn Hông, about sixty kilometers north of the capital, Kong Le was visited by Kaysone, who had come to settle the details of distribution of Soviet aid and coordination of Neutralist and Pathet Lao troops in future operations. On January 1, Kong Le's troops took control of the Plain of Jars and Khang Khay after skirmishing with some of the 9,000 Phoumist troops and an equal number of Hmong guerrillas in the vicinity and recovered large quantities of supplies. The following day, the Neutralists occupied Xiangkhoang, and United States advisers and Phoumist troops were evacuated from the Muang Phônsavan airfield.

Quinim and Tiao Sisaleumsak established themselves at Khang Khay and urged Souvanna Phouma, who was in Cambodia, to join them. Souvanna Phouma said that he was still legally prime minister but would resign at once if Phoumi's government were validated in accordance with the constitution. Souvanna Phouma argued that the National Assembly's vote of no confidence on December 11 was not valid because it had taken place in neither the royal capital nor the administrative capital. He regarded the king's dealings with the Revolutionary Committee as beyond the king's authority. When the National Assembly met in Vientiane and voted confidence in the Boun Oum government on January 4, Souvanna Phouma ignored the action.

The Widening War

The Soviet airlift, which continued despite United States protests to Moscow, transformed the Plain of Jars into a vast armed camp, fully resupplying Kong Le. For the first time, the Pathet Lao were equipped with heavy weapons allowing them to play a major role in their military alliance with Kong Le's troops in support of Souvanna Phouma's government. There was, moreover, another and more important factor: the commitment of significant numbers of North Vietnamese troops to the fighting, exactly what Souvanna Phouma and Brown had

The Anousavari, in Vientiane, is built of cement and has bas-relief on the sides and temple-like ornamentation along the top and cornices; a stairway leads to the top of the monument, which provides panoramic views of the city. Courtesy Gina Merris

feared. Kong Le requested four battalions of North Vietnamese troops on January 7. Two of these linked up with his forces on Route 7 and down Route 13. The third was engaged in military action at Tha Thom, a key defense point south of the Plain of Jars. The fourth took up a position north of the plain.

In Xiangkhoang, the Hmong once again blew up the bridges on Route 7 in a desperate effort to interfere with North Vietnamese truck convoys rolling westward. The Royal Lao Army had been quietly supplying arms to the Hmong since at least March 1957 to enable them to resist the Pathet Lao, but the North Vietnamese influx created a sudden need for arms far in excess of what the Laotians could supply, even with the help of Thailand. The Hmong, under their military leader Vang Pao, had taken up positions in the mountains surrounding the Plain of Jars and asked to talk to United States officials. Vang Pao requested quick delivery of arms, but United States officials were concerned that the Hmong would not fight, and the arms might fall into communist hands. Vang Pao said all 7,000 volunteers would fight, but they needed the arms in three days or they would have to fall back to less exposed positions. United States airdrops of arms from stocks in Okinawa began three days later, signaling the beginning of a heroic Hmong resistance.

International Pressure and the Advent of the Second Coalition

Souvanna Phouma reaffirmed his position that his was the legal government of Laos. In an interview, he spoke bitterly about his nemesis, Parsons, and said that "the Savannakhét group" was committed to the policy of military confrontation that had failed in the past. He believed Laos should conserve its ancient traditions and monarchy and urged a political settlement along the lines negotiated in 1957.

Phoumi's failure to advance on the Plain of Jars made a deep impression on the new administration of United States president John F. Kennedy. If Phoumi had his difficulties with Kong Le's outnumbered battalion, he was no match for the North Vietnamese. The North Vietnamese-Pathet Lao counteroffensive that opened in January drove Phoumi's poorly motivated troops and their United States military advisers back—a retreat that irrevocably changed the balance of forces in Laos.

The United States embassy in Vientiane had accurate intelligence on the numbers and movements of North Vietnamese military units in Laos, as opposed to the alarming reports emanating from Phoumi's headquarters. Central Laos and the entire length of the road from the Sala Phou Khoun junction south to Vangviang was in North Vietnamese-Pathet Lao hands by mid-March.

Contact between emissaries of the two sides was finally made by officers under a truce flag at the village of Ban Hin Heup on the Vientiane-Louangphrabang road. Tripartite truce talks opened in the nearby village of Ban Namone, with the ICC, reconvened by the cochairmen of the Geneva Conference, Britain, and the Soviet Union, present. The three negotiators were Nouhak, Pheng Phongsavan, and General Sing Ratanassamay. A cease-fire declared on May 3 did not prevent the Pathet Lao from capturing Xépôn, an important crossroads on the Ho Chi Minh Trail, or put an end to the fighting in the Hmong country. As part of the plan to find a settlement, an enlarged Geneva Conference convened on May 16.

Expansion of Pathet Lao Influence

There were thus two rival royal governments in Laos from the beginning of 1961, the Boun Oum-Phoumi Nosavan government at Vientiane and the Souvanna Phouma government at Khang Khay. The Pathet Lao, protected by the presence of thousands of North Vietnamese troops, constituted a third faction in what became a rightist-Neutralist-leftist division.

The idea of neutralism had been expressed by Kong Le in his earliest speeches in Vientiane, which described the goals of his coup d'état as stopping the fighting among the Laotians and enacting a policy of friendship with all foreign countries, especially Laos's neighbors. At Khang Khay, Soviet diplomats mingled with officials of missions from Beijing and Hanoi, with which relations had been established on May 5. Kong Le's troops readily adopted the unofficial name Neutralist Armed Forces. Souvanna Phouma seized the opportunity of having a sizeable number of adherents on hand at Khang Khay, including many Lao students returned from abroad, to form the Neutralist Party (Lao Pen Kang—known as the Neutralists). He was confident the party would outpoll the Pathet Lao's LPF in a free election.

Although publicly deferring to Souvanna Phouma on matters of government policy, the Pathet Lao secretly extended their influence at the grassroots level, using their proven methods of propaganda and organization. In villages under their control, the Pathet Lao installed their own personnel alongside the existing administration—for example, a *khana muang* (liberated district) alongside a *chao muang* (district chief), a *khana seng* (liberated subdistrict) alongside a *pho tasseng* (subdistrict chief), and a *khana ban* (liberated village) alongside a *pho ban* or *nai ban* (village chief). Access to the Pathet Lao-administered areas was forbidden to outsiders, even after the formation of the coalition government.

A hierarchy of politico-military participation and responsibility tied the villagers to a chain of command. All resources in villages under Pathet Lao control were mobilized into both a horizontal and a vertical structure that included organizations of women, youth, and monks. Villagers were easily susceptible to Pathet Lao control, making a Pathet Lao village a world unto itself. Children acted as couriers and lookouts; young people joined the village self-defense units, the lowest level of guerrilla organization; adults acted as porters for the regular guerrilla units; and women made clothing, prepared food, and looked after the sick and wounded.

Protracted Diplomacy

At the reconvened Geneva Conference, the Neutralists were represented by Quinim, the rightists by Phoui Sananikone, and the Pathet Lao by Phoumi Vongvichit. The separate delegations served until they agreed on forming a unified government to sign the final agreement. All Laos's neighbors were represented, as were the three ICC member countries and their cochairmen, and the United States and France.

The summit meeting between John F. Kennedy and Nikita Khrushchev in Vienna on June 3–4, 1961, coincided with the crisis over the North Vietnamese-Pathet Lao cease-fire violations at the besieged Hmong outpost of Padong. The Hmong abandoned Padong in early June and established a new base at Long Chieng. Kennedy protested North Vietnam's involvement to Khrushchev and pointed out that the United States was supporting Laos's neutrality. Both leaders agreed that the conflict in Laos should not bring their two countries into confrontation. The idea of neutralizing Laos had been suggested to Kennedy as early as January.

For the next year, an enormous effort of persuasion involving all the great powers went into getting the Laotian parties to agree to form a coalition government. The effort included meetings among princes Souvanna Phouma, Boun Oum, and Souphanouvong in Zurich and Vientiane and protracted diplomatic consultations in Vientiane, Xiangkhoang, Rangoon, Moscow, Paris, and Geneva.

Phoumi finally had to be disabused of the notion that he could count on unqualified United States and Thai support. Sarit favored supporting the negotiation policy. Phoumi favored peace but felt that Souvanna Phouma was the wrong choice to lead a new government. W. Averell Harriman, the intermediary, and a United States delegation held a tense and acrimonious meeting with Phoumi and his cabinet at the general's office in Vientiane. Phoumi repeated his opposition to Souvanna Phouma, and Harriman warned him he was leading his country to disaster. The meeting ended inconclusively. Phoumi further demonstrated his intransigence by building up his forces at Nam Tha, a town in northwestern Laos without strategic importance, thereby inviting attack. When the North

Vietnamese and Pathet Lao attacked, camouflaging their violation of the cease-fire with the usual propaganda about mutinies
in the opposing ranks, the defenders fled toward the Mekong,
leaving most of their weapons behind. Phoumi may have
hoped the debacle would precipitate Thai or United States
armed intervention, but it did not. In the end, he agreed to the
coalition.

Souvanna Phouma's new government took office on June
23, 1962, the second coalition in Laos's modern history. In
accordance with the principle of tripartism, seven cabinet seats
were allocated to the Neutralists, four seats each to the rightists
and Pathet Lao, and four to nonparty people. The rapprochement between Souvanna Phouma and Kennedy was manifested
by the former's visit to Washington in July at the conclusion of
the Geneva Conference. Unlike in 1954, representatives of
each of the fourteen participating nations signed the final document, the Declaration on the Neutrality of Laos and its Protocol.

Renewed Strains

The strains imposed on the Neutralists by their alliance of
convenience with the Pathet Lao were now manifested. In addition, the presence of the North Vietnamese army that this alliance implied did nothing to support neutralism. As if to
confirm their doubts, the Neutralists were subjected to communist propaganda. Deuane Sunnalath, Kong Le's subordinate,
allowed himself to be subverted by this political influence and
started publishing his own newspaper, *Khao Pathan Van* (Daily
News), full of anti-United States propaganda. Most of Kong
Le's followers remained fiercely loyal, however, and the dissidents, who called themselves Patriotic Neutralists, remained a
minority.

On April 1, 1963, less than a year after the Geneva agreement, Foreign Minister Quinim was assassinated in Vientiane.
Protesting the lack of security, Pathet Lao members of the coalition immediately left town. Following a series of incidents in
which one of Kong Le's closest aides was assassinated and a
United States plane on a supply flight to Kong Le authorized
by Souvanna Phouma was shot down by Deuane's troops, fighting broke out in the Neutralist camp. Kong Le pulled his men
back from Khang Khay and set up a new command post at
Muang Souy on the western edge of the Plain of Jars. Kong Le

was running short of supplies, however, because the Soviet airlift had ended, and the North Vietnamese were in a position to block supplies by road.

An estimated 10,000 North Vietnamese were still present in Laos, despite the stipulation their government had signed at Geneva that withdrawal of all foreign troops be completed by October 7. In preparation for a massive escalation of the conflict in South Vietnam, North Vietnam had expanded the Ho Chi Minh Trail through eastern Laos and garrisoned it with support troops. North Vietnamese troops also were present in northern Laos, where they were engaged almost continuously in pressuring the Hmong guerrillas. All United States military advisers had been withdrawn by the deadline, but clandestine operations continued, and supply and reconnaissance flights still were conducted over such heavily contested areas as the Plain of Jars. Antiaircraft fire took its toll on such flights, and as a result, the planes began attacking targets on the ground in Laos beginning in 1964.

The "Secret War"

United States support of Souvanna Phouma's government in the face of continuing North Vietnamese aggression did not constitute, technically speaking, a violation of the terms of the 1962 Geneva Protocol, as Radio Hanoi and Radio Pathet Lao charged. It did not involve Laos in a military alliance, and there were no United States military bases or ground troops in Laos. Supply flights to RLG outposts were flown by civilian companies under charter to Souvanna Phouma's government. United States military pilots in civilian clothes, their names deleted from Department of Defense rosters, flew forward air control missions over Laos. United States pilots killed or captured in Laos often were officially described as lost "in Southeast Asia." CIA advisers assisted the guerrilla units of General Vang Pao's Hmong army, which, along with irregular forces in the south, was supplied with rice, arms, and pay by CIA operatives based at Udon Thani in Thailand. The total number of CIA personnel involved in this effort never exceeded 225 and included some fifty case officers.

On the periphery of the plenary sessions at Geneva, Harriman and his deputy, William H. Sullivan, had arrived at an informal understanding with Soviet deputy foreign minister Georgi M. Pushkin to the effect that as long as the United

States did not technically violate the Geneva Protocol the Soviet Union would not feel compelled, out of consideration of its ally in Hanoi, to respond to United States activities in Laos. The official curtain of secrecy associated with this arrangement gave rise later to statements in Congress that the United States was engaged in a "secret war" in Laos, a perspective that absolved the Ho Chi Minh government of responsibility for its support of the communist-dominated resistance movement in Laos since 1945.

Souvanna Phouma was having problems of his own because of the peculiar nature of the Cold War in Laos. In April 1964, he visited Hanoi and Beijing. Premier Zhou Enlai reiterated China's support for the 1954 and 1962 Geneva agreements and advised Souvanna Phouma to dissociate the Laos question from the Vietnam question, a difficult task. Hanoi seemed to have succeeded in its strategy of making "one battlefield" out of Indochina—Cambodia, Laos, South Vietnam—and the Ho Chi Minh Trail now extended through Laos and Cambodia.

After a new tripartite meeting on the embattled Plain of Jars, Souvanna Phouma returned to Vientiane without any result and announced his intention to resign. Two rightist generals took advantage of the situation, staged a coup attempt, and arrested Souvanna Phouma. Only concerted action by Western ambassadors in the capital secured his release. Souvanna Phouma pledged to merge the rightist and Neutralist factions.

There was further infighting among the generals. In February 1965, General Phoumi, whose business dealings had earned him many enemies on the noncommunist side, left for Thailand.

With the formal merger of their faction with the rightists, Neutralist leaders increasingly felt their lives to be in danger. Kong Le eventually took refuge in the Indonesian embassy in Vientiane, leaving Laos soon after for the safety of Paris. He was replaced as commander of Neutralist troops by General Seng-souvanh Souvannarath.

From 1965 to 1973, the civil war seesawed back and forth in northern Laos, characterized by short but often very intense engagements. Because of the large areas contested, even North Vietnamese regular divisions in Laos, such as the 316th, were used in small-unit engagements during the dry season to deny control of territory and population to the other side. Population control was particularly important, because that was where recruitment for military training and transport occurred. The Hmong, in particular, suffered. Aside from the casualties, entire villages periodically had to escape the fighting, disrupting crop growing and livestock tending.

An exception to the rule of small-scale engagements was the major North Vietnamese-Pathet Lao offensive against Vang Pao that began in mid-December 1971 and lasted until the end of April 1972. This battle involved more than twenty North Vietnamese battalions and some 10,000 Hmong irregulars and Royal Lao Army defenders. After blasting the last defensive positions on the Plain of Jars with newly introduced 130mm guns with a thirty-kilometer range, the North Vietnamese advanced on Longtiang. They captured a number of positions on a ridge dominating the airfield before being driven off with heavy loss of life on both sides. The Hmong halted an attack of T–34 tanks against the airfield by skillfully placing land mines.

Since 1963 Souvanna Phouma had kept vacant the cabinet seats allotted to the LPF, as he had done in the case of Phoumi's seat as interior minister in his August 30, 1960, government. When the National Assembly rejected his budget in debate in September 1966, he obtained a vote in the King's Council to dissolve the assembly and hold elections for a new assembly the following year. Elections were held again on January 2, 1972; forty-one of the fifty-nine deputies elected were new. The LPF boycotted the elections. The prime minister kept up contact with Souphanouvong in his cave headquarters in Houaphan, occasionally using the ICC and Soviet and North Vietnamese ambassadors as messengers.

Powerless to stop the war and acquiescing in the diplomatic fiction that the 1962 Geneva Agreement was still in effect, Souvanna Phouma endured the revilement of Radio Pathet Lao, which called him a traitor, a capitulationist, and a tool of United States aggressors. The war drained Laos's manpower resources and pushed Souvanna Phouma into agreeing to introduce Thai artillery units on the royalist side and also helped to identify him with the rightist faction. As a result of the war, a peak number of 378,800 internally displaced persons were being cared for by the RLG in October 1973. Souvanna Phouma never gave up hope of resuming negotiations when conditions became more favorable.

The Unknown Soldiers Memorial, in Vientiane, was built after the
revolution to commemorate the Pathet Lao who died during
the Second Indochina War.
Courtesy Gina Merris

The Third Coalition and the Lao People's Democratic Republic

Negotiations in Paris in the autumn of 1972 between the
United States and North Vietnam created a favorable environment for reaching a cease-fire agreement in Laos. Negotiations
opened in Vientiane on October 17, 1972, and went on inconclusively between Pheng Phongsavan, representing Souvanna
Phouma, and Phoumi Vongvichit, representing the Pathet Lao.
Souvanna Phouma was hopeful that the United States would
keep up the pressure. But the situation had changed drastically
during the previous decade. There were now only two sides in
the negotiations, and the Pathet Lao insisted that their opponents be referred to as "the Viangchan government side."

Moreover, the United States was on its way out of Indochina—whether by its Vietnamization policy or by negotiations with Hanoi. Nonetheless, there was no guarantee that Hanoi would respect the provisions of negotiated agreements on Laos, and the ability of the United States to enforce compliance was not as great as Souvanna Phouma imagined. The pressure grew to conclude the negotiations rapidly.

The Vientiane Agreement

The two sides signed the peace agreement in Vientiane on February 21, 1973. A new coalition government was to be formed. Vientiane and Louangphrabang were to be neutralized by the arrival of Pathet Lao security contingents. A cease-fire was to take effect from noon on the following day. Unlike in 1962, however, there were no solemn guarantees by fourteen signatories of Laos's neutrality. The agreement was strictly between Laotians, with the ICC more powerless than ever to verify its execution.

By the time of the cease-fire, United States aircraft had dropped almost 2.1 million tons of bombs on Laos, approximately the total tonnage dropped by United States air forces during all of World War II in both the European and Pacific theaters. Most bombs were dropped on the Ho Chi Minh Trail, which had grown into a major transportation route for the North Vietnamese. The cessation of United States bombing allowed the North Vietnamese-Pathet Lao supply convoys to move with impunity, enabling them to initiate armed actions that they camouflaged with accusations of cease-fire violations by RLG forces. The United States, in protest against some of the most flagrant cease-fire violations, sent its planes back into action on limited missions. This enabled the Pathet Lao to claim that the United States had violated the Vientiane Agreement.

An uneasy lull settled on the Hmong country north of Vientiane. Air power had allowed the Hmong to maintain a tenuous balance of force with their adversaries. However, the air strip at Longtiang was empty, and the Royal Lao Air Force T–28s, on which General Vang Pao had often relied, had been pulled back to Vientiane on orders from Souvanna Phouma. The United States air armada that had operated from bases in Thailand was withdrawn. With the loss of air cover, no area in Hmong territory was safe from artillery bombardment.

Although their CIA advisers remained temporarily at Long-tiang, the Hmong were beginning to feel deserted. With the war winding down in Vietnam and the military government in Thailand overthrown in a student revolt in October 1973, United States interest in Laos waned.

The Origins of the Prisoner of War/Missing in Action Question

The unconditional return of prisoners of war (POWs) from all the countries of Indochina was, in the words of Henry A. Kissinger, the chief United States negotiator at Paris, "one of the premises on which the United States based its signature of the Vietnam agreement." Kissinger said he had received "categorical assurances" from the North Vietnamese delegation in Paris that United States POWs captured in Laos would be released in the same time frame as those from North Vietnam and South Vietnam, that is, by March 28, 1973.

Under the provisions of Chapter II, Article 5, of the Vientiane Agreement, the two sides were obligated to repatriate all persons held captive regardless of nationality within sixty days of the formation of the coalition government. When the cease-fire came, it was generally assumed that the Pathet Lao held a large number of United States citizens they or the North Vietnamese had captured in Laos, and the Department of Defense listed some 555 United States personnel as unaccounted for—either as POWs, missing in action (MIA), or killed in action/body not recovered. The Pathet Lao had released a number of United States prisoners after the formation of the 1962 coalition. There was considerable uncertainty surrounding the POW/MIA question, however, because the Pathet Lao had neither provided lists of those who had fallen into their hands nor adhered to international conventions on treatment of POWs, in keeping with their contention that the United States was guilty of an aggressive, undeclared war against Laos. Conditions of detention in jungle prison camps were harsh in the extreme, as attested to by the few who managed to escape. Prisoners had no medicine, and they had to supplement their ration of rice, both meager and dirty, with beetles and rats.

Soth Petrasy, permanent representative of the Pathet Lao delegation in Vientiane, told Phone Chantaraj, editor of the Vientiane newspaper *Xat Lao* (The Lao Nation), five days prior to the signing of the Vientiane Agreement that the Pathet Lao leadership had a detailed accounting of United States prisoners and the locations where they were being held and that they would be released after the cease-fire. He added: "If they were captured in Laos, they will be returned in Laos." On the day the Vientiane Agreement was signed, the United States chargé d'affaires obtained confirmation from Soth of his previous statements and requested further details. Although Soth proposed to send a message to Xam Nua asking for the number and names of United States citizens held captive, this information was not forthcoming.

The United States embassy began pressing for the release by March 28 of prisoners captured in Laos. The question was whether the Pathet Lao would consider themselves bound by the agreement with its implication that they followed the orders of the North Vietnamese. Resolution of the matter was further complicated by the fact that procedures for prisoner exchanges stipulated in the Vientiane Agreement had still to be negotiated by the two sides in Laos.

On March 26, Soth informed the United States that the Pathet Lao would release eight prisoners in Hanoi on March 28. These prisoners, whose names had previously been given to United States officials by the North Vietnamese in Paris, had been held in North Vietnam for some time. On March 27, the Pathet Lao delivered a *note verbale* to the United States embassy that stated this fulfilled their POW release obligations and demanded that the United States pressure the Vientiane government to negotiate "seriously" for implementing the political provisions of the agreement. The Pathet Lao rejected subsequent United States requests to dissociate the question of United States POWs from other matters covered by the Vientiane Agreement. The North Vietnamese, for their part, did not respond to Kissinger's requests for clarification of the discrepancy between the number of POWs and MIAs carried by the Department of Defense and the small number of POWs released.

The protocol giving effect to the Vientiane Agreement was signed on September 14, 1973. Paragraph 18 made the two-party Joint Central Commission to Implement the Agreement responsible for implementing provisions for exchanges of prisoners and information. The names of personnel who had died in captivity were to be exchanged within fifteen to thirty days, and all prisoners were to be released within sixty days after formation of the coalition government. However, the only United

States citizen released by the Pathet Lao in Laos in accordance with these provisions was a civilian pilot captured after the cease-fire. For the next twenty years, representatives of the new regime would sit at a table and calmly inform visiting United States officials and families of POW/MIAs that they knew nothing about the fate of United States POWs and MIAs in Laos (see Bilateral Relations, ch. 4).

Formation of the Third Coalition

The Provisional Government of National Union (PGNU), Laos's third experiment with coalition government, was finally constituted on April 5, 1974, following one last desperate coup attempt by rightist officers in exile against Souvanna Phouma. Cabinet posts were assigned, with a vice premier and five ministers from each side plus two chosen by mutual consent. Under each minister was a vice minister from the other side. The makeup of the National Political Consultative Council, an unelected pseudo-National Assembly, was similarly balanced.

Paragraph 14 of the September 14, 1973, protocol provided for the withdrawal of all foreign troops from Laos within sixty days of the PGNU's formation, the same deadline as for prisoner exchanges. Once again the United States met the deadline. Although it terminated the mission of Group 959 after the cease-fire, North Vietnam did not withdraw its estimated 38,500 regular troops from Laos. Among other provisions that occupied the Joint Central Commission to Implement the Agreement was the demarcation of the cease-fire line and the neutralization of the two capitals.

Because of the Pathet Lao ministers' opposition, the PGNU barred the traditional opening of the National Assembly on May 11, Constitution Day. The king voiced his displeasure over the PGNU's decision to circumvent the constitution and not convene the National Assembly, elected in 1972. The dissolution of the National Assembly and the holding of new elections, matters that had not been specifically included in the Vientiane Agreement or its protocol, embroiled the PGNU in endless argument. The king did not attend the session of the National Political Consultative Council in Louangphrabang, which, under the chairmanship of Souphanouvong, adopted a far-ranging eighteen-point political program. One of the points in the National Political Consultative Council's program was a demand that the United States pay reparations for war damages.

The Communist Seizure of Power

On March 27, 1975, North Vietnamese-Pathet Lao forces launched a strong attack against Vang Pao's Hmong defenders. The attackers rapidly captured the Sala Phou Khoun road junction and then drove south along Route 13 as far as Muang Kasi. Souvanna Phouma, wishing to avoid bloodshed, ordered Vang Pao only to defend himself and refused to allow air strikes in his support. The Pathet Lao singled out the Hmong as enemies to be shown no quarter. Pathet Lao radio broadcasts spoke of "wiping out" these special forces who had stood in their way for fifteen years.

Realizing that the Hmong were being abandoned and the penalty they faced if left to the mercy of the Pathet Lao, Vang Pao requested evacuation for his soldiers and their families to safe haven in Thailand. The CIA station at Udon Thani offered to evacuate families of key officers. Vang Pao requested an airlift for 5,000. Facing an ultimatum, Vang Pao and twelve Hmong leaders signed a treaty on May 10 reminding the United States of the pledges made to them and agreeing to leave Laos and never return. In the next days, a motley collection of planes piloted by United States volunteers, Hmong, and Lao flew out a few hundred Hmong. Vang Pao himself left on May 14, eluding the T–28s at Vientiane.

Meanwhile, a campaign of intimidation against rightist members of the PGNU and military officers gathered momentum in Vientiane. Operating under the umbrella of a coalition of twenty-one "organizations standing for peace and national concord," a standard communist tactic, the demonstrators used inflation and other popular grievances to mobilize support for the eighteen-point program of the National Political Consultative Council. Souvanna Phouma tried at first to ban the demonstrations but later gave in and sided with their aims. The May Day holiday provided the pretext for the largest demonstration to date, followed a week later by a demonstration against the rightist army and police. Demonstrators occupied the compound of the United States aid mission, forcing termination of the aid program. Four rightist ministers, including the defense minister, Sisouk na Champasak, fled. Another minister, Boun Om, was assassinated in the capital.

Elsewhere, takeovers of government offices and orchestrated demonstrations led to the entry of Pathet Lao troops into Pakxé, Savannakhét, Thakhek, and other towns during May "to secure their defense." People's revolutionary committees surfaced to seize administrative power from the remnants of the RLG. Officials and military officers who chose not to flee were summoned to "seminars." On August 23, the Pathet Lao completed its seizure of local power with the takeover of the Vientiane city administration by a revolutionary committee. The Pathet Lao announced that military units had requested Pathet Lao "advisers," thereby facilitating the integration of the army.

Throughout this time, the elite communist leaders who were making the decisions remained out of sight. Kaysone Phomvihan, in a speech in Vieng Xay on October 12, declared that "the revolution will speed up." Simultaneously, the National Political Consultative Council established new screening procedures for candidates for election that effectively eliminated all those who had not supported the LPF. Suddenly, in the last week of November, the NPCC convened in Xam Nua. Also in November, elections were held in the "new zone," the former RLG zone. Eligible voters were required to vote for a list of candidates whose names were distributed the evening before. Candidates were local party administrators, whose identities had been kept secret up to then. On November 28, demonstrators demanded the dissolution of the PGNU and the National Political Consultative Council as inappropriate to the situation. The next day, Souvanna Phouma and Souphanouvong flew to Louangphrabang and persuaded the king to abdicate.

Establishment of the Lao People's Democratic Republic

The National Congress of People's Representatives, recreating the mise-en-scène of 1945, met in the auditorium of the former United States community school on December 1. Sisana Sisan delivered the opening speech on behalf of the preliminary committee for convening the National Congress of People's Representatives. So far only the LPF and other front organizations and delegations from the various provinces were listed as attending among the 264 delegates. The preliminary committee thereupon dissolved itself.

Prince Souphanouvong, named to the presidium of the National Congress, said in his speech that the congress would "study" the king's abdication, the dissolution of the PGNU and the National Political Consultative Council, and the political report on abolishing the monarchy and establishing a people's democratic republic. This last item was read by Kaysone, who was also on the congress presidium. For most of the world, it was the first look at the man who, for thirty years, had led the revolution in Laos from behind the scenes in Vietnam and in the caves of Houaphan. Kaysone presided at the December 2 session. He began by reading a motion to establish the Lao People's Democratic Republic, which was passed by acclamation. Kaysone then nominated Souphanouvong to be president of the country. Again, the vote was unanimous. Next, Nouhak took the podium to say it was necessary to elect a Supreme People's Assembly. He proposed Souphanouvong as president of the Supreme People's Assembly and then read a list of forty-four names. This vote was also unanimous.

Officially, the party—which had been renamed the Phak Pasason Pativat Lao (Lao People's Revolutionary Party—LPRP; see Glossary) at its Second Party Congress in 1972—played no role in the National Congress. But it began making its public appearance immediately thereafter in indirect ways; for example, banners carrying revolutionary slogans and messages of congratulations from North Vietnamese, Soviet, and Chinese leaders began to appear. With power firmly in its grasp, the LPRP no longer had any reason to hide its identity. For the first time, the party publicly identified the seven members of its Political Bureau (Politburo). From this point, the party alone made decisions in the Lao People's Democratic Republic. Gone were the "democratic freedoms" that had been extolled in the National Political Consultative Council's eighteen points. The Neutralist Party and other noncommunist parties disappeared, leaving a one-party regime. Those who objected could leave. Some 350,000 availed themselves of this opportunity over the next few years, leaving behind their homes and belongings, and, in many cases, even their loved ones.

"Seminar Camps" and the Death of King Savang Vatthana

"Seminar camps," also called reeducation centers, were the centerpiece of the new regime's policy toward the enemies it had defeated. The LPRP's Marxist-Leninist dogma allowed no respite in the class struggle, and those identified as its former enemies were the presumed saboteurs and subversives of the socialist phase of the revolution that was just getting under way. After its victory, the regime made people judged unfit to participate in the new society in their present frame of mind construct a series of camps, known only by their numbers. They included Camp 01 at Sop Hao; Camp 03 near Na Kai, newly given the Pali name Viangxai, meaning "Victorious Town"; Camp 05 near Muang Xamteu; and Camps 04 and 06 near Muang Et, all in Houaphan. A camp was also built at Muang Khoua on the Nam Ou, and others were built in the center and south. There are no official figures on the numbers of people sent for reeducation, because the camp network was kept a secret from the outside world. The only information was brought out by former inmates and their families. Various published estimates have put the number of inmates at 30,000, at 37,600, and at 50,000.

Even before the communist takeover, the first groups of high-level officials, including provincial governors and district chiefs, had been transported to the camps, arriving in full dress uniform. They had received letters signed by Souvanna Phouma ordering them to attend an important meeting in Vientiane. After an overnight stay in Vientiane, the group was flown to the Plain of Jars, where a festive atmosphere prevailed. The officials, about seventy in all, were feted with food and a movie, and North Vietnamese advisers were present. They were then flown to Houaphan, separated into small groups, and organized into work parties.

In August and September 1977, a group of twenty-six "reactionary" high-ranking officials and military officers in Camp 05 were accused of plotting a coup and arrested. These persons were taken away to Camp 01. They included Pheng Phongsavan, the minister who had signed the Vientiane Agreement; Touby Lyfoung, the Hmong leader; Soukhan Vilaysan, another of Souvanna Phouma's ministers who had been with him in the Lao Issara and had risen to become secretary general of the Neutralists; and Generals Bounphone Maekthepharak and Ouan Ratikoun. All died in Camp 01. Thus, those who played roles in the modern history of Laos were relegated by the regime to the status of nonpersons and their fate placed in the hands of their prison guards. Others, like Tiao Sisoumang Sisaleumsak, a minister in Souvanna Phouma's 1960 government, General Sengsouvanh Souvannarath, commander of the Neutralist forces, Khamchan Pradith, an intellectual and diplomat, and even Sing Chanthakoummane, a lieutenant in the Second Paratroop Battalion in 1960, were held in seminar camps for fifteen years or more before being released. Souvanna Phouma was allowed to live quietly in Vientiane until his death in January 1984.

The new regime feared that ex-King Savang Vatthana, who until March 1977 had lived quietly in the royal palace as a private citizen with the meaningless title of adviser to President Souphanouvong, would become a symbol of popular resistance. As a result, he was suddenly spirited away by helicopter to Houaphan along with Queen Khamboui and Crown Prince Say Vongsavang. Imprisoned in Camp 01, the crown prince died on May 2, 1978, and the king eleven days later of starvation. The queen died on December 12, 1981. According to an eyewitness, all were buried in unmarked graves outside the camp's perimeter. No official announcement was made. More than a decade later, during a visit to France in December 1989, Kaysone confirmed reports of the king's death in an innocuous aside that attributed it to old age.

The party did not dare abolish the Buddhist community of monks and novices, the clergy (*sangha*), of which the king had been the supreme patron. It did, however, attempt to reshape the *sangha* into an instrument of control. In March 1979, the Venerable Thammayano, the eighty-seven-year-old Sangha-raja of Laos, the country's highest-ranking abbott, fled by floating across the Mekong on a raft of inflated car tubes. His secretary, who engineered the escape, reported that the Sangha-raja had been confined to his monastery in Louangphrabang and was forbidden to preach. Ordinary monks were not forbidden to preach, but their sermons were commonly tape recorded and monitored for signs of dissidence. As a result of these pressures, the number of monks in Laos decreased sharply after 1975 (see Buddhism, ch. 2).

Postwar Relations with the United States

Perhaps more understandable than its brutality toward its own people was the party's hostility toward the formerly large United States aid program, which had been directed at supporting the RLG. Even so, the public humiliations inflicted on the departing aid mission personnel—forced to leave behind everything they could not carry aboard a plane—were excessive by any standard. Aid projects such as the Operation Brotherhood hospital at Longtiang were abandoned overnight. In spite of Souvanna Phouma's assurances to the United States ambassador that the government would provide continuity in

Monk crossing Wat Xieng Thong yard, Louangphrabang
Courtesy Gina Merris

medical services, foreign nurses and other technicians were not replaced.

No record exists of any discussion by the United States embassy—staffed at the chargé d'affaires level after the departure in April 1975 of Ambassador Charles S. Whitehouse—of United States "participation" in healing war wounds or of the reconstruction aid mentioned in Article 10c of the Vientiane Agreement. Even had the United States been predisposed to discuss these matters, the conditions of the takeover by the LPRP would have precluded it. Ambassadorial relations resumed in 1992.

Another issue was opium production, which, in Laos as in the rest of the Golden Triangle of Laos-Burma-Thailand, had grown as the demand for the opium derivative heroin grew. Opium production and trade became a source of tension in relations between the two governments. Laos resented official

United States pressure as an attempt to shift the blame for the problem (see Bilateral Relations, ch. 4; Narcotics and Counternarcotics Issues, ch. 5).

Developments in the Lao People's Democratic Republic

In spite of the regime's revolutionary rhetoric about self-reliance on the march to socialism, Western aid was simply replaced over the 1970s and 1980s by aid from "fraternal countries" of the Soviet bloc. Living standards declined further. Nongovernmental organizations, including some from the United States, in cooperation with local officials, established a few small-scale aid projects that reached out to real needs in the areas of health, education, and economic development.

Kaysone and his colleagues, following the well-known examples of Soviet and East European party leaders, led carefully protected lives behind the walls of their guarded compounds in the capital, secluded from public scrutiny and shielded from any manifestation of hostility, their movements kept secret. The minister of interior, Somseun Khamphithoun, whose ministry was responsible for the operation of the seminar camps, was never seen publicly in Vientiane. Corruption, widespread in the years of the United States civilian and military aid programs, resumed with the new opportunities presented by the "economic opening" beginning in 1986.

The first Supreme People's Assembly, appointed by the National Congress on December 2, 1975, rapidly faded into obscurity, although its twice-yearly meetings were reported in the controlled press. In 1988, perhaps because the regime wished to give itself some semblance of popular underpinning, it suddenly announced that elections would be held for a new Supreme People's Assembly. Elections were held on June 26, 1988, for 2,410 seats on district-level people's councils and on November 20, 1988, for 651 seats on province-level people's councils. On March 26, 1989, elections were held for seventy-nine seats on the Supreme People's Assembly. Candidates in all elections were screened by the party. Sixty-five of the seventy-nine members of the assembly were party members (see Legislature, ch. 4).

In the area of foreign relations, Laos joined the ranks of the "socialist camp" on December 2, 1975. Gone was any pretense of neutrality. In the new state of affairs where "peace" had at long last been achieved and no one paid attention to the presence of "fraternal" foreign troops on Laotian soil, the delegations of the ICC in Laos returned to their respective countries, leaving behind piles of unpaid bills.

In accordance with the organic links between the Vietnamese and Laotian parties that have been acclaimed by the highest party leaders, Laos has been tied more closely to Vietnam than to any other country. The term *special relations* (in Lao, *khan phoua phan yang phiset*) to describe the linkage between the two parties and governments had come into use as early as November 1973 when Le Duan, first secretary of the Vietnamese party, visited Viangxai (see Bilateral Relations, ch. 4). Thereafter, special relations was the term increasingly emphasized in joint statements. In July 1977, Laos and Vietnam signed the twenty-five-year Treaty of Friendship and Cooperation. They also agreed to redefine their common border, which was demarcated in 1986. In early 1989, the Vietnamese troops that had been stationed in Laos continuously since 1961 were reported to have been withdrawn.

Despite some incidents along their common border, Thailand took an accommodating stand toward the country. Opening the border to trade and eliminating the "sanctuary" problem were affirmed as goals in a 1979 joint communiqué between Kaysone and the Thai prime minister, Kriangsak Chomanand, which was subsequently cited by Laotians as the touchstone of their relations with Thailand (see Bilateral Relations, ch. 4). Following a series of shooting incidents in 1984 involving rival claims to three border villages, a major dispute arose in December 1987 over territory claimed by Laos as part of Botèn District in Xaignabouri and by Thailand as part of Chat Trakan District in Phitsanulok Province. The fighting that ensued claimed more than 1,000 lives before a cease-fire was declared on February 19, 1988. The origin of the dispute was the ambiguity of the topographic nomenclature used in the 1907 Franco-Siamese border treaty over the area of the Nam Heung, up which Fa Ngum's army had traveled in the fourteenth century. After 1975 the sanctuary problem also defied solution for a decade, with the Hmong and communist rebels occupying some of the old Lao Issara resistance bases in Thailand. However, a series of working-level meetings between the two sides were arranged that served to defuse the conflict, and relations improved markedly in the late 1980s.

Although official relations between Laos and China were strained by the Sino-Vietnamese War of 1979, the two countries maintained diplomatic relations, and local trade continued across their common border. The ending of the brief war saw a rapid and steady improvement in mutual ties and exchanges of visits at all levels. Kaysone visited Beijing, and a border demarcation commission completed its work to mutual satisfaction.

Laos seemed at last to have achieved stable relations with its neighbors. Centuries-old conflicts that had repeatedly seen foreign invaders trampling Laotian soil with their elephants or tanks, Laotians conscripted by this or that pretender to the throne, pagodas built and then destroyed, and the countryside laid waste, had receded. Peace brought the prospect of a better life, if not yet participation in a multiparty democracy. It was as if after so much suffering Laotians had turned inward, seeking the fulfillment that had always come from their families, their villages, their *sangha*, and their pride in the moments of glory in their country's long history.

$$*\qquad*\qquad*$$

No complete history of Laos exists in English, but there are three very useful bibliographies. The most useful for the beginner, because of the annotations, is Helen Cordell's *Laos*. The compiler's introductory essay also provides an informative overview of the country and its people. A far more extensive bibliography, but lacking annotation except for subject matter headings, is William W. Sage and Judith A. N. Henchy's *Laos: A Bibliography*. Finally, Martin Stuart-Fox and Mary Kooyman's *Historical Dictionary of Laos* contains a much more narrow selection of writings on Laos.

For the modern period before 1975, Arthur J. Dommen's *Conflict in Laos: The Politics of Neutralization* and Hugh Toye's *Laos: Buffer State or Battleground* are still standard. Maha Sila Viravong's *Phongsavadan Lao* (History of Laos), although flawed and somewhat dated, is still useful. MacAlister Brown and Joseph J. Zasloff's *Apprentice Revolutionaries: The Communist Movement in Laos, 1930–85* provides detailed information on the civil war years. No history of the Lao People's Democratic Republic in English has yet appeared, and in view of the secretiveness of the regime, writing about it is difficult. Readers interested in following current events are advised to rely on the translations provided by the Foreign Broadcast Information Service's *Daily Report: East Asia.*

Primary source materials are available in both the French and United States archives. The former deal mainly with the colonial period. The latter contain so far declassified diplomatic correspondence of the Department of State through 1960, with the exception of that dealing with the POW/MIA issue for 1973–92 declassified at a Senate committee's request. All Department of Defense documents relating to the POW/ MIA issue are available at the Library of Congress. Documentation of the CIA's role in Laos is still withheld by the CIA.

Foreign scholars have not had access to the archives of the Indochinese Communist Party, the Vietnamese Communist Party, or the Lao People's Revolutionary Party (with the exception of some work by Japanese scholars in Hanoi dealing with the period of the 1940s and early 1950s; e.g., Moto Furuta and Masaya Shiraishi's *Indochina in the 1940s and 1950s*). These archives seem unlikely to be opened short of an upheaval similar to that which befell the parties of Eastern Europe and the Soviet Union.

Much scholarly writing on Laos history appears in periodicals, such as *Asian Survey, Journal of Southeast Asian Studies, Pacific Affairs,* and *Péninsule.* (For further information and complete citations, see Bibliography.)

Chapter 2. The Society and Its Environment

Detail of a glass mosaic depicting scenes of village life covering the walls of the "Library," a small building on the grounds of Wat Xieng Thong, Louang-phrabang; an example of sixteenth-century Buddhist architecture.

LAOS IS A RURAL COUNTRY whose relatively low population density has allowed the continuation of a village society reliant on subsistence agriculture. The lack of a national government infrastructure and effective transportation networks has also contributed to the relative independence and autonomy of most villages. Residence in a village thus has been an important aspect of social identity, particularly for lowland Lao ethnic groups. For many upland ethnic groups, clan membership is a more important point of social identification. For all groups, the village community has a kinship nexus, although structures differ. Rice is the staple food for all Laotians, and most families and villages are able to produce enough or nearly enough each year for their own consumption.

Laos is ethnically diverse; the population includes more than forty ethnic groups, which are classified within three general families of Lao Sung (upland Lao), Lao Theung (midland Lao), and Lao Loum (lowland Lao). The country is officially a multiethnic nation, with Lao as the official language, but relationships among the different groups have sometimes been characterized by misunderstandings and competition over natural resources. The different ethnic groups have substantially different residential patterns, agricultural practices, forms of village governance, and religious beliefs.

Only the national capital of Vientiane and a few other provincial capitals can be considered urban. These small cities are market and administrative centers that attract trading and communications activity, but they have developed very little manufacturing or industrial capacity. Daily and seasonal life in all sectors of the society is affected by the monsoon. Rice production determines periods of heavy and slack work, which are mirrored in school vacations, religious festivals, and government activity.

Most lowland Lao and some midland groups practice Theravada Buddhism, but also believe in spirits of places or of deceased persons. Upland and most midland ethnic groups are animist, with religious practices oriented toward protective or guardian spirits commonly associated with places or with a family or clan. Shamans or other spirit practitioners are recognized

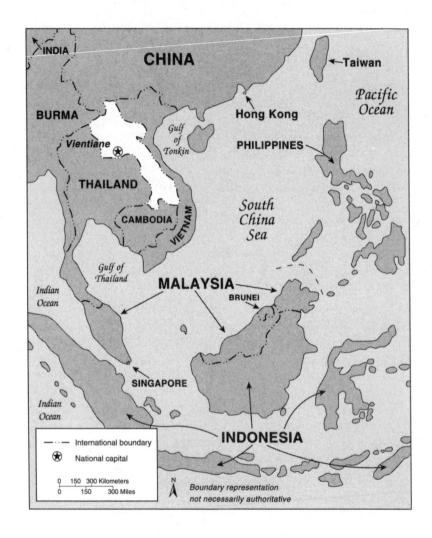

Figure 3. Laos in Its Southeast Asian Setting, 1994

and respected for their divinatory and healing powers among most ethnic groups, whether Buddhist or not.

Education and social services remain rudimentary at best but are improving. In lowland villages, traditional education was provided to boys and young men through the Buddhist temples. Although this practice continues in some areas, in general it has been supplanted by a national education system, which, unfortunately, is hampered by limited financial resources and a lack of trained teachers. Western medical care is seldom available outside provincial or a few district centers and even then is very limited. Child and infant mortality is high, and life expectancy is the lowest in Southeast Asia; the population, however, is increasing at a rapid rate. Since the end of World War II, significant differences in education, health, and demographic conditions have prevailed among the ethnic groups and between rural and urban populations.

The Physical Environment

Laos, a landlocked nation that covers 236,800 square kilometers in the center of the Southeast Asian peninsula, is surrounded by Burma, Cambodia, China, Thailand, and Vietnam (see fig. 3). Its location has often made it a buffer between more powerful neighboring states, as well as a crossroads for trade and communication (see Developments in the Nineteenth Century, ch. 1; Foreign Trade, ch. 3). Migration and international conflict have contributed to the present ethnic composition of the country and to the geographic distribution of its ethnic groups.

Topography

Most of the western border of Laos is demarcated by the Mekong River, which is an important artery for transportation (see fig. 4). Khong Falls at the southern end of the country prevents access to the sea, but cargo boats travel along the entire length of the Mekong in Laos during most of the year. Smaller power boats and pirogues provide an important means of transportation on many of the tributaries of the Mekong. The Mekong has thus not been an obstacle but a facilitator for communication, and the similarities between Laos and northeast Thai society—same people, same language—reflect the close contact that has existed across the river for centuries. Also, many Laotians living in the Mekong Valley have relatives and friends in Thailand. Prior to the twentieth century, Laotian kingdoms and principalities encompassed areas on both sides of the Mekong, and Thai control in the late nineteenth century extended to the left bank. Although the Mekong was established as a border by French colonial forces, travel from one side to the other has been significantly limited only since the establishment of the Lao People's Democratic Republic (LPDR, or Laos) in 1975.

The eastern border with Vietnam extends for 2,130 kilometers, mostly along the crest of the Annamite Chain, and serves as a physical barrier between the Chinese-influenced culture of Vietnam and the Indianized states of Laos and Thailand. These mountains are sparsely populated by tribal minorities, who traditionally have not acknowledged the border with Vietnam any more than lowland Lao have been constrained by the 1,754-kilometer Mekong River border with Thailand. Thus, ethnic minority populations are found on both the Laotian and Vietnamese sides of the frontier. Because of their relative isolation, contact between these groups and lowland Lao has been mostly confined to trading.

Laos shares its short—only 541 kilometers—southern border with Cambodia, and ancient Khmer ruins at Wat Pho and other southern locations attest to the long history of contact between the Lao and the Khmer. In the north, the country is bounded by a mountainous 423-kilometer border with China and shares the 235-kilometer-long Mekong River border with Burma.

The topography of Laos is largely mountainous, with elevations above 500 meters typically characterized by steep terrain, narrow river valleys, and low agricultural potential. This mountainous landscape extends across most of the north of the country, except for the plain of Vientiane and the Plain of Jars in Xiangkhoang Province. The southern "panhandle" of the country contains large level areas in Savannakhét and Champasak provinces that are well suited for extensive paddy rice cultivation and livestock raising (see Crops and Farming Systems, ch. 3). Much of Khammouan Province and the eastern part of all the southern provinces are mountainous. Together, the alluvial plains and terraces of the Mekong and its tributaries cover only about 20 percent of the land area.

Only about 4 percent of the total land area is classified as arable. The forested land area has declined significantly since the 1970s as a result of commercial logging and expanded swidden, or slash-and-burn, farming (see Forestry, ch. 3).

Climate

Laos has a tropical monsoon climate, with a pronounced rainy season from May through October, a cool dry season from November through February, and a hot dry season in March and April. Generally, monsoons occur at the same time across the country, although that time may vary significantly

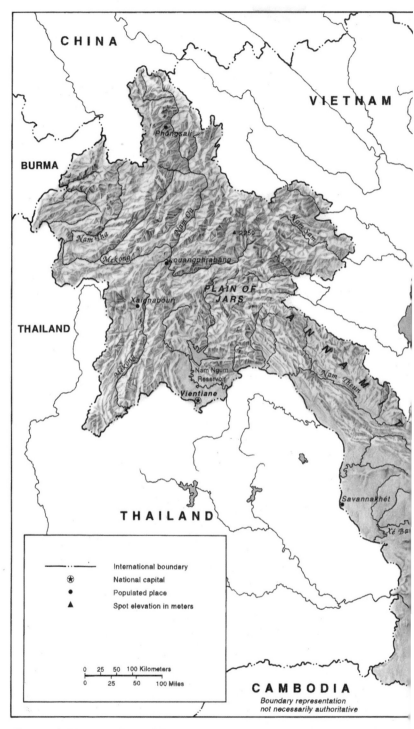

Figure 4. Topography and Drainage

84

from one year to the next. Rainfall also varies regionally, with the highest amounts—3,700 millimeters annually—recorded on the Bolovens Plateau in Champasak Province. City rainfall stations have recorded that Savannakhét averages 1,440 millimeters of rain annually; Vientiane receives about 1,700 millimeters, and Louangphrabang (Luang Prabang) receives about 1,360 millimeters. Rainfall is not always adequate for rice cultivation, however, and the relatively high average precipitation conceals years where rainfall may be only half or less of the norm, causing significant declines in rice yields. Such droughts often are regional, leaving production in other parts of the country unaffected. Temperatures range from highs around 40°C along the Mekong in March and April to lows of 5°C or less in the uplands of Xiangkhoang and Phôngsali in January.

Transportation Routes

Because of its mountainous topography and lack of development, Laos has few reliable transportation routes. This inaccessibility has historically limited the ability of any government to maintain a presence in areas distant from the national or provincial capitals and has limited interchange and communication among villages and ethnic groups (see Transportation and Telecommunications, ch. 3). The Mekong and Nam Ou are the only natural channels suitable for large-draft boat transportation, and from December through May low water limits the size of the craft that may be used over many routes. Laotians in lowland villages located on the banks of smaller rivers have traditionally traveled in pirogues for fishing, trading, and visiting up and down the river for limited distances. Otherwise, travel is by ox-cart over level terrain or by foot. The steep mountains and lack of roads have caused upland ethnic groups to rely entirely on pack baskets and horse packing for transportation.

The road system is not extensive. However, a rudimentary network begun under French colonial rule and continued from the 1950s has provided an important means of increased intervillage communication, movement of market goods, and a focus for new settlements. In mid-1994, travel in most areas was difficult and expensive, and most Laotians traveled only limited distances, if at all. As a result of ongoing improvements in the road system during the early 1990s, however, it is expected that in the future villagers will more easily be able to seek medical care, send children to schools at district centers, and work outside the village.

Natural Resources

Expanding commercial exploitation of forests, plans for additional hydroelectric facilities, foreign demands for wild animals and nonwood forest products for food and traditional medicines, and a growing population have brought new and increasing attention to the forests. Traditionally, forests have been important sources of wild foods, herbal medicines, and timber for house construction. Even into the 1990s, the government viewed the forest as a valued reserve of natural products for noncommercial household consumption. Government efforts to preserve valuable hardwoods for commercial extraction have led to measures to prohibit swidden cultivation throughout the country (see Agriculture and Forestry, ch. 3). Further, government restrictions on clearing forestland for swidden cropping in the late 1980s, along with attempts to gradually resettle upland swidden farming villages (*ban*—see Glossary) to lowland locations suitable for paddy rice cultivation, had significant effects on upland villages. Traditionally, villages have relied on forest products as a food reserve during years of poor rice harvest and as a regular source of fruits and vegetables. By the 1990s, however, these gathering systems were breaking down in many areas. At the same time, international concern about environmental degradation and the loss of many wildlife species unique to Laos has prompted the government to consider the implications of these developments.

Population

The first comprehensive national population census of Laos was taken in 1985; it recorded a population of 3.57 million (see fig. 5). Annual population growth was estimated at between 2.6 and 3.0 percent, and the 1991 population was estimated at 4.25 million. The national crude birth rate was estimated at about forty-five per 1,000, while the crude death rate was about sixteen per 1,000. Fertility rates were consistently high from ages twenty through forty, reflecting a lack of contraceptive use. Each woman bore an average of 6.8 children.

Birth control techniques were not generally available to the population before the late 1980s, although there was limited use of oral contraceptives from the late 1960s through 1975. The government took a pronatalist stance, believing that the country was underpopulated. The overall population density was only eighteen persons per square kilometer, and in many districts the density was fewer than ten persons per square kilometer. Population density per cultivated hectare was considerably higher, however, ranging from 3.3 to 7.8 persons per hectare. Because high fertility and poor nutrition contribute to the poor health of women and high infant and child mortality, since the late 1980s the Federation of Women's Unions has advocated a policy of birth spacing to improve the health of women and their children. Official prohibitions on contraceptive technology were relaxed, but use of contraception was still low as of mid-1994 and virtually nonexistent in villages distant from provincial capitals or the Thai border. Regional differences in birth rates as of late 1988—forty per 1,000 in Vientiane and Bolikhamxai provinces versus forty-eight per 1,000 in other provinces—reflected uneven access to contraception (see table 2, Appendix).

Ethnic Diversity

The population is ethnically diverse, but a complete classification of all ethnic groups has never been undertaken. Before the Indochina wars, sources commonly identified more than sixty different groups, whereas the 1985 census listed forty-seven groups, some with populations of only a few hundred persons. Discrepancies in the number of groups resulted from inconsistent definitions of what constitutes an ethnic group as opposed to a subgroup, as well as incomplete knowledge about the groups themselves. The 1985 census distinguished three general ethnic group classifications reflecting common origin and language grouping and noted significant differences among the groups comprising the three families. Because detailed ethnographic information about many groups is lacking—especially for the midland groups—and because the sheer number of ethnicities represented in Laos is so great, the discussion of ethnic groups concentrates on one or two representative examples of each of the three larger groupings; other groups may differ on a number of points (see fig, 6; table 3, Appendix).

The Lao Loum (see Glossary), or lowland Lao, constitute the majority of the population—66 percent—and comprise several ethnic groups that began to move from the north into the Southeast Asian peninsula about 1,000 years ago. All Lao Loum speak languages of the Tai-Kadai family—for example, Lao, Lue, Tai Dam (Black Tai), and Tai Deng (Red Tai). Lao Loum

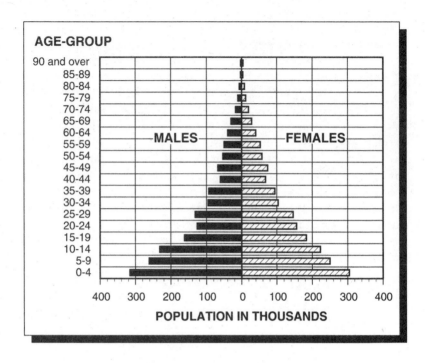

Figure 5. Population by Age and Gender, 1985

Source: Based on information from National Committee of Plan, *Population Census of 1985*, Vientiane, 1986.

prefer to live in lowland valley areas and base agricultural production on paddy rice.

The Lao Theung (see Glossary), or midland Lao, are of Austroasiatic origin and are probably the autochthonous inhabitants of Laos, having migrated northward in prehistoric times. Originally paddy rice farmers, they were displaced into the uplands by the migrations of the Lao Loum and in 1993 accounted for about 24 percent of the national population. The cultural and linguistic differences among the many Lao Theung groups are greater than those among the Lao Loum or Lao Sung (see Glossary), or upland Lao. Groups range from the Kammu (alternate spellings include Khamu and Khmu) and Lamet in the north, to the Katang and Makong in the center, to the Loven and Lawae in the far south.

The Lao Sung make up about 10 percent of the population. These groups are Miao-Yao or Tibeto-Burmese speaking peoples, who have continued to migrate into Laos from the north within the last two centuries. In Laos most highland groups live on the tops or upper slopes of the northern mountains, where they grow rice and corn in swidden fields. Some of these villages have been resettled in lowland sites since the 1970s. The Hmong (see Glossary) are the most numerous Lao Sung group, with villages spread across the uplands of all the northern provinces. Mien (Yao), Akha, Lahu, and other related groups are considerably smaller in numbers and tend to be located in rather limited areas of the north.

Government policy emphasizes the multiethnic nature of the nation and in many ways works to reduce the discrimination against midland and upland minorities by some lowland Lao (see Education, this ch.). Use of the three general ethnic group classifications emphasizes the commonality of Lao nationality but obscures significant differences among the smaller groups. Most Laotians categorize ethnic groups in terms of these three broad categories, and villagers themselves, when asked their ethnicity by outsiders, are likely to respond Lao Loum, Lao Theung, or Lao Sung, rather than their specific ethnicity.

Although ethnic differences are seldom a direct source of conflict, historical patterns of exploitation and competition for natural resources have led to tensions and occasional overt conflicts, some of which persisted in the early 1990s. For example, lowland Tai-Lao migrants displaced the Lao Theung groups into the uplands beginning a millennium ago, dominated them politically, and exploited them as well. The Lao Theung were frequently referred to as "Kha," a derogatory term meaning *slave*, which reflected their social, if not necessarily legal, status. (Slave trade did exist in the south of Laos during the eighteenth and nineteenth centuries, usually involving the Lao Theung.) Rites surrounding the coronation of the Lao king in Louangphrabang, as well as annual ceremonies of renewal, include rituals in which the king makes symbolic payment to Lao Theung representatives for the land, and they in turn acknowledge the legitimacy of the king.

French colonial rule tended to strengthen the position of lowland Lao, both by granting them access to education and by commonly appointing them as district and provincial governors regardless of the ethnic makeup of a region. In the early 1900s, Lao Theung and Lao Sung groups carried out several rebellions against Lao-Thai as well as French authority but all

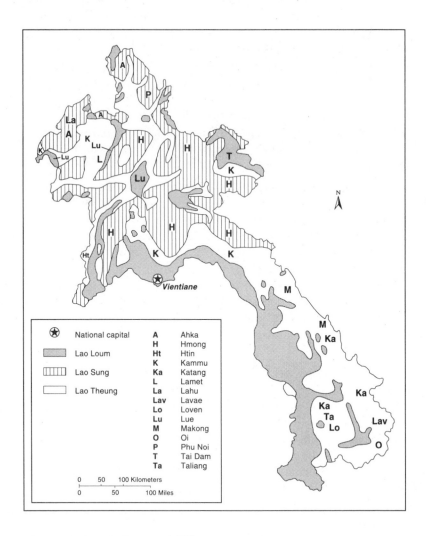

Figure 6. Ethnic Groups, 1992

Source: Based on information from United Nations Children's Fund, *Children and Women in the Lao People's Democratic Republic,* Vientiane, 1992; and Laos, National Committee of Plan, *Population Census of 1985,* Vientiane, 1986.

were eventually suppressed, leaving unresolved tensions. The court, administration, and national symbols continued to be defined in terms of Tai-Lao cultural traditions. During the 1950s, significant numbers of Lao Theung and Lao Sung were recruited by the leftist Pathet Lao (Lao Nation—see Glossary), and these groups played an important role in the military struggle (see The Coming of Independence, ch. 1). Since 1975 the number of Lao Theung and Lao Sung in the national and provincial administrations has increased, although in 1993 they were still underrepresented (see Government Structure, ch. 4).

National borders have not created significant barriers to the movement and settlement patterns of the different Lao ethnic groups because Laotian villagers have traditionally moved in search of better land for rice farming. About 5 million Hmong lived in southern China in the early 1990s, as opposed to about 200,000 in Vietnam, a similar number in Laos, and about 90,000 in northern Thailand. Kammu settlements existed both in northern Laos and northern Thailand, and many of the midland groups in the center of the country had villages in both Laos and Vietnam. The lowland Lao historically lived on both sides of the Mekong, with early Lao kingdoms encompassing much of the Khorat Plateau in present-day Thailand. Cultural and linguistic differences between the Lao Loum and the Thai Isan—what the Thai call the inhabitants of the Khorat Plateau in northeast Thailand—were primarily a result of the expansion of the Thai state and its influence in that region since 1945. Significant political changes in Laos since 1975 also contributed to a growing cultural distance.

The Refugee Population

During the Second Indochina War (1954–75), particularly between 1960 and 1973, large numbers of Laotians were displaced from their villages, either to escape frequent bombings or as a result of forced relocations by one side or the other seeking to consolidate control over an area. In the eastern zone controlled by the Pathet Lao, many villages were abandoned, and the inhabitants either lived in caves, fled across the border to Vietnam (where, despite the massive United States aerial war, the bombing was less intense than in the areas from which they had moved), or moved to refugee villages or camps in Royal Lao Government (RLG—see Glossary) areas (see Toward Neutrality: The First Coalition; The Attempt to Restore Neutrality; International Pressure and the Advent of the Second Coalition; The Third Coalition and the Lao Democratic People's Republic, ch. 1). These villages were established along Route 13 from Savannakhét to Pakxan and continued north of Vientiane. In addition, many Hmong and Mien villages that had allied with the RLG were frequently forced to move as a result of the changing battle lines and were regularly supplied by the RLG and United States.

At the end of the war, an estimated 700,000 persons, or about 25 percent of the population, were in some way displaced from their original homes. Many of these refugees began to return to their villages, or at least to the same general area, after the cease-fire of 1973, emptying many of the refugee villages along Route 13. The United Nations High Commissioner for Refugees (UNHCR—see Glossary) provided some assistance in transportation and initial rice supplies, and after 1975 the government also assisted to the extent possible with its meager resources. Hmong who sided with the RLG were forced to flee after 1975.

Not all internal refugees returned to their home districts, however. Some chose to remain in more populated areas near the Mekong and the larger towns, continuing to farm land that they had cleared during the war. The fall of the RLG and increased control by government cadres over daily activities in the villages also caused many villagers to flee the country. Many ended up in refugee camps in Thailand. The outmigration occurred in three phases. An initial flight of RLG officials and Westernized elite began in 1975. A second period of departures by many more ordinary villagers occurred between 1977 and 1981. These villagers were responding as much to economic hardship caused by poor weather and government mismanagement of the agricultural sector as to political control measures. A later period of less rapid departure lasted through the late 1980s. In all, more than 360,000 Laotians—about 10 percent or more of the population—fled the country between 1975 and 1992. This group included nearly all Western-educated Laotians, and, as political scientist Martin Stuart-Fox has noted, the loss of the intelligentsia may have set the country back an entire generation. Some upland minorities who had supported the RLG and the United States military effort also fled immediately, while other groups continued a guerrilla insurgency, which was not brought under control until after about 1979 (see Threats to National Security, ch. 5).

By the end of 1992, approximately 305,000 Laotian refugees had been permanently resettled in third countries, most commonly in the United States and France. Forty thousand Laotians—mostly Hmong—remained in refugee camps in Thailand, and 12,000 refugees had been voluntarily repatriated to Laos under the supervision and with the assistance of the UNHCR. International agreements mandated the resettlement or repatriation of all remaining refugees in Thailand by the end of 1994.

Even without the circumstances of war, Laotian villagers traditionally have moved in search of better prospects. Because of the overall low population density, if farmland near a village became scarce or its quality declined, part or all of a village might decide to relocate where there was more potential. This pattern occurs more frequently among upland semimigratory peoples, where there is a regular pattern of movement linked to the use of swidden fields. Even the lowland Lao, however, have a history of village fragmentation in search of new lands, although their investment in household or village infrastructure has tended to stabilize the population. Since the mid-1980s, the government has encouraged or compelled a number of upland villages farming swidden rice to resettle in lowland environments—a pattern also used by the RLG to more easily control villagers. In some instances, assistance in relocation and initial land clearing has been provided, while in others people have been left to fend for themselves in their new locations.

Rural-Urban Distribution

In the early 1990s, over 85 percent of the Laotian population was rural, typically living in villages ranging from ten to 200 households, or up to about 1,200 persons. Towns grew during the Second Indochina War as villagers fled to escape United States bombing. After 1975 many rural migrants returned to farming. Most of the sixteen province capitals or centers can be considered towns, although a few, such as Phôngsali, Attapu, and Xiangkhoang, are not much more than market centers, with populations well under 5,000 surrounded by a somewhat denser network of neighboring villages. In 1985 Vientiane had a population estimated at about 250,000, with municipal water and electricity systems, a variety of housing, and more developed educational and health facilities than were available elsewhere in the country.

The major provincial centers are Louangphrabang—the former royal capital—Savannakhét, and Pakxé, with populations ranging from 20,000 to 109,000 and a range of services and urban amenities. The other provincial capitals are distinguished by several government buildings, a regular market—although not always daily—at least one hotel and restaurant, and occasional air service. Towns are primarily administrative and market centers, with little or no industrial manufacturing outside of Vientiane (see Industry and Services, ch. 3). Aside from Vientiane and a few other provincial towns, growth has been limited, and the general pattern of existence held over many generations. In 1994, most of the 121 district centers were little more than large villages with the addition of a middle school and a few score officials.

Rural Life

Laotian society is above all else characterized by semi-independent rural villages engaged in subsistence agricultural production. Ethnic, geographic, and ecological differences create variations in the pattern of village life from one part of the country to another, but the common threads of village self-reliance, limited regional trade and communication, and identification with one's village and ethnic group persist regardless of the setting. Rural trade networks, however, have been a part of life since the 1950s. Except near the larger towns and in the rich agricultural plains of Vientiane and Savannakhét, villages are spaced at least several kilometers apart and the intervening land is variously developed as rice paddy and swidden fields or maintained as buffer forest for gathering wild plants and animals, fuelwood, and occasional timber harvest.

Ethnicity differentiates the villages but is usually not a source of conflict or antagonism. Nearly all villages are ethnically homogeneous, although a few include two or more distinct groups. Ethnic mixing often has resulted from different groups migrating to a new settlement site at about the same time, or a larger village at a crossroads or river transit point developing into a minor trading center. Ethnic identity is never absolutely immutable. Some minority Laotian individuals have adopted lowland Lao behavior and dress patterns, or intermarried with lowland Lao, and have effectively acculturated to lowland society. In some units, military service has also brought together Laotians of different ethnic groups, both before and after 1975.

Only since 1975 has there been any sense of national unity among most rural villagers. Precolonial governments depended more on a system of control at the district level, with the *chao muang* (district chief) maintaining his own allegiance and tribute to the state (see Government Structure, ch. 4). Administrative practices under the French and during the post-World War II period were confined primarily to provincial and a few district centers. The government was able to extract taxes with some facility but had little impact on the daily lives or thoughts of most villagers. However, since 1975, the government has expended considerable energy and resources on national unification, so that even isolated villages recognize the role of local government and consider themselves at some level to be part of a Laotian state.

Lowland Lao Society

Lao Loum (Laotian of the valley) have been the dominant group—numerically, politically, and economically—since the founding of the Kingdom of Lan Xang in the fourteenth century. The Lao of the Lao Loum ethnic group comprise just over 50 percent of the total population. Other related lowland groups include the Lue and Phu Thai, who together make up an additional 15 percent of the population. Groups such as the Tai Dam and Tai Deng are included by government statistics in the general category Phu Thai despite linguistic and cultural differences from other lowland groups. Variations occur regionally and among different ethnic subgroups, but the general patterns are relatively uniform. Most officials in the RLG were Lao Loum, and despite increases in the number of minority officials in the government, the lowland Lao held a clear majority in the early 1990s. Lowland cultural patterns are frequently considered the norm in designing policy or setting development priorities.

Lao Loum traditionally live in stable independent villages situated near lowland rivers or streams. At higher elevations, villages are located in valley areas that give as much access as possible to land suitable for paddy rice cultivation. Villages are self-contained and range from around twenty to over 200 households, although they typically contain forty or fifty houses and 200 to 300 people. Usually, villages are separated by rice fields or unused land. In rural areas, there might be five kilometers or more between villages, whereas in more densely populated areas only one kilometer or less separates the settlements. Most villages have grown in population over time, and if good land becomes scarce in the vicinity, it is not uncommon for some families to migrate to another area, either individually or as a group. Individual households usually move to another village where the family has kin or friends, but larger groups have often migrated to unsettled areas. Such village fission or relocation continued into the early 1990s, although migrants had to obtain permission from the district administration before settling in a new site.

The traditional independence and relative isolation of lowland villages has been reduced since the late 1980s. Although commerce in forest products—for example, sticklac—dates to colonial times, as roads have improved and marketing networks expanded, the government has encouraged commercial production for trade and export. As long as the open economic policies of the New Economic Mechanism are operating, the process of integrating lowland villages into a national socioeconomic system will likely continue (see Agriculture and Forestry; Foreign Trade, ch. 3).

Lao Loum houses are built on wooden piles, with the floor from one to two and one-half meters above the ground. This style keeps the living area above the mud of the rainy season, provides a shady area under the house to work or rest during the day, and allows the house to catch breezes for natural cooling. Depending on the wealth and resources of the family, the walls and floor may be made of woven split bamboo or sawn wood; the roof is constructed from grass thatch, bamboo, wood shingles, or corrugated steel roofing sheet. Some older houses in well-off villages are roofed with clay tiles, but this style was no longer common in the early 1990s. A separate rice granary is built in the house compound, also on posts using similar construction. Livestock is sometimes kept under the house.

Houses commonly range from five by seven meters to eight by twelve meters, with the smallest size typical of a newly established household or a family that has recently moved. Most houses are built with a porch on the long side that is used for visiting and as a public area. The interior is divided into one or two sleeping rooms, a common room for visiting and eating, and a separate kitchen area or side porch. Household furnishings are simple: mats or mattresses and blankets for sleeping on the floor, a low woven bamboo and rattan table for eating, and a few pots and dishes for cooking and eating. Lao Loum sit on the floor and eat from common bowls of soup or other dishes. Steamed rice is distributed among two or three common baskets placed around the edge of the table.

*Rice padi house, with
bamboo drying outside,
Vientiane
Courtesy Gina Merris*

*Louangphrabang family
at home
Courtesy Gina Merris*

Lao Loum households average between six and eight persons, but may reach twelve or so in exceptional cases. The family structure is typically nuclear or stem: a married couple and their unmarried children, or an older married couple together with one married child and his or her spouse plus unmarried children and grandchildren. Because kinship is reckoned bilaterally and flexibly, Lao Loum may maintain close social relationships with kin who are only distantly related by blood. Terms of address for persons in an older generation indicate whether the relationship is through the father's or mother's side and distinguish between elder and younger siblings.

Marriage occurs through a blend of traditional and modern practices. In earlier generations, marriages may have been arranged by the families, but at least since the 1960s, most couples usually have made their own choice, which is communicated to the parents. A bride-price is negotiated, which often defrays the expenses of the wedding. The wedding takes place at the home of the bride's family, with whom the couple initially resides, either in the same house or nearby. The groom helps with farming in the bride's family for several years until the couple feels they are economically ready to establish a separate household. Even then, they may continue to farm jointly with the older generation and either divide the harvest or eat from a common granary. A bride may sometimes move into her husband's household, but uxorilocal residence is somewhat more common. Initial uxorilocal residence combined with the sequential establishment of separate households by each older sibling frequently leaves the youngest daughter and her husband to care for the aged parents and ultimately to inherit the house. All the children divide lands and other valuables.

Polygyny is traditionally allowed but uncommon since the LPDR government outlawed it shortly after coming to power. Further, having multiple wives generally was restricted to the elite because it required the ability to maintain a larger household. However, many men have mistresses. Divorce may be initiated by either party. If a couple encounters domestic difficulties, the two families usually address the problem first. If necessary, the village elders join the attempt to resolve the couple's differences and achieve a reconciliation. After a divorce, both husband and wife may return to their families of birth, unless either can make a living other than from farming. Children of divorce may remain with either parent. In the case of a spouse's death, the widow or widower may return to her or his natal household but more commonly maintains an independent household or remarries. The choice often hinges on the ages of children; if none are old enough to help in the fields, the family has a difficult time surviving without extra help.

The lowland Lao village economy is centered on paddy rice cultivation, and most village activities and daily life revolve around rice production. Glutinous, or sticky, rice is the staple food; because it has a high starch content, sticky rice must be steamed rather than boiled. It is eaten with the fingers and dipped in soup or a vegetable or meat dish. Most Lao Loum villages are self-sufficient in rice production, although the production of individual households within a village varies. Household work centers on paddy production from the beginning of the rains in May through December when all the rice has been brought to storage. Periods of intense work occur at the time of transplanting and harvesting, and cooperative work groups are often organized among several families to help get the tasks completed in a timely manner.

Where level terrain is inadequate, lowland Lao also practice swidden rice farming. This method is less efficient than paddy rice cultivation, which provides higher and more stable yields for less work. In certain villages, swidden rice is grown only in some years as a supplement to paddy rice production, whereas in others it is planted regularly in small quantities. Some Lao Loum villages have no land suitable for rice paddies and are completely dependent on swidden rice production. Newly established villages may first clear fields and plant swidden rice for a year or two before plowing and bunding the fields to convert them to paddies.

In addition to paddy rice, most households also have a small vegetable garden and some fruit trees, either in the house compound or near a stream or other water source. Other crops include cotton, tobacco, and sugarcane, but they are usually planted only in small quantities for personal use. Villagers also raise chickens, ducks, and pigs, as well as a buffalo or two for plowing the fields and perhaps a pair of cattle for pulling a cart. In general, rural households are largely self-sufficient, growing their own food, making their own tools and clothes, and trading any surplus for soap, kerosene, medicines, and kitchen or household goods.

Hunting, fishing, and gathering traditionally play an important role in the household economy, although as the population has increased and wild areas have been degraded, access to these resources has gradually deteriorated. Homemade rifles are used to hunt small deer, wild pigs, and small game such as squirrels and birds; fish are caught with a variety of nets, traps, or hooks. Bamboo shoots, mushrooms, fruit, medicinal or culinary roots, and leaves are gathered in the forest according to the season. Men hunt and fish with throw nets and hooks, while women fish with dip nets and baskets and collect roots and wild vegetables.

Household tasks are typically divided according to gender, but the divisions are not rigid, and men and women often perform tasks interchangeably. For example, both sexes cut and carry firewood. Women and children traditionally carry water for household use and to cultivate kitchen gardens. Women do most of the cooking, household cleaning, and washing and serve as primary caretakers for small children. They are the main marketers of surplus household food and other petty production, and women are usually the commercial marketers for vegetables, fruit, fish, poultry, and basic household dry goods. Men typically market cattle, buffalo, or pigs and are responsible for the purchase of any mechanical items. Intrafamily decision making usually requires discussions between husband and wife, but the husband usually acts as the family representative in village meetings or other official functions. In farming work, men traditionally plow and harrow the rice fields, while women uproot the seedlings before transplanting them. Both sexes transplant, harvest, thresh, and carry rice.

Occupational specialization in the village is low; virtually everyone is a rice farmer first. Some villagers may have special skills in weaving, blacksmithing, or religious knowledge, but these skills are supplementary to the fundamental task of growing enough rice and vegetables for the family. Social and economic stratification tends to be low within any one village, although villages may differ substantially one from another. Status accrues to age, wealth, skill in specific tasks, and religious knowledge. Factions based on kinship or political alliance may exist in a village but usually do not obstruct overall village cooperation and governance.

Traditionally, lowland Lao villages are led by a village chief (*pho ban* or *nai ban*) and one or two assistants who are elected by the villagers, although district or province officials sometimes use their positions to influence the results. Respected

elders, including women, form an advisory group that medi-
ates intravillage disputes. Since 1975 villages have been governed by an administrative committee headed by a village
president (*pathan ban*) and several other persons with responsibilities for such specific areas as economic and population
records, self-defense militia, agriculture, women's affairs, and
youth affairs. All members are in principle elected by popular
vote, although for about a decade after 1975, party cadres at
the village level were supposed to have taken an active role to
ensure that acceptable candidates'were selected.

Even under the present political system, however, village
leaders have little or no formal authority and govern through
consensus and the use of social pressure to ensure conformity.
Village meetings are held infrequently, but are usually well
attended with different viewpoints on issues expressed openly.
If a consensus on an issue is not reached, leaders will delay
decisions to allow further discussion outside the meeting with
all members of the community. Typical issues might include
whether to build or expand a village school or dig a community
well, or how to organize the annual ceremony for the village
protective spirit. Historically, religious and ceremonial activities and ties with the Buddhist temple or monastery (*wat*) have
been very important in village life and a focus of considerable
time and expenditure.

Each family contributes equal amounts of labor, material,
and money to village projects. Once a decision is made to
undertake a project, a committee is appointed to manage the
details and keep track of the contributions to ensure that everyone does his or her share. Systems of rotating labor groups for
village projects are common; for example, groups of ten households may supply one worker per household every three to
seven days, depending on the number of groups, until the
project is finished. Some large projects, such as building a
school, may continue for several years, with work taking place
during the dry season when farming tasks are not heavy or
when funds are available to purchase materials.

Households also cooperate informally, especially in agricultural work. Labor exchange occurs for almost every task associated with rice farming, although it is most common for
transplanting, harvesting, and threshing. There are two different patterns of farm exchange. In central and southern Laos,
villagers call on many other households, sometimes the entire

village, for one day's help to complete a specific task such as transplanting. No specific repayment is required, but the family is obligated to help others in the village if they are unable to finish work in time. In northern villages, mutual assistance is organized on the basis of exchanges between families that should even out over the year; a day's work transplanting may be repaid by a day's work threshing. The contributions of men, women, and children over sixteen are considered equal, regardless of the task.

Houses are typically built by hand using local materials, and once the householder has collected enough wood, bamboo, and/or thatching grass, he will ask his neighbors and relatives to assist in the house raising. It usually takes twenty people a day or two to assemble the frame and raise the heavy timbers. Once the heavy work is completed, the owners finish construction over the ensuing weeks. In this work as well as farm labor exchange, the host family provides a meal to all those coming to help. For common farmwork, the meal is relatively simple and usually includes a chicken or duck and a bottle of local rice liquor. For a house raising, the meal is more elaborate—a pig or small ox and considerably more liquor after the task is done. Illness, death, or other household emergencies also elicit help from one's neighbors.

Lowland Lao are almost all Buddhists, and most villages have a *wat*, which serves as both a social and religious center (see Buddhism, this ch.). Whereas small villages may have only one or two monks in residence plus a few novice monks, larger villages may have up to six monks plus novices (see Religion, this ch.). Many villagers assemble at the *wat* for prayers on the days of each lunar quarter; on days of major religious festivals, they carry out more elaborate ceremonies and may organize a *boun* (religious fair) at the *wat*. Before the development of a national education system, boys and young men received basic religious and secular education at the *wat*. The *wat* is frequently used as a place for village meetings because the hall is often the only building large enough to accommodate everyone at once. Most villages have a small *wat* committee to oversee the maintenance of the building, organization of the fair, and the general welfare of the monks and novices. The committee members are selected by consensus on the basis of their morality and religious sincerity and usually have been monks at some time in their lives.

Lowland Lao in formal dress celebrating the opening of Lane Xang Bank, Louangphrabang Courtesy Gina Merris

Lowland Lao in formal dress in front of Wat Xieng Thong dressed for the Lao New Year in typical Louangphrabang style Courtesy Ernest Kuhn

Although they are Buddhists, Lao Loum also respect the power of *phi* (spirits), which may be associated with a place or a deceased person. More important for village organization is the cult of a village protective deity, or *phi ban*, which is typically celebrated yearly. Many villages have abandoned this practice in the face of increased modernization and official discouragement by the government. However, some villages continued through the early 1990s to offer an annual sacrifice to the *phi ban* in a ceremony that both reaffirmed the importance of the village as a unique social unit and aimed to secure the continued good fortune of the village and its inhabitants.

Midland Lao Society

Lao Theung (Laotian of the mountain slopes) make up about 24 percent of the population and consist of at least thirty-seven different ethnic groups ranging in population from nearly 400,000 (the Kammu) to fewer than 100 (the Numbri). Many of the groups have additional members in Thailand or Vietnam. Of the three main ethnic classifications, the differences among the Lao Theung groups are greater than among the Lao Loum or Lao Sung. Little is known about many of these groups, and reasonably complete ethnographic accounts are available only for a few. Most Lao Theung groups reside in a relatively limited geographic area; for example, the Nyaheun, Sedang, and Lavae mostly live in the far southern provinces of Attapu and Saravan (Salavan), whereas the Lamet reside near the border between Bokeo, Oudômxai, and Louang Namtha provinces. The Kammu live scattered throughout the north, from Xiangkhoang to Bokeo.

The Lao Theung speak languages of the Austroasiatic family, and although some languages are closely related, such as Kammu, Lamet, and Sam Tao, others are mutually incomprehensible. None of the languages has developed a written script. The geographer Christian Taillard has suggested that the Lao Theung were originally paddy rice farmers displaced by Tai migrants into the hills and mountains and forced to turn to swidden rice production. However, Karl Gustav Izikowitz's ethnography of the Lamet reports that historically they had been swidden farmers and did not cultivate paddy rice even in areas where suitable land was available. Certainly within the last two centuries, all the Lao Theung have been characterized as swidden farmers and as semimigratory because they have occasionally relocated their villages as swidden areas were exhausted.

The Kammu and Lamet, who are found in northern Laos, have different social organization and agricultural ecology than the ethnic groups in southern Laos.

Most Lao Theung villages (based primarily on descriptions of the Kammu) are located on mountain slopes but not at the peaks or ridges—the name Lao Theung means roughly "the Lao up there." Since the 1950s, however, a growing number of villages have been established at lower elevations near rivers or roads; villages grew up as roads were beginning to be rebuilt and expanded. Sometimes these villages were founded by people fleeing the war, and sometimes they arose out of the people's desire to be closer to transportation, markets, and social services. After 1975 many Hmong and some Kammu were driven out by the Pathet Lao and the Lao People's Army (see Glossary). Since the 1980s, the government has encouraged upland swidden farming minorities to relocate to lowland areas in order to reduce upland swidden farming and forest clearing. Kammu and Lamet villages, as well as those of some other midland groups, are relatively permanent, some remaining over fifty years in a location. Traditionally, villages managed the rotation of swidden fields in such a way as to sustain agricultural production over long periods. Individual households might move from a village to another location, or villages might merge with a second village being established a short distance away; however, the usual pattern was sedentary. Midland groups inhabiting central Laos generally have been more mobile, with villages relocated after a decade or so. It is not clear, however, whether this is a long-standing pattern or a response to the unsettled conditions during the Second Indochina War.

Lao Theung villages are usually somewhat smaller than most Lao Loum villages, commonly ranging between twenty and thirty households, but sites with fifty households and 300 or more inhabitants have been reported. Houses in Lamet and Kammu villages are clustered without apparent organization or orientation, but individual sites are selected with the advice of a village spirit practitioner. Lamet villages are commonly divided into two segments by the men's common house located in the middle of the village, but a similar practice has not been recorded for the Kammu. Traditionally, in Kammu households, there is a separate common house for adolescent boys and strangers, but this practice has not been continued in many new settlements established after 1975.

The houses are built on wooden or bamboo piles between one and two meters above the ground and are at least five by seven meters in size. Usually they are larger. Construction materials include woven bamboo or sawn lumber for floors and walls and grass thatch or bamboo shingle roofing. A kitchen hearth is located inside the house, and an open porch is built on at least one end of the house. A separate rice barn, also built on piles, may be located in the village near the house (Kammu) or on the edge of the village (Lamet). Villages are commonly built near a small stream to provide drinking and washing water, which is often diverted through a bamboo aqueduct to facilitate filling buckets and bathing.

Almost all Lao Theung groups rely on swidden rice cultivation as the basis of their household economy. Lamet and Kammu prefer glutinous rice, but some other groups prefer to eat ordinary rice. A small field house is almost always built in the fields, and all or part of the family may sleep there for days during the farming season rather than walk back to the village every day.

Swidden rice seldom yields as much as paddy fields, and the labor needed to keep weeds under control is the major constraint to expanding the area farmed. Corn, cassava, and wild tubers are thus important components of the diet to supplement a frequently inadequate rice supply. As a consequence of low rice yields, Lao Theung are generally considered to be the poorest of the three ethnic groupings in Laos. Men often come to towns to work as coolies.

In addition to farming, Lao Theung engage in hunting and gathering in the forests surrounding the village. Men shoot or trap small game and occasionally a wild pig or deer. Both women and men regularly collect bamboo and rattan sprouts, wild vegetables, mushrooms, tubers, and medicinal plants, the latter marketed by women. Fishing is common for some groups but seldom practiced by others, perhaps as a consequence of living in an upland environment distant from large streams.

Damrong Tayanin, an anthropologist of Kammu origin, has described a pattern of land tenure for the Kammu in which households own a large number of separate fields that are farmed over a twelve- to fifteen-year rotation; other households recognize these ownership rights. The claimed fields are divided among the offspring of each generation. However, no other studies mention any Lao Theung group respecting permanent rights to swidden fields. In all cases, fields that are cleared and farmed are allowed to revert to fallow after a year or two. Depending on the population-to-land balance, these fields might be allowed to lie fallow for three to over fifteen years before being cleared again. After each harvest, individual households select the fields they will clear and farm the following year. Sometimes this choice is an individual decision, but sometimes a group of households cooperates to clear and fence a single large area, which is then divided. Or, a village decides which area to clear and divide among all the families in the village. Once a field is abandoned, anyone may clear it and farm. Fallow periods shorter than five to seven years lead to gradual degeneration of the swidden system, however, because they do not allow adequate regrowth of vegetation to restore the soil fertility.

Almost all Lao Theung groups are patrilineal. Kammu and Lamet households average between six and seven persons but may be as large as twelve or fourteen persons. The ideal household consists of parents and children, wives of married sons, and grandchildren. Married sons eventually establish separate households, but a family might be temporarily augmented by a son-in-law who must live and work with the bride's parents for several years in partial payment of the bride-price. The Kammu and Lamet have eight and seven totemic clans, respectively, which provide a basis for social organization and the regulation of marriage. For the Lamet, the clans are exogamous, and each village contains at least two clans, thus providing the possibility of marriage exchanges. Kammu group the clans according to three categories—quadruped, bird, or plant— depending on the clan's totem. The totem is a plant or animal that was instrumental in either saving or killing the legendary clan ancestor. One must marry someone from another clan, and more particularly, men should marry real or classificatory mother's brothers' daughters. Each group of clans (for example, quadruped) always gives brides to one of the others (for example, bird) and receives brides from the third (for example, plants) in a circular relationship. Thus, a village must have all three clan categories represented for marriage exchanges to proceed.

Lamet clans help in establishing relationships between persons both inside and outside a village. In the village, members of the same clan are likely to develop cooperative relationships in farming, and a man traveling outside his village might seek out fellow clan members when arriving in another village. For the Kammu, however, clan membership appears relevant only for facilitating interhousehold cooperation and for regulating marriage relationships within a village. Should a family move to another village, it may change its clan membership in order to fit into the three-group marriage exchange circle.

Marriage choices are made by the groom and bride. Once a couple agrees to marry, their parents negotiate a bride-price. Among the Lamet, the bride's family also sends a dowry. Because there are few opportunities to acquire significant wealth in villages, Kammu and Lamet young men have frequently migrated to towns or to Thailand since the 1920s to work for several years until they acquire the funds needed for a bride-price. Among the Lamet, unmarried adolescent males sleep in the communal men's house, although they work with their families during the day.

Polygyny traditionally has been allowed, but it is rare, because few men can afford a second wife. Whereas a Lamet man may marry two sisters, this practice is prohibited among the Kammu; a widow may marry her husband's brother in either culture. If he chooses not to marry her, however, the brother is still responsible for her support. Initial residence after marriage is usually patrilocal, but if the groom is unable to pay the full agreed-upon bride-price, he may be obligated to live and work in his in-laws's household for several years in lieu of the bride-price. Upon the parents' death, the sons divide items of value and, according to Damrong, rights to swidden fields and fallows. Material possessions are generally limited and include not much more than livestock, farm and household equipment, or perhaps a few silver coins—used in traditional dress—or ingots. Wooden and bronze drums were important symbols of Lamet and Kammu household wealth in the past, but most appear to have been lost or sold during the Indochina wars.

Gender role differentiation in both farming and household activities is considerably greater among the Lao Theung than among the Lao Loum. Men are primarily responsible for clearing and burning swidden fields, although women may assist in clearing the smaller brush. Men punch holes for seed and the women follow, dropping and covering the seed with topsoil. Both sexes weed the fields, but the women are primarily responsible for this time-consuming task. Harvest is a joint activity. In the house, women cook, care for children, husk rice, cut firewood, and haul water. Women also gather roots, shoots, and other wild vegetative products. Men weave baskets, repair farm tools, and hunt small game. Men are also more likely than women to manage household finances and engage in trade, typically selling livestock and collected forest products or scrap metal from the war in exchange for rice. Izikowitz reports a significant trade of surplus rice by the Lamet and Kammu to neighboring lowland Lao villages in exchange for salt and metal implements in the 1920s and 1930s but notes that rice sales were declining because of competition from other producers. Since at least the 1970s, few Lao Theung have produced any surplus rice. Women may sell vegetables, chickens, or occasionally handicrafts locally but do not have the important market role of lowland Lao women. Where villages have access to primary schools, both boys and girls attend for a few years, but girls are much more likely to drop out before boys do (see Education, this ch.).

As in all villages in Laos, village governance is managed by an elected administrative committee consisting of a president and several other members in charge of economic affairs, self-defense, agriculture, and so on (see Government Structure, ch. 4). Traditionally, the village has a chief who is the intermediary between the village and the national government. Important decisions are made by elders, who in the absence of a written script memorize agreements among village members.

Both Kammu and Lamet villages have a ritual leader (*lkuun* in Kammu, *xemia* in Lamet), who officiates at important spirit rituals that affect the entire village. This position is hereditary in the male line. Kammu and Lamet, as most Lao Theung, are animists and are respected by their lowland neighbors as being especially proficient in protecting against or propitiating spirits that may cause illness or accidents. Ancestral spirits are an important aspect of household religious and safety rituals, but above the grandparents' generation they are generalized, and the spirits of specific persons are not worshiped. Kammu and Lamet revere rather than fear the spirits of their ancestors, who protect the household and village against harm as long as they are respected and are offered sacrifices. Rituals are also performed at the start of any important undertaking, for example, at the beginning of rice planting or building a house. Taboos restrict certain activities; for example, Lamet cannot make or repair tools inside the family house but do this work in the communal men's house.

Lao Theung are socially, economically, and politically the most marginal group of the three ethnic classes. During the Second Indochina War, many Lao Theung supported the Neo Lao Hak Xat (Lao Patriotic Front—LPF; see Glossary), the political party of the Pathet Lao—or actively fought with the Pathet Lao. Ethnic differences and resentments against lowland Lao dominance likely stimulated some of this support, as did effective Pathet Lao recruitment activities in the remote eastern areas populated principally by Lao Theung groups. During the years immediately after 1975, Lao Theung cadres gained numerous mid-level positions in the new government, but later many were replaced by lowland Lao with greater technical training and experience. Provincial and district officials are more likely to be Lao Theung in provinces with pronounced minority populations, and geographical isolation and poor education are still barriers to the integration of all Lao minorities in national affairs. The traditional subsistence swidden agricultural societies of the Lao Theung, which involved little trade with other groups, led to a marginal economic existence for many villages in the early 1990s. Numerous individual Lao Theung have adopted lowland behavioral patterns and successfully pass as lowland Lao, but prejudicial attitudes attributed to many lowland Lao continue to affect social and economic opportunities for many Lao Theung villages.

Upland Lao Society

Lao Sung (Laotian of the mountain top) include six ethnic groups, of which the Hmong, Akha, and Mien (Yao) are the most numerous. As of 1993, the Hmong numbered over 200,000, with settlements throughout the uplands of northern Laos. About the same number of Hmong live in northern Vietnam, and approximately 90,000 live in Thailand; this number does not include the 30,000 Hmong that were living in Thai refugee camps at the end of 1992. Some 60,000 Akha reside in Louang Namtha, Phôngsali, and Bokeo provinces. The other upland groups are the Phu Noi, found in Phôngsali and northern Louangphrabang provinces, the Mien (in Bokeo and Louang Namtha provinces), and small populations (fewer than 10,000) of Lahu and Kui located in the far northwest. The 1985 census also classified the 6,500 Hô (Haw)—Chinese originally from Yunnan Province—with the Lao Sung. All these groups have significant populations outside Laos, and the bulk of the ethnographic information available is from studies conducted in neighboring countries.

The Lao Sung are the most recent migrants to Laos, having arrived from the north in a series of migrations beginning in the early nineteenth century. Hmong entered northwestern Vietnam from China prior to 1800, and early settlements in northeastern Laos were reported around the turn of the nineteenth century. Pioneering settlements gradually extended westward, crossing the Mekong around 1890 and reaching Tak in northern Thailand around 1930. Mien migrations, in contrast, seem to have come southeast through Burma and Thailand before reaching Laos. All Lao Sung settlements are located in the north, with only Hmong villages found as far south as Vientiane.

Lao Sung typically live on mountain tops, upland ridges, or hillsides over 1,000 meters in elevation. The name Lao Sung means "the Lao up high." Most groups are considered to be semimigratory; villages are moved to new locations when swidden farming resources in the old locale have been exhausted. Yet some villages have continued for more than 100 years, with individual households moving in or out during this period. Although all Lao Sung traditionally live in the uplands and engage in swidden farming, their housing styles, diet, farming techniques, kinship systems, and social organization vary from one group to another.

The Hmong make up more than two-thirds of the Lao Sung. Hmong villages in Laos, Vietnam, and Thailand have traditionally been found on mountain or ridge tops, with sites selected according to principles of geomancy. Before the 1970s, villages seldom consisted of more than twenty or thirty households. Hmong rely on swidden farming to produce rice, corn, and other crops, but tend to plant a field until the soil is exhausted, rather than only for a year or two before allowing it to lie fallow. Consequently, the fields farmed by a village would gradually become too distant for easy walking, and the village would relocate to another site. The new site might be nearby or might be many kilometers distant.

The Hmong fled China (where they were traditionally paddy rice farmers) to escape persecution and pacification campaigns, gradually migrating through Vietnam and Laos into Thailand. They adopted swidden farming in these regions by necessity because lowland basins were already settled. Small

111

groups of households would leave an established village to start another village in relatively uninhabited upland areas. In turn, other families moving from older settlements would settle an area that had been vacated, always in search of better farmlands than those that had been left behind. As the population of both Hmong and other neighboring groups increased, it ultimately became impossible to find new unclaimed lands, and the pioneering settlement pattern ended sometime between 1960 and 1975 in western Laos and northern Thailand. Villages in the old settled areas of eastern Laos— Xiangkhoang and Louangphrabang—in many cases have been in one location for more than thirty or fifty years and have grown in size to as many as sixty or eighty households and more than 500 persons.

Hmong houses are constructed directly on the ground, with walls of vertical wooden planks and a gabled roof of thatch or split bamboo. In size they range from about five by seven meters up to ten by fifteen meters for a large extended household. The interior is divided into a kitchen/cooking alcove at one end and several sleeping alcoves at the other, with beds or sleeping benches raised thirty to forty centimeters above the dirt floor. Rice and unhusked corn are usually stored in large woven bamboo baskets inside the house, although a particularly prosperous household may build a separate granary. Furnishings are minimal: several low stools of wood or bamboo, a low table for eating, and kitchen equipment, which includes a large clay stove over which a large wok is placed for cooking ground corn, food scraps, and forest greens for the pigs. Almost every house has a simple altar mounted on one wall for offerings and ceremonies associated with ancestral spirits.

The Hmong swidden farming system is based on white (nonglutinous) rice, supplemented with corn, several kinds of tubers, and a wide variety of vegetables and squash. Rice is the preferred food, but historical evidence indicates that corn was also a major food crop in many locations and continues to be important for Hmong in Thailand in the early 1990s. Most foods are eaten boiled, and meat is only rarely part of the diet. Hmong plant many varieties of crops in different fields as a means of household risk diversification; should one crop fail, another can be counted on to take its place. Hmong also raise pigs and chickens in as large numbers as possible, and buffalo and cattle graze in the surrounding forest and abandoned fields with little care or supervision.

Hmong have traditionally grown opium in small quantities for medicinal and ritual purposes. From the beginning of their colonial presence, the need for revenue prompted the French to encourage expanded opium production for sale to the colonial monopoly and for payment as head taxes. Production, therefore, increased considerably under French rule, and by the 1930s, opium had become an important cash crop for the Hmong and some other Lao Sung groups. Hmong participate in the cash market economy somewhat more than other upland groups. They need to purchase rice or corn to supplement inadequate harvests, to buy cloth, clothing, and household goods, to save for such emergencies as illness or funerals, and to pay bride-prices. In the isolated upland settlements favored by the Lao Sung, opium poppies, a cold-season crop, are typically planted in cornfields after the main harvest. Opium, a sap extracted from the poppy plant, is almost the only product that combines high value with low bulk and is nonperishable, making it easy to transport. It is thus an ideal crop, providing important insurance for the household against harvest or health crises. The government has officially outlawed opium production, but, mindful of the critical role it plays in the subsistence upland economy, has concentrated efforts on education and developing alternatives to poppy farming, rather than on stringent enforcement of the ban (see Narcotics and Counternarcotics Issues, ch. 5). It also established a special police counternarcotics unit in August 1992.

Lao Sung farming is not mechanized but depends on household labor and simple tools. The number of workers in a household thus determines how much land can be cleared and farmed each year; the time required for weeding is the main labor constraint on farm size. Corn must be weeded at least twice, and rice usually requires three weedings during the growing season. Peppers, squash, cucumbers, and beans are often interplanted with rice or corn, and separate smaller gardens for taro, arrowroot, cabbage, and so on may be found adjacent to the swiddens or in the village. In long-established villages, fruit trees such as pears and peaches are planted around the houses.

In response to increasing population pressure in the uplands, as well as to government discouragement of swidden farming, some Hmong households or villages are in the process of developing small rice paddies in narrow upland valleys or relocating to lower elevations, where, after two centuries as swidden farmers, they are learning paddy technology, how to train draft buffalo, and how to identify seed varieties. To varying degrees, this same process is also occurring with other Lao Sung groups in the early 1990s as it had under the RLG.

✓ Hmong households traditionally consist of large patrilineal extended families, with the parents, children, and wives and children of married sons all living under the same roof. Households of over twenty persons are not uncommon, although ten to twelve persons are more likely. Older sons, however, may establish separate households with their wives and children after achieving economic independence. By the 1990s, a tendency had developed in Laos for households to be smaller and for each son and his wife to establish a separate household when the next son married. Thus, the household tends toward a stem family pattern consisting of parents and unmarried children, plus perhaps one married son. Following this pattern, the youngest son and his wife frequently inherit the parental house; gifts of silver and cattle are made to the other sons at marriage or when they establish a separate residence. In many cases, the new house is physically quite close to the parents' house.

✓ Hmong reckon kinship patrilineally and identify fifteen or sixteen patrilineal exogamous clans, each tracing their descent back to a common mythical ancestor. There are several subdivisions in Hmong society, usually named according to features of traditional dress. The White Hmong, Striped Hmong, and Green Hmong (sometimes called Blue Hmong) are the most numerous. Their languages are somewhat different but mutually comprehensible, and all recognize the same clans. Each village usually has at least two clans represented, although one may be more numerous. Wives almost always live with their husband's family.

Marriage is traditionally arranged by go-betweens who represent the boy's family to the girl's parents. If the union is acceptable, a bride-price is negotiated, typically ranging from three to ten silver bars, worth about US$100 each, a partial relic from the opium trade. The wedding takes place in two installments, first at the bride's house, followed by a procession to the groom's house, where a second ceremony occurs. Sometimes the young man arranges with his friends to "steal" a bride; the young men persuade the girl to come out of her house late at night and abduct her to the house of her suitor. Confronted by

*A member of the People's
Revolutionary Youth Union
Courtesy Gina Merris*

*Hmong children
Courtesy Harvey Follender*

the fait accompli, the girl's parents usually accept a considerably lower bride-price than might otherwise be demanded. Although some bride stealing undoubtedly involves actual abductions, it more frequently occurs with the connivance of the girl and is a form of elopement.

As a result of a government directive discouraging excessive expenditures on weddings, some districts with substantial Hmong populations decided in the early 1980s to abolish the institution of the bride-price, which had already been administratively limited by the government to between one and three silver bars. In addition, most marriages reportedly occurred by "wife stealing" or elopement, rather than by arrangement. In the past, males had to wait for marriage until they had saved an adequate sum for the bride-price, occasionally until their mid-twenties; with its abolition, they seemed to be marrying earlier. Hmong women typically marry between fourteen and eighteen years of age.

The Hmong practice polygyny, although the government officially discourages the custom. Given the regular need for labor in the swidden fields, an additional wife and children can improve the fortunes of a family by changing the consumer/worker balance in the household and facilitating expansion of cropped areas, particularly the labor-intensive opium crop. Yet the need to pay a bride-price limits the numbers of men who can afford a second (or third) wife. Anthropological reports for Hmong in Thailand and Laos in the 1970s suggested that between 20 and 30 percent of marriages were polygynous. However, more recent studies since the mid-1980s indicate a lower rate not exceeding 10 percent of all households. Divorce is possible but discouraged. In the case of marital conflict, elders of the two clans attempt to reconcile the husband and wife, and a hearing is convened before the village headman. If reconciliation is not possible, the wife may return to her family. Disposition of the bride-price and custody of the children depend largely on the circumstances of the divorce and which party initiates the separation.

Hmong gender roles are strongly differentiated. Women are responsible for all household chores, including cooking, grinding corn, husking rice, and child care, in addition to regular farming tasks. Patrilocal residence and strong deference expected toward men and elders of either sex often make the role of daughter-in-law a difficult one. Under the direction of her mother-in-law, the young bride is commonly expected to carry out many of the general household tasks. This subordinate role may be a source of considerable hardship and tension. Farm tasks are the responsibility of both men and women, with some specialization by gender. Only men fell trees in the swidden clearing operation, although both sexes clear the grass and smaller brush; only men are involved in the burning operation. During planting, men punch the holes followed by the women, who place and cover the seeds. Both men and women are involved in the weeding process, but it appears that women do more of this task, as well as carry more than half of the harvested grain from the fields to the village. Harvesting and threshing are shared. Women primarily care for such small animals as chickens and pigs, while men are in charge of buffalo, oxen, and horses. Except for the rare household with some paddy fields, the buffalo are not trained but simply turned out to forage most of the year.

As with all Laotian ethnic groups, there is virtually no occupational specialization in Hmong villages. Everyone is first and foremost a subsistence farmer, although some people may have additional specialized skills or social roles.

Hmong are animists, although a small number have converted to Christianity as a result of contact with Protestant and Roman Catholic missionaries. Most believe that spirits are a common cause for illness. Shamans (*txiv neeb*) who can treat spirit-induced illness are respected and play an important role in the village, often being consulted to tell fortunes. Shamans may be either male or female and are usually "chosen" by the spirits after the former have suffered a long illness. Other men and women may know curing rites but do not enter a trance as a shaman does (see Religion, this ch.).

Village stratification is limited but based primarily on clan membership and wealth. Often the clan that founded a village dominates it, either because of numerical majority or because early settlement facilitated access to the better fields. A family's wealth derives primarily from work and good luck. The ability to produce enough rice, or even a little to sell, and a decent opium harvest depend on having enough workers in the family to clear and care for more extensive swidden fields than average. Livestock, particularly buffalo and cattle, are another important source of mobile wealth. This wealth, however, is subject to loss through disease, just as savings of silver, livestock, or cash can be lost almost overnight if the family experiences a serious illness that reduces the workforce at a critical time or that requires the sacrifice of chickens, pigs, or even a buffalo for curing rituals. Proceeds from sales of opium and livestock not immediately consumed are usually converted into silver bars or jewelry for safekeeping.

In contrast to the Buddhist *wat* or the men's common house in Lao Loum, Kammu, and Lamet villages, there is no building or other central point in a Hmong village. Hmong cultural norms are more individualistic, and the household is more important than the village. Despite greater overall village permanence than in former times, individual households may come and go, usually in search of better opportunities but occasionally because of conflict with relatives or neighbors. The decline of migrating villages has been a gradual process since the 1940s. As opportunities for pioneering settlements have disappeared, households often relocate to be near other clan members or less-distant relatives.

Village governance is usually in the hands of a president and administrative committee, but clan elders have important consultative or advisory roles in all decisions. Interhousehold cooperative relationships occur less often than among the Lao Loum and appear limited to labor exchanges for some farming tasks and assistance at house raisings. Most cooperation takes place among brothers or cousins, and it is primarily close kin who can be relied upon for assistance in the case of family hardship or emergency. Lacking any other resource, Hmong will look for help from any other member of the same clan.

Hmong and other Lao Sung groups have traditionally lived in villages distant from Lao Loum or Lao Theung settlements, although trade in rice, forest products, and other market goods has stimulated contact between the groups. As the population of both Lao Sung and Lao Loum groups increased after the war, Lao Sung expansion of swidden fields had an impact on the watersheds of Lao Loum rice paddies. Northern Lao Loum who cannot produce enough rice on limited paddy fields have also begun to clear swiddens in the middle elevations. For the most part, there has been no overt conflict, and trade and casual contact have continued, but long-standing ethnic prejudice continued to color interethnic relations in these regions of closer contact and competition for land in the early 1990s.

At the same time that roads in remote provinces were being improved and international trade opened in the late 1980s, the Thai government imposed a ban on logging and timber exports following extensive deforestation and catastrophic floods. Thai logging companies quickly turned to Laos as an alternate source of tropical hardwoods. This suddenly increased demand for tropical timber has stimulated additional competition for hitherto unvalued forestland and provoked increased criticism of upland swidden farming groups. Although traditional levels of swidden farming did not cause the same level of land and forest damage as have recent logging activities, government statements increasingly have attributed rapid deforestation to swidden clearing and have envisioned the abolition of all upland swidden cultivation soon after the year 2000. Thus, in the 1990s, there may be more pressure on arable land in the uplands than previously. However, other analysts have noted the great impact of legal and illegal logging, as well as the encroachment of lowland Lao farmers into the uplands since the end of the Second Indochina War. A continuing low-level insurgency against the government, substantially led by Hmong refugees who formerly fought for the RLG, is a further source of official mistrust directed at some Hmong and other minority groups. Government efforts to resettle Hmong and other swidden farming communities in lowland sites are motivated by security concerns—as was the case under the RLG in the 1960s and 1970s—and by competition for timber, but may lead to increased disaffection of the minorities affected.

The Pattern of Rural Life

For Lao Loum, Lao Theung, and Lao Sung, the rhythm of life is strongly tied to the changing seasons and the requirements of farming. For swidden farming villages, the work year begins in January or February when new fields are cleared. This time of the year is also good for hunting and for moving to a new village. Opium farmers harvest the resin between January and March, depending on location and variety of poppy, but otherwise there are few agricultural activities. Swidden fields are burned around March and must be planted in May or June, just before the first rains. From the time the seeds sprout until August, work revolves around the never-ending task of weeding. Hunting and fishing continue, and with the coming of the rains, the forest begins to yield new varieties of wild foods.

For paddy farmers, the agricultural year begins with the first rains, when a small seedbed is plowed and planted. The seedlings grow for a month or so while the remaining fields are plowed and harrowed in preparation for transplanting. Transplanting requires steady work from every able-bodied person over a period of about a month and is one of the main periods of labor exchange in lowland villages.

Swidden farmers begin the corn harvest as early as September, and short-season rice varieties mature soon after the corn. Paddy rice seldom ripens before October, however, and the harvest may continue through early December in some areas, although mid-November is more usual. Even late swidden rice is finished by early November. Harvesting and threshing the rice are the principal activities during the second period of intense work in the farm year. Dry-season rice farmers repeat the same cycle, but vegetables, tobacco, or other cash crops require a more even labor input over the season.

Food availability parallels the seasons. Wild foods and fish are abundant during the rainy season, although the months just before the corn ripens may be difficult if the previous year's harvest was inadequate. Fruit is available during the rainy and cool dry seasons, but becomes scarce, as do most vegetables, from March through May. Hmong and Mien celebrate their new year in December or January, when the harvest is complete but before the time to clear new fields. Lowland Lao celebrate their new year on April 15, also shortly before the start of the farming year. The harvest is marked by the That Luang (see Glossary) festival, on the full moon of the twelfth lunar month, which falls in late November or early December (see Buddhism, this ch.).

Because most roads are in poor condition, travel in the rainy season is generally difficult, and villagers tend to stay close to home because of farmwork as well as the ever-present mud. The dry season brings easier land travel and the free time it allows. Since the late 1980s, a few rural villagers have begun to travel to regional population centers in search of temporary wage employment, often in construction.

Urban Society

With a population of somewhat over 250,000 in 1985, Vientiane is the only city of any size in Laos. Three provincial capitals have populations of more than 20,000—Louangphrabang with 20,000, Savannakhét with 109,000, and Pakxé with 50,000. The 1985 census classified 15 percent of the population as "urbanized," but this figure includes the populations of all district centers, most of which are little more than large villages of 2,000 to 3,000 persons. The expanded marketing and commercial opportunities resulting from economic liberalization in 1986 have somewhat stimulated urban growth. Vientiane planners anticipate an annual population expansion of 5.4 percent through the year 2000, and many of the more rural provincial capitals also are growing at a significant rate in the early 1990s.

Urban centers, for the most part, have developed from villages that expanded or grew together around an administrative or trading center. Louangphrabang is the historical capital of the kingdom of Lan Xang, and Vientiane and Pakxé are also centers of earlier kingdoms. Migration of the Lao Loum into the region resulted in the establishment of *muang* (see Glossary), semi-independent principalities, which sometimes formed a larger state entity but which always preserved a certain autonomy as a result of transportation and communication difficulties. Many of the original districts have since become district centers, and the word itself is used for this political division (see Party Structure, ch. 4). Although district centers rarely had more than a few thousand people as the mid-1990s approached, they serve as secondary administrative posts and marketing centers for the surrounding villages and are the location of the medical clinic and lower-secondary school—grades six through eight—for the vast majority of the rural population.

Population displacement during the Second Indochina War caused growth in some cities—Vientiane, Louangphrabang, and the main lower Mekong Valley towns—but depopulation of centers in the eastern liberated zones. Xiangkhoang was destroyed by bombing in 1969, and Xam Nua and Phôngsali were virtually depopulated. These provincial capitals have been revived since 1975, but their geographic isolation inhibits rapid growth. The capital of Xiangkhoang was relocated twenty kilometers north to the village of Phônsavan. Administrative centers of several districts were also relocated after 1975 in order to make them more central to all villages in the district.

Historically, towns were located along major rivers or in upland valleys and were primarily populated by Lao Loum and small populations of Vietnamese merchants, artisans, and civil servants (imported by the French), as well as by Chinese and Indian traders. Migration of refugees during the Second Indochina War brought an increased minority population, which grew even faster after 1975 because officials of the new regime, many of whom were Lao Theung and Lao Sung, moved into administrative posts in Mekong towns. So many Chinese and Indian merchants left Laos during the war that these groups accounted for only a small portion of the urban population in 1994. Many Vietnamese who were sympathetic to the RLG also fled, although an unknown number of advisers from North Vietnam were posted to Vientiane and other major centers. The Vietnamese population was nevertheless unlikely to exceed a few thousand in any towns other than Vientiane and Savannakhét.

All provincial capitals were centers of marketing, administration, education, and health care, but not of manufacturing because there was almost no industrial production outside the Vientiane area (see Industry and Services, ch. 3). As of mid-1994, each capital had at least one upper-secondary school—often the only one in the province—along with specialized technical schools for agriculture, teacher training, or public health (see Education, this ch.). Almost every province capital also had a hospital, but the quality of care and the availability of medicines—although greater than that in villages—were frequently limited.

Everywhere, the basic village character of society is evident. Even in Vientiane, a substantial number of the inhabitants are paddy rice farmers, either as their main occupation or as important supplemental work. Government officials' salaries are inadequate to support a family, and many officials rely on family members to secure their basic rice supply by farming. Cities and towns are also important markets for vegetables and fruit produced in the nearby villages; the trade volume remains small outside of Vientiane but has stimulated the gradually increasing market orientation of rural producers.

Traditional festivals and religious ceremonies are observed in towns much as in villages and are often organized on the basis of a neighborhood, which is typically defined by the boundaries of a formerly separate village. Family life-cycle ceremonies frequently draw guests from outside the neighborhood but rely on close neighbors and relatives to help with food and other preparations, as in a village.

Between 1975 and 1990, urban amenities such as hotels, restaurants, and cinemas were virtually absent outside of Vientiane, Savannakhét, and Louangphrabang. A few towns had government-operated guest houses for official travelers and one or two restaurants with a limited menu. Travelers in most district centers and even some provincial capitals could find a meal only by making arrangements with a family or the caretaker assigned to the guest house. Town markets are also limited in size and number. After the economic reforms of the late 1980s, however, private restaurants and hotels opened in most provincial centers and larger districts. Official travel increased, and, more important, Laotian merchants, foreign delegations, and tourists again began to travel within the country.

Sanitation services and utilities are not widespread. As of mid-1994, only a few of the larger towns had municipal water systems, and none had sewerage services. Electrification is a limited but important feature of urban life (see Industrial Output and Employment, ch. 3). Outside of the Vientiane area, Thakhek, Louangphrabang, and Savannakhét, most district centers did not have electricity in the early 1990s. Even in towns, electric power is limited to a few hours a day. Automobile batteries and voltage inverters are widely used as a power source to watch television or listen to a stereo cassette player.

The presence of a foreign diplomatic and aid community has had a significant effect on the economy of Vientiane, both in terms of direct aid and through employment of Laotians by the missions and as domestic help (see Foreign Aid, ch. 3). In response, Vientiane merchants stock imported consumer goods such as electronics, clothing, and food, items purchased by Laotians much more than by foreigners. A once dormant service sector of automobile and truck repair, tailors, barbers, and hairdressers has begun to revive. Patrons at restaurants and the six disco establishments are also predominantly Laotians, reflecting the increased income available to private-sector businessmen and employees of foreign organizations. Foreign assistance in Vientiane during the early years of the LPDR helped to develop several upper-secondary schools and technical-training schools and improve the two main hospitals.

However, Laotian cities have failed to attract the rural population, as cities do in other countries, because they offer little
obvious economic opportunity and because the rural areas
offer the possibility of making a decent living within communities that have not been socially or economically fragmented by
the forces of modernization. Further, the government initially
had explicitly anti-urban policies. Other towns have experienced less in-migration than Vientiane; this pattern is likely to
change if economic opportunities arise in secondary towns or
if competition for land and forest resources—or restrictions on
access—increases to the point of reducing the rural standard of
living. Nevertheless, even if a town does not dominate the
region, it has an impact on the lives of people living in the surrounding area. The larger the population of a town, the
greater the town's impact on the region. For example, farmers
within about fifteen kilometers of Louangphrabang grow vegetables for sale in the town market. In Vientiane, this radius
expands to forty kilometers; some village residents commute
up to thirty kilometers each way to government or private jobs
in the capital. Through these contacts, new ideas and material
goods filter into rural areas.

Religion

Buddhism

Buddhism was the state religion of the Kingdom of Laos,
and the organization of the Buddhist community of monks and
novices, the clergy (*sangha*), paralleled the political hierarchy.
The faith was introduced beginning in the eighth century by
Mon Buddhist monks and was widespread by the fourteenth
century (see Early History, ch. 1). A number of Laotian kings
were important patrons of Buddhism. Almost all lowland Lao
were Buddhists in the early 1990s, as well as some Lao Theung
who have assimilated to lowland culture. Since 1975 the communist government has not opposed Buddhism but rather has
attempted to manipulate it to support political goals, and with
some success. Increased prosperity and a relaxation of political
control stimulated a revival of popular Buddhist practices in
the early 1990s.

Lao Buddhists belong to the Theravada tradition, based on
the earliest teachings of the Buddha and preserved in Sri
Lanka after Mahayana Buddhism branched off in the second

century B.C. Theravada Buddhism (see Glossary) is also the dominant school in Thailand and Cambodia.

Theravada Buddhism is neither prescriptive, authoritative, nor exclusive in its attitude toward its followers and is tolerant of other religions. It is based on three concepts: *dharma* (see Glossary), the doctrine of the Buddha, a guide to right action and belief; karma (see Glossary), the retribution of actions, the responsibility of a person for all his or her actions in all past and present incarnations; and *sangha*, within which a man can improve the sum of his actions. There is no promise of heaven or life after death but rather salvation in the form of a final extinction of one's being and release from the cycle of births and deaths and the inevitable suffering while part of that cycle. This state of extinction, nirvana, comes after having achieved enlightenment regarding the illusory nature of existence.

The essence of Buddhism is contained in the Four Noble Truths taught by the Buddha: suffering exists; suffering has a cause, which is the thirst or craving for existence; this craving can be stopped; and there is an Eightfold Path by which a permanent state of peace can be attained. Simply stated, the Eightfold Path consists of right understanding, right purpose, right speech, right conduct, right vocation, right effort, right thinking, and right meditation.

The average person cannot hope for nirvana at the end of this life, but by complying with the basic rules of moral conduct, can improve karma and thereby better his or her condition in the next incarnation. The doctrine of karma holds that, through the working of a just and impersonal cosmic law, actions in this life and in all previous incarnations determine which position along the hierarchy of living beings a person will occupy in the next incarnation. Karma can be favorably affected by avoiding these five prohibitions: killing, stealing, forbidden sexual pleasures, lying, and taking intoxicants. The most effective way to improve karma is to earn merit (*het boun*—literally, to do good—in Lao). Although any act of benevolence or generosity can earn merit, Laotians believe the best opportunities for merit come from support for the *sangha* and participation in its activities.

Traditionally, all males are expected to spend a period as a monk or novice prior to marriage and possibly in old age, and the majority of Lao Loum men probably did so until the 1970s. Being ordained also brings great merit to one's parents. The period of ordination need not be long—it could last only for the three-month Lenten retreat period—but many men spend years in the *sangha* gaining both secular and religious knowledge. Study of the Pali language, in which all Theravada texts are written, is a fundamental component of religious training. Ordination as a monk also requires a man to comply with the 227 rules of the monastic order; novices—those under twenty years old—must obey seventy-five rules; and lay persons are expected to observe the five prohibitions. Only a few women, usually elderly, become Buddhist nuns; they live a contemplative and ascetic life but do not lead religious ceremonies as do monks.

Monks are trying to develop detachment from the world and, thus, may have no possessions but must rely on the generosity of people for food and clothing. These gifts provide an important opportunity for the giver to earn merit. Women are more active than men in preparing and presenting rice and other food to monks, who make their morning rounds through the town carrying a bowl to receive offerings that are their only nourishment for the day. In villages where there are only a few monks or novices, the women of the village often take turns bringing food to the *wat* each morning. Attendance at prayers held at the *wat* on the quarter, full, and new moon of each lunar cycle also provides a regular means of gaining merit.

Major religious festivals occur several times a year. The beginning and end of the Lenten retreat period at the full moon of the eighth and eleventh months are occasions for special offerings of robes and religious articles to the monks. During Buddhist Lent, both monks and laity attempt to observe Buddhist precepts more closely. Monks must sleep at their own *wat* every night—rather than being free to travel—and are expected to spend more time in meditation. Offerings to monks and attendance at full-moon prayers are also greater than at other times. Vixakha Bouxa, which celebrates the birth, enlightenment, and death of Buddha at the full moon of the sixth month—usually May—corresponds with the rocket festival (*boun bang fai*), which heralds the start of the rains. The date of Boun Phavet, which commemorates the charity and detachment of Prince Vessantara, an earlier incarnation of the Buddha, varies within the dry season, and, aside from its religious orientation, serves as an important opportunity for a village to host its neighbors in a twenty-four-hour celebration centering on monks reciting the entire scripture related to Ves-

*Monk standing by the door
of That Luang, Vientiane
Courtesy Gina Merris*

*Monks sawing logs for
charcoal, Louangphrabang
Courtesy Gina Merris*

santara. That Luang, a Lao-style stupa, is the most sacred Buddhist monument in Laos and the location of the nationally important festival and fair in November.

For the Lao Loum, the *wat* is one of the two focal points of village life (the other is the school). The *wat* provides a symbol of village identity as well as a location for ceremonies and festivals. Prior to the establishment of secular schools, village boys received basic education from monks at the *wat*. Nearly every lowland village has a *wat*, and some have two. Minimally, a *wat* must have a residence building for the monks and novices (*vihan*), and a main building housing the Buddha statues (*sim*), which is used for secular village meetings as well as for prayer sessions. Depending on the wealth and contributions of the villagers, the buildings vary from simple wood and bamboo structures to large, ornate brick and concrete edifices decorated with colorful murals and tile roofs shaped to mimic the curve of the *naga*, the mythical snake or water dragon. An administrative committee made up of respected older men manages the financial and organizational affairs of the *wat*.

Buddhist ceremonies generally do not mark events in a life-cycle, with the exception of death. Funerals may be quite elaborate if the family can afford it but are rather simple in rural settings. The body lies in a coffin at home for several days, during which monks pray and a continual stream of visitors pays their respects to the family and shares food and drink. After this period, the body is taken in the coffin to a cremation ground and burned, again attended by monks. The ashes are then interred in a small shrine on the *wat* grounds.

Beginning in the late 1950s, the Pathet Lao attempted to convert monks to the leftist cause and to use the status of the *sangha* to influence the thoughts and attitudes of the populace. The effort was in many ways successful, despite efforts by the RLG to place the *sangha* under close civil administrative control and to enlist monks in development and refugee assistance programs. Political scientist Stuart-Fox attributed the success of the Pathet Lao to the inability of the Lao Loum elite to integrate the monarchy, government, and *sangha* into a set of mutually supportive institutions. Popular resentment of the aristocracy, division of the *sangha* into two antagonistic sects, the low level of its religious education and discipline, and opposition to foreign (i.e., Western) influence all contributed to the receptiveness of many monks to Pathet Lao overtures.

The politicization of the *sangha* by both sides lowered its status in the eyes of many, but its influence at the village level augmented popular support for the Pathet Lao political platform, which paved the way for the change in government in 1975.

The LPDR government's successful efforts to consolidate its authority also continue to influence Buddhism. In political seminars at all levels, the government taught that Marxism and Buddhism are basically compatible because both disciplines state that all men are equal, and both aim to end suffering. Political seminars further discouraged "wasteful" expenditures on religious activities of all kinds because some monks were sent to political reeducation centers and others were forbidden to preach. The renunciation of private property by the monks was seen as approaching the ideal of a future communist society. However, Buddhist principles of detachment and nonmaterialism are clearly at odds with the Marxist doctrine of economic development, and popular expenditures on religious donations for merit making are also seen as depriving the state of resources. Thus, although overtly espousing tolerance of Buddhism, the state undercut the authority and moral standing of the *sangha* by compelling monks to spread party propaganda and by keeping local monks from their traditional participation in most village decisions and activities. During this period of political consolidation, many monks left the *sangha* or fled to Thailand. Other pro-Pathet Lao monks joined the newly formed Lao United Buddhists Association, which replaced the former religious hierarchy. The numbers of men and boys being ordained declined abruptly, and many *wat* fell empty. Participation at weekly and monthly religious ceremonies also dropped off as villagers under the watchful eye of local political cadre were fearful of any behavior not specifically encouraged.

The nadir of Buddhism in Laos occurred around 1979, after which a strategic liberalization of policy occurred. Since that time, the number of monks has gradually increased, although as of 1993, the main concentrations continue to be in Vientiane and other Mekong Valley cities. Buddhist schools in the cities remain but have come to include a significant political component in the curriculum. Party officials are allowed to participate at Buddhist ceremonies and even to be ordained as monks to earn religious merit following the death of close relatives. The level of religious understanding and orthodoxy of the *sangha*, however, is no higher than it had been before 1975, when it was justly criticized by many as backward and unobservant of the precepts.

From the late 1980s, stimulated as much by economic reform as political relaxation, donations to the *wat* and participation at Buddhist festivals began to increase sharply. Festivals at the village and neighborhood level became more elaborate, and the That Luang festival and fair, which until 1986 had been restricted to a three-day observance, lasted for seven days. Ordinations also increased, in towns and at the village level, and household ceremonies of blessing, in which monks were central participants, also began to recur. Although the role of Buddhism has been permanently changed by its encounter with the socialist government, it appears that Buddhism's fundamental importance to lowland Lao and to the organization of Lao Loum society has been difficult to erase, has been recognized by the government, and will continue for the foreseeable future.

• Animism

Despite the importance of Buddhism to Lao Loum and some Lao Theung groups, animist beliefs are widespread among all segments of the Lao population. The belief in *phi* ✓ (spirits) colors the relationships of many Lao with nature and community and provides one explanation for illness and disease. Belief in *phi* is blended with Buddhism, particularly at the village level, and some monks are respected as having particular abilities to exorcise malevolent spirits from a sick person or to keep them out of a house. Many *wat* have a small spirit hut built in one corner of the grounds that is associated with the *phi khoun wat*, the beneficent spirit of the monastery.

Phi are ubiquitous and diverse. Some are connected with the universal elements—earth, heaven, fire, and water. Many Lao Loum also believe that they are being protected by *khwan* (thirty-two spirits). Illness occurs when one or more of these spirits leaves the body; this condition may be reversed by the *soukhwan*—more commonly called the *baci*—a ceremony that calls all thirty-two *khwan* back to bestow health, prosperity, and well-being on the affected participants. Cotton strings are tied around the wrists of the participants to keep the spirits in place. The ceremony is often performed to welcome guests, before and after making long trips, and as a curing ritual or after recovery from an illness; it is also the central ritual in the

Lao Loum wedding ceremony and naming ceremony for new-born children.

Many Lao believe that the *khwan* of persons who die by acci-dent, violence, or in childbirth are not reincarnated, becoming instead *phi phetu* (malevolent spirits). Animist believers also fear wild spirits of the forests. Other spirits associated with spe-cific places such as the household, the river, or a grove of trees are neither inherently benevolent nor evil. However, occa-sional offerings ensure their favor and assistance in human affairs. In the past, it was common to perform similar rituals before the beginning of the farming season to ensure the favor of the spirit of the rice. These ceremonies, beginning in the late 1960s, were discouraged by the government as successive areas began to be liberated. This practice had apparently died out by the mid-1980s, at least in the extended area around Vientiane.

Ceremonies oriented to the *phi* commonly involve an offer-ing of a chicken and rice liquor. Once the *phi* have taken the spiritual essence of the offering, people may consume the earthly remains. The head of a household or the individual who wants to gain the favor of the spirit usually performs the ritual. In many villages, a person, usually an older man believed to have special knowledge of the *phi*, may be asked to choose an auspicious day for weddings or other important events, or for household rites. Each lowland village believes itself pro-tected by the *phi ban*, which requires an annual offering to ensure the continued prosperity of the village. The village spirit specialist presides over this major ritual, which in the past often involved the sacrifice of a water buffalo and is still an occasion for closing the village to any outsiders for a day. To *liang phi ban* (feed the village spirit) also serves an important social function by reaffirming the village boundaries and the shared interests of all villagers.

Most Lao Theung and Lao Sung ethnic groups are animists, for whom a cult of the ancestors is also important, although each group has different practices and beliefs. The Kammu call spirits *hrooy*, and they are similar to the *phi* of the Lao Loum; the house spirit is particularly important, and spirits of wild places are to be avoided or barred from the village. Lamet have similar beliefs, and each village must have one spirit practitio-ner (*xemia*), who is responsible for making all the sacrifices to village spirits. He also supervises the men's communal house and officiates at the construction of any new houses. When a spirit practitioner dies, one of his sons is elected by the married men of the village to be his successor. If he has none, one of his brother's sons is chosen. Ancestor spirits (*mbrong n'a*) are very important to the Lamet because they look out for the well-being of the entire household. They live in the house, and no activity is undertaken without informing them of it. Ancestor spirits are fond of buffalos; thus buffalo skulls or horns from sacrifices are hung at the altar of the ancestors or under the gable of the house. Numerous taboos regarding behavior in the house are observed to avoid offending ancestral spirits.

Hmong also believe in a variety of spirits (*neeb*), some associated with the house, some with nature, and some with ancestors. Every house has at least a small altar on one wall, which is the center of any ritual related to the household or its members. Annual ceremonies at Hmong New Year renew the general protection of the household and ancestral spirits. The spirit of the door is important to household well-being and is the object of another annual ceremony and sacrifice. As with other Lao groups, illness is frequently attributed to the action of spirits, and spirit practitioners are called to carry out curing rites. Two classes exist: ordinary practitioners and shamans. Ordinary priests or the household head conduct the household ceremonies and ordinary divinations. The shaman may be called on to engage in significant curing rituals.

According to Hmong belief, spirits reside in the sky, and the shaman can climb a ladder to the heavens on his magical horse and contact the spirits there. Sometimes illness is caused by one's soul climbing the steps to the sky, and the shaman must climb after it, locate it, and bring it back to the body in order to effect a cure. During the ritual, the shaman sits in front of the altar astride a wooden bench, which becomes his or her horse. A black cloth headpiece covers vision of the present world, and as the shaman chants and enters a trance, he or she begins to shake and may stand on the bench or move, mimicking the process of climbing to heaven. The chant evokes the shaman's search and the negotiations with the heavenly spirits for a cure or for information about the family's fortune.

Hmong shamans are believed to be chosen by the spirits, usually after a serious or prolonged illness. The illness would be diagnosed by another shaman as an initiatory illness and confrontation with death, which was caused by the spirits. Both men and women can be summoned in this way by the spirits to be shamans. After recovery from the illness, the newly chosen shaman begins a period of study with a master shaman, which may last two or three years, during which time he or she learns the chants, techniques, and procedures of shamanic rites, as well as the names and natures of all the spirits that can bring fortune or suffering to people. Because the tradition is passed orally, there is no uniform technique or ritual; rather, it varies within a general framework according to the practice of each master and apprentice.

Education

Education Prior to the Lao People's Democratic Republic

Of the many ethnic groups in Laos, only the Lao Loum had a tradition of formal education, reflecting the fact that the languages of the other groups had no written script. Until the mid-twentieth century, education was primarily based in the Buddhist *wat*, where the monks taught novices and other boys to read both Lao and Pali scripts, basic arithmetic, and other religious and social subjects. Many villages had *wat* schools for novices and other village boys. However, only ordained boys and men in urban monasteries had access to advanced study.

During the colonial period, the French established a secular education system patterned after schools in France, and French was the language of instruction after the second or third grade. This system was largely irrelevant to the needs and life-styles of the vast majority of the rural population, despite its extension to some district centers and a few villages. However, it did produce a small elite drawn primarily from the royal family and noble households. Many children of Vietnamese immigrants to Laos—who made up the majority of the colonial civil service—also attended these schools and, in fact, constituted a significant proportion of the students at secondary levels in urban centers. Post-secondary education was not available in Laos, and the few advanced students traveled to Hanoi, Danang, and Hué in Vietnam and to Phnom Penh in Cambodia for specialized training; fewer still continued with university-level studies in France.

The Pathet Lao began to provide Lao language instruction in the schools under its control in the late 1950s, and a Laotian curriculum began to be developed in the late 1960s in the RLG schools. In 1970 about one-third of the civilian employees of the RLG were teachers, although the majority of these were poorly paid and minimally trained elementary teachers. At that time, there were about 200,000 elementary students enrolled in RLG schools, around 36 percent of the school-age population.

Education since 1975

An important goal of the LPDR government was to establish a system of universal primary education by 1985. The LPDR took over the existing RLG education system that had been established in the 1950s and restructured it, facing many of the same problems that had also confronted previous governments. The French system of education was replaced with a Laotian curriculum, although lack of teaching materials has impeded effective instruction. An intensive adult literacy campaign was initiated in 1983–84, which mobilized educated persons living in villages and urban neighborhoods to bring basic reading and writing skills to over 750,000 adults. Largely as a result of this campaign, those able to read and write increased to an estimated 44 percent. According to the United Nations (UN), by 1985 those able to read and write were estimated at 92 percent of men and 76 percent of women of the fifteen to forty-five age-group. Because few reading materials are available, especially in the rural areas, many newly literate adults lose much of their proficiency after a few years.

The decision to establish universal education led the government to focus its efforts on building and staffing schools in nearly every village. Because resources are limited, most schools are poorly constructed—of bamboo and thatch—and staffed by only one or two teachers who are paid low wages, usually in arrears. Many village schools have only one or two grades, and books, paper, or other teaching materials are conspicuous by their scarcity.

School enrollment has increased since 1975. In 1988 primary school enrollment was estimated at 63 percent of all school-age children. In 1992–93 an estimated 603,000 students were in primary school, compared to 317,000 students in 1976 and 100,000 students in 1959. However, the goal of achieving universal primary education was postponed from 1985 to 2000 as a result of the lack of resources.

Because teachers are paid irregularly, they are forced to spend significant amounts of time farming or in other livelihood activities, with the result that in many locations classes are actually held for only a few hours a day. Because of irregular classes, overcrowding, and lack of learning resources, the average student needed eleven to twelve years to complete the five-year primary course in the late 1980s. Repetition rates ranged from 40 percent for the first grade to 14 percent for the fifth grade. Dropouts also were a significant problem, with 22 percent of all entering first graders leaving school before the second grade. In the late 1980s, only 45 percent of entering first graders completed all five years of primary school, up from 18 percent in 1969.

Performance statistics vary according to rural-urban location, ethnic group, and gender. Enrollment and school quality are higher in urban areas, where the usefulness of a formal education is more evident than in rural farming communities. Isolated teachers confronted with primitive rural living and teaching conditions have a difficult time maintaining their own commitment as well as the interest of their pupils. Ethnic minority students who have no tradition of literacy and who do not speak Lao have a particularly difficult time. Unless the teacher is of the same or similar ethnic group as the students, communication and culturally appropriate education are limited. Because of these factors, in the late 1980s the enrollment rate for the Lao Sung was less than half that of the Lao Loum; enrollment was also low for Lao Theung children.

Girls are less likely than boys to attend school and attend for fewer years—a discrepancy that was declining, however, in the early 1990s. In 1969 only 37 percent of students in primary school were girls; by 1989, however, 44 percent of primary school students were girls. Because of Lao Sung cultural attitudes toward girls' and women's responsibilities, girls in these groups accounted for only 26 percent of all students.

Secondary education enrollment has expanded since 1975 but as of mid-1994 was still limited in availability and scope. In 1992–93 only about 130,000 students were enrolled in all post-primary programs, including lower- and upper-secondary schools, vocational programs, and teacher-training schools. The exodus of Laotian elite after 1975 deprived vocational and secondary schools of many of their staff, a situation that was only partly offset by students returning from training in socialist countries. Between 1975 and 1990, the government granted over 14,000 scholarships for study in at least eight socialist countries; just over 7,000 were to the Soviet Union, followed by 2,500 to Vietnam, and 1,800 to the German Democratic Republic (East Germany).

In mid-1994, the school year was nine months. The typical sequence includes five years of primary school, followed by three years of lower-secondary school and three years of upper-secondary school. Some students go directly from primary or lower-secondary school to vocational instruction, for example, in teacher-training schools or agriculture schools.

Local secondary education is concentrated in the provincial capitals and some district centers. Dropout rates for students at secondary and technical schools are not as high as among primary students, but the gender and ethnic group differentials are more pronounced. In the late 1980s, only 7 percent of lower-secondary students were Lao Sung or Lao Theung, a rate that dropped to 3 percent in upper-secondary school. For most students who do not live in a provincial center, attendance at secondary school requires boarding away from home in makeshift facilities. This situation further discourages students in rural areas from pursuing further education, with additional differential impacts on girls and minorities. Vientiane has the majority of advanced schools, including the national teachers' training school at Dong Dok, the irrigation college at Tad Thong, the agriculture college at Na Phok, the National Polytechnic Institute, and the University of Medical Sciences. Even so, the level of training available at these schools is low.

In 1986 the government began to reform the education system, with the goals of linking educational development more closely to the socioeconomic situation in each locality, improving science training and emphasis, expanding networks to remote mountainous regions, and recruiting minority teachers. The plan envisioned making education more relevant to daily realities and building increased cooperation in educational activities among the various ministries, mass organizations, and the community. However, the ability to implement this program through its scheduled completion in 2000 depends on a significant budgetary increase to the educational sector in addition to receiving significant foreign aid. Education accounted for only 8 percent of government expenditures in 1988, down from a 10 to 15 percent range during the preceding seven-year period, and cultural expenditures also were not accorded a high priority.

Although more school texts and general magazines are being printed, poor distribution systems and budgetary constraints limit their availability throughout the country (see Mass Media, ch. 4). Overall, 3.9 million books were printed in 1989, including school texts published by the Ministry of Education, and novels, stories, and poems published by the Ministry of Information and Culture. Translations into Lao of various Russian-language technical, literary, and children's books were available through the Novosti press agency. Almost all these materials are inexpensive paperbound editions. Distribution of school texts is improving, and magazines and novels can occasionally be found in district markets distant from Vientiane. Thai printed material—for the most part, magazines and books—was available after the late 1980s in a few shops. Yet, in the early 1990s, it was rare to see a book or any other reading material in rural villages, with the exception of political posters or a months-old edition of the newspaper *Xieng Pasason* (Voice of the People) pasted on a house wall.

Health And Welfare

Public Health

Health and health care in Laos were poor in the early 1990s. Although diets are not grossly inadequate, chronic moderate vitamin and protein deficiencies are common, particularly among upland ethnic groups. Poor sanitation and the prevalence of several tropical diseases have further eroded the health of the population. Western medical care is available in few locations, and the quality and experience of practitioners are, for the most part, marginal, a situation that has not improved much since the 1950s.

The life expectancy at birth for men and women in Laos was estimated in 1988 at forty-nine years, the same as in Cambodia but at least ten years lower than in any other Southeast Asian nation. High child and infant mortality rates strongly affected this figure, with the Ministry of Public Health estimating the infant mortality rate at 109 per 1,000 and the under-five mortality rate at 170 per 1,000 in 1988. The United Nations Children's Fund (UNICEF—see Glossary) believed these figures underestimated the true mortality rate but still represented decreases from comparable rates in 1960. Regional differences were great. Whereas the infant mortality rate for Vientiane was about 50 per 1,000, in some remote rural areas it was estimated to be as high as 350 per 1,000 live births; that is, 35 percent of all children died before the age of one.

Children's deaths are primarily caused by communicable diseases, with malaria, acute respiratory infections, and diarrhea the main causes of mortality as well as morbidity. Vaccination against childhood diseases was expanding, but in 1989 Vientiane's municipal authorities still were unable to vaccinate more than 50 percent of targeted children. Other provinces have much lower rates of immunization. Malaria is widespread among both adults and children, with the parasite *Plasmodium falciparum* involved in 80 to 90 percent of the cases.

In the first malaria eradication program between 1956–60, DDT was sprayed over much of the country. Since 1975 the government has steadily increased its activities to eradicate malaria. The Ministry of Public Health operates provincial stations to monitor and combat malaria through diagnosis and treatment. Prevention measures involve chemical prophylaxis to high-risk groups, elimination of mosquito breeding sites, and promotion of individual protection. The campaign has had some success: the ministry reported a decline in the infected population from 26 percent to 15 percent between 1975 and 1990.

As of 1993, diarrheal diseases were also common, with regular outbreaks occurring annually at the beginning of the rainy season when drinking water is contaminated by human and animal wastes washing down hillsides. Only a few rural households have pit or water-seal toilets, and people commonly relieve themselves in the brush or forested areas surrounding each village. For children in these villages, many of whom are chronically undernourished, acute or chronic diarrhea is life-threatening because it results in dehydration and can precipitate severe malnutrition.

Although nutrition appears to be marginal in the general population, health surveys are of varying quality. Some data indicate that stunting—low height for age—in the under-five population ranged from 2 to 35 percent, while wasting—low weight for height—probably does not exceed 10 percent of the under-five population. These figures reflect village diets based predominantly on rice, with vegetables as a common accompa-

*Laotians bringing offerings to a temple in Ban Houayxay, near the
Thai border, in Bokeo Province
Courtesy Randall C. Merris
Musicians in Vientiane help to raise funds for wat restoration.
Courtesy Gina Merris*

niment and animal protein—fish, chicken, and wild foods— eaten irregularly. Children aged six months to two years—the weaning period—are particularly susceptible to undernutrition. The nutritional status of adults is related closely to what is being grown on the family farm, as well as to dietary habits. For example, fresh vegetables and fruits are not highly valued and therefore are not consumed in adequate amounts. As a result, it is likely that vitamin A, iron, and calcium deficiencies are common in all parts of the country.

Acquired Immune Deficiency Syndrome

Permissive attitudes of Laotian men toward sex and prostitution facilitated the transmission of human immunodeficiency virus (HIV) during the 1980s and 1990s, making HIV infection and acquired immune deficiency syndrome (AIDS) a growing concern. In 1992 a focused sample of about 7,600 urban residents identified one AIDS case and fourteen persons who tested HIV positive. No other statistics were available as of mid-1994.

The government convened a conference on AIDS in 1992, which noted the potential for a rapid spread of HIV in the population. Participants at the conference agreed that the spread of AIDS in Laos was inevitable, and, in fact, would likely be through young men who migrated to towns and then returned to their villages, as well as through women who entered the sex trades because of economic necessity. The numbers of HIV-positive people could increase to more than 10,000 within the next few years, although these numbers would likely not expand at the same rate as in Thailand—even though Thai men demonstrate similar attitudes toward sex and prostitution—because Laos's national policies forbid open prostitution. Through the early 1990s, Laos avoided widespread prostitution such as that found in neighboring countries, but it is likely to increase, as is the temporary migration of Laotian women to neighboring countries to work in the sex industry. Other possible routes of HIV infection include users of injectable illicit drugs and medical injections using unsanitary syringes. Should AIDS spread significantly in Laos, it will not only have a devastating effect on rural labor and the national economy, but will put impossible stress on the health care system. As the best means of preventing an epidemic, the conference report emphasized education in all sectors of the population through a variety of methods, including the media.

Health Infrastructure

Despite government promises that the urban-oriented health system inherited from the RLG would be expanded to support rural primary health care and preventative programs, little money had been allocated to the health sector as of 1993. According to figures from 1988, less than 5 percent of the total government budget was targeted for health, with the result that the Ministry of Public Health was unable to establish a management and planning system to facilitate the changes envisioned. UNICEF considered the effort to construct a primary health care system to have failed entirely.

Official statistics identified hospitals in fifteen of the sixteen provinces, plus several in Vientiane, and clinics in 110 districts and more than 1,000 *tasseng* (subdistricts—see Glossary). In reality, most subdistrict clinics are unstaffed, unequipped, and unsupplied, and in 1989 only twenty of the district clinics actually provided services. The physical condition of the facilities is poor, with clean water and latrines unavailable at most health posts, and electricity unavailable at 85 percent of district clinics, rendering vaccine storage impossible. Drugs and equipment stored in the central warehouses are seldom distributed to outlying provinces, and in most situations, patients had to purchase Western pharmaceuticals from private pharmacies that import stock from Thailand or Vietnam.

The number of health care personnel has been increasing since 1975, and in 1990 the ministry reported 1,095 physicians, 3,313 medical assistants, and 8,143 nurses. Most personnel are concentrated in the Vientiane area, where the population per physician ratio (1,400 to one) is more than ten times higher than in the provinces. In 1989 the national ratio was 2.6 physicians per 10,000 persons.

Training of medical personnel at all levels emphasizes theory at the expense of practical skills and relies on curricula similar to those used prior to 1975. International foreign aid donors supported plans for a school of public health, and texts were written and published in Lao. As of 1990, however, the school did not exist because of delays in approval of its structure and difficulties in finding trainers with the appropriate background.

Rural and provincial health personnel work under conditions similar to their counterparts in education: salaries are low and seldom paid on time, necessary equipment and supplies are unavailable, and superiors offer little supervision or encouragement. In these circumstances, morale is low, job attendance sporadic, and most health care ineffectual. In general, the population has little confidence in the health care sector, although some village medics and a few district or provincial hospitals are respected by their communities.

Use of traditional medical practitioners remains important in urban as well as rural locations. Healers who know how to use medicinal plants are often consulted for common illnesses. The Institute of Traditional Medicine of the Ministry of Public Health formulates and markets a number of preparations from medicinal plants. Spirit healers are also important for many groups, in some cases using medicinal plants but often relying on rituals to identify a disease and effect a cure. Many Laotians find no contradiction in consulting both spirit curers and Western-trained medical personnel.

In the absence of a widespread system of health workers, local shops selling drugs became an important source of medicines and offered advice on prescriptions. However, these pharmacies are unregulated and their owners unlicensed. As a consequence, mis-prescription is common, both of inappropriate drugs and incorrect dosages. In rural areas, vendors commonly make up small packets of drugs—typically including an antibiotic, several vitamins, and a fever suppressant—and sell them as single-dose cures for a variety of ailments.

Social Welfare

Despite statistics indicating that Laos is one of the poorest countries in the world, it has for the most part been spared the acute problems often associated with underdevelopment and poverty. Famine and serious epidemics have been absent in the twentieth century, urban slums have not existed, and debt bondage has been unknown. Because the rural economy was not effectively monetized through at least the early 1980s, households usually countered seasonal crop shortages by increasing their gathering activities and relying on wild tubers and other foods as insurance crops. Most villages have customs regarding the provision of rice loans—sometimes interest-free—to families experiencing a bad year. Most shelter in rural areas is self-built and not dependent on land ownership or access to money. Thus, it is possible for most families to survive at least at a subsistence level, although for many the material standard of living is not high. Chronic marginal food production and lack of access to or inability to afford medical care and education remain pervasive problems, however.

No reliable statistics regarding income distribution or the extent of poverty were available as of mid-1994. A 1988 survey of income distribution in urban Vientiane found an average household monthly income of about K35,000 (for value of the kip—see Glossary), or US$70, with the most common income between K25,000 and K30,000 per month—about $US55 at the 1988 exchange rate. With 4.5 persons per average household, the modal figure implied an annual per capita income of about US$150, far below the UN poverty line of US$275. Whether this survey included noncash income from agricultural production or other exchange is unknown, however; family crop production is still an important element in the economy of many urban Vientiane families. These limited statistics emphasize the relative sensitivity of urban residents to prices and cash income, particularly when compared with rural villagers who are more insulated from the effects of inflation and market behavior.

The government does not maintain a social welfare system, but the National Committee for Social Welfare and War Veterans operates a number of "orphans' schools" in some province centers and administers retirement pay to government officials. This retirement pay, however, is as insignificant as the officials' salaries were before retirement. Orphans, handicapped persons, and elderly persons living in rural villages are usually supported and cared for by their relatives, although the level of support depends on the economic resources of the caretakers. Lowland Lao are traditionally tolerant of mentally handicapped members of their community, and these persons, although not economically productive, are allowed to live with their families and move around the village at will. This family approach to social welfare operates in the towns as well, often on a neighborhood basis but particularly relying on extended kinship networks. As a consequence, urban beggars were unknown between 1975 and about 1987, although a small number appeared in Vientiane after that date, perhaps reflecting the increase in urban economic differentiation as much as any increase in acute poverty.

Regional and ethnic discrepancies remain the greatest source of poverty and poor living conditions. Many lowland villages are prosperous, regularly produce a rice surplus, and assist a small number of less well-off households within their boundaries. Other villages, particularly those in the uplands or of minorities who have recently relocated to lowland sites, are less well off and often unable to produce enough rice for village consumption. In these situations, the ability to produce other salable commodities, whether livestock, opium, or vegetables, or to find wage-labor jobs, is critical to the well-being of the household and the village. In settings where an entire village is rice-deficient, interfamily exchanges and rice loans cannot ameliorate the basic shortage affecting the community. Acute regional crop shortfalls in several years between 1989 and 1993 were largely met by rice imports provided through foreign aid. As market networks expand and as the economy becomes increasingly monetized and population growth and resettlement increase pressure on land resources, the number of villages in marginal economic situations can be expected to increase.

Future Trends

In mid-1994 Laotian society was in a period of transition. Although firmly based in self-sufficient village agricultural patterns, it is beginning to experience social and economic change stimulated by government policies and slowly growing communication with urban centers and neighboring modernizing countries. Most Laotians, however, have little experience outside their district of residence and are able to live simply and relatively comfortably on the food and other products they produce or gather themselves. Limited but expanding trade provides basic consumer goods that make life more comfortable or save labor. Trade also provides a stimulus to produce somewhat more than the family needs for its immediate consumption. Nevertheless, villages in mountainous regions are less advantaged and less connected to the market network and to government influence than those on the plains and river valleys, and some are chronically unable to produce enough food to meet their needs.

As the market economy expands and rural farmers find opportunities for cash crop production, village labor exchange relationships and other forms of cooperation are likely to begin to break down. These changes have already begun in the villages on the Vientiane plain, although in outlying provinces traditional cooperation networks remain more firmly in place. Not surprisingly, social and economic stratification increases in villages more closely linked to urban areas or markets, where some families are quicker to exploit economic or educational opportunities. Landownership remains relatively equal, but unclaimed good quality land for paddy rice production is extremely difficult to locate, thus removing one factor that served to minimize stratification in the past. At the end of the twentieth century, competition for lowland farms and increased pressure and restrictions on upland swidden farming may combine to change the character of rural landownership and farming. Genuinely landless families are likely to increase in number, and urban populations also will likely continue to expand at a moderate rate, depending on the continued establishment of manufacturing enterprises in provincial centers.

Substantial changes occurred in the education and health systems after 1975, but both sectors are severely underfunded and fail to meet the expectations of government policy makers. Education is more likely to improve, and as schools improve, expand their curriculum, and become more widespread, rural youth will gradually acquire the outlook and skills needed for work and life in an increasingly open and market-oriented society. Whether improved education also brings political inquiry and change remains to be seen.

Past performance of the state health sector does not generate much optimism regarding future developments. In the early 1990s, economic growth and stratification were already creating a demand for health care that remained unmet by the government sector, and since the late 1980s, significant numbers of people have traveled to Thailand for treatment of serious illnesses. Private health providers may increase, in much the same way as private pharmacies have opened to meet the demand for medications that cannot be obtained through the state health system.

Religious traditions that were initially threatened by the communist government have made a resurgence, and economic prosperity in lowland Lao areas has stimulated increased donations to and support of the Buddhist *wat* in many villages. As of mid-1994, most ethnic minorities maintained animist traditions as well, but were criticized formally and informally by officials for being superstitious.

At least through the 1990s, the traditional elements of Laotian society will very likely continue, and society will maintain its predominantly rural character. Self-sufficiency is not widely at risk, although there are certain ethnic groups and regions of the country experiencing inadequate food production and continued lack of access to productive resources. Ethnic diversity will certainly continue to be a factor in government development policy as well as intervillage relationships but is unlikely to be a source of serious conflict.

*   *   *

There have been few contemporary works on Laotian society, and only one researcher, anthropologist Grant Evans, has been able to carry out formal ethnographic or sociological studies in Laos since 1975. Most recent books and articles have focused on economic and political affairs. For information about society, it is necessary to search for certain less accessible reports prepared for development projects, as well as older sources. For some of the better sources, knowledge of French is necessary. The best books as of the early 1990s were Evans's *Lao Peasants Under Socialism*, Australian political scientist Martin Stuart-Fox's *Laos: Politics, Economics, Society*, and French social geographer Christian Taillard's *Le Laos: Stratégies d'un état-tampon*. The UNICEF report, *Children and Women in the Lao People's Democratic Republic*, is not easily available but provides an excellent up-to-date overview of the economic, health, education, and agricultural sectors, as well as the socioeconomic status of women and children.

A number of monographs or journal articles on post-1975 Laos are noteworthy. These include Evans's *Agrarian Change in Communist Laos*; an article entitled "'Rich Peasants' and Cooperatives in Socialist Laos," and another article entitled "Reform or Revolution in Heaven? Funerals among Upland Tai." Carol Ireson's study, "Women's Forest Work in Laos," outlines women's roles regarding gathering of wild foods and other resources in rural areas. Three short studies produced for the Swedish development aid mission also provide useful details of contemporary village life in rural areas: Agneta Håkangård's "Road 13: A Socio-Economic Study of Villagers, Transport and Use of Road 13 S, Lao P.D.R.;" Jan Ovesen's "Anthropological Reconnaissance in Central Laos: A Survey of Local Communities in a Hydropower Project Area;" and Ing-Britt Trankell's "On the Road in Laos: An Anthropological Study of Road Construction and Rural Communities." Martin Stuart-Fox and Rod Bucknell's "Politicization of the Buddhist Sangha in Laos" analyzes the religious changes occurring through the early 1980s.

Several works based on research during the RLG period remain valuable. Jacques Lemoine's *Un village Hmong vert du Haut Laos* is the only comprehensive source on the Hmong in Laos, as is Karl Gustav Izikowitz's dated, but still fundamentally useful account of the Lamet, *Lamet: Hill Peasants in French Indochina.*

Several publications on the Kammu produced with the collaboration of Kristina Lindell, Damrong Tayanin, and their coworkers provide detailed descriptions of Kammu life in Laos prior to the revolution. See particularly Lindell, et al., *The Kammu Year: Its Lore and Music*; Damrong and Lindell's *Hunting and Fishing in a Kammu Village*; and Damrong's "Environment and Nature Change in Northern Laos."

Articles by Christian Taillard and Georges Condominas provide an understanding of the social dynamics of lowland Lao village life unavailable elsewhere, particularly Taillard's "Le village Lao de la région de Vientiane: Un pouvoir local face au pouvoir étatique" and "Le dualisme urbain-rural au Laos et la récupération de l'idéologie traditionnelle" and Condominas's "Phiban Cults in Rural Laos." Martin John Philip Barber's "Migrants and Modernization: A Study of Change in Lao Society" also contains valuable information on village social structure in the Vientiane area. (For further information and complete citations, see Bibliography.)

Chapter 3. The Economy

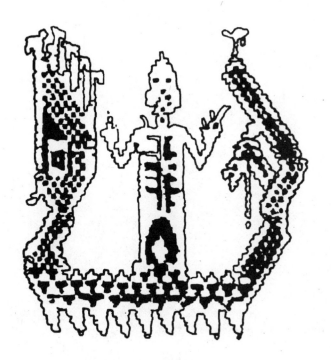

Detail from a Red Tai textile, with a spirit figure and a naga *(mythical snake or water dragon, associated with the rains and rivers) performing a healing and spirit-appeasing ceremony; a* naga *almost forms the shape of a boat.*

IN THE EARLY 1990s, the Lao People's Democratic Republic (LPDR, or Laos) was among the ten poorest countries in the world, according to a World Bank (see Glossary) ranking, with a per capita gross national product (GNP—see Glossary) in 1991 of just US$200. Its labor force is poorly trained and educated, its infrastructure severely damaged from years of inadequate maintenance, and its ability to feed itself precariously dependent upon the weather. Development expenditure is financed almost entirely by foreign aid, and, by 1991, exports financed only 40 percent of imports. By the beginning of the 1990s, however, Laos, while still an impoverished country highly dependent on foreign aid for its development, had taken some essential steps toward a free-market economy.

Despite the many obstacles to economic development that remained in the early 1990s, however, in little more than a decade, starting in 1979, the government had deliberately shifted the focus of its economic policy away from socialist goals and had made great strides. Many state-owned enterprises, which had been draining the nation's treasury through subsidies, were privatized, and tax collection was boosted tremendously, helping to bring the fiscal deficit under control. Liberal laws on foreign investment and trade were passed, precipitating a surge of investment activity. Prices of many commodities were freed from government controls, domestic transport restrictions were lifted, and the cooperative farming system was ended.

The Seventh Resolution, passed at a plenary session of the Central Committee by the ruling Phak Pasason Pativat Lao (Lao People's Revolutionary Party—LPRP; see Glossary) in late 1979, marked the start of the country's shift toward a market-oriented economy. The resolution affirmed the government's commitment to begin to open to a market economy, as the necessary path to economic development. Since its inception in 1975, the government, in theory, has recognized private property and private enterprise. However, they were not encouraged, and, in fact, the provincial governments of Louangphrabang (Luang Prabang) and Phôngsali abolished private trade and traders through 1987. The objectives of the First Five-Year Plan (1981–85) included self-sufficiency in food production, defined as the equivalent of 350 kilograms of paddy rice and other foodstuffs per capita per year, and the collectivization of agriculture. The plan also focused on developing industrial activity, increasing trade with Thailand, improving the shattered rural infrastructure, and increasing export revenues, all goals that received much greater attention as the tentative steps toward a market-oriented economy continued.

Growth during the plan period was slower than had been anticipated, however, and the government decided to take bolder steps toward reform. At the Fourth Party Congress in 1986, the Second Five-Year Plan (1986–90) was endorsed, and a new national development strategy was introduced. The New Economic Mechanism, as this program was called, was designed to expose the economy to world market forces gradually, without sacrificing the nation's goal of food self-sufficiency. To implement this plan, many facets of the economy were decentralized. Although the central authorities continued to set policy guidelines, responsibility for administering and financing many programs for economic and social development was delegated to the provinces. About a year after the congress, the new policy was promulgated into regulations, and changes became rapid and extensive.

The second plan also sought to encourage foreign and private investment. Among the reforms called for under the New Economic Mechanism were the lifting of numerous trade regulations and the creation of opportunities for foreign investment. In a major shift from its economic dependency on Vietnam, Laos began to look toward Thailand—and, later, toward other socialist countries—for private investment, technology transfer, and trade. Through the improvement of transportation and communications systems, encouragement of the private sector, and development of the agroforestry industrial processing sector, it was hoped that non-food imports could be reduced and exports increased, thus improving the balance of payments. Although Laos showed an overall balance of payments surplus in 1985 and 1986, the current account deficit had been increasing, and during those years exports financed less than 30 percent of imports. The government took a new interest in environmental protection and sought to limit the practice of swidden, or slash-and-burn, cultivation as a means of protecting its forest resources and encouraging cash cropping. It proved difficult, however, to bring about such a change because of negative effects on upland farmers' livelihoods. Traditional swidden agriculture does not adversely affect forest resources to the same extent that commercial exploitation does.

Many reforms were carried out successfully during the late 1980s, but the Second Five-Year Plan ended with economic performance lagging well behind planned achievements. Not least among the disappointments was the need to import rice during the droughts of 1987 and 1988, underlining the fact that an objective identified over ten years earlier—sustained self-sufficiency in food—had not been met.

Despite economic failures, however, the Fifth Party Congress, held in March 1991, reaffirmed the government's commitment to the development of a market-oriented economy. The Third Five-Year Plan (1991–95) proposes a "strategy" that aims to continue progress made under the previous two plans: improving the country's infrastructure, promoting exports, and encouraging import-substitution industries. In August 1991, the Supreme People's Assembly (SPA) approved a new constitution—the first since the previous constitution was abolished in 1975 (see The Constitution, ch. 4). Among its provisions is the affirmation of the right to private ownership; the words "democracy and prosperity" replaced "socialism" in the national motto.

Agriculture and Forestry

Agriculture in the Economic System

At least 5 million hectares of Laos's total land area of 23,680,000 hectares are suitable for cultivation; however, just 17 percent of the land area (between 850,000 and 900,000 hectares) is, in fact, cultivated, less than 4 percent of the total area. Rice accounted for about 80 percent of cultivated land during the 1989–90 growing season, including 422,000 hectares of lowland wet rice and 223,000 hectares of upland rice, clearly demonstrating that although there is interplanting of upland crops and fish are found in fields, irrigated rice agriculture remains basically a monoculture system despite government efforts to encourage crop diversification. Cultivated land area had increased by about 6 percent from 1975–77, but in 1987 provided citizens with less than one-fourth of a hectare each, given a population of approximately 3.72 million in 1986. In addition to land under cultivation, about 800,000 hectares are used for pastureland or contain ponds for raising fish. Pastureland is rotated, and its use is not fixed over a long period of time.

In the early 1990s, agriculture remained the foundation of the economy. Although a slight downward trend in the sector's contribution to gross domestic product (GDP—see Glossary) was evident throughout the 1980s and early 1990s—from about 65 percent of GDP in 1980 to about 61 percent in 1989 and further decreasing to between 53 and 57 percent in 1991—a similar decrease in the percentage of the labor force working in that sector was not readily apparent. Some sources identified such a downward trend—from 79 percent in 1970 to about 71 percent in 1991—but both the LPDR's State Planning Commission and the World Bank reported that 80 percent of the labor force was employed in agriculture in 1986. Available evidence thus suggests that the percentage of the labor force employed in agriculture in fact remained relatively steady at about 80 percent throughout the 1970s and 1980s.

Agricultural production grew at an average annual rate of between 3 and 4 percent between 1980 and 1989, almost double its growth rate in the preceding decade, despite two years of drought—in 1987 and 1988—when production actually declined. Paddy rice production declined again in 1991 and 1992, also because of drought. By 1990 the World Bank estimated that production was growing at an increasingly faster rate of 6.2 percent. Increased production, long one of the government's goals, is a result, in part, of greater use of improved agricultural inputs during the 1970s and 1980s. The area of land under irrigation had been expanding at a rate of 12 percent per annum since 1965, so that by the late 1980s, irrigated land constituted between 7 and 13 percent of total agricultural land. Although still a small percentage, any increase helps to facilitate a continued rise in agricultural productivity. Small-scale village irrigation projects rather than large-scale systems predominate. Use of fertilizers increased as well, at an average annual rate of 7.2 percent; given that commercial fertilizer use had been virtually nonexistent in the late 1970s, this, too, is an important, if small, achievement in the government's pursuit of increased productivity. In addition, the number of tractors in use nearly doubled during the decade, from 460 tractors in 1980 to 860 in 1989.

Crops and Farming Systems

Most farmers employ one of two cultivation systems: either the wet-field paddy system, practiced primarily in the plains and valleys, or the swidden cultivation system, practiced primarily in the hills. These systems are not mutually exclusive, especially among the Lao Loum (see Glossary), or lowland Lao, in areas remote from major river valleys (see Lowland Lao Society, ch. 2). Swidden cultivation was practiced by approximately 1 million farmers in 1990, who grew mostly rice on about 40 percent of the total land area planted to rice.

Swidden agriculture is highly destructive to the forest environment because it entails shifting from old to new plots of land to allow exhausted soil to rejuvenate, a process that is estimated to require at least four to six years. The extent of destruction, however, depends on the techniques used by the farmers and the overall demographic and environmental circumstances that relate to the length of the fallow period between farming cycles. Further, traditional agricultural practices allowed for forest regeneration and not the stripping of forest cover, which is a current commercial logging practice. Swidden fields are typically cultivated only for a year, and then allowed to lie fallow, although Kammu (alternate spellings include Khamu and Khmu) anthropologist Tayanin Damrong reports that at least through the 1970s some fields were planted two years in a row. An increasing population, encroachment on traditional swidden farming areas by other villages or ethnic groups, and gradual deterioration of the soil as a result of these pressures have led to increasingly frequent shortfalls in the harvests of midland swidden farmers.

The swidden farming process begins with clearing the selected fields in January or February, allowing the cut brush and trees to dry for a month, and then burning them. Rice or other crops are seeded by dibble shortly before the rains begin in June, and the growing crops must be weeded two or three times before the harvest in October. Swidden farming households are seldom able to harvest a rice surplus; in fact, the harvest usually falls one to six months short of families' annual rice requirements.

Swidden cultivation is less productive than wet-field cultivation because it requires between ten and fifty times as much land per capita—if one includes the fallow fields in the calculation—yet produces just 20 percent of the national rice harvest.

Mature fallows or young forests have other benefits such as wild food gathering, animal habitat, and watershed protection. Government policy since the introduction of the New Economic Mechanism has discouraged the practice of swidden cultivation because it works against the goals of increased agricultural productivity and an improved forest environment. Also, the government wishes to control the population in close clusters. Farmers have resisted the change, however, largely because wet-field cultivation often is not feasible in their areas and because no alternative method of subsistence has presented itself, especially given the lack of markets and infrastructure necessary for cash-cropping to be an attractive, or even a possible, venture. Further, government traders' defaults on purchase contracts with farmers in the late 1980s made farmers with better physical access to markets skeptical about cash-crop production. In general, despite government efforts to increase export-oriented agricultural production, the "rice monoculture" persisted in Laos through the early 1990s.

Rice

Rice is the main crop grown during the rainy season, and, under usual conditions, rainfall is adequate for rice production.However, if rain ceases to fall for several weeks to a month at a critical time in the rice growing cycle, yields will be significantly affected. Upland rice varieties, although adapted to a lower moisture requirement, are also affected by intermittent rains because farmers have no means of storing water in their fields.

Rice accounted for over 80 percent of agricultural land and between 73 percent and 84 percent of total agricultural output of major crops throughout the 1980s, except in 1988, and into the early 1990s (see table 4, Appendix). Rice paddies also yield fish in irrigation ditches in *na* (lowland rice fields). Production of rice more than doubled between 1974 and 1986, from fewer than 700,000 tons to 1.4 million tons; however, drought in 1987 and 1988 cut annual yields by nearly one-third, to about 1 million tons, forcing the government to rely on food aid for its domestic requirements. In 1988 and 1989, some 140,000 tons of rice were donated or sold to Laos. With improved weather and the gradual decollectivization of agriculture—an important measure under the New Economic Mechanism—rice production surged by 40 percent in 1989. The increase in production reflected the importance of the agricultural sector

Sticky rice harvest, Vientiane
Rice padi, Louangphrabang
Courtesy Gina Merris

to the economy and was largely responsible for the economic recovery following the droughts. In 1990 production continued to increase, although at a much slower rate, and the point of self-sufficiency in rice was reached: a record 1.5 million tons. Sufficiency at a national level, however, masks considerable regional differences. The southern Mekong provinces of Khammouan, Savannakhét, and Champasak regularly produce surpluses, as do Vientiane and Oudômxai provinces, but an inadequate transportation system often makes it easier for provinces with shortages to purchase rice from Thailand or Vietnam than to purchase it from other provinces.

According to some sources, the percentage of the labor force engaged in rice production declined gradually, by over 30 percent between 1986 and 1991, a trend encouraged by the government because it tended to increase export-oriented production. Some feared, however, that this trend would threaten sustained self-sufficiency in food, another key goal of the government. But sustained self-sufficiency more likely depends on a continued increase in the use of agricultural inputs such as fertilizers and improved strains of rice, and on the implementation of extension and research services, rather than on the actual number of workers involved in planting.

The overall increase in rice production throughout the 1980s was the result of higher productivity per hectare, rather than of an increase in the land area planted in rice; in fact, the area planted in rice decreased during the 1980s, from 732,000 hectares in 1980 to 657,000 hectares in 1990. Because farmers make little use of fertilizers or irrigation, however, most land still yielded only one annual crop in the early 1990s, despite government efforts to foster the use of double-crop rice.

Other Crops

Only about 150,000 hectares were planted with major crops other than rice in 1990, an increase from approximately 80,000 hectares in 1980. Principal non-rice crops include cardamom—sometimes considered a forestry product—coffee, corn, cotton, fruit, mung beans, peanuts, soybeans, sugarcane, sweet potatoes, tobacco, and vegetables. The only crop produced for export in substantial quantities is coffee. Although the total area planted to these crops is small relative to the area planted to rice, it increased from 10 percent of the total cropped area in 1980 to about 18 percent in 1990. The increase in part reflects the drop in rice production during the drought years;

it also demonstrates some success in the government's push to diversify crops. Yields for all the major crops except coffee, vegetables, and cardamom—for which some figures are only available from 1986—increased gradually between 1980 and 1990, most notably corn (by 70 percent), fruit (by 65 percent), peanuts (by 28 percent), and mung beans (by 25 percent) (see table 5, Appendix). Despite increasing agricultural output, however, Laos is still an importer of food, heavily dependent on food aid.

Statistics for agricultural production do not reflect either the nature of the subsistence agricultural economy or the importance of opium to the hill economy. Opium, legal in Laos and once even accepted as a tax payment, is a lucrative cash crop for the Lao Sung (see Glossary)—including the Hmong (see Glossary)—who have resisted government efforts to replace opium production with the production of other goods, for which the market is much less profitable (see Upland Lao Society, ch. 2). Opium production provides the funds necessary to the household when there is a rice deficiency, common among swidden farmers. Crop substitution programs, however, have had some effect, and to some extent tougher laws against drug trafficking and government cooperation on training programs have also contributed to reduced output.

In 1994 Laos remained the third largest producer of illicit opium for the world market, according to United States drug enforcement officials (see Narcotics and Counternarcotics Issues, ch. 5). These officials estimate that the potential yield of opium declined 47 percent—from 380 tons in 1989 when a memorandum of understanding on narcotics cooperation between the United States and Laos was signed—to an estimated 180 tons in 1993. The 22 percent decline in opium production in 1993 from 1992, however, was largely attributed to adverse weather conditions.

Livestock

The government encourages animal husbandry through programs for cattle breeding, veterinary services, cultivation of pasture crops, and improvement of fish, poultry, and pig stocks. Between 1976–78 and 1986–88, the stock of all farm animals increased greatly: cattle by 69 percent to 588,000 head; goats by 128 percent to 73,000; pigs by 103 percent to 1.5 million; horses by 59 percent to 42,000; buffaloes by 55 percent to 1 million; and chickens by 101 percent to 8 million. Increases, however, would have been significantly greater without diseases and a persistent shortage of animal feed. Disease is a serious problem: there is a significant annual mortality of chickens and pigs in most villages, and buffaloes are also frequently subject to epidemics.

Fishing

For many Laotians, freshwater fish are the principal source of protein; per capita consumption averages 5.1 kilograms annually. Fishpond culture began in the mid-1960s, and production—mainly carp raised in small home lots—grew an average 30 percent annually thereafter, the highest rate in Asia between 1975 and 1985. The Mekong districts in the south have especially high potential for greater increases in fish production. In the 1982–84 period, the average annual catch was 20,000 tons, all of which was consumed domestically.

Forestry

In the 1950s, forests covered 70 percent of the land area; yet, by 1992, according to government estimates, forest coverage had decreased by nearly one-third, to just 47 percent of total land area. Despite the dwindling expanse, timber (including ironwood, mahogany, pine, redwood, and teak) and other forestry products (benzoin (resin), charcoal, and sticklac) constitute a valuable supply of potential export goods. The forest has also been an important source of wild foods, herbal medicines, and timber for house construction and even into the 1990s continues to be a valued reserve of natural products for noncommercial household consumption. Since the mid-1980s, however, widespread commercial harvesting of timber for the export market has disrupted the traditional gathering of forest products in a number of locations and contributed to extremely rapid deforestation throughout the country (see Environmental Problems and Policy, this ch.).

Deforestation increased steadily throughout the 1980s, at an annual average rate of about 1.2 percent in the first half of the decade according to the United Nations (UN) and other monitoring agencies. This rate represents the destruction of about 150,000 to 160,000 hectares annually, as compared with annual reforestation of about 2,000 hectares. The government, however, reported a deforestation rate double this figure. Deforestation results from clearing forestland for shifting cultivation and removing logs for industrial uses and fuel. The volume of logs (roundwood) removed for industrial purposes increased by about 70 percent between 1975–77 and 1985–87, to about 330,000 cubic meters; however, this volume was dwarfed by that removed for domestic (fuel) purposes. Between 1980 and 1989, the volume of logs removed for fuel increased by about 25 percent, to about 3.7 million cubic meters; only about 100,000 cubic meters were removed for industrial purposes. By 1991 these figures had increased to approximately 3.9 million cubic meters and 106,000 cubic meters, respectively.

Following the introduction of the New Economic Mechanism, decentralization of forest management to autonomous forest enterprises at the provincial level encouraged increased exploitation of forests. At the central and provincial levels, autonomous forest enterprises are responsible for forest management.

Timber resources have been commercially exploited on a small scale since the colonial period and are an important source of foreign exchange. In 1988 wood products accounted for more than one-half of all export earnings. In 1992 timber and wood products were almost one-third of the total principal exports.

The government needed to reconcile its opposing objectives of decentralized forestry management and environmental protection. In January 1989, the government imposed a ban on logging—initially announced in January 1988 as a ban on the export of unprocessed wood—although exemptions are granted on a case-by-case basis. This measure was followed by the imposition of high export taxes on timber and other wood products, included in the June 1989 tax reforms. Toward the end of 1989, logging was again permitted, but only based on quotas extended to individual forestry enterprises. In response to the restrictions, production of unprocessed logs (roundwood or timber) decreased slightly in 1989, but, according to the Asian Development Bank (see Glossary), production more than recovered the following year. The effect of the restrictions is most clearly shown in the export statistics for 1989—exports of timber and wood products had decreased by 30 percent from the previous year. In 1991 a new decree banned all logging until further notice, in hopes of controlling widespread illegal logging and subsequent environmental destruction. However, there was little practical impact, and illegal logging remains widespread. The smuggling of logs to Thailand also is significant.

Agricultural Policy

Agriculture, the most important sector of the economy, clearly benefited from the introduction of the New Economic Mechanism. The changes positively affected performance by establishing a consistent policy that induced increased agricultural production over a number of years—before the droughts in 1987 and 1988—particularly in paddy production.

In June 1988, in line with the policies described by the New Economic Mechanism, the government passed a resolution to reform the agricultural sector. As announced at the Fourth Party Congress in 1986, the principal goal was to reorient the sector toward a market economy. The abolition of the much hated agricultural tax as well as the socialist restrictions on marketing helped to create necessary incentives for farmers.

The major change was in the pricing policy. The practice of setting low producer prices for a wide range of crops was ended, boosting incomes in rural areas. (In 1987 the procurement price of rice was only 30 percent of the market price).

Other changes were implemented. Restrictions on internal trade of agricultural products were removed, allowing free markets to operate, at least for important crops such as rice. Laws also were enacted to guarantee farmers' rights to private ownership of land, including the right to use, transfer commercially, and bequeath. Tax exemptions for specified periods also were decreed.

The reforms emphasize the government's belief that further increasing and diversifying agricultural production requires the participation and encouragement of the private sector. Food security, as always, remains a key objective, but the focus of the new agricultural policy is on the production of cash crops that can be processed—to increase their value—and then exported. The means for reaching that goal include the popular 1989 measure of abandoning the poorly developed attempts at establishing the socialist infrastructure of agriculture—a cooperative farming system.

The primary objective of the cooperative farming system, based on the Vietnamese model, had been to help the nation achieve self-sufficiency in food. Reflecting the government's pursuit of this goal, the number of government-assisted cooperative farms nearly tripled between 1978, when the drive to reorganize agriculture began, and the introduction of the New Economic Mechanism in 1986. At that time, cooperative farms numbered about 4,000 and employed about 75 percent of the agricultural labor force, although most were cooperatives only on paper, and there was no practical cooperative management. By 1988, however, employment in the cooperatives had decreased and included only 53 percent of all rural families and about half of all rice fields.

The distribution and sale of collectively managed land to families began in 1989. Most families in the old settled areas had their original land returned, which they still recognized. By mid-1990 most state farms and agricultural cooperatives had been disbanded. This move, in conjunction with the removal of many restrictions on food prices and the distribution of agricultural goods, helped to precipitate a modest growth in agricultural output of about 7 percent in 1990.

At the Fifth Party Congress in March 1991, the government reiterated the basic objective of its agricultural policy: a shift from subsistence production to cash crop production through crop diversification and improved linkages to export markets. Although rural farmers have limited experience in marketing their farm produce and are cautious about participating actively in the market, they are beginning to produce and sell their specialized crops and livestock and buy manufactured goods on a regular basis. At the congress, the government also affirmed its support for the private ownership of land and its intent to protect farmers' rights to long-term use of land, to bequeath land to their children, and to transfer their land rights in exchange for compensation. These assurances, among other improvements in the economic atmosphere, are an attempt to make Laos more attractive to foreign investors.

Environmental Problems and Policy

Laos suffers from a number of environmental problems, the most important of which are related to deforestation. Expanding commercial exploitation of the forests, plans for additional hydroelectric facilities, foreign demand for wild animals and non-wood forest products for food and traditional medicines, and a growing population put increasing pressure on the forests. Deforestation not only destroyed at least 150,000 to

160,000 hectares of valuable forest annually in the 1980s, but also caused erosion—leading to siltation of reservoirs, navigation channels, and irrigation systems downstream—and reduced groundwater levels. The practice of swidden cultivation not only contributes greatly to deforestation, but also in 1987 made Laos one of eleven countries in the world that together were responsible for over 80 percent of net world carbon emissions amounting to a per capita emission of ten tons annually, compared with the world average of 1.17 tons per capita. Further, during the Second Indochina War (1954–75), Laos was heavily bombed and left with tons of unexploded ordnance and bomb craters that ultimately altered the local ecology.

The government's desire to preserve valuable hardwoods for commercial extraction and to protect the forest environment, as well as international concern about environmental degradation and the loss of many wildlife species unique to Laos, have motivated efforts to prohibit swidden cultivation throughout the country (see Natural Resources, ch. 2). This policy has had a significant effect on the livelihoods of upland villagers dependent on swidden cultivation of rice. Traditionally, villagers relied on forest products as a food reserve during years of poor rice harvest and as a regular source of fruits and vegetables. By the 1990s, however, these gathering systems were breaking down in many areas. The government has restricted the clearing of forestland for swidden cropping since the late 1980s and is attempting to resettle upland swidden farming villages in lowland locations where paddy rice cultivation is possible. However, both the government's inability to ensure compliance with the measures and the attraction of Thai money for forest products inhibits implementation of the restrictions.

Although a lack of environmental planning, surveys, and legislation diminishes the likelihood of substantial improvement of the environment in the near future, a number of decrees have been issued to encourage environmental protection. These decrees include general principles for protecting forestland; prohibitions on cutting certain tree species; regulations on hunting, fishing, and the use of fire during the dry season; and regulations on the management and protection of forestland, wildlife, and fish. The use of manure and compost have been encouraged to help rejuvenate soil. Managed burning also encourages many forms of forest growth.

Rural housing and rice padis, Louangphrabang
Harvesting vegetables outside Vientiane
Courtesy Gina Merris

The government's commitment to environmental protection is affirmed in the constitution and in its policy of finding new occupations for swidden cultivators. In 1991 the Ministry of Agriculture and Forestry established a land use program under the National Forest Resource Conservation and Development Strategy. The program reserves 17.0 million hectares, including 9.6 million hectares for forest protection, 2.4 million hectares for wildlife reserves and national parks, and 5.0 million hectares for production. The commitment, however, is mainly on paper: the highest priority park—Nam Theun—will be flooded by a hydroelectric dam by 2000.

Industry and Services

Industrial Output and Employment

Estimates of the industrial sector's contribution (including construction) to GDP vary, but most sources find it to be slowly increasing, from about 10 percent in 1984 to about 17 percent in 1993. The World Bank estimated the sector's contribution at 14 percent in 1989. Most sources also indicated an increase in the percentage of the labor force employed in the sector, from about 5 percent in 1970 to about 7 percent in 1980. However, World Bank figures available in mid-1993 indicated that the sector employed only just over 2 percent of the labor force in 1986. All sources agree that the growth of the industrial sector had increased throughout the 1980s; the World Bank estimated an average annual growth rate of 3.4 percent between 1980 and 1989, despite negative growth in the drought years of 1987 and 1988 during which exports of hydroelectricity were substantially lowered. By 1990 the growth rate had leveled off, from a surge of nearly 32.0 percent in 1989 to about 12.7 percent in 1992. The virtual end of the command economy fueled the 1989 industrial boom and supported steady growth for at least the medium term. Principal activities in the industrial sector include manufacturing, construction, mining, processing agricultural and forestry goods, and producing hydroelectricity.

Manufacturing

There is a paucity of any real industry in Laos outside of timber harvesting and electricity generation. Nonetheless, "manufacturing" represents about half of all industrial activity. Other manufacturing activities include the production of agricultural tools, animal feed, bricks, cigarettes, detergents, handicrafts, insecticides, matches, oxygen, plastics, rubber footwear, salt, soft drinks and beer, textiles and clothing, and veterinary products. Manufacturing employed only approximately 2 percent of the labor force in 1991. As of 1994, the garment industry was "booming," with investment from China, France, Taiwan, and Thailand; there were more than forty garment factories in the Vientiane area.

The manufacturing subsector was composed of over 600 factories and plants, of which one-third were state-owned in 1991. Most manufacturing is for domestic consumption and is centered in the Vientiane area. As of mid-1994, there was little manufacturing in or near Laotian towns. In 1989 and 1990, there was a rapid increase in cottage industries such as cotton spinning and weaving, traditional village crafts, basket-weaving, and the production of alcoholic beverages. As part of the informal business sector, however, cottage industries are not covered by national statistics.

Between 1980 and 1990, over 80 percent of manufacturing was in the production of clothing, food and beverages, metal products, tobacco products, and wood products (see table 6, Appendix). Industrial roundwood production increased 71 percent between 1975–77 and 1985–87 to an annual average of 330,000 cubic meters and then declined to 309,400 cubic meters in 1990. Sources differ over the growth trend for lumber production; the UN reported a decrease in production of 61 percent between 1980 and 1988, and the Asian Development Bank showed an increase of nearly 400 percent in the same period. Cigarette production rose from 1.10 billion units per year from 1981–84; to 1.12 billion units in 1985 and an estimated 1.20 billion units per year for 1986–90. Statistics over a lengthy period of time for the production of other major goods are not readily available; however, the Asian Development Bank estimated that the value of metal products, food and beverages, and clothing (at 1991 prices) had increased greatly between 1980 and 1990, by 55 percent, 195 percent, and 196 percent, respectively (see table 7, Appendix). A general upward trend in the growth of production is borne out by official LPDR statistics from the first half of the decade. The World Bank reported that the manufacturing subsector grew by 35 percent in 1989, slowing to about 4 percent the following year.

Energy

Mountainous terrain and heavy annual rainfall give Laos

considerable hydroelectric potential. The Mekong River and its tributaries in Laos have an estimated hydroelectric potential of between 18,000 and 22,000 megawatts, or roughly half that of the river as a whole. The remaining potential belongs to Cambodia and other riparian countries. Total installed capacity in 1991 was 212 megawatts, the majority of it hydroelectric, or only about 1 percent of the potential.

Production of hydroelectricity, the country's major export until 1987, expanded slowly throughout the 1980s, from 930 thousand megawatt-hours in 1980 to about 1.1 million megawatt-hours in 1989, an increase of about 17 percent. The majority of electricity produced—approximately 75 to 80 percent, as of 1992—is exported to Thailand, which has an agreement to purchase all surplus electricity. The remainder is supplied to power networks for domestic consumption. Through 1986 the sale of electricity to Thailand was the country's most important source of foreign exchange. Despite increased production, in 1987 hydroelectricity yielded its place as the principal export to wood products, because of the drought, which lowered water levels, and a reduction in the unit price of electricity to Thailand. By 1991 a new agreement between Laos and Thailand had raised the unit price of electric power.

The largest hydropower facility in Laos is the Nam Ngum dam, sited on the Nam Ngum River, north of Vientiane. The Nam Ngum plant began operation in 1971 with an installed generating capacity of thirty megawatts; by 1987 additional turbines had increased capacity to 150 megawatts. In the early 1970s, the Nam Ngum facility provided electricity to Vientiane; the supply was gradually extended to surrounding villages on the Vientiane plain. As of the early 1990s, approximately 80 percent of the power produced at Nam Ngum was exported to Thailand; some was diverted to the south for town and village electrification.

A second hydroelectric dam was completed at Xeset near Saravan (Salavan) in southern Laos in 1991. The Xeset plant has an installed capacity of twenty megawatts.

About twenty smaller hydropower facilities and diesel plants supply additional power. Since the mid-1980s, Thakhek and Savannakhét had access to a regular power supply through a repurchase agreement with Thailand whereby a cable under the Mekong diverts power from the Thai electrical grid; villages along Route 9 east of Savannakhét have been receiving electricity since the late 1980s. Louangphrabang has seasonal access to power from a hydroelectric dam supplemented by diesel generators. A power transmission line from Nam Ngum to Louangphrabang is scheduled for completion in the mid-1990s and will bring electrification to many villages near Route 13 that previously relied on kerosene lamps and battery-operated florescent lights.

Hydroelectric capacity will further increase as a result of agreements signed either for construction of new facilities or for conducting feasibility studies for additional sites. Thailand is the primary investor in the hydroelectric sector; Australia, Denmark, Finland, Japan, Norway, and Sweden also have companies with interests in various projects.

As of 1992, other provincial centers relied primarily on diesel generators, which are run for three to four hours nightly and serve only a fraction of the surrounding population. Most district centers do not have electricity other than small private generators that light the houses of a few dozen subscribers for several hours each evening. Automobile batteries and voltage inverters are used as a means of supplementing the limited hours of power. These devices enable Laotians to watch television and listen to stereo cassette players, even in remote locations.

Despite assistance from the International Development Association, the Asian Development Bank, the United Nations Development Programme (UNDP—see Glossary), and other donors to increase rural electrification services, national consumption of electricity increased slowly. The average annual increase between 1970 and 1980 was 14.5 percent—an overall increase of 287 percent—to 325 million kilowatt-hours. After 1980 the growth of consumption slowed greatly, to an average annual rate of just 1.5 percent, reaching 365 million kilowatt-hours in 1988. Per capita consumption was just 93.6 kilowatt-hours, one of the lowest rates in the region.

According to the World Bank, energy consumption grew at an average annual rate of 4.2 percent between 1965 and 1980, slowing to 1.8 percent in the 1980–90 period. Fuelwood constitutes about 85 percent of total energy consumption. Per capita consumption of fuelwood is between one and three cubic meters annually, accounting for more than ten times the consumption of wood for commercial purposes. Total usage— including fuelwood and charcoal—was 3.9 million cubic meters in the 1985–87 period, a 21 percent increase over the 1975–77 period (see Forestry, this ch.). In 1985 hydroelectric power accounted for approximately 5 percent of annual energy consumption. Most consumption was in Vientiane; domestic use accounted for about 89 percent in 1983 and industrial use only about 10 percent. The transportation sector, especially civil aviation, which consumes imported petroleum products, accounted for the remaining 5 percent of energy consumption.

The cost of fuel imports—primarily from the Soviet Union until 1991—has placed a heavy burden on the economy, constituting nearly 19 percent of all imports in 1986. In 1989 approximately 124,000 tons of petroleum fuel were imported, an increase of nearly 40 percent over the preceding year (see Transportation, this ch.).

In 1987 an oil pipeline of 396 kilometers was laid from Vientiane to the border with Vietnam, close to the port of Vinh, facilitating the import of oil from the Soviet Union. The pipeline's capacity is 300,000 tons annually, considerably in excess of the annual national oil consumption rate of approximately 100,000 tons.

Mining

Assessments of mineral reserves are imprecise, because even by 1991 most of the country had not been geologically surveyed in a detailed manner. According to 1991 estimates, deposits of gemstones, gold, gypsum, iron, lead, potash, silver, tin, and zinc have relatively high commercial development potential, but mining activity is on an extremely small scale. In addition, Laos has small deposits of aluminum, antimony, chromium, coal, and manganese, as well as potential for oil and natural gas. In 1989 exploration agreements for oil and gas were signed with British, French, and United States companies.

Mining operations are carried out by state mining enterprises and supervised by the Department of Geology and Mines and small-scale miners. Production of tin—the principal mineral export—decreased 50 percent between 1975 and 1988, to about 240 tons. Gypsum production increased 167 percent between 1980 and 1988, to about 80,000 tons. Salt production increased 233 percent between 1981 and 1988, to eleven tons. Coal production increased more than 600 percent between 1982 and 1988, to about 800 tons. In addition to commercial enterprises, some individual households pan for alluvial gold

Loading a truck onto a boat on the Mekong River, Vientiane
Mekong River transport, Louangphrabang
Courtesy Gina Merris

on the Mekong as well as on small streams during the dry season to supplement household incomes.

Further development of the mineral sector is contingent upon the willingness of private companies to invest. However, the lack of adequate data, a trained labor force, dependable and adequate infrastructure, and legislation (a mining code was being drafted as of 1991) inhibit private companies from major investments. Nonetheless, private investment was growing as of 1993.

Construction

Throughout the 1980s, the construction subsector grew at an average annual rate of 1.1 percent, surging by 24 percent in 1989. Vigorous growth continued the following year at a rate of 15 percent, reflecting a big increase in private demand for new construction. Several sources estimate the construction subsector's contribution to the gross national product (GNP—see Glossary) at about 5 percent throughout the decade. According to one estimate, the construction subsector employed more than one-fourth of all industrial workers in 1986.

Services

Estimates of the services sector's contribution to GDP—including wholesale and retail trade, transport and communications, tourism, and public administration—vary. However, the trend throughout the 1980s was an increasing share, from about 15 percent of GDP in 1982 to about 25 percent in 1991. Employment in the services sector, as a percentage of the labor force, increased from 13 percent in 1960 to 17 percent in 1980, remaining fairly stable through 1989. The sector grew at an average annual rate of between 3 and 6 percent from 1980 to 1989, reaching a growth rate of about 13 percent in 1989 but slowing to about 6 percent the following year.

Wholesale and Retail Trade

According to government statistics, the number of retail shops increased dramatically—by 44 percent—in just one year, to 21,600 in 1991, reflecting the response to relaxed restrictions on private trade and entrepreneurship as well as a renewed social acceptability of petty trade. Of these establishments, 97 percent are privately owned. During the same period, the number of state-owned shops decreased by one-third, to 600 stores. Wholesale and retail trade grew at a rate of 20 percent in 1989 and 1990. Retail trade was worth about K563,000 million (for value of the kip—see Glossary) in 1991, an increase of 38 percent over the preceding year.

Tourism

In line with the government's desire to increase foreign exchange earnings, Western tourists were first permitted to enter Laos in 1988, although just 600 persons visited, well within the official limit of 1,000. The following year, 2,600 tourists visited, and in 1990, the figure increased by 130 percent, to approximately 6,000 tourists. The Ministry of Trade was assigned responsibility for the development of the tourism industry in 1989. In the following year, the government monopoly on the industry was removed, and nine private tourist agencies were authorized. As of 1992, tourism was somewhat limited to group travel. However, if an individual has a Laotian sponsor who provides individual sponsorship assurances, it is possible to receive a visa without being a member of an organized tour group.

Industrial Policy

The organization of the industrial sector prior to 1986 was centered on the state. Between 1979 and 1984, most state-owned enterprises incurred huge losses, and industrial sector output decreased by 10 percent. At the same time, gross industrial production began to shift slightly to the private sector: private industrial output as a percentage of gross industrial output doubled to 8 percent between 1980 and 1983, whereas state output decreased slightly from 93 percent to 89 percent. In the early 1980s, a slow increase in the number of private enterprises began, reflecting both the government's newly relaxed policy on the private sector and the private sector's greater efficiency and profitability compared to that of the state sector.

Following the introduction of the New Economic Mechanism, the private sector's involvement in industry increased even more, as industrial management was decentralized and most prices—except prices of basic utilities, air transport, postal service, and telecommunications—were freed from price controls. In 1988 Decree 19 granted state-owned enterprises expanded financial and managerial responsibilities.

As a result of these changes, some state-owned enterprises were forced to curtail production sharply or to close down entirely, precipitating a short-run drop in manufacturing output. It was not until March 1990, however, that the government provided a legal basis for the actual privatization of state-owned enterprises, through the promulgation of Decree 17. Under this decree, most state-owned enterprises were transformed into enterprises under other forms of ownership, through leasing, sale, joint ownership, or contracting with workers' collectives. Exceptions included enterprises deemed necessary to the nation's security or economic and social health, such as utilities and educational facilities. The extension of credit to unprofitable state-owned enterprises was discontinued, and state-owned enterprises were required to set prices and salaries at free market levels. By the end of the year, the private sector's contribution to net material product (see Glossary) had increased dramatically, to 65 percent.

The government reported at the Fifth Party Congress in 1991 that its "disengagement" policy was succeeding; two-thirds of the approximately 600 state-owned enterprises had been either partially privatized or leased to domestic or foreign parties. The remaining state-owned enterprises were granted greater autonomy in making investment decisions and setting input and output targets, in hopes of improving their productivity.

Transportation and Telecommunications

Because of its mountainous topography and lack of development, Laos has few reliable transportation routes, and as of mid-1994, there were no railroads. This inaccessibility has historically limited the ability of the government to maintain a presence in areas distant from the national or provincial capitals and to some extent limits communication among villages and ethnic groups (see Population; Rural Life, ch. 2). The Mekong and Nam Ou are the only natural channels suitable for large draft boat transportation, and from December through April low water limits the size of the craft that may be used on many routes. Between 1985 and 1990, freight and passenger traffic increased at rates of 14 percent and 8 percent, respectively. This occurred largely as a result of the government's abolishment, in 1986, of restrictions on the interprovincial movement of goods, which had artificially isolated markets throughout the country. In 1991 approximately 91 percent of freight traffic—measured in ton-kilometers—was carried by road and 9 percent by river, whereas 95 percent of passenger traffic—measured in passenger-kilometers—was carried by road, 3 percent by river, and the remaining 2 percent by domestic air service.

As of 1991, freight transport services were provided by four state transport enterprises, a number of provincial transport enterprises, and the private sector. The state has a monopoly on freight transport between Laos and ports in Vietnam. Although no longer regulated by provincial government, the private sector's participation in road transport remains severely restricted by government regulations; in 1990 the private sector accounted for just 13 percent of freight transport and 43 percent of passenger transport. According to the Asian Development Bank, it is considered unlikely that the transportation subsector will eventually be a focus of the government's privatization efforts because poor road conditions, lack of spare parts, an aging vehicle fleet, and low transport tariffs—in some cases below operating costs—make such a move doubtful, at least for the short term. The Ministry of Communications, Transport, Posts, and Construction oversees transport and telecommunications.

Roads

Laos had a minimal road network in the early 1990s. By 1991 the country's total road length was about 13,970 kilometers, an increase of just 22 percent over 1976. Of the total length, 24 percent, or 3,353 kilometers, is paved and 30 percent gravel; the remaining roads are trails unusable during the rainy season.

Route 13, a main north-south road, was built under French colonial rule. The highway parallels the Mekong and extends from the Cambodian border to Louangphrabang; the quality of the road varies over its length. Together with a few trans-mountain roads, Route 13 connects Laos with Vietnam and provides a rudimentary national road system. In addition, there are three east-west roads, Routes 7, 8, and 9, which are linked to Routes 7, 8, and 9 in Vietnam to facilitate access to Vietnamese seaports (see fig. 7).

In the late 1960s, China constructed a network of paved roads in northern Laos, linking most of the northern provin-

Laos: A Country Study

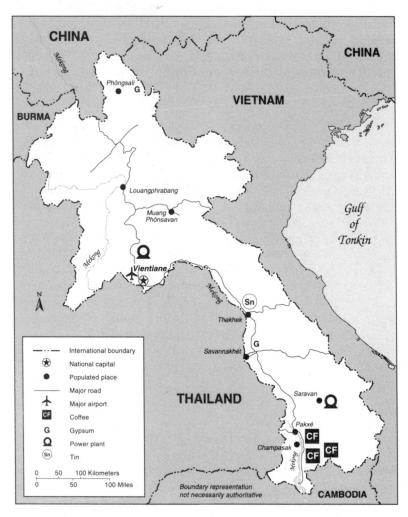

Figure 7. Transportation and Selected Industrial and Agricultural Activity, 1994

Source: Based on information from Germany, Statistisches Bundesamt, *Länderbericht Laos, 1990,* Wiesbaden, October 1990, 11.

cial capitals and for the first time facilitating motorized transportation across this region. These roads enabled government officials to reach some hitherto remote areas of the country, which helped begin the process of national integration that continues in the 1990s. These roads were maintained in reasonably good repair into the 1990s, providing an important new means of increased intervillage communication and move-

ment of market goods, as well as a locale for additional settlements. However, as of 1993, the link between this network and
Louangphrabang was a 100–kilometer stretch of dirt track pass-
able only during the dry season.

During the 1990s, all major routes in the center and south
are being improved and/or surfaced, and a larger network of
feeder roads is gradually being constructed by provincial governments. Development of these roads will facilitate a greater
government presence at the village level and easier travel by villagers to district and provincial centers. Such improved transportation will also assist villagers seeking medical care and
those sending children to school at district centers. Improved
transportation may also be an additional stimulus to villagers
looking for wage labor outside the village; tribal groups in
northern Laos have engaged in seasonal labor in northern
Thailand since at least the 1930s.

As roads improve and marketing networks expand, the government has encouraged commercial production for trade and
export. As a result, the independence and relative isolation of
lowland villages have been reduced. Travel, whether for visiting
or marketing—particularly the extensive market network developed as a result of the long-standing opium trade—or because
of military conscription, broadens the outlook of villagers and
makes then aware of the relationships between Laos and its
neighbors, of national policy issues, and of the possibility of a
different material standard of living. Lao in lowland villages
travel by oxcart over level terrain, or on foot. The steep mountains and lack of roads have caused upland ethnic groups to
rely entirely on pack baskets and pack horses for transportation. Wheeled vehicles traditionally have not been used. Travel
in most areas is still difficult and expensive, and most villagers
travel only limited distances if at all.

Despite the fact that the road network is the backbone of the
transportation network, it had received very little maintenance
work prior to 1985. The protracted war and period of government reorganization, limited financial resources, and lack of
maintenance equipment have contributed to the road network's deterioration. The deterioration has had serious consequences throughout the economy, including hindering
domestic and foreign trade, discouraging foreign investors,
and slowing domestic revenue collection.

In early 1990, an agreement was signed with Thailand and Australia for the construction of the 750–meter Friendship Bridge—which opened in April 1994—across the Mekong River, linking Thailand and Laos by road for the first time. As a result, tourism is expected to increase dramatically and freight transport costs to decrease, facilitating regional trade.

Motor Vehicles

In 1987 there were about 30,000 motor vehicles, divided equally between commercial and private vehicles; this number represents an increase of about 67 percent from 1979. Between 1977 and 1990, the number grew by an estimated 12.3 percent annually. Although government statistics estimated close to 1 million vehicles in 1990, this estimate included scrapped vehicles.

Inland Waterways

Inland waterways, including the Mekong River, constitute the second most important transport network in the country. There are about 4,600 kilometers of navigable waterways, including sections of the Mekong, the Ou, and nine other rivers. The Mekong accounts for about 1,330 kilometers of the total navigable length. Although the Mekong flows through Laos for approximately 2,030 kilometers, it is only navigable for about 70 percent of this length, mainly because of rapids and low water levels in the dry season. Between Vientiane and Savannakhét, the river can accommodate boats with between seventy and 140 deadweight tons; otherwise it can carry between fifteen and fifty deadweight tons, depending on the season. Residents of lowland villages located on the banks of smaller rivers have traditionally traveled in pirogues for fishing, trading, or visiting up and down the river for limited distances.

Both public and private trade associations handle river traffic, including the State River Transport Company, based in Vientiane. In mid-1987 the State Water Transport Company had thirty-seven boats, most built with help from Vietnam. There are state warehouses at Savannakhét, Xénô, and Vientiane, in addition to a number of ports. River transportation has improved as government policy has emphasized expanded trade with Vietnam and with rural regions.

Civil Aviation

Lao Aviation, the national airline, services domestic and foreign points from Wattai Airport, the primary airport, located outside Vientiane. Domestic air service was already somewhat well developed prior to the beginning of the Indochina War years and offered limited international service from the 1950s. Lao Aviation has domestic flights to provincial capitals, including Louangphrabang, Louang Namtha, Pakxé, Saravan, and Xiangkhoang. Improvements in civil air service are encouraged by the government as a way to boost tourism and commercial appeal. New airports and renovations—primarily expansion projects, so as to have the capability to handle larger aircraft—are planned for Khamkeut, Louang Namtha, Louangphrabang, Oudômxai, and Phôngsali. As of mid-1993, however, work had not begun. International service is provided to Hanoi, Bangkok, Saigon, Phnom Penh, and Kunming and Guangzhou in China. Flights to Burma, Chiang Mai (Thailand), Hong Kong, Singapore, and Taipei are in the planning stages. Lao Aviation has formed a joint venture with firms from Australia, Thailand, and the United States to increase and upgrade its international flights.

Telecommunications

In mid-1994, the Lao telecommunications system was rudimentary, with a telephone system that serves primarily government offices and broadcast facilities in only a few large towns. In 1986 there were approximately 8,000 telephones for the entire country, or fewer than 2 telephones per 1,000 people. There reportedly was a substantial expansion of telephone lines in Vientiane beginning in 1989, but no updated figures are available.

One powerful amplitude modulation (AM) station is located in Vientiane; the other nine AM stations are low-powered transmitters scattered in other cities. Seven shortwave stations broadcasting in six tribal languages reach remote areas, including one that broadcasts in Cambodian, French, Thai, and Vietnamese to neighboring countries in Southeast Asia. The capital also has two lower-power television transmitters and one frequency modulation (FM) station. The number of radios increased from 350,000 in 1980 to 520,000 in 1990.

The first domestic television service was established in 1983, and the second, in 1988, broadcasting from Savannakhét.

Southern Laos receives transmissions from Thailand, and all of Laos receives satellite-relayed transmissions from a ground satellite station linked to Intersputnik. There were about 31,000 television sets in 1990.

International communications improved greatly with the installation in 1990 of a new satellite ground station. In 1991 agreements were concluded with China and France to relay their broadcasts to Laos by satellite.

Public Finance

, The Budget Deficit

Laos ran a fiscal deficit throughout the 1980s. The deficit expanded greatly in the second half of the decade, from about 12 percent of GDP in 1985 to between 25 percent and 30 percent of GDP in 1988 and 1989. This deficit was fueled by both a sharp decrease in non-tax revenue (mainly from surpluses of state-owned enterprises) and a large jump in expenditures, particularly for wages and salaries (see table 8, Appendix). By 1990, however, the deficit had decreased (relatively) to about 17 percent of GDP and was continuing to decrease as previously implemented reforms, especially of taxes and the banking system, took effect.

Government Revenue

From the outset of the founding of the LPDR in 1975, development expenditures depended primarily on foreign aid, continuing a pattern begun in the 1950s. In July 1990, more than half of the state's total revenue came from foreign aid and loans. Until 1988 the bulk of current government revenue—excluding capital receipts—came from non-tax sources, mainly from surpluses of state-owned enterprises. Revenue increased nearly four times between 1984 and 1986, and again by more than one-half between 1986 and 1988, almost entirely from non-tax sources. Tax collection is difficult because of the widely dispersed population and poor organization and management of the collection process.

An annual rice tax was assessed on all paddy land. The tax collected was in principle divided between provincial and national budgets, but in practice much was retained in the district of collection for in-kind salary support of local officials and military personnel. Where villages had schools, a portion of the tax collected was delivered to the local teachers(s). The paddy tax rate varied between sixty and 120 kilograms per hectare, depending on the quality of the land and was reduced to forty to 100 kilograms per hectare in the early 1990s. The paddy tax rate amounted to roughly 5 percent of the seasonal yield but could be forgiven in the event of a crop failure. A separate, lower tax was assessed on swidden rice fields. Collection from more remote villages without road access was always problematic. Since March 1993, the land tax has been assessed in cash. The rates vary between 500 to 6,000 kip per hectare, depending on land quality and productivity. Between 1983 and 1986, an improved system of business taxation was implemented; despite this, by 1987 the share of non-tax sources had exceeded 90 percent of current revenue, from about 70 percent in the early 1980s.

Substantial qualitative changes in fiscal management beginning in 1988 were introduced at most levels of government, and the implementation of limited tax reforms changed the fiscal situation dramatically, with 75 percent of state revenue coming from taxes. Non-tax revenues declined by 62 percent, however, as the traditional revenue source—profits from the state-owned enterprises—continued to decrease; thus, current revenue increased only by 42 percent. To increase revenue, Decree 47—on the national tax and customs system—was promulgated in June 1989; the decree broadened the tax base by expanding coverage of personal income and corporate taxes and improving collection and revenue administration methods. Import, profit, and turnover taxes were also increased. Fiscal revenue responded positively to the new tax reforms, increasing substantially from 1989, to about 11 percent of GDP in 1990; revenue from taxes alone increased by 62 percent. Transfers from public enterprises rose by 63 percent in 1990 over 1989 figures, and other non-tax revenue increased as well, including lease payments to the government and overflight charges. The composition of revenue remained about 75 percent tax-based through the early1990s.

Government revenue actually dropped from 11 percent of GNP in 1986 to 9.6 percent in 1990. However, its annual growth rate increased dramatically, from 9 percent in 1987 to 63 percent in 1990—partially a rebound from the drop in revenue in 1989. GNP also is subject to dramatic fluctuations, falling from almost US$2.4 billion in 1985 to about US$600 million in 1988. By 1991 GNP had increased to approximately

US$1 billion, from approximately US$863 million the previous year.

Government Expenditure

Capital expenditures rose slowly throughout the 1980s, from about 55 percent of total expenditures in 1983 to about 66 percent in 1988; however, by 1989 they had begun to decrease as a result of limited absorptive capacity, a critical factor in the economic picture because it seriously affects economic development. Wages and salaries accounted for the largest portion of expenditures, increasing from 11 percent of expenditures in 1983 to 42 percent in 1988. A substantial amount of this portion in the late 1980s was spent on salary increases and arrears payments: many civil servants had not been paid for up to two years. Subsidies to state-owned enterprises make up most of the remainder of expenditures, but by the end of the decade these subsidies were cut back in response to the reforms of 1988 and 1990. Expenditures for operation and maintenance of basic infrastructure remained inadequate throughout the 1980s. Defense expenditure is an important part of the government budget; however, no figures are available (see The Defense Budget, ch. 5).

Government expenditure as a percentage of GDP increased from 10.7 percent in 1986 to 14.2 percent in 1990; capital expenditure increased from 7.7 percent to 12.1 percent in the same period. However, although the growth rate of total government expenditure increased from 8.3 percent in 1987 to 65 percent in 1990 as wage and salary payments increased, growth in capital expenditure slowed dramatically, from 14.9 percent to slightly negative growth in the same period, because of limited absorptive capacity and decreased aid from nonconvertible currency area countries.

Policy

A new "vertical management system" for budgetary allocation was implemented in 1991, directed by the Ministry of Finance. Under this system, all revenue collected by provincial and local authorities is integrated into the national budget, and all expenditures are linked to a national budget expenditure plan. The primary purpose of the system is to ensure that local-level expenditures are consistent with national planned expenditures.

The Financial Sector

The Banking System

In March 1988, Decree 11 on the reform of the banking system was passed, separating commercial bank functions from central bank functions. The Vientiane branch of the old State Bank, the Banque d'État de la République Démocratique Populaire du Laos (RDPL), became the central monetary agency. In June 1990, the Central Banking Law was passed, establishing the Bank of the Lao People's Democratic Republic, or Central Bank, to replace the State Bank. Under this law, the Central Bank assumes responsibility for regulation and supervision of commercial and regional banks; maintenance of foreign exchange reserves; issuance and supervision of money for circulation; licensing, supervision, and regulation of financial services; and management of the monetary and credit system. The Central Bank has about ninety regional branches; as of 1991, the government was considering separating these branches into three regional banks, serving the southern, northern, and central regions.

Other branches of the former State Bank were transformed into autonomous commercial banks to promote private investment. These banks are responsible for accepting savings deposits from enterprises, government departments, and individuals, and for granting credit to state entities, joint ventures, and individuals for capital investment and business start-ups or expansion. Commercial banks are prohibited from granting credit to economic units experiencing deficits and losses. These banks do not receive subsidies, although they do render 60 percent of their profits to the government.

By 1991 Laos had seven commercial banks, including the Joint Development Bank—a Lao-Thai joint venture—and six wholly state-owned banks. Government policy encourages privatization of these six banks. However, in part because of the absence of laws governing banking activities and in part because of the relatively small size of the economy, foreign bankers have not expressed much interest in these ventures.

The Foreign Trade Bank (Banque pour le Commerce Extérieur Lao—BCEL), a subsidiary of the Central Bank, is the country's foreign exchange and foreign trade bank. By Decree 48 of July 1989, the Central Bank is assigned sole responsibility for setting and managing the exchange rate. BCEL was granted autonomy in November 1989 and was charged with handling foreign exchange transactions relating to trade; as of 1991, BCEL had arrangements with sixty-four banks internationally. However, a Foreign Exchange Decree was scheduled to go into effect soon after 1991, allowing all commercial banks already authorized to deal in foreign exchange to carry out foreign exchange transactions themselves, thus removing BCEL's monopoly on such activities. Information on the status of this decree was unavailable as of mid-1994.

Responsibility for state-owned enterprise debts was transferred to the commercial banks, giving them enormous liquidity problems. To alleviate the precarious situation, in 1989 the government allowed foreign banks to begin operations in Laos. That October the Joint Development Bank became the first private commercial bank permitted to operate since 1975, followed soon thereafter by the Thai Military Bank. In addition, new reform measures stipulate that enterprises will have to clear all debts owed to the banks before being considered for new loans. In 1990 the Asian Development Bank granted Laos a soft loan of US$25 million to recapitalize the banking system.

Interest rates on commercial bank deposits with the Central Bank are uniform across the country and are generally higher than rates for enterprises depositing at the commercial banks. Since August 1989, only minimum interest rates have been set by authorities; banks are allowed to set specific rates on their own. Interest rates on deposits vary from bank to bank, depending on the type and currency of deposits. The annual rate on kip deposits at the end of 1991 was between zero and 1.2 percent for most banks; fixed deposits in kip earned between 16 and 24 percent annually, and deposits in United States dollars at some banks, including BCEL, earned 7 percent annually. Rates for loans depend on the term and currency of the loan and on the sector for which the investment is intended. Loans for the agriculture and forestry sectors carry rates ranging from 7 to 12 percent, for example, and loans for the services sector carry rates between 12 and 30 percent.

Money and Prices

By Decree 14 of March 1988, prices of most goods are no longer set by the government; exceptions include basic utility and mineral prices. Instead, a new system of "unified prices"—free market prices—was instituted. As a result, prices of

A street scene in Vientiane
A motorized cart—typical means of transportation in
Louangphrabang
Courtesy Gina Merris

rationed and subsidized goods such as rice, sugar, cloth, and petroleum increased, and procurement prices were raised by 50 percent to 100 percent.

In addition, in 1988 the wages of state employees, previously paid through coupons redeemable for subsidized goods at state stores, began to be gradually remonetized. Very high inflation. rates soon caused a real drop in annual wages, however, and low rates of tax collection gave the government less revenue to spend on wages. As a result, large arrears built up on salaries that are quite small. In 1990 salaries were increased by 83 percent, and arrears began to be paid off, contributing to the increase of 65 percent in government expenditure. Once paid, however, salaries almost immediately go again into arrears. Moreover, the salary increase is not sufficient for state employees to recoup real losses from inflation.

Money Supply and Inflation

Money supply—measured by both M1 (demand deposits and currency outside banks) and M2 (M1 plus quasi-money such as checking accounts)—expanded between 1980 and 1989 (statistics are available only from 1980 on), in part because of the remonetization of government salaries, rising wage and price levels in industry, and extension of credit to indebted state-owned enterprises. World Bank figures indicated that money supply as measured by M2 increased at an annual rate of between 35 and 75 percent—except for 1984, when money supply was steady—until 1987, when, fueled by increases in domestic credit to public enterprises and foreign currency deposits from public enterprises, it jumped by over 300 percent. During the next two years, the money supply continued to grow rapidly, reaching a growth rate close to 90 percent in 1989.

The average annual inflation rate was about 11.5 percent from 1985 to 1989. In 1989, however, inflation increased dramatically, to 52 percent, fueled by the massive increase in the money supply and a devaluation of the kip and exacerbated by a reduction in foreign exchange caused by the ban on forestry exports and the temporary reduction in exports of hydroelectricity to Thailand. Monetary policy was tightened in 1990; credit allocated to unprofitable state-owned enterprises was restricted through Decree 17 and through higher interest rates. As a result, growth in M2 was held to just 2.3 percent in

1990. Lower food prices as a result of good harvests in 1989 and 1990 following the years of drought also helped to slow inflation to about 20 percent; inflation continued to decline slowly through 1994—to about 9 percent.

The Balance of Payments

The Foreign Exchange Rate

In June 1976, the "liberation kip" replaced the old kip at a rate of twenty to one. Three years later, following a massive collapse of the value of the currency, a "new kip," or National Bank kip, was introduced, worth 100 liberation kip, and the official exchange rate was fixed at thirty-five new kip to one United States dollar. A system of multiple exchange rates has been implemented in an effort to control inflation; different rates are applied to the transactions of businessmen, tourists, senders of remittances, and aid agencies. In September 1987, however, with a devaluation of the commercial rate of roughly 900 percent relative to the United States dollar, the multiple rates were abandoned in favor of a single floating exchange rate applicable to all transactions.

The exchange rate is adjusted periodically relative to the dollar. In 1988 it stabilized at about K340 to the dollar, in part because the government stopped accepting United States dollars and Thai baht in payment for commercial or customs taxes, thus reducing holdings of kip. By late 1989, the kip had been devalued by 100 percent—relative to the 1987 rate—where it remained stable at about K700 to the dollar through 1992. The exchange rate was K721 to the dollar in June 1994—in part because of the government's decision to allow the free exchange of hard currencies.

In September 1990, Decree 53 ordered that all transactions within the country be conducted exclusively in kip; in practice, however, foreign currencies remain in daily use because consumers do not have enough confidence in their own currency. The kip, Thai baht, and United States dollar are used interchangeably. Under Decree 16, state-owned enterprises and private enterprises are allowed to maintain accounts in both kip and foreign exchange.

Foreign Trade

Foreign trade figures for Laos do not reflect the large volume of illegal trade in opium and other products, mostly with Thailand; some estimates put smuggling at half of all trade, legal and illegal. Although Laos continued to run a trade deficit throughout the 1980s and early 1990s, the volume of trade increased substantially during the latter half of that period. The increase was the result of increased production of exportable goods, the shift in trade patterns from the Soviet bloc to the convertible currency bloc, especially Thailand, and the removal of many regulations on trade, as the government continues to implement the orders of the New Economic Mechanism. Despite these improvements, however, by 1990 exports still financed only about 40 percent of imports (see table 9, Appendix).

Exports

According to World Bank and International Monetary Fund (IMF—see Glossary) estimates, merchandise exports grew from about US$40.0 million in 1982—the first year statistics were available—to about US$64.3 million in 1987, when droughts and lower prices for Thailand—the only buyer—cut revenue from exports of hydroelectricity by 40 percent (see table 10, Appendix). As a result, the value of exports dropped to US$57.8 million by 1988 but recovered the following year and continued to expand, reaching US$77.9 million in 1991— an overall increase in exports of 95 percent from 1982 to 1991. Between 1982 and 1988—when they decreased by 10 percent— exports grew at an average annual rate of 6.8 percent; however, after trade reforms were enacted, the growth rate increased— to 10.7 percent between 1988 and 1991. Exports increased again in 1992 and 1993 to an estimated US$133 million (free on board) and US$203 million, respectively.

Principal exports are hydroelectricity and timber and wood products. In addition, much smaller quantities of coffee, gypsum, and tin concentrates are exported. The composition of major export commodities did not change throughout the 1980s; however, the relative importance of the commodities did. In 1987 lower export earnings from hydroelectricity precipitated a shift toward exports of forestry products. The value of hydroelectricity exports decreased from US$30 million in 1986 to US$12 million in 1987, while the value of timber and wood exports increased from US$8 million to US$33 million. Timber and wood products thus replaced hydroelectricity as the major export, and despite restrictions on logging and high export taxes implemented in 1989—which decreased its share of total exports by 36 percent—timber and wood products remained the major export through 1992.

Imports

Although the level of imports remained relatively stable beginning in the mid-1980s, droughts and the subsequent need to import rice influenced import totals. Principal imports include manufactured goods, including transport equipment; food items, including rice; and fuel. According to 1986 UN statistics, manufactured goods accounted for 53.5 percent of imports—of which 14.1 percent was transport equipment; food items for 20.8 percent—of which 16.2 percent was cereals, including rice; and 18.9 percent for petroleum. Limited information shows that the composition of imports did not change significantly through 1989. A substantial portion of imports is linked to aid programs, although a government source indicated that these imports accounted for a slowly decreasing share of total imports, from about 40 percent in 1982 to about 28 percent in 1987.

Trade Partners

Although the overall composition of trade did not change significantly throughout the 1980s and early 1990s, the direction of trade did change. Until 1989 major trading partners were from nonconvertible currency areas—mainly China, the Soviet Union, and Vietnam; Laos also traded with Bulgaria, Czechoslovakia, Mongolia, and Poland. From 1984—the first year with accurate data—to 1988, the nonconvertible currency area accounted for over half of all imports. Although the nonconvertible currency area never had a monopoly on exports (mostly because the largest export until 1987, hydroelectricity, was sold only to Thailand) it accounted for over half of the total trade volume through the end of the decade. However, following the easing of some trade restrictions in 1988 and the improvement of relations with Thailand, including a reduction in the Thai list of 273 strategic goods in which trade has been prohibited, the pattern of trade began to shift in favor of the convertible currency area. Bilateral trade with Thailand increased 26 percent over 1987, and imports from the nonconvertible currency area dropped to about 35 percent of total imports.

Eager to avoid Thai domination of its foreign trade, Laos sought to improve relations with China, and in December 1989 the two countries signed their first bilateral agreement in a decade, including notes on cross-border trade. As a result, trade with China grew by roughly 40 percent in 1990. Despite the positive effect of this move on the growth of regional trade, new agreements with members of the former Soviet bloc work against the trend. In 1990, at a Soviet-Lao Cooperation Commission meeting, it was determined that henceforth Soviet exports and loans would be paid for in convertible currencies at world prices. Previously, payments had been made in nonconvertible currencies and often on barter terms. Trade with Vietnam also shifted to a hard currency basis. In addition, the eventual disintegration of the Soviet Union clinched the shift in trade patterns toward the convertible currency area: in 1991 trade with the nonconvertible area accounted for just 2 to 3 percent of total imports and total exports. The convertible currency area was more than able to make up for this loss: trade volume actually increased that year, although by only 4.3 percent.

Major trading partners from the convertible currency area include Britain, France, Japan, Malaysia, Singapore, and Thailand. Of these, Malaysia, Singapore, and Thailand accounted for roughly 45 percent of imports from 1970 to 1978; their share increased to about 51 percent by 1987. Similarly, Japan's share of imports from the convertible currency area increased from 7 percent in 1978 to 19 percent in 1987. The United States accounted for less than 1 percent of imports from the convertible currency area in 1987, although the LPDR's first trade mission to the United States in 1991 signaled its eagerness to expand trade. Malaysia, Singapore, and Thailand accounted for 65 percent of Laos's exports to the convertible currency area in 1987, up from 43 percent in 1978. This increase in regional trade made up for the decrease in the shares in exports from the United States and Japan: from 33 percent to 6 percent for Japan, and from 9 percent to 4 percent for the United States. Thailand's removal of the ban on trade in strategic goods in late 1989 gave regional trade another boost.

Trade Balance

The trade deficit increased from US$92.2 million in 1982 to US$114.9 million in 1991, reaching a decade high of US$151.9

*Construction of a Thai
bank, Vientiane
Courtesy Gina Merris*

*Gasoline station,
Louangphrabang
Courtesy Gina Merris*

million in 1987, the first year of the drought (see table 11, Appendix). Before 1987 the deficit had increased by an average annual rate of 10.9 percent. However, after the introduction of the New Economic Mechanism and subsequent loosening of many restrictions on trade, it actually began to decrease at an annual average of 7 percent, although in 1991 it increased slightly, by 3.2 percent. The deficit was largely financed through external assistance, including direct grants and highly concessional loans, and constituted approximately 16 percent of GDP in 1989–90. As the deficit decreased in response to increasing export volumes, the country's trade position also improved in terms of import financing. Between 1982 and 1987, exports financed less than one-third of imports, but beginning in 1990, import financing improved considerably, with exports financing over 40 percent of imports. This fact put Laos in a more secure position in view of sharply decreased foreign aid from the nonconvertible currency area.

Trade Policy

Trade policy prior to the introduction of the New Economic Mechanism had been highly restrictive, revolving around the centralized allocation of goods for export. In 1988, however, in line with the New Economic Mechanism, the government began to progressively decentralize some of its trade-oriented responsibilities, including planning and arranging trade contracts with foreign suppliers. Trade, controlled by the ministries of trade and finance, is conducted by about twenty-four state trading companies and some provincial trading companies. Several measures promulgated in March 1988 modified trade policy. According to Decree 16, the government became the sole exporter through state import-export organizations. Under Decree 13, the State Committee for Foreign Economic Relations and Trade, provincial administrative committees, and municipalities are empowered to supervise the management and control of import and export activities. The decree also authorizes trade agents at LPDR embassies worldwide to make direct trade contacts.

Decree 18 identifies a number of "strategic" goods, including coffee, tobacco, wood products (such as timber, sawn wood, pressed wood, and rattan), other forestry products (such as benzoin and sticklac), and minerals, for which the state has an export monopoly: in short, all the major export commodities. Only the central government's import-export organization, the Lao Import-Export Company (Société Lao Import-Export), and certain provincial and state enterprises are permitted to export these goods to fulfill national trade agreements with the nonconvertible currency area. All importing units are required to submit plans for their trading operations to the State Committee for Foreign Economic Relations and Trade in order to formulate the national import-export plan. However, importers are permitted to trade in all commodities not on the strategic or restricted lists. Under Decree 18, export businesses are permitted to export goods on the strategic list directly, after national requirements have been met. The decree thus considerably liberalizes trade regulations. The main reason for the restriction on trade in strategic goods is that the government has to plan its supply of export goods to coincide with its multiyear trade arrangements with the nonconvertible currency area countries. After 1990, however, this issue was moot because the trade volume with these countries dropped to a negligible amount.

The import of certain items, including automobiles and military vehicles, fertilizers, drugs, and "decadent cultural products and pictures," is subject to quotas and other restrictions. In addition, trade in certain goods is entirely prohibited, including poisons, weapons, and other goods related to national security.

At the end of the 1980s, the authority of the Lao Import-Export Company had begun to diminish because import-export licenses were being granted to increasing numbers of private organizations. By 1991 the national trade company was slated for privatization.

Transit

Because Laos is a landlocked country, its foreign trade volume is highly dependent on transit routes through neighboring countries. Bangkok serves as the major port, but the Vietnamese ports of Da Nang—the most distant from Vientiane at 1,000 kilometers—and Cua Lo—the closest to Vientiane at 460 kilometers—are also used. The Express Transit Organization of Thailand has a monopoly on the LPDR's transit business through Thailand, initially imposed as a way to regulate trade in strategic goods. Transshipment of goods through Vietnam and especially Thailand increases the prices of Laos's goods greatly—by as much as 60 percent, or, according to some sources, as much as 300 percent—severely reducing the competitiveness of export commodities on the world market. In December 1991, and again in the fall of 1993, Cambodia offered Laos the use of its seaport at Kompong Som, but Cambodia's poor infrastructure and lawlessness make this an empty gesture.

As of 1991, limitations on trade resulting from transshipment began to ease. Plans were made to establish a Thai-Lao joint venture responsible for handling transit goods to Laos, with the potential of cutting transit costs in half. To further reduce the Thai company's monopoly on transshipment of goods to Laos, Thai import duties on more than twenty agricultural goods, including one of Laos's major exports, coffee, were reduced from a 40 to 80 percent range to a maximum of 20 percent. By 1991 Thailand had expanded from three to eight the number of approved border transit points with Laos. Completion of the first bridge over the Mekong, which opened in April 1994, is likely to further encourage regional trade.

Direct Foreign Investment

Policy

The Foreign Investment Law of July 1988 is modeled on legislation that has already been adopted in Vietnam and China. Laos seeks to encourage foreign investment as a means of facilitating economic development as called for by the New Economic Mechanism. The government hopes that foreign investment projects will help to shift the economy from a subsistence to a commodity production basis by improving the management skills of the labor force; introducing advanced technology to the manufacturing sector; fostering economic, scientific, and technological cooperation with other countries; and increasing the production of goods for export.

The Foreign Investment Law allows investors to enter into three types of investment arrangements. The first type of arrangement, contractual or cooperative businesses, entails investment in existing state or private companies, or with Laotian individuals; in this way, the law is more liberal than comparable legislation in either Vietnam or China. The second type of arrangement, joint ventures, requires foreigners to invest a minimum of 30 percent of total capital. In general, terms for either of these arrangements are not to exceed twenty years. The third type of arrangement, private ventures, requires foreigners to invest 30 percent of total capital, up to a maximum of 100 percent. Terms are generally limited to fifteen years. Tax exemptions or reductions for joint ventures and private enterprises are available for two to six years after the first year of profit, depending on the size of the investment, the volume of goods exported as a result of the project, the location of the project, and the sector on which it focuses.

Tax incentives—a reduction of 2 to 5 percent in the profit tax—are also used to encourage foreign investment. In order to qualify for the reduction, a foreign investment project has to meet three of the following criteria: the project will export more than 70 percent of the goods it produces; will obtain domestically more than 70 percent of the raw materials it uses; will use advanced technology; will aim to overcome unfavorable natural or socioeconomic conditions; will contribute to national economic development despite low profit margins; or will be established before 1995. The Foreign Investment Law allows foreign investors to remit profits to the countries of their choice; in addition, it prohibits the nationalization of their capital and property.

Other laws also seek to facilitate foreign investment. In early 1989, Decree 27 established the Foreign Investment Management Committee to centralize foreign investment approval procedures, thus enabling the Foreign Investment Law to be implemented. The Lao Chamber of Commerce was established in January 1990 to assist in attracting new business ventures. Private domestic and foreign investments have been encouraged by the gradual improvement of the legal environment, including the passage of laws regarding property rights (1990), contractual obligation (1990), inheritance (1990), crime (1990), civil procedures (1990), and labor (1991). The 1991 approval of the constitution, which protects the right to private ownership, is also an important factor in encouraging foreign investment. Also, as of late 1993, an arbitration law was being drafted that will provide a legal mechanism for the settlement of disputes. There was an informal arbitration procedure, but the lack of a law or decree made decisions nonbinding.

Investment Projects

Decree 20 of 1988 identifies sectors open to foreign investment under the Foreign Investment Law: these include agriculture and forestry; industry; communication, transportation, and construction; and services and tourism. Five criteria are used to judge the desirability of investment projects: whether the project uses advanced techniques, technology, and scientific management to produce goods that could compete in the world market and make efficient use of energy, raw materials, and equipment; provides export merchandise or services that generate foreign-exchange earnings and use domestic raw materials as much as possible; has low labor requirements but provides managerial and/or technical training; involves infrastructure development, especially of roads, bridges, and irrigation; and is deemed by the government to be important to economic development. Projects are discouraged if they do not conform to economic and social development, or disturb the sovereignty, order, or security of the country; seriously damage the environment; make long-run use of imported materials and do not promote import substitution; create large debts; or are prohibited by the government.

The law spurred a steady increase in foreign direct investment. Within one year of the law's promulgation, Laos received

124 investment proposals, of which sixty were approved that same year.

As of 1992, some 109 proposals had been accepted out of a total of about 200, worth about US$231 million, of which the government share is roughly 3 percent; most are worth less than US$5 million each. Almost 50 percent of the proposals were signed with Thai companies. Most proposed investment is in foreign trade, manufacturing, handicrafts, services, tourism, and the agriculture, forestry, and mining sectors. About ten proposals were subsequently canceled, usually because of a failure to receive expected financing.

Despite the positive response of foreign investors to liberalization measures, in the early 1990s, foreign investment is still handicapped. Hindrances include the poor infrastructure, the unskilled labor force, and the lack of an intellectual property rights law, although regulations on patents and industrial property have been drafted.

Foreign Aid

Between 1975 and 1990, total foreign aid to Laos, including grants and loans, was approximately US$2.3 billion. Of this sum, only 65 percent had been spent as of 1989, of which grants and loans made up approximately equal quantities. Fifty-five percent of spent aid derived from the nonconvertible currency area, 17.8 percent from convertible currency area countries, and 27.2 percent from international organizations and financial institutions (see table 12, Appendix).

According to the World Bank and the IMF, long-term loans increased nearly threefold, from about US$38.8 million in 1982 to about US$111.4 million in 1988. Drawings on loans received from the nonconvertible currency area had averaged 73 percent of the total annually through 1988; in 1989, however, drawings from the area dropped to 23 percent of the total, and by 1991 they were nonexistent. In January 1991, the Soviet Union suspended all its aid and credits to Laos although loan repayments were postponed until the end of the decade. Drawings from the convertible currency area during this period increased, but not enough to support spending at the level of the mid-1980s; by 1991 drawings on all loans received had dropped nearly 50 percent from 1988. In response, grants from the convertible currency area, which had decreased from

Women in the market at Talat, Louangphrabang, selling
water buffalo legs, ears, and innards
Courtesy Gina Merris

approximately US$45.4 million in 1985 to just US$14.7 million in 1989, spiraled to US$63.9 million in 1991.

Aid from the nonconvertible currency area was primarily from the Soviet Union and Vietnam. Until 1991 Soviet aid constituted over half of all aid to Laos, including the stationing of over 1,000 Soviet technical personnel in Laos, and donations of construction equipment, vehicles, and aircraft. The second largest donor was Vietnam, which sent roughly 5,000 advisers and technicians to the country and participated in the joint exploitation of mineral and forest resources.

The cutback in aid from the nonconvertible currency area caused Laos to seek improved ties with Western nations. Australia, Japan, and Sweden accounted for virtually all foreign aid from the convertible currency area until 1988; but by 1990, their combined share had dropped to about 78 percent because other developed nations began to increase their aid programs to Laos. Japan and France became more important aid donors in the early 1990s. The United States does not have an "aid program" in the traditional sense because Laos is a communist country and is prohibited from receiving aid under the Foreign Assistance Act of 1961 (as amended). The crop

197

substitution program, begun in October 1989 following reassessment of the country's involvement in the world opium trade, is possible because of separate legislative authority. In December 1990, following an improvement in Chinese-Laotian relations, China pledged a US$9.3 million credit for a five-year economic and technical cooperation program in Laos.

Other aid is provided by international organizations such as the UNDP, the Asian Development Bank, the International Development Association, and the IMF. Multilateral organizations provide large loans in support of government reforms; in 1990 and 1991, the IMF and the Asian Development Bank made loans worth US$37 million for this purpose.

Aid to Laos covers a wide range of activities, including technical and capital assistance for such projects as hydroelectric power stations (Sweden), a livestock vaccination program (the UNDP), and scholarships for agricultural study (Thailand). The IMF approved a US$50 million loan in 1993 in support of economic development, inflation reduction, and compensation for depleted reserves. Other loans have been granted for such infrastructure development as road construction, hydropower projects, and telecommunications systems. Aid has also been extended for irrigation projects and forestry and fisheries programs.

Other types of aid include loan forgiveness: in 1991 Japan and Germany forgave loan liabilities worth US$32.3 million. Despite the country's continued striving to reach food self-sufficiency, it relies on food aid for its domestic needs during years of poor harvest. In 1988 and 1989, for example, 140,000 tons of food aid were donated or sold to Laos to make up for shortfalls caused by drought. Food aid in cash or in kind was donated to Laos in 1991 by the Food and Agriculture Organization and the UNDP, and by the United States, Australia, Thailand, and the Netherlands.

Although foreign grants and loans remain sufficient to finance Laos's trade deficit and development expenditure, at least for the medium term, poor absorptive capacity, the result (in part) of a poorly educated and trained labor force, reduces its ability to make efficient use of the available funds. The balance of payments actually went into surplus in 1989 and 1990. However, there remains the question of whether flows from the convertible currency area will continue to increase enough to make up for the losses from the nonconvertible currency area.

Because the country's fiscal and trade position is not likely to improve dramatically in the early 1990s, this is an important concern.

External Debt

The total external debt grew by an average annual rate of 22.5 percent from 1985 to 1989, slowing to 8.5 percent annually through 1991. Debt to the nonconvertible currency area is large but difficult to quantify, in part because available statistics often use different ruble-to-dollar exchange rates. World Bank figures showed that between 68 and 77 percent of the external debt was held by countries from the nonconvertible currency area through 1991. However, debt service to nonconvertible currency area countries as a percentage of total debt service decreased from about 33 percent of the total in 1984 to less than 10 percent in 1990. Debt service as a ratio of total exports increased from 10.2 percent in 1984 to a high of 16 percent in 1988, when it began a slow decline to nearly 10 percent in 1990, as exports increased (see table 13, Appendix). Although statistics on debt as a percentage of GDP are highly variable, sources agree that external debt constituted considerably more than 60 percent of GDP throughout the 1980s, surpassing total GDP in 1987 or 1988.

Through mid-1987, Laos was able to meet its non-ruble debt repayment schedule mainly because many multilateral loans had been made on highly concessional terms—about 99 percent of all long-term debt throughout the 1980s. Japan, which accounted for approximately 33 to 45 percent of all debt to bilateral donors in the convertible currency area in the late 1980s, eased debt pressures by forgiving parts of its debt. In the nonconvertible currency area, the Soviet Union allowed trade deficits of up to 400 percent of the value of imports annually; deficits at year's end were then converted into long-term loans. In 1991 the Soviet Union agreed to reschedule some of its long-run debt payments and to continue accepting repayments in commodities, rather than switching over to a hard currency basis as had previously been agreed by the Soviet-Lao Cooperation Commission.

Prospects for Growth

By the start of the 1990s, Laos had obtained some impressive results from the implementation of economic reforms under the New Economic Mechanism. Although the experiment in cooperative farming had ended as an ideological failure, rice harvests had reached self-sufficiency levels in favorable weather conditions. New decrees also guarantee farmers the right to long-term use and transfer of property. In response to the encouragement of the manufacturing and services sectors through privatization, investment promotion, and other means, these sectors have slowly begun to supplant agriculture's share of GDP. The private retail sector has blossomed. Removal of restrictions on interregional transit and improvement of foreign relations with Thailand have fueled growth in the transport subsector, simplified trade activities, and are likely to reduce the prices of many goods. The potential for tourism as a foreign exchange earner has brightened as foreign investors join with Laotian companies to provide improved aviation and tourism services. The opening of the Friendship Bridge between Thailand and Laos symbolizes the new relationship with countries outside the former Soviet bloc: trade with and aid from both developed and neighboring countries have increased. Despite an inflationary surge in the late 1980s, the reduction of credit to money-losing state-owned enterprises and a tight monetary policy helped to bring inflation down to more manageable levels in the early 1990s. Tax reform has also worked to slow the increase in the fiscal deficit.

Despite these successes, however, many of the troubles that saddled Laos at the beginning of the 1990s remain. Perhaps the two most crucial constraints continue to be a poorly educated and trained labor force and a limited, poorly maintained transportation network with endemic problems. Many of Laos's most experienced and educated citizens fled the country in the late 1970s, and the poorly run and underfunded educational system is inadequate to make up for this important loss of managerial and technical skill. Similarly, insufficient investment in operations and maintenance over the years has resulted in a road system poorly equipped to handle the increased traffic that liberalization precipitated. Without a better educated and trained labor force and an improved infrastructure, measures to increase foreign investment and encourage export-oriented production are not likely to yield sustainable economic progress. Even the push to privatize state-owned enterprises and encourage efficient, profit-oriented production depends upon the availability of trained managers to direct production. Thus, the sustainability of reforms implemented by the start of the 1990s depends, at least in part, upon the ability of the government to turn its attention to the long-term infrastructure and human capital requirements of a market-based economy.

* * *

Writing about the LPDR economy presents special challenges because the measurement of crucial variables such as population, size of the labor force, GDP, trade and aid flows, and other economic indicators differs from source to source. In addition, information is often out of date; most of the few important books that cover the economy, such as Martin Stuart-Fox's *Laos: Politics, Economics, and Society*, were published before the New Economic Mechanism was introduced.

Among the most useful sources available are various World Bank publications, including *World Tables*, and especially *Historically Planned Economies, A Guide to the Data*, as well as the IMF's *Balance of Payments Statistics Yearbook*. Frequently conflicting statistical information is given in such publications as the Organisation for Economic and Co-operation and Development's *Geographical Distribution of Financial Flows to Developing Countries*, and the UN's *The Least Developed Countries Report*. Three extremely useful publications with a wide variety of statistics that frequently coincide with those of other sources are the UN's *Statistical Yearbook for Asia and the Pacific* and *Economic and Social Survey of Asia and the Pacific*, and the Asian Development Bank's *Asian Development Outlook*. Of these publications, the first is perhaps the only up-to-date publication with reasonably detailed sectoral and production time series. For a more historical perspective on the growth of various economic sectors, the *Asian Economic Handbook* and the Laos government's *10 Years of Socio-Economic Development in the Lao People's Democratic Republic* are very informative, if not always in agreement with other sources.

For information on specific sectors, a number of publications provide very useful data. The World Resources Institute's *World Resources* statistical tables contain otherwise scarce information on forestry and agricultural activities, deforestation, energy, and pollution. Two publications are indispensable for information on trade and investment: the UN's *Traders' Manual for Asia and the Pacific: Lao People's Democratic Republic* and Laurence J. Brahm and Neill T. Macpherson's *Investment in the Lao People's Democratic Republic*. A collection of papers from the Asian Development Bank and the Thai-Canada Economic Cooperation Foundation's *Thai-Lao Forum on Investment and Trade Opportunities in Lao PDR* provide some excellent sectoral background information.

A number of excellent, although brief, surveys of the economy are available, including Martin Stuart-Fox's article "Laos in 1991: On the Defensive" and the section on Laos in *The Far East and Australasia*; the latter publication also contains some useful statistical tables. For the most wide-ranging, up-to-date information, the Economist Intelligence Unit's *Country Profile* and *Country Report* series for Indochina are essential; see also *Asian Survey*'s annual summary and the annual *Asia Yearbook* series. The increase in foreign investment in Laos and the general upswing in private activity in the marketplace may result in the dissemination of more accurate, comprehensive, and timely information about the economy. (For further information and complete citations, see Bibliography.)

Chapter 4. Government and Politics

Parallel dragons form the sides of long steps leading to Wat Houa Xieng in Louangphrabang.

AS A TRADITIONAL SOCIETY until 1975, Laos was a conservative monarchy, dominated by a small number of powerful families. In 1975 it was transformed into a communist oligarchy, but its social makeup remained much the same. In the 600-year-old monarchy, the Lao king ruled from Louangphrabang (Luang Prabang), while in other regions there were families with royal pretensions rooted in the royal histories of Champasak (Bassac), Vientiane (Viangchan), and Xiangkhoang (Tran Ninh). They were surrounded by lesser aristocrats from prominent families, who in turn became patrons to clients of lower status, thus building a complex network of allegiances. The king reigned from Louangphrabang but did not rule over much of the outlying regions of the country.

In December 1975, with the declaration of the Lao People's Democratic Republic (LPDR, or Laos), the king abdicated. Although Laos was reorganized as a communist "people's democracy," important vestiges of traditional political and social behavior remained. The aristocratic families were shorn of their influence, but a new elite with privileged access to the communist roots of power emerged, and clients of lower status searched them out as patrons. In addition, some of the old families who had links to the new revolutionary elite managed to survive and wield significant influence. As newly dominant elites replaced the old, they demanded a similar deference.

Lao Loum (lowland Lao; see Glossary) families continue to wield the greatest influence (see Lowland Lao Society, ch. 2). Despite the rhetoric of the revolutionary elite concerning ethnic equality, Lao Theung (midland Lao; see Glossary) and Lao Sung (upland Lao; see Glossary) minorities are low on the scale of national influence, just as they were in pre-1975 society. However, the power of the central government over the outlying regions has remained tenuous; the government still relies upon bargains with tribal chieftains to secure the loyalty of their peoples.

Although manifesting many of the characteristics of a traditional Lao monarchy dominated by a lowland Lao Buddhist elite, the country also has exhibited many of the characteristics of other communist regimes. It has shown a similar heavy bureaucratic style, with emphasis within the bureaucracy on political training and long sessions of criticism and self-criticism for its civil servants. Laos imported from its Vietnamese mentor the concept of reeducation centers or "seminar camps," where, during the early years of the LPDR, thousands of former Royal Lao Government (RLG—see Glossary) adversaries were incarcerated. This communist overlay on traditional society, however, has been moderated by two important factors: Lao Buddhism and government administrative incompetence in implementing socialist doctrine. Thus, what emerged in Laos has been a system aptly labeled by Prince Souvanna Phouma, former prime minister of the RLG, as "socialisme à la laotienne" (Lao-style socialism).

The mélange of traditional politics, accompanied by patron-client relations, with communist-style intra-institutional competition, has produced a unique political culture. Power centers tend to cluster around key personalities, and those in power become targets of opportunity for members of their extended family and friends (see Leadership, this ch.)

The Lao People's Revolutionary Party

Whereas communist parties in the former Soviet Union and Eastern Europe have crumbled, in Laos, the ruling communist party, the Phak Pasason Pativat Lao (Lao People's Revolutionary Party—LPRP; see Glossary) has retained undiluted political control. The constitution, adopted in August 1991, notes simply in Article 3 that the LPRP is the "leading nucleus" of the political system. LPRP statutes, revised following the Fifth Party Congress held in 1991, leave no doubt regarding the dominant role of the party:

> The party is . . . the leading core of the entire political system, hub of intelligence, and representative of the interest of the people of all strata. The party formulates and revises the major lines and policies on national development in all spheres; finds solutions to major problems; determines the policies regarding personnel management, training of cadres, and supplying key cadres for different levels; controls and supervises activities of party cadres and members, state agencies and mass organizations.

Origins of the Party

The LPRP has its roots in the Indochinese Communist Party

(ICP), founded by Ho Chi Minh in 1930. (Ho Chi Minh led the struggle for Vietnamese independence and was the president of the Democratic Republic of Vietnam (North Vietnam) from 1945 until his death in 1969.) The ICP, composed entirely of Vietnamese members in its early years, formed the Committee for Laos (or a "Lao section") in 1936. Only in the mid-1940s did the Vietnamese communist revolutionaries step up active recruitment of Laotian members. In 1946 or early 1947, Kaysone Phomvihan, a law student at the University of Hanoi, was recruited, and Nouhak Phoumsavan, engaged in a trucking business in Vietnam, joined in 1947.

In February 1951, the Second Congress of the ICP resolved to disband the party and to form three separate parties representing the three states of Indochina (see The Pathet Lao, ch. 1). However, it was not until March 22, 1955, at the First Party Congress, that the Phak Pasason Lao (Lao People's Party—LPP) was formally proclaimed. (The name LPRP was adopted at the Second Party Congress in 1972.) It seems likely that from 1951 to 1955, key Laotian former members of the ICP provided leadership for the "resistance" movement in Laos, under the tutelage of their Vietnamese senior partners. In 1956 the LPP founded the Neo Lao Hak Xat (Lao Patriotic Front—LPF), the political party of the Pathet Lao (Lao Nation—see Glossary), to act as the public mass political organization. Meanwhile, the LPP remained clandestine, directing the activities of the front.

The Vietnamese communists provided critical guidance and support to the growing party during the revolutionary period. They helped to recruit the leadership of the Laotian communist movement; from its inception, the LPRP Political Bureau (Politburo) was made up of individuals closely associated with the Vietnamese. The Vietnamese furnished facilities and guidance for training not only the top leadership, but also the entire Laotian communist movement. The Vietnamese assigned advisers to the party, as well as to the military forces of the LPF. Under the guidance of North Vietnamese mentors, LPRP leaders shaped a Marxist-Leninist party, political and mass organizations, an army, and a bureaucracy, all based upon the North Vietnamese model.

From their perspective, Laotian communists had not compromised their legitimacy as a nationalist movement by their dependence on Hanoi. During the revolutionary period prior to 1975, when LPRP leaders looked to the North Vietnamese for a sense of overall direction and cohesion, they found many common interests. Both parties faced the same enemies: first France and then the United States. They held a similar view of the world and of the desirable solution to its problems. In some cases, this affinity was strengthened by family relations (for example, Kaysone, whose Vietnamese father, Luan Phomvihan, had been a secretary to the French resident in Savannakhét) or marriage ties (Souphanouvong and Nouhak had Vietnamese wives).

Following the First Party Congress, it was seventeen years until the Second Party Congress was convened, in February 1972. The Third Party Congress met ten years later, in April 1982; the Fourth Party Congress convened in November 1986, and the Fifth Party Congress in March 1991.

Party Structure

The LPP steadily grew from its initial 300 to 400 members ("25 delegates representing 300 to 400 members" were said to have attended the founding congress of the party). By 1965 there were 11,000 members; by 1972, as it prepared to enter into the final coalition with the RLG, it had grown to some 21,000 members; by 1975, when the party seized full power, it claimed a membership of 25,000; and by 1991, at the convening of the Fifth Party Congress, the LPRP claimed its membership had increased to 60,000.

The LPRP has been organized in a manner common to other ruling communist parties, with greatest similarity to the Vietnamese Communist Party. As in other such parties, the highest authority is the party congress, a gathering of party cadres from throughout the country that meets on an intermittent schedule for several days to listen to speeches, learn the plans for future party strategy, and ratify decisions already taken by the party leadership.

Next in the party hierarchy—since the elimination of the Secretariat in 1991—is the Central Committee, made up of members of the party elite who fill key political positions throughout the country (see fig. 8). The Central Committee is charged with leading the party between congresses. In addition to members of the Politburo and former members of the Secretariat, the committee includes key government ministers, leading generals of the army, secretaries of provincial party committees, and chairpersons of mass organizations.

When the LPRP first revealed itself to the public in 1975, the Central Committee comprised twenty-one members and six alternates. By the Fourth Party Congress, its size had expanded to fifty-one members and nine alternates. The average age of a Central Committee member in 1986 was fifty-two, with the oldest seventy-seven and the youngest thirty-three. The number of women on the Central Committee rose from three to five, including Thongvin Phomvihan, then Secretary General Kaysone's wife, who was chair of the LPRP's People's Revolutionary Youth Union and, in 1982, the first woman appointed to the Central Committee.

At the Fifth Party Congress, the Central Committee stabilized in size at fifty-nine members and took on a few younger, more educated men to replace deceased or retired members. At the time, the oldest member was seventy-seven, the youngest thirty-five; 22 percent of the members were over sixty, 30 percent between fifty and fifty-nine, and 40 percent under forty-nine. Only two women were full members of the Central Committee, and two continued as alternates. Thongvin Phomvihan—who had ranked thirty-fifth in 1986—was removed, accompanied by rumors of excessive political influence in her business activities. Notwithstanding this setback to Kaysone's family fortune, their son, Saisompheng Phomvihan, was appointed to the Central Committee, ranking forty-fifth, and was named governor of Savannakhét Province in 1993. This appointment inspired some private muttering about the emerging "princelings," including Souphanouvong's son, Khamsai Souphanouvong, number thirty-four on the Central Committee, who became minister of finance.

Despite the party's rhetoric asserting ethnic equality, the Central Committee has been dominated by lowland Lao. Upland minorities remain sparsely represented at the highest levels of party leadership. Only four members of ethnic minority groups were reported on the Central Committee elected at the Fifth Party Congress.

The Central Committee is served by a number of subordinate committees. These committees include, most importantly, the Office of the Central Committee, and five other offices: Organization Committee; Propaganda and Training Committee; Party and State Control Committee; Administrative Committee of the Party and State School for Political Theory; and Committee for the Propagation of Party Policies.

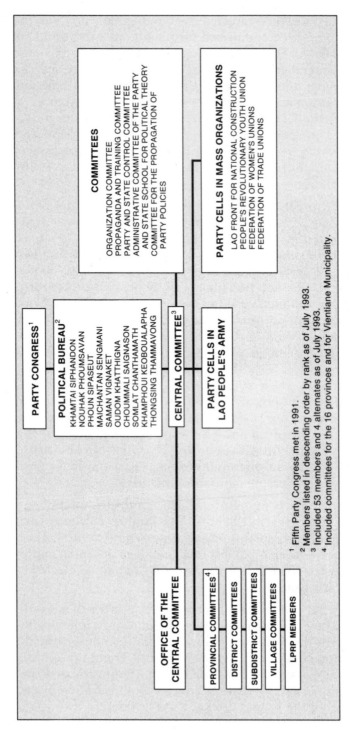

Figure 8. Organization of the Lao People's Revolutionary Party (LPRP), 1993

Source: Based on information from Martin Stuart-Fox, *Laos: Politics, Economics, and Society*, London, 1986, 61.

Since 1972 the genuine center of political power, as in other communist parties, has resided in the Politburo. Membership of the Politburo, and formerly that of the Secretariat, is drawn from the Central Committee. A small group of men—seven in 1972 and eleven by 1993—have provided the critical leadership of the communist movement in Laos. A signal attribute of this group has been its remarkable cohesion and continuity. The Politburo has been dominated for more than fifteen years of communist rule by the same stalwart band of revolutionary veterans. The twenty-five Laotian former members of the ICP who founded the LPP in 1955, and from whom the Politburo was drawn, remained in almost identical rank until illness and age began to take their toll in the 1980s. Kaysone was named secretary general of the then secret LPP upon its establishment, a post he retained until his death in 1992. Nouhak retained his number-two position on the Politburo into 1993. It was not until the Fifth Party Congress that Souphanouvong, Phoumi Vongvichit, and Sisomphone Lovansai (ranking third, fourth, and seventh, respectively) were retired with honorific titles as counselors to the Central Committee. Prime Minister Khamtai Siphandon was promoted to succeed Kaysone as chief of the party, and Phoun Sipaseut advanced a notch in rank. In 1991 the Politburo numbered ten, including only two new members.

Although the exact manner of Politburo decision making has never been revealed, a collegiality, based on long years of common experience, appears to have developed. In addition to their powerful position on the Politburo, members exercise additional political power—perhaps even more than in most other communist systems—through important posts within the governmental structure. In fact, for many years, five Politburo members also held seats on the Secretariat.

At the Fifth Party Congress, the party abolished the nine-person Secretariat of the Central Committee and changed the designation of the head of the party (Kaysone) from secretary general to chairman. Until it was abolished, the Secretariat wielded influence second only to that of the Politburo. The Secretariat issued party directives and acted on behalf of the Central Committee when it was not in session, in effect managing the day-to-day business of the party. Khamtai Siphandon became party chairman in November 1992, but it is not certain whether he will accrue the same power and influence as his predecessor.

Each of the sixteen provinces (*khoueng*—see Glossary) is directed by a party committee, chaired by a party secretary, who is the dominant political figure in the province. At a lower level are 112 districts (*muang*—see Glossary), further divided into subdistricts (*tasseng*—see Glossary), each with their own party committees. Administratively, subdistricts have been abolished in principle since around 1993, but implementation has been uneven across provinces. It is unknown whether subdistrict-level party committees have also been abolished. At the base of the country's administrative structure are more than 11,000 villages (*ban*—see Glossary), only some of which have party branches.

Semisecrecy of the Lao People's Revolutionary Party

Unlike other communist regimes, the LPRP has long maintained a semisecrecy about its mode of operation and the identity of its rank-and-file members. However, the LPRP follows the standard communist practice of planting party members within all principal institutions of society—in government, in mass organizations, and, formerly, in agricultural collectives. These individuals serve as leaders and transmit party policy. They also act as the eyes and ears of the central party organization. Although party members are admonished not to reveal themselves, it is not difficult for knowledgeable persons to pick out the party members in their organization. In each ministry, for example, the key power wielders are party members. All party members do not, of course, hold positions of authority. Some occupy the lower ranks, serving, for example, as messengers, drivers, and maintenance personnel.

By the late 1980s, some of the LPRP's semisecrecy had eroded. Party leadership lists, which, during revolutionary and early postrevolutionary days had been secret, were published. But a quasi-clandestine attitude remains among the party rank and file that can be explained by several factors. Clandestine behavior is an old habit that is not easily shed. Secrecy adds to the party's mystery, inspires anxiety and fear, and contributes to control. In view of its long history of revolutionary activity, party veterans fear infiltration and subversion. LPRP pronouncements during its first decade of rule frequently alluded to "CIA and Thai-reactionary-inspired agents," and later, when relations with China grew tense, to the danger of "big power hegemonism." Moreover, party leaders appear to lack confidence in the quality of their membership, speaking from time to time about "bad elements" within the party.

The LPRP is relatively small compared with other incumbent parties. For example, the 40,000 members that the party claimed in 1985 represented 1.1 percent of the population (estimating 3.5 million inhabitants). In 1979 the Vietnamese Communist Party had 1.5 million members in a population of 53 million, or approximately 3 percent.

Ideology of the Lao People's Revolutionary Party

When LPRP leaders came to power in 1975 as victorious revolutionaries guided by Marxism-Leninism, they retained a zeal for creating a "new socialist society and a new socialist man." They declared their twin economic goals as the achievement of "socialist transformation with socialist construction." They asserted that in establishing the LPDR in 1975, they had completed the "national democratic revolution." (The national goal had been to expel the French colonialists and the United States imperialists. The democratic goal was to overthrow "reactionary traitors, comprador bourgeoisie, bureaucrats, reactionaries, feudalists and militarists. . . .") The LPRP claimed that it had won the national democratic revolution by winning a "people's war" with a "worker-peasant" alliance, under the secret leadership of the LPRP working through a national front. It proclaimed a commitment to "proletarian internationalism" and the "law of Indochinese solidarity," and at the same time defined Vietnam and the Soviet Union as friends and the "unholy alliance" among United States imperialism, Chinese "great power hegemonism," and Thai militarism as enemies.

By the late 1980s, as communism was undergoing a radical transformation in the Soviet Union and Eastern Europe, Kaysone and his colleagues on the Politburo still professed an adherence to Marxism-Leninism, but they emphasized the necessity for Laos to pass through a stage of "state capitalism." Following Mikhail Gorbachev's example of perestroika, Kaysone proclaimed in 1989 that state enterprises were being severed from central direction and would be financially autonomous. V.I. Lenin's New Economic Policy was frequently cited to legitimize the movement toward a market economy and the necessity to stimulate private initiative.

By the early 1990s, even less of the Marxist-Leninist rhetoric remained. The party has continued to move internally toward more free-market measures and externally toward reliance upon the capitalist countries and the international institutions on which they depend for investment and assistance. The "law" of Indochinese solidarity has been amended, and the LPDR's "special relations" with its former senior partner are no longer invoked, even though party spokesmen still insist that Laos retains a solid friendship and "all-round cooperation" with Vietnam (see Bilateral Relations, this ch.).

Despite this erosion of communist ideology, retaining exclusive political power remains a primary goal of the party. In a speech in 1990, Secretary General Kaysone asserted the basis of legitimacy of the party:

> The party is the center of our wisdom. It has laid down the correct and constructive line, patterns, and steps compatible with realities in our country and hence has led the Lao people in overcoming difficulties and numerous tests to win victory after victory, until the final victory. History has shown that our party is the only party which has won the credibility and trust of the people. Our party's leadership in our country's revolution is an objective requirement and historic duty entrusted to it by the Lao multiethnic people. Other political parties which had existed in our country have dissolved in the process of historical transformation. They failed to win the control and support of the people because they did not defend the national interest or fight for the interests and aspirations of the people.

Leadership

Internal Stability and External Influences

Since the LPDR was proclaimed in December 1975, its leadership has been remarkably stable and cohesive. The record of continuous service at the highest ranks is equaled by few, if any, regimes in the contemporary world. Laotian leaders have an equally impressive record of unity. Although outside observers have scrutinized the leadership for factions—and some have postulated at various times that such factions might be divided along the lines of Marxist-Leninist ideologues versus pragmatists or pro-Vietnamese versus nationalists (or pro-Chinese), there is no solid evidence that the leadership is seriously divided on any critical issues.

In 1975 the Laotian communist leaders, most of whom had spent the revolutionary decade from 1964 to 1974 operating from Pathet Lao headquarters in the caves of Sam Neua Province (now Houaphan), came down from the mountains to Vientiane to direct the new government. At the outset of their accession to power, they were suspicious, secretive, and inaccessible, and lower-level cadres were maladroit in imposing heavy bureaucratic controls. Travel within the country was limited, personal and family behavior was monitored by newly organized revolutionary administrative committees, cadres were assigned to disseminate propaganda, and seminars were held to provide political education for all sorts of groups. During these early years, the party squandered much of the goodwill and friendly acceptance from a population tired of war and the corruption of the old regime.

At first, Laotian communist leaders were committed to fulfilling their revolutionary goals of fundamentally altering society through "socialist transformation and socialist construction." After 1979 the regime modified its earlier zealous pursuit of socialism and pursued more liberal economic and social policies, in much the same manner as Vietnam.

For more than a decade after 1975, the Vietnamese continued to exercise significant influence upon the Laotian leadership through a variety of party, military, and economic channels. By the end of the 1980s, however—in particular following the collapse of the Soviet Union and the Soviet bloc in 1991 and diminishing assistance from the Soviet Union to Vietnam and Laos—Vietnam turned inward to concentrate on its own problems of development. This emboldened Laotians leaders to jettison even more of their socialist ideological baggage, abandon agricultural collectivization, and move toward a market economy. Laos was also free to pursue an independent foreign policy. The single most important vestige of the former communist system was the solitary ruling party, the LPRP.

Key Leaders

Kaysone Phomvihan was preeminent leader of both the party and the state until his death in November 1992. Kaysone's unusual career had taken him through two decades of revolution and almost another two decades of independence. Born in 1920, Kaysone studied at the Faculty of Law at the University of Hanoi where, in 1942, he joined the struggle against the

French colonialists, according to his official biography. Kaysone was known in Hanoi by his Vietnamese name, Quoc.

For at least a decade after independence, Kaysone avoided contact with the masses, Western diplomats, and journalists, remaining heavily guarded and secretive, in some ways continuing an earlier shadowy revolutionary style. Kaysone's caution may have been influenced by concern for his safety because several attempts had been made on his life during the first few years of his rule. During 1989 and 1990, however, Kaysone moved about more freely in Laos and showed himself more openly to the outside world. For the first time, he made state visits to Japan, China, and Sweden. He gave interviews to Western journalists and was more available to meet with Western officials. His public statements suggested that he was impressed by the level of development he had seen in affluent nations and that he was open to new techniques to bring economic progress to Laos under the leadership of the LPRP.

Although the political careers of most communist leaders in Europe and Asia had been terminated when fundamental new policies were introduced to their regimes, Kaysone continued his leadership without challenge, showing unusual political agility and ideological flexibility. Kaysone had long embraced Marxism-Leninism, following the pattern of his Vietnamese and Soviet mentors. When evidence of change in the communist world began to appear, Kaysone propounded the New Economic Mechanism in 1986, invoking Lenin, but soon moved control of state enterprises to autonomous firms, and by 1989 edged more deliberately toward a market economy (see Industrial Policy, ch. 3). Kaysone appeared to be a pragmatic communist leader, open to the ideas of outsiders and zealous for— although unsuccessful at producing—economic growth.

Upon Kaysone's death, the person who had been second in party Politburo rank for as long as Kaysone had been first, Nouhak Phoumsavan, born in 1914, was passed over as party chairman—presumably for reasons of age and ill health—in favor of the third-ranking member, General Khamtai Siphandon. In keeping with the Laotian communist practice of maintaining continuity and honoring seniority, however, Nouhak was promoted from deputy prime minister to president of state.

As of 1994, the new LPRP chairman, Khamtai, also retained his government post as prime minister, suggesting that he had consolidated his role as the preeminent political leader. Born

Khamtai Siphandon, Prime
Minister, Lao People's
Democratic Republic
Courtesy Embassy of the Lao
People's Democratic
Republic, Washington

Nouhak Phoumsavan,
President, Lao People's
Democratic Republic
Courtesy Embassy of the Lao
People's Democratic
Republic, Washington

in 1924 in Champasak Province, Khamtai is the youngest surviving member of the group that founded the Neo Lao Issara
(Free Laos Front—see Glossary) in 1950 and the LPP in 1955.
He is thought to have spent part of World War II (1939–45) in
India and was employed as a postal worker in southern Laos
after the war. He joined the Lao Issara (Free Laos—see Glossary) in 1946 and remained with the Pathet Lao group that
split with the Lao Issara in 1949 (see The Coming of Independence, ch. 1). Assigned to military and political functions in
the southern Laos sector, Khamtai was elected to the Central
Committee of the Neo Lao Issara in 1950. According to a biography published in the Vietnamese newspaper, *Nhan Dan* (People), Khamtai was appointed chief of staff of the Lao People's
Liberation Army (LPLA—see Glossary) in 1954, and in 1957

he was elected to membership in the Central Committee of the LPP. He directed the party's propaganda and training functions during 1959 and 1960 and in 1961 was named supreme commander of the LPLA. In 1962 he was appointed to the Standing Committee of the party's Central Committee and named deputy secretary of the General Military Committee.

Khamtai moved steadily forward in the LPRP Politburo to the third ranking position, serving as minister of national defense from 1975 to 1991 and as deputy prime minister before his elevation to the post of prime minister in 1991. Khamtai's background in the military establishment, which has been a conservative force in Laotian politics, is thought to make him particularly sensitive to security concerns. He has a reputation as a hardliner and appears to be more inclined toward secrecy than Kaysone. Before assuming the post of prime minister, he had little exposure to Westerners, although his contacts increased when he took on his new task.

The deputy prime minister for foreign affairs in 1994 was Phoun Sipaseut, a veteran Politburo member who headed the Ministry of Foreign Affairs for seventeen years. Below him, in the rank of minister of foreign affairs, was Somsavat Lengsavat, who ranked fifty-first in the LPRP Central Committee. In Kaysone's time, an "inner cabinet" of six party leaders carried the major decision-making responsibility for the government. Of this group, only three members were living as of mid-1994—Nouhak, Khamtai, and Phoun. It is uncertain whether Kaysone's successors will continue the inner cabinet, but there appears to be some generational conflict between the leaders who were educated by service in the secret revolutionary party and those who may have studied abroad—very likely in France—before 1975 and whose membership in the party came during a more open era. One of the vice ministers of foreign affairs in 1992, for example, studied at the French military academy, Saint Cyr, as did a former minister of external economic relations. The latter was dealing very adroitly in 1991 with foreign donors, and at the Fifth Party Congress, his rank on the Central Committee rose from twenty-sixth to sixteenth. His counterpart in the Ministry of Finance, however, a former provincial governor with more than three decades of service in the revolutionary movement, was propelled from forty-third to tenth in the Central Committee and gained membership in the Politburo.

The Constitution

Development of the Constitution

On August 14, 1991, sixteen years after the establishment of the LPDR, the Supreme People's Assembly (SPA), the country's highest legislative organ, adopted a constitution. Although the SPA had been charged with drafting a constitution in 1975, the task had low priority. It was not until the Third Party Congress that party Secretary General Kaysone stated that the LPRP should "urgently undertake the major task . . . of preparing a socialist constitution at an early date." Laotian press reports subsequently revealed that a constitutional drafting committee was working informally under the chairmanship of Politburo member Sisomphone Lovansai, a specialist in party organization, with the help of East German advisers. Despite the proclaimed urgency of the task, only on May 22, 1984, did the SPA Standing Committee formalize the appointment of Sisomphone to head a fifteen-person drafting committee.

Although the political institutions had functioned without a written constitution for fifteen years, the lack of a constitution created serious drawbacks for the country. International development agencies were reluctant to invest in Laos given the absence of a fixed, knowable law. Amnesty International, in a 1985 report on Laos, asserted that without a constitution or published penal and criminal codes, citizens were "effectively denied proper legal guarantees of their internationally recognized human rights." Even the party newspaper, *Xieng Pasason* (Voice of the People), commenting in June 1990 on the absence of a constitution and a general body of laws, acknowledged that "having no laws is . . . a source of injustice and violation, thus leading to a breakdown of social order and peace, the breeding of anarchy, and the lack of democracy."

Reasons for the leisurely pace of constitution drafting, unusually slow even for the plodding bureaucracy, were not readily apparent. Vietnam had adopted a revised constitution in 1980 and Cambodia in 1981, only two years after the ouster of the Khmer Rouge. According to some reports, progress in Laos had been blocked by differences within the Politburo over certain substantive clauses. Perhaps most important, the party leadership, accustomed to rule without question, may have assigned a low priority to producing a document that might eventually lead to challenging their authority, despite rhetoric to the contrary. Further, the public seemed not to care.

After the new SPA was elected in March 1989, it formally appointed a seventeen-member constitutional drafting committee. The National Radio of Laos reported that the drafting committee was working "under the close supervision of the Political Bureau and the Secretariat of the Party Central Committee." Six members of the drafting committee were members of the Central Committee; two of these members also served on the SPA, which also had six members on the drafting committee.

In April 1990, after securing approval of its document from the LPRP Politburo and the Secretariat, the SPA finally made public the draft constitution. With its publication, the party Central Committee issued Directive Number 21, on April 30, 1990, calling for discussion of the draft, first among party and government officials and then among the public. The discussions, although orchestrated by party cadres, did not always please party authorities. An LPRP spokesman released a memo complaining that "people in many major towns" had dwelled too much on what the constitution had to say about the organization of the state. In June a member of the Central Committee cautioned against demonstrations to "demand a multiparty system" and warned that demonstrators would be arrested. Competing parties would not be tolerated, he asserted, adding that "our multi-ethnic Lao people have remained faithfully under the leadership of the LPRP." In a later pronouncement, he said that "the Party has proved to the people in the last 35 years that it is the only party that can take care of them" and he lectured that "too many parties invite division." A Central Committee directive, dated June 14, 1990, hinted at the quality of the public discussion, noting that "in many cases where people were convoked to a meeting, they were simply given question and answer sheets to study."

Not all discussions of the draft constitution were perfunctory, however. Undoubtedly inspired by the examples of Eastern Europe and the Soviet Union—where the monopoly of power by communist parties had crumbled—a group of some forty government officials and intellectuals began criticizing the country's one-party system in a series of letters and meetings in April 1990. Organized in the unofficial "Social Democratic Club," the group called for a multiparty system in Laos.

One member of the group, an assistant to the minister of science and technology, submitted a letter of resignation to Prime Minister Kaysone in which he labeled Laos a "communist monarchy" and a "dynasty of the Politburo," declaring that the country should "change into a multi-party system in order to bring democracy, freedom and prosperity to the people."

Criticism of the draft document gathered strength in the succeeding months; Laotian students in Paris, Prague, and Warsaw joined in the call for free elections. Criticism broadened as a group of young, educated party cadres associated with nonparty bureaucrats—many educated in France and Canada—targeted veteran party leaders. These groups charged that the new policies of the old guard were fostering corruption and increased social and economic inequality. It was not until October 1990 that the government finally cracked down on these calls for democratic reforms, with the arrest of several protesters, including a former vice minister in the State Planning Commission and a director in the Ministry of Justice who were sentenced to long prison terms in Houaphan.

Thus, although the constitution purports to guarantee freedom of speech and petition and its framers give lip service to the desirability of public discussion, the ruling party sent a clear message with these arrests that it will not tolerate challenges to its exclusive exercise of power. Veteran party leaders were clearly more impressed by the political models of Vietnam and China than by the examples of Eastern Europe and the Soviet Union. Although willing to experiment with economic liberalization, party leaders seemed determined to retain political domination—if they could—through a Leninist-style party.

Highlights of the Constitution

The 1991 constitution, which contains elements of an earlier revolutionary orthodoxy, is clearly influenced by the economic and political liberalization within Laos, as well as by the dramatic changes in the socialist world and the international balance of forces. The constitution specifies the functions and powers of the various organs of government and defines the rights and duties of citizens. Several chapters prescribing the structure of the state define the function and powers of the National Assembly (the renamed SPA), the president, the government, the local administration, and the judicial system. The constitution has little to say, however, about the limitations on

View of the Mekong River from Phousi courtyard, Louangphrabang
Courtesy Gina Merris

government. In foreign policy, the principles of peaceful coexistence are followed.

The constitution legally establishes a set of authorities that resembles the traditional differentiation among executive, legislative, and judicial branches of government. The delineation does not imitate any particular model (neither Vietnamese, nor Russian, nor French), but it pays respect to the idea of a basic blueprint of responsibilities lodged in designated institutions. There is room for evolution of government authority, but there are also specific boundaries.

Government outside Vientiane has developed an independence over the years, reflecting the exigencies of the Pathet Lao armed struggle and of economic self-reliance during the postwar socialist pitfalls. The constitution eliminated elected people's councils at the provincial and district level as necessary "no more," in an effort to fit the state apparatus to the needs of building and developing the regime under "the actual conditions of the country." Again, the will of the ruling party determines which road the administration follows in regard to local governance, but the constitution has left governors, mayors, and district and village chiefs free to "administer their regions and localities without any assistance from popularly elected bodies." The leading role of the party within the administration of the nation overall is illustrated by the fact that party Politburo members are found in state offices—the offices of the president of state, and prime minister, deputy prime ministers (two), chair of the National Assembly, minister of defense, and chair of the Party and State Inspection Board.

The first words of the Preamble refer to the "multi-ethnic Lao people," and frequent use of this term is made throughout the text, a clear rhetorical attempt to promote unity within an ethnically diverse society. The "key components" of the people are specified as workers, farmers, and intellectuals. The Preamble celebrates a revolution carried out "for more than 60 years" under the "correct leadership" of the ICP.

The dominant role played by the LPRP, however, is scarcely mentioned, and the constitution is almost silent about the party's functions and powers. One brief reference to the ruling party is made in Article 3, which states that the "rights of the multi-ethnic people to be the masters of the country are exercised and ensured through the functioning of the political system with the Lao People's Revolutionary Party as its leading nucleus."

Article 5 notes that the National Assembly and all other state organizations "function in accordance with the principle of democratic centralism." This stricture is an obvious reference to the Marxist-Leninist principle, which calls for open discussion within a unit but prescribes that the minority must accede to the will of the majority, and lower echelons must obey the decisions of higher ones.

Article 7 calls upon mass organizations, such as the Lao Front for National Construction, the Federation of Trade Unions, the People's Revolutionary Youth Union, and the Federation of Women's Unions, to "unite and mobilize the people." The Lao Front for National Construction, the successor to the LPF, served as the political front for the party during the revolutionary struggle. Its mandate is to mobilize political support and raise political consciousness for the party's goals among various organizations, ethnic groups, and social classes within society. Other mass organizations are assigned to pursue these goals among their target populations of workers, youths, and women.

The constitution proclaims that the state will respect the "principle of equality among ethnic tribes," which have the right to promote "their fine customs and culture." Further, the state is committed to upgrading the "socio-economy of all ethnic groups."

Regarding religion, the state "respects and protects all lawful activities of the Buddhists and of other religious followers." Buddhist monks and other clergy are reminded that the state encourages them to "participate in the activities which are beneficial to the country" (see Buddhism, ch. 2).

The chapter on the socioeconomic system does not mention the establishment of socialism, a principal goal of earlier dogma. Instead, the objective of economic policy is to transform the "natural economy into a goods economy." Private property appears to be assured by the statement that the "state protects the right of ownership," including the right of transfer and inheritance. The state is authorized to undertake such tasks as managing the economy, providing education, expanding public health, and caring for war veterans, the aging, and the sick (see Health and Welfare, ch. 2). The constitution admonishes that "all organizations and citizens must protect the environment."

A chapter on the rights and obligations of citizens sets forth a cluster of well-known rights found in modern constitutions, including freedom of religion, speech, press, and assembly. Women and men are proclaimed equal, and all citizens can vote at age eighteen and hold office at twenty-one. In return, citizens are obliged to respect the laws, pay taxes, and defend the country, which includes military service (see Manpower and Conditions of Service, ch. 5). In commenting on this chapter in 1990, Amnesty International, clearly concerned about past human rights abuses, criticized the document for what was *not* included. Amnesty International noted the absence of provisions for protecting the right to life, abolishing the death penalty, guaranteeing the inalienability of fundamental rights, prohibiting torture, safeguarding against arbitrary arrest and detention, protecting people deprived of their liberty, and providing for a fair trial. No safeguards exist to protect the rights to freedom of opinion and expression, peaceful assembly and association, and independence of the judiciary.

Laos is made up of provinces, municipalities, districts, and villages. The constitution gives no clear guidance on provincial and district responsibilities except to specify that the leaders at each echelon must ensure the implementation of the constitution and the law and must carry out decisions taken by a higher level. In spite of the party's inclination to centralize decision making, provinces and localities have enjoyed a surprising degree of autonomy in shaping social policy. This independence is partly a result of limited resources and poor communications with Vientiane. But the central government has also encouraged direct contacts along the borders with China, Thailand, and Vietnam, and trading agreements with neighboring jurisdictions.

Although it is unlikely that the constitution will immediately change the embedded patterns of the Laotian political system or threaten the dominant role of the party, it has the potential to protect human rights and respect for the law, by the rulers as well as the ruled. The crumbling of communist regimes in Eastern Europe and the Soviet Union as well as strains in communist systems elsewhere, accompanied by widespread movements for democracy, suggest that Laos will not be immune to growing demands for a more dependable rule of law.

Government Structure

Bureaucratic Culture

The historical evolution of Laos created identifiable layers of bureaucratic behavior. Traditional royal customs and Buddhist practices set the foundation. Next, there was an overlay of French influence, the product of colonial rule from 1890 to 1954. During this period, several generations of Laotian bureaucrats were trained and often placed in subordinate rank to French-imported Vietnamese civil servants. The administration used French as the official language and followed French colonial administrative practices. From 1954 to 1975, there was an increase in United States influence, and the United States provided training and educational opportunities for future bureaucrats as well as employment in United States agencies. Because of its brevity, however, the United States impact was far less pervasive than the French.

When the communists seized power in 1975, a new layer of bureaucrats—strongly influenced by North Vietnam and the Soviet Union and its allies—was added. Many of the French-trained and United States-influenced bureaucrats fled across the Mekong River. Of those who stayed, perhaps 10,000 to 15,000 were sent to "seminar camps," or reeducation centers (see "Seminar Camps" and the Death of Savang Vatthana, ch. 1; Detention Centers, ch. 5). The few Western-trained bureaucrats who remained possessed French- or English-language skills and the technical competence needed to deal effectively with the Western foreign aid donors so critical to the economy. The Western-trained bureaucrats were essential because not many of the new revolutionary cadres who moved into key positions of bureaucratic authority had much formal education, knowledge of a foreign language, or competence in the technical and managerial skills necessary to run a national economy. The few cadres in each ministry who were capable of managing the economy were often unavailable because there were so many demands for their services: for example, meeting with visiting foreign delegations, traveling to international meetings, and attending political training sessions.

Since its inception, the LPDR bureaucracy has been lethargic and discouraged individual initiative. It has been dangerous to take unorthodox positions. Some officials have been arrested on suspicion of corruption or ideological deviation: for example, "pro-Chinese" sentiment. Initiative has been further constrained by the lack of legal safeguards, formal trial procedures, and an organized system of appeal. The beginnings of a penal code, which the SPA endorsed in 1989, and the promulgation of a constitution in 1991, however, may solidify the system of justice and provide a clear definition as to what constitutes a crime against socialist morality, the party, or the state.

The lethargy of the bureaucracy is understandable within the cultural context of Laos. As a peasant society at the lower end of the modernization scale, the LPDR has adopted few of the work routines associated with modern administration. Foreign aid administrators frequently point out that Laotian administrators have difficulty creating patterns or precedents, or learning from experience. Laotians are known for their light-hearted, easy-going manner. This *bo pinh nyang* (never mind—don't worry about it) attitude is reflected in the languid pace of administration. Official corruption has also been acknowledged as problematic.

Kaysone acknowledged the bureaucracy's low level of competence. In his report to the Fourth Party Congress in 1986, he chided those in authority who gave "preference only to (their friends) or those from the same locality or race; paying attention to only their birth origin, habits and one particular sphere of education." Patronage is but one area that has come under scrutiny and resulted in admonishments to strengthen inspection and control. Kaysone further railed against "dogmatism, privatism, racial narrow-mindedness, regionalism and localism."

Executive

The president of the country is elected by a two-thirds vote of the National Assembly for a term of five years. One surprising constitutional provision transforms the presidency from a ceremonial position to one with important political power. The president appoints and can dismiss the prime minister and members of the government, with the approval of the National Assembly—parliamentary responsibility that has not yet occurred in the short life of the current constitutional regime. He also presides over meetings of the government, "when necessary," and appoints and dismisses provincial governors and mayors of municipalities as well as generals of the armed forces, upon the recommendation of the prime minister. In addition, the president receives and appoints ambassadors and declares states of emergency or war.

The powers accorded to the president grew perceptibly during the drafting process of the constitution, but the sudden death of Kaysone, who had moved from prime minister to state president after the promulgation of the constitution, temporarily introduced doubts regarding the relative power potential of the two offices. Nonetheless, the president of state heads the armed forces and has the right and duty to promulgate laws and issue decrees and state acts.

The primary organization for administration is the government, which consists of the prime minister—its head—and deputy prime ministers, ministers, and chairs of ministry-equivalent state committees. The prime minister, appointed by the president with the approval of the National Assembly, serves a five-year term. Duties of this office include the guidance and supervision of the work of government ministries and committees, as well as of the governors of provinces and mayors of municipalities. The prime minister appoints all the deputies at these levels of government, as well as the local district chiefs (see fig. 9).

Legislature

The National Assembly, the country's supreme legislative body, is to be elected every five years. Significantly, this designation was used in RLG and French colonial times, before the introduction of the title "Supreme People's Assembly" in late 1975. It is located in a new building, far larger than the previous structure built in colonial times, and contains an auditorium seating 800 persons.

The National Assembly makes decisions on fundamental issues and oversees administrative and judicial organs. Its most significant powers include electing and removing the president of state, the president of the Supreme People's Court, and the prosecutor general, "on the recommendation of the National Assembly Standing Committee." Its prestige has been further enhanced by the constitutional mandate to "make decisions on

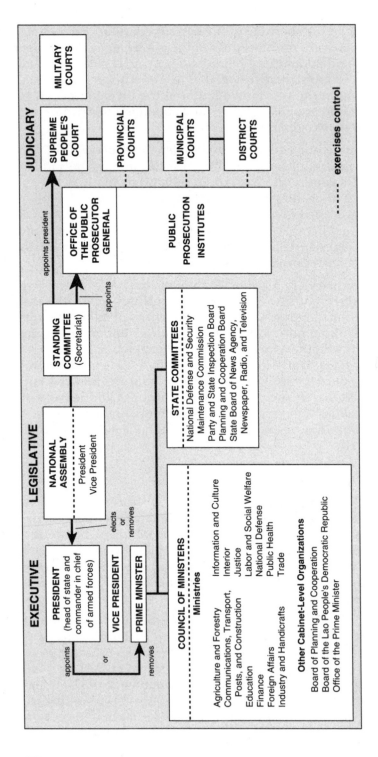

Figure 9. Structure of the Government, 1993

the fundamental issues of the country" and to "elect or remove the President of state and the Vice President of state," by a two-thirds vote, and to approve the removal of members of the government on the recommendation of the president of state. Its powers encompass amending the constitution, determining taxes, approving the state budget, endorsing or abrogating laws, and electing or removing the two top judicial figures in the system. Members of the National Assembly have the "right to interpellate the members of the government." The National Assembly also ratifies treaties and decides questions of war and peace. These powers may prove to be limited, however, by a provision in the constitution that the National Assembly will generally meet in ordinary session only twice a year. The Standing Committee meeting in the interim may convene an extraordinary session if it deems this necessary.

The constitution does not specify the number of members in the National Assembly, whose candidates are screened by the LPRP. The 1989 election placed seventy-nine members in this body, representing districts of between 40,000 and 50,000 persons each. The election campaign lasted two months, and candidates appeared before voters at night in local schools or pagodas. Voting consisted of crossing out unfavored candidates, and every ballot contained at least two candidates. The number of party members elected by this process was officially placed at sixty-five.

Between sessions, the Standing Committee of the National Assembly, consisting of the president and the vice president elected by the National Assembly and an unspecified number of other members, prepares for future sessions and "supervise[s] and oversee[s] the activities of the administrative and judicial organizations." It is empowered to appoint or remove the vice president of the Supreme People's Court and judges at all levels of the lower courts. Its supervisory role can be reinforced by National Assembly committees established to consider draft laws and decrees and to help in the supervision and administration of the courts. The special National Assembly Law passed March 25, 1993, specifies five substantive areas for National Assembly committees: secretarial; law; economic planning and finances; cultural, social, and nationalities; and foreign affairs. The membership of the committees includes not only National Assembly members but also chiefs and deputy chiefs, who "guide the work," and technical cadres.

Judiciary

The development of the legal and judicial system did not begin until almost fifteen years after the state was proclaimed. In November 1989, a criminal code and laws establishing a judicial system were adopted. In 1993 the government began publishing an official gazette to disseminate laws, decrees, and regulations.

In 1990 the judicial branch was upgraded. New legislation provided a draft of a criminal code, established procedures for criminal cases, set up a court system, and established a law school. Moreover, the Ministry of Justice added a fourth year of studies to a law program for training magistrates and judges.

Also in 1990, the functions of the Supreme People's Court were separated from those of the Office of the Public Prosecutor General. Until then, the minister of justice served as both president of the court and director of public prosecutions.

Although the implementation of judicial reforms proceeded slowly and had not significantly improved the administration of justice by mid-1994, the new legal framework offers the possibility of moving away from the arbitrary use of power toward the rule of law. In late 1992, however, the government suspended the bar until it formulates regulations for fees and activities of (the few) private lawyers who are able to advise in civil cases. Lawyers are not allowed to promote themselves as attorneys-at-law. Theoretically, the government provides legal counsel to the accused, although in practice persons accused of crimes must defend themselves, without outside legal counsel. This situation is changing, however, and the assessors (legal advisers)—who are often untrained—and the party functionaries are being increasingly replaced by professional personnel trained at the Institute of Law and Administration.

The constitution empowers the National Assembly to elect or remove the president of the Supreme People's Court and the public prosecutor general on the recommendation of its Standing Committee. The Standing Committee of the National Assembly appoints or removes judges (previously elected) of the provincial, municipal, and district levels.

Further evidence of an attempt to shift toward a professional judicial system is found in the public prosecution institutes provided for at each level of administration. The task of these institutes is to control the uniform observance of laws by all ministries, organizations, state employees, and citizens. They prosecute under the guidance of the public prosecutor general, who appoints and removes deputy public prosecutors at all levels.

Challenges to the Regime

Human Rights

Human rights have been gaining a measure of respect in Laos. In the early years of the LPDR, party authorities arbitrarily sent people labeled as social deviants—"prostitutes, addicts, gamblers, hippies, thieves, and lost children"—to seminar camps. Political opponents associated with the former RLG—perhaps as many as 30,000 to 50,000—were also confined to these camps.

By the late 1980s, there was a slight liberalization in the granting of human rights. Many, although not all, of the seminar camps had been closed, and some former inmates were assigned to labor and construction units and collective farms near the camps. It became easier for a citizen to travel within the country and gain permission to cross the Mekong River to Thailand or travel abroad. As of April 1994, any Laotian with an identification card and foreigners with valid visas were permitted to travel anywhere in the country—with specific travel papers—except to a few unspecified "restricted areas." Restrictions on Buddhist religious practices became more relaxed, and even high-level government officials routinely attended Buddhist functions. The number of Buddhist monks increased, with some 30,000 reported to be practicing in 1991 (see Buddhism, ch. 2). The agents of state internal security, principally the police and other cadres of the Ministry of Interior, seemed less oppressive. In 1991 twenty-five detainees who had been held at seminar camps since 1975 were released. The number the government was known to be holding as of 1993 had diminished to fewer than twelve, all former officials or military officers of the RLG. The LPDR claimed that the remaining detainees were free to travel in Houaphan Province, where they were confined.

Nonetheless, many freedoms remain inaccessible. The government controls most large public gatherings, and, except for religious, athletic, and communal events, generally organizes them. Political demonstrations, protest marches, and other "destabilizing subversive activities" are expressly banned by the new penal code. The constitution guarantees the freedoms of speech and the press, but the exercise of these freedoms is subject to a wide range of government controls (see Mass Media, this ch.).

Insurgents

A small-scale insurgency that has existed since 1975 continues in the early 1990s, although at a much lower level than in previous years. This insurgency has never seriously threatened the regime, but it is troublesome because the insurgents commit sabotage, blow up bridges, and threaten transport and communications. The great majority of insurgents are Hmong (see Glossary), led by ex-soldiers from United States Central Intelligence Agency (CIA)-supported units who fought against Pathet Lao and North Vietnamese troops in the 1960s. Hmong groups, most of them formerly associated with the RLG, draw recruits and support from Hmong refugee camps and operate from bases in Thailand with the cooperation of local Thai military officers. As relations between Thailand and Laos continued to improve in the 1990s, support for this insurgent activity declined (see Foreign Policy, this ch.). Resistance spokesmen claim that their principal source of funds for weapons and supplies comes from Laotian expatriate communities overseas, including the 180,000 Laotians in the United States.

Even though the government lacks widespread public support, insurgency is less a measure of discontent than evidence of a serious ethnic problem. The LPDR, like the RLG that preceded it, has been dominated by lowland Lao. The two governments exemplify the traditional Lao disdain for upland peoples, in spite of Pathet Lao rhetoric in favor of ethnic equality. On the one hand, because many Hmong fought on the side of the "American imperialists," government leaders feel additionally suspicious of them. On the other hand, Hmong and other upland minorities who served with the United States-supported forces have been suspicious and uncomfortable under their former enemies. Thus, a core of insurgents, composed largely of ethnic minorities, continues to fight against the authorities. It will be extremely difficult—perhaps impossible—for the government to pacify them, especially without help from Vietnamese military units, if the insurgents enjoy access to sanctuary in Thailand along the easily crossed, 1,000-kilometer Mekong River border.

In the early 1980s, Hmong insurgents claimed that the Lao People's Army (LPA—see Glossary) was using lethal chemical agents against them. The Hmong refugees in Thailand often referred to the chemical agents as "poisons from above;" foreign journalists used the term "yellow rain." The government vehemently denied these charges. The United States Department of State noted in 1992 that "considerable investigative efforts in recent years have revealed no evidence of chemical weapons use" in the post-1983 period.

Refugees

From 1975 to 1985, after the communists had seized power and were consolidating their hold, some 350,000 persons fled across the Mekong River to Thailand and, in most cases, resettled in third countries. By the late 1980s and early 1990s, this outflow had declined substantially. In 1990, for example, an estimated 1,000 to 2,000 lowland Lao and 4,000 to 5,000 upland Lao departed illegally for Thailand. The Thai government refused to admit these refugees as immigrants. Emigrants who claim to be "victims of communism" may face more problems being accepted for third-country resettlement as a result of the end of the Cold War. Moreover, Laos has become more liberal in granting exit permits to those desiring to emigrate.

By the early 1990s, almost as many Laotians were returning to Laos as were leaving. Under a voluntary repatriation program worked out in 1980 by Laos and the United Nations High Commissioner for Refugees (UNHCR—see Glossary), nearly 19,000 Laotians had voluntarily returned to their homeland by the end of 1993, and an estimated 30,000 more had returned without official involvement. Most of the returnees are lowland Lao. Of the approximately 30,000 Laotian refugees remaining in camps in Thailand in 1993, the majority are upland Lao. Approximately 1,700 Laotian refugees remain in China. Émigrés who had resettled in third countries are returning in increasing numbers to visit relatives and, in a few cases, to survey business opportunities in the more liberal economy.

Political Opposition

Over the centuries, residents of the Laotian Buddhist kingdom developed gentle techniques of accommodation, often searching for more powerful patrons either outside the country or within. Authorities governed during the early years after

1975 with little popular support, but most Laotians simply submitted to their authority because they had little alternative. However, the authorities were not harsh compared to other communist regimes of the 1970s and 1980s, most of which—by mid-1994—had toppled.

The relatively passive Laotian political culture inspires few direct challenges to one-party domination, and party authorities firmly assert the limits of political dissent. LPRP spokesmen invoke a litany of explanations to justify the party's monopoly of power—for example, the country is too underdeveloped and the people too little educated to permit more than one party. Further, there are too many ethnic groups, and open political participation would lead to disunity and chaos. Political stability, provided by the leadership of a single party, is said to be necessary for economic growth. The LPRP has also pointed out the corrupt multiparty system of the RLG. An abiding political reality, however, is that those who have power wish to retain it.

Restrictions on political opposition do not appear to be a serious issue among a majority of the population, although a small number of educated Laotians in intellectual, student, and bureaucratic circles have raised a few protests. Despite the toll of age and failing health among the aged Politburo members, the leadership governs without active opposition. Even when communist leaders were unceremoniously dumped in Eastern Europe, vigorously challenged in the Soviet Union, and confronted by students in China, communist leaders in Laos retained their hold as they guided the regime into the uncharted realm of reform. It is not clear why there was so little challenge to these aging leaders. They maintained a cohesion among themselves, perhaps a product of their many years as comrades in revolution, living in caves and dodging United States bombs. They may also have earned an enduring respect from party stalwarts who followed them during twenty-five years of revolution. Whether the government will encounter political opposition from a broader segment of Laotian society as it moves to a more market-oriented economy and increasingly opens its doors to Western influence remains to be seen.

Mass Media

Information and communication have been tightly controlled in Laos since the days of French colonialism. During

Main entrance of the Royal Palace, Louangphrabang, with an honor guard at rest in front of the doors in 1975. The palace is now a national museum.
Courtesy Ernest Kuhn

the years of revolutionary struggle against the RLG, the LPRP relied heavily upon radio broadcasts in the Lao and Hmong languages. Starting in 1960, with technical assistance from North Vietnam, these radio broadcasts, lasting four hours a day, reached a largely illiterate and mountain-dwelling audience. Press operations, oriented to the towns of the Mekong Valley, were conducted secretly, if at all, by the clandestine Pathet Lao. Radio broadcasters never mentioned the official name of the party until a few months before the seizure of power in December 1975.

Given such a heritage of party control, it is not surprising that the postrevolutionary operation of the mass media is a tightly controlled party monopoly without private participation. The joint party-government organization of the media is reflected in the Ministry of Information and Culture and the State Board of News Agency, Newspaper, Radio, and Television. The party maintains the more narrowly focused Propaganda and Training Committee, whose chairman is also the head of the state board. The overall goal of the press is stated as making the mass media into a link among the party, the state, and the masses.

In mid-1994 the official media consisted of the party-sponsored daily newspaper, *Xieng Pasason* (The Voice of the People), in Lao language only. Khaosan Pathet Lao (Lao News Agency), a news service of the Committee of Information, Press, Radio and Television Broadcasting, distributes daily bulletins in Lao, English, and French. The National Radio of Laos, the state-owned radio service, has a national network and seven regional stations that broadcast in Lao and tribal languages. The four government-owned Laotian television stations broadcast daily for a few hours each. Regional stations broadcast in Lao and in tribal languages.

Other media are specialized for particular audiences. For example, the daily *Vientiane Mai* (Vientiane News), covers local matters of significance to the party. The journal *Sangkhom Thoulakit* (Society and Business), in Lao, targets readers interested in Vientiane business and society. A theoretical quarterly, *Aloun Mai* (New Dawn), established in 1985, appears with some regularity to disseminate major speeches by party leaders, among other official pronouncements. An arts and letters monthly, *Vannasin*, is surviving, but the print output of various mass organizations such as the People's Revolutionary Youth

Union's *Noum Lao* (Lao Youth), a fortnightly journal, or those of the Federation of Women Unions is only intermittent. *Lao Dong* (Labor) is the fortnightly journal of the Federation of Trade Unions.

Laotian media output is sporadic and relatively insignificant compared with the impressions made by Thai television, radio, and commercials, and the daily newspapers carried into Vientiane by international travelers. Given the proximity of Thai radio and television, Thailand both remains an open window to a different economic system and provides a perspective on the news. Further, outside information and culture have proven to be too pervasive to be worth eradicating by surveillance or jamming.

So far as publishing is concerned, the Ministry of Information and Culture held a seminar in 1992, which reviewed its activities over the previous sixteen years and worked out a "plan of action" for the coming period that included "provisional regulations on publication, printing, and distribution in the Lao PDR." Reinforcement of this type of intellectual planning is achieved through periodic conferences with delegations from the official news agencies of Vietnam and Cambodia, and through visits to China. A delegation of Thai writers was also entertained.

Foreign Policy

More than most countries, Laos suffers the constraints of physical location in shaping its foreign policy. Historically, the landlocked Laotian kingdom of Lan Xang, situated along the middle stretch of the Mekong River, had to contend with the predatory kingdoms of Burma to the north, Vietnam to the east, and Siam (present-day Thailand) to the west. After these kingdoms' seventeenth-century period of ascendancy, the lowland Lao kingdom broke up into the principality of Louangphrabang (Luang Prabang), which survived by offering tribute to both east and west, and Vientiane and Champasak (Bassac), which were reduced by the end of the eighteenth century to tributaries of Siam. Vietnam then asserted suzerainty over Xiangkhoang and Khammouan to the west (see Early History, ch. 1). Thus, the foreign relations of the Laotians reflected their geography—landlocked and narrowly confined by valleys and mountains that supported a limited, overwhelmingly agricultural population exposed to more numerous and productive neighbors. In addition, the lack of national cohesion among various tribal groups subsisting in the mountains diminished the thrust of Laotian statehood.

Starting in 1893, Laotian kingdoms were subjected to the "protection" of France, which reasserted Vietnamese claims against Siam to all Laotian territories east of the Mekong River and in Xaignabouri and Champasak. This period of subordination was followed by the intervention of the United States and Thailand after 1954, succeeded by the Vietnamese communists after 1975. More recently, since 1989, foreign policy has veered back toward more independence, in relinquishing both Marxist-Leninist ideology and the special influence of Vietnam.

The geographical and demographic confines of Laos have not been the only constraints on its foreign policy. Given the weakness of the state, the international environment has largely determined both the opportunities and the limits of national strategy. The most obvious recent example is the economic collapse and political breakup of the Soviet Union and the consequent retrenchment of its economic assistance throughout Indochina. This series of events helped cause Vietnam's withdrawal of its troops from Cambodia and Laos by 1990, which encouraged Thailand to reenter Indochina as a field for business. In turn, Vietnam sought to normalize relations with China, which also withdrew its military support from Cambodia.

These policy shifts redefined the conceivable strategies for a government concerned with economic development and political leeway. The shibboleths of Marxism-Leninism and state-organized agriculture and industry were no longer appropriate. In need of economic advice and investment, Laos looked beyond Vietnam and the Soviet bloc to the United Nations Development Programme (UNDP—see Glossary) and other international organizations and to aid from a few Western nations and Japan. Besides increasing dramatically the presence of Thai traders and investors, Laos responded positively to suggestions from the International Monetary Fund (IMF—see Glossary) and advice from various United Nations (UN) agencies (see Foreign Aid, ch. 3). At the same time, it began to establish a legal foundation for the protection of business risk-takers. Thus, the road to "national uplift" no longer stretched through the alien fields of Soviet/Vietnamese collectivism; people in Mekong Valley towns could see more products in their markets, and peasants began to believe that communal agriculture was a government imposition not likely to return.

Despite the security gained during the French protectorate, Laos lost ground economically because of its slowness in absorbing European technology and in developing trade beyond its borders. By and large, it failed to tap the mineral resources beneath its mountains, except for tin, which was mined by the French, and to investigate its oil potential. It did next to nothing to build an infrastructure for international trade. Even if a railroad system and reliable roads had been built, Laos still would have confronted potential controls over its access to the sea from Thailand or Vietnam. The hydroelectric capacity of the country has, however, provided a major export that Thailand cannot afford to do without (see Industrial Output and Employment, ch. 3).

Because the rugged Annamite Mountains separate the Mekong Valley from Vietnamese population centers to the east, physical communication with the Thai nation to the west has always been easier than communication with Vietnam, even before the Friendship Bridge across the river was completed in April 1994. Thus, the threat of Thai intervention across the Mekong River cannot be treated lightly by the LPDR's military planners, particularly under dry season conditions. At the same time, the ease of Vietnamese infiltration through the Annamite Mountains was thoroughly demonstrated during the years of the Ho Chi Minh Trail, which led across southeastern Laos into the Republic of Vietnam (South Vietnam).

Basic Goals

The basic goals of foreign policy have not differed from one regime to another. National security or survival are fundamental concerns, and both the RLG and the LPDR have striven to preserve a Laotian state, even though their philosophies for organizing and serving the people differed fundamentally. In the 1990s, ideology shifted away from relentless Marxism-Leninism to "state capitalism" and single-party "democracy." Such formulations place Laos outside any rigid ideological camp and leave the national agenda open to the general promise of economic development. Officially, the government has dedicated itself to a foreign policy of peace, "independence, friendship and non-alignment," with the instrument for achieving those conditions being the LPRP.

In the 1940s, the ICP provided the most assertive challenge to colonialism. With the ending of French and United States dominance over the Laotian peoples, the communist-inspired LPRP has wrestled with the next challenge—economic and national development. The success of that undertaking and the survival of the party that has assumed it remains in the balance in the 1990s. The key to success, however, lies in developing and maintaining fruitful foreign relations.

Bureaucratic Complications

A serious need for skilled technical and economic personnel still hinders the government's dealings with international agencies and businesspeople. Thousands of the most trained and enterprising citizens fled the country after 1975. A related problem for foreign policy makers is the relative lack of young university graduates who are fluent in English and familiar with international economics. The several thousand Laotian students sent between 1975 and the late 1980s to the Soviet Union and its East European allies for several years of training often have returned without tangible or relevant skills. The hundreds of training years provided in the Soviet Union did not produce a solid base of junior diplomatic officers intellectually prepared to move easily among UN economic development agencies or in Western state capitals. In the 1990s, education in Western states has become essential for advancement. As the horizon broadened for Laotian diplomats and businesspersons, elite families in Laos sought training in United States or Australian universities. Thailand is also willing to pick up some of the demand for educational opportunity, and other Association of Southeast Asian Nations (ASEAN—see Glossary) states are also a potential source for scholarships.

Recruitment of a professional foreign service is no easier in these circumstances. Moreover, party experience seems to count more heavily than sophistication in language and diplomatic training, even in the realm of foreign relations.

Economic Factors

The retarded economic diversification and development of Laos has constrained its foreign policy opportunities and generated its dependency in succession upon France, the United States, and the Soviet bloc. Following the economic collapse of the Soviet Union, Laos has become heavily dependent upon

Grand Presidential Palace, Vientiane
Courtesy Gina Merris

the advice and contributions of UN agencies and the readiness of regional states such as Australia, Japan, and Thailand to invest in its economy. Sweden has also made significant economic contributions.

There has been a dramatic shift away from maintaining basic solidarity with a military/political bloc of mentors—first, the United States regional security alliance and then the "special relations" of Vietnamese-influenced Marxism-Leninism—to maximizing donor-recipient relations with UN agencies, state donors, and private investors. Although the universe of relations has not essentially grown, especially with Russia cutting back on its assistance, the expectation of genuine economic progress has begun to creep into economic dealings with outsiders. By moving resolutely and responding to Thai and Chinese gestures, Laos has broadened its range of donors, trading partners, and investors. The presence of Thai traders and investors has increased dramatically.

The degree to which Laos has depended upon outside donors and investors, and which ones, has been a function not only of need but also of political choice, a dependence that was carefully controlled during Kaysone Phomvihan's tutorship. Without his pervasive leadership, foreign economic relations might have fallen victim to internal rivalries between ministries and factions within the party.

Through legislation enacted by the National Assembly in 1991 of a basic criminal and investment code and the creation of a judiciary, however, Laos opened its doors wider to serious investors. In addition, the stabilization of foreign exchange rates and inflation signaled major steps toward engaging constructively with countries outside the ideological blocs within which it used to confine itself. The new institutions require a few years of serious testing, but a Burma-like return to stagnation seems unlikely, even with Kaysone's departure from the helm. The tantalizing images of Thailand's growth and prosperity, conveyed by television along the Mekong border, and increasingly easier travel across the river—in both directions— make the economic policy of openness seem all but irreversible.

Bilateral Relations

Relations with Vietnam

Relations with Vietnam had secretly set the strategy for the LPRP during the struggle to achieve full power, and the "sudden" opportunity to establish the LPDR in 1975 left no leeway to consider foreign policy alignments other than a continuation of the "special relations" with Vietnam. The relationship cultivated in the revolutionary stage predisposed Laos to Indochinese solidarity in the reconstruction and "socialist construction" phases and all but ensured that relations or alignments with China and Thailand would be wary and potentially unfriendly. Further, the LPRP, unlike the Cambodian communists under Pol Pot, was far too accustomed to accepting Vietnamese advice to consider striking out on its own. The final seizure of power by the hitherto secret LPRP in 1975 brought both a public acknowledgment of the previously hidden North Vietnamese guidance of the party and genuine expressions of gratitude by the LPRP to its Vietnamese partners. The challenge facing the ruling group—the construction of a socialist society—was seen as a natural extension of past collaboration with North Vietnam. The revolution was simply entering a new phase in 1975, and the LPRP leaders congratulated themselves upon ousting the "imperialists" and looked forward to advice and economic as well as military support, which was not available from any neighbor or counterrevolutionary state.

LPRP leaders were accustomed to discussing policies as well as studying doctrine in Hanoi. They formalized governmental contacts with their mentors at biannual meetings of the foreign ministers of Cambodia, Laos, and Vietnam starting in 1980 and through the joint Vietnam-Laos Cooperative Commission, which met annually to review progress of various projects. Other levels of cooperation between Laos and Vietnam existed, for example, party-to-party meetings and province-to-province exchanges, as well as mass organizations for youths and women. Meetings of the commission were held regularly.

The primary channels for Vietnam's influence in Laos, however, were the LPRP and the LPA (see Structure and Administration of the Armed Forces, ch. 5). In the LPRP, long-standing collaboration and consultation at the very top made special committees unnecessary, whereas in the LPA, the Vietnamese advisers, instructors, and troops on station constituted a pervasive, inescapable influence, even though they scrupulously avoided public exposure by sticking to their designated base areas. Cooperation in the military field was probably the most extensive, with logistics, training, and communications largely supplied by Vietnam throughout the 1970s and 1980s (heavy ordnance and aircraft were provided by the Soviet Union).

The phrase "special relations" came into general use by both parties after 1976, and in July 1977, the signing of the twenty-five-year Lao-Vietnamese Treaty of Friendship and Cooperation legitimized the stationing of Vietnamese army troops in Laos for its protection against hostile or counterrevolutionary neighbors. Another element of cooperation involved hundreds of Vietnamese advisers who mentored their Laotian counterparts in virtually all the ministries in Vientiane. Hundreds of LPRP stalwarts and technicians studied in institutes of Marxism-Leninism or technical schools in Hanoi.

The resources that Vietnam was able to bestow upon its revolutionary partner were severely limited by the physical destruction of war and the deadening orthodoxy of its economic structures and policies. It could, however, put in a good word for its Laotian apprentices with the Soviet Union, which in turn could recommend economic assistance projects to its East European satellite states. Yet, Vietnam's influence on Laos was determined by economic assistance and ideology as well as by geographical and historical proximity. The two nations fit together, as the leaders liked to say, "like lips and teeth." Vietnam provided landlocked Laos a route to the sea, and the mountainous region of eastern Laos provided Vietnam a forward strategic position for challenging Thai hegemony in the Mekong Valley.

During the 1980s, Vietnam's regional opponents attributed to it a neocolonial ambition to create an "Indochina Federation." This phrase can be found in early pronouncements of the ICP in its struggle against the French colonial structures in Indochina. The charge, exaggerated as it was, lost its currency once Vietnam withdrew its troops from Cambodia in 1989 and subsequently from Laos. Laos's dependence on Vietnam since 1975 could then be perceived as a natural extension of their collaboration and solidarity in revolution rather than as domination by Vietnam.

With the departure of Vietnamese military forces—except for some construction engineers—and the passing of most senior Vietnamese revolutionary partners, the magnetism of the special relationship lost its grip. Further, Vietnam was never able to muster large-scale economic aid programs. It launched only 200 assistance projects between 1975 and 1985, whereas the Soviet Union generated considerably more in the way of contributions. In 1992 the long-standing Vietnamese ambassador to Laos, a veteran of fourteen years' service, characterized the relationship as composed "d'amitié et de coopération multiforme entre les pays" (of friendship and diverse cooperation between the two countries). This pronouncement was far less compelling than the "objective law of existence and development" formulation sometimes expressed in the past.

Although Vietnam's historical record of leadership in the revolution and its military power and proximity will not cease to exist, Laos struck out ahead of Vietnam with its New Economic Mechanism to introduce market mechanisms into its economy. In so doing, Laos has opened the door to rapprochement with Thailand and China at some expense to its special dependence on Vietnam. Laos might have reached the same

*One of the royal elephants in
a New Year's parade in
Louangphrabang in 1975,
ridden by its Lao Theung
handler
Courtesy Ernest Kuhn*

point of normalization in following Vietnam's economic and diplomatic change, but by moving ahead resolutely and responding to Thai and Chinese gestures, Laos has broadened its range of donors, trading partners, and investors independent of Vietnam's attempts to accomplish the same goal. Thus, Vietnam remains in the shadows as a mentor and emergency ally, and the tutelage of Laos has shifted dramatically to development banks and international entrepreneurs.

Relations with Thailand

In some respects, Thailand can be seen as a greater threat to the country's independence than Vietnam because of its closer cultural affinity (Theravada Buddhism—see Glossary), its easier access, and its control over the railroad and highway routes to the sea. The Mekong River, which both sides have an interest in making a "river of true peace and friendship"—as their respective prime ministers called for in 1976—also provides a north-south artery during the rainy season.

Relations with Thailand have been uneven. An alarming patrol boat shooting incident occurred in 1980, but this brief encounter was overshadowed by the border disputes and military clashes of 1984 and 1987 in Xaignabouri Province west of the Mekong. These conflicts originated in rival claims to forest

247

resources based on maps from the early days of the French protectorate.

The determination in 1988 of Thai prime minister Chatichai Choonhaven to open up the Indochina market abruptly turned a deadly conflict into a wave of goodwill gestures and business ventures. Kaysone paid an official visit to Bangkok in 1989, his first since the brief 1979 rapprochement with Prime Minister General Kriangsak Chomanand. These gestures were followed by official visits by Princess Maha Chakkri in March 1990 and Crown Prince Maha Wachirolongkon in June 1992. An irony of this process of reacquaintance was the dropping from the Politburo in 1992 of Army Chief of Staff General Sisavat Keobounphan, who had dealt closely and effectively with the Thai military command in restoring neighborly relations, but who apparently was considered by his party colleagues to have indulged in personal gains. Indeed, this corruption of a senior party leader symbolizes the fear among some Laotian leaders that Thailand, with its materialism and business strength and greed, "wants to eat us."

Two political issues slowed rapprochement during the 1980s: first, the continuing issue of Laotian migrants and refugees remaining in temporary camps—whom Thailand had no desire to accept as immigrants—and second, Laotian and Hmong resistance groups who used the camps as a base. The Hmong constituted half of the camp dwellers and were expected to avoid repatriation the longest, out of fear of reprisal and hope for national autonomy. Thailand announced in July 1992, however, that Laotian refugees who have not returned home or found third-country resettlement by 1995 will be classified as illegal immigrants and face deportation.

In the first few years of rapprochement, Thai businesspersons have not threatened to buy up long-term economic opportunities in Laos because they seem to seek shorter-term commercial ventures. Yet the possibility of heavy interdependence generated by Thai investors remains. A Thai business presence in Laos will probably depend on the continuing demonstration of Laos's independence from Vietnam.

The persistence of a resistance movement since 1975 is attributable to permissive policies on the part of Thailand on behalf of their former Laotian cohorts. With the demise of the Cold War, the motivation to harass the LPDR and its Vietnamese military partners has dwindled. The Ministry of Foreign

Affairs will continue to press the Thai military command to live up to its March 1991 agreement to disarm rebels and discourage Laotian sabotage operations. At the same time, Thailand has made clear its unwillingness to assimilate Hmong refugees.

The threat of a return of Vietnamese troops remains as a cautionary note to the Thai military, who prefer to keep Laos as a buffer rather than a military line of contact with the Vietnamese. The Friendship Bridge should open the interior to more foreign trucking and commerce and more openly reveal any foreign military presence in Laos.

The exodus of tens of thousands of middle-class lowland Lao and mountain dwelling Hmong across the Mekong into Thailand created a tense border that Thailand preferred to close off to commerce of any kind. Future Laotian-Thai relations, however, have a visible path toward mutually beneficial trade and investment, which need not be obscured by refugees or economic migrants, by one-sided economic dealings of an exploitative kind, or by inflamed border disputes. An improved trade relationship has been achieved in spite of past feelings of superiority or victimization, and growing interdependence may make the path easier to follow.

Relations with China

Relations with China have traditionally consisted of trade and aid, largely in road construction in the northern provinces of Laos, without directly challenging the interests of Thailand or Vietnam in the central and southern regions. However, Vietnam's invasion of Cambodia in December 1978 to unseat then prime minister Pol Pot, which provoked China into a limited invasion of Vietnam—approximately nineteen kilometers deep—to "teach Vietnam a lesson," put Laos in a dangerous bind. It did not want to further provoke China, but it was not able to oppose its special partner, Vietnam. The Laotian leadership survived the dilemma by making slightly delayed pronouncements in support of Vietnam after some intraparty debate and by sharply reducing diplomatic relations with China to the chargé d'affaires level—without a full break. The low point in Sino-Laotian relations came in 1979, with reports of Chinese assistance and training of Hmong resistance forces under General Vang Pao in China's Yunnan Province (see Internal Threats and Resistance Movements, ch. 5).

This hostile relationship gradually softened, however, and in 1989 Prime Minister Kaysone paid a state visit to Beijing. In 1991 Kaysone chose to spend his vacation in China rather than make his customary visit to the Soviet Union. Diplomatic and party-to-party relations were normalized in 1989. Trade expanded from the local sale of consumer goods to the granting of eleven investment licenses in 1991—including an automotive assembly plant. Following the establishment of the Laotian-Chinese Joint Border Committee in 1991, meetings held during 1992 resulted in an agreement delineating their common border. China's commercial investments and trade with Laos expanded quietly, but not dramatically, in 1993 and early 1994.

Unlike its other neighbors, China has not historically dominated the Laotians. In the final analysis, China represents the most powerful remaining communist state to which Laos might turn for support against Thai or Vietnamese hegemony.

Relations with the Soviet Union

The Soviet Union and Soviet-bloc involvement with Laos originated as a secondary element in the East-West contest over the communist-led revolution in Vietnam and in the Sino-Soviet rivalry that this contest exacerbated. Even though the Laos subtheater was formally neutralized by the Geneva Agreement of 1962, the superpower involvement in Laos continued in the form of military supplies, advice, and diplomatic and propaganda support to the opposing sides up to the end of the war. The succeeding period of coalition government in Vientiane lasted fewer than two years and left the Soviets not only enjoying the prestige of supporting the winning party—the Marxist-Leninist LPRP, which by then had publicly revealed itself—but also holding the bag of vast economic development needs in a nation losing its most skilled persons across the border to the West. The Soviet Union had helped its friends prevail over the opponents of the revolution, but the Marxist-Leninist model for building up an overwhelmingly agricultural nation was not effective with the complaisant Lao peasantry.

Since 1989, aid from the Soviet Union and its successor states—which once accounted for more than half the aid to Laos and approximately 1,500 technicians and advisers—has slowly dwindled. The memorial to Soviet efforts in Laos lies in dozens of projects such as bridges, roads, airports, hospitals, and broadcast facilities; in tons of military equipment, includ-

Boats on the Mekong River, Louangphrabang
Courtesy Gina Merris

ing MiG jet fighters and air transports; and in the hundreds of students with a faltering command of the Russian language, some of whom are trained for such jobs as railroad operator or circus clown, for which Laos has no market.

The Laotian leadership has resolutely sought to take up the slack among its previous bilateral and multilateral donors. By 1990 bilateral external assistance disbursed by Russia was down to 36 percent of the total, from a previous 60 percent; Hungary, the German Democratic Republic (East Germany), Mongolia, and Vietnam contributed a mere 3.7 percent. The number of student fellowships to the Soviet Union—usually 300 per year—decreased dramatically. The downward spiral continued as the Russians shifted their dwindling influence in the region to cooperation with the five permanent members of the UN in settling the war in Cambodia. And, in a further move away from dependence, the coming generation of national leaders was eager to obtain useful education in the West for their children, even if they could still get by with Vietnamese and French.

Relations with the United States

Relations with the United States suffered some of the same

cutbacks as those experienced by Vietnam and Cambodia after the United States withdrawal from Indochina in 1973, but there were important differences. After 1975 Laos provided the United States the only official window to its former enemy states in Indochina. The United States was also willing to treat all departing Laotians as political refugees entitled to asylum, with hopes that third countries might eventually accept them for resettlement. And, in spite of the full economic and diplomatic embargo imposed by the United States on Vietnam and Cambodia in 1975, United States diplomatic relations with Laos facilitated such occasional humanitarian aid projects as food and prosthetics. In this manner, the door to full diplomatic relations was kept ajar.

Diplomatic relations with the United States were never broken, even though the United States Agency for International Development (AID) and the United States Information Agency (USIA) both withdrew, under harassment, and diplomatic representation in Vientiane and in Washington was reduced to the level of chargé d'affaires, with a limit of twelve persons and no military attachés. Relations eventually were reciprocally restored to the ambassadorial level in the summer of 1992.

A tentative agreement to allow United States Peace Corps personnel in Laos fell through in the spring of 1992. The admission of Peace Corps workers was initially approved but then rejected by the Ministry of Foreign Affairs. Apparently some party leaders feared that the volunteers might have a subversive impact on the Laotians, especially if deployed outside Vientiane. As of 1993, a country agreement was on the table, and the Peace Corps remained interested in sending volunteers but was waiting for Laos to initiate a program.

Other United States agencies run small programs in Laos. In 1992 AID made a US$1.3 million grant for a prosthetics project. Because AID does not have an office in Laos, the program is administered from AID's office in Bangkok. The United States Information Service, the overseas branch office of the USIA, reopened a one-officer post in Vientiane in October 1992. The post concentrates on supporting English-language teaching activities and publications, press activities, and cultural and educational exchanges. Two Laotian Fulbright grantees were in the United States in 1993.

Since the establishment of the LPDR, Laos and the United States have cooperated in varying degrees on two major issues of high priority to the United States. One is the search for information on the more than 500 United States servicemen listed as missing in action (MIA) in Laos (see The Origins of the Prisoner of War/Missing in Action Question, ch. 1; Relations with the United States, ch. 5). This problem has proved to be a surprisingly durable issue, which delayed an otherwise uncomplicated and mutually beneficial rapprochement between the two countries. Starting in 1985, Laos treated the MIA issue seriously enough to undertake joint searches of known wartime crash sites of United States aircraft. However, the United States Senate Select Committee on Prisoner of War/MIA Affairs concluded in January 1993 that "The current leaders of Laos, who are the successors to the Pathet Lao forces that contended for power during the war, almost certainly have some information concerning missing Americans that they have not yet shared." Further cooperation has brightened the atmosphere of Laos-United States relations, even though a full accounting of United States military personnel lost in the Laos theater of war can probably never be achieved.

The second long-standing issue is the production and export of opium. In April 1993, Laos received a national interest certification on the issue of cooperation in counternarcotics activities. Opium traffic out of Laos is a tangible irritant to relations, however, particularly because of the suspicion that high-ranking Laotian officials, especially those in the military, are involved in protecting the trade. The United States Drug Enforcement Administration worked with the LPDR to maintain Laos's eligibility—despite its opium trade—as a potential United States aid recipient. In 1990 an economic aid project worth US$8.7 million was provided to help the hill tribes that grow poppies turn to substitute crops. Thus, the legal barriers to expanding Laos-United States consultation and commerce were essentially removed. Yet most-favored-nation treatment for imports such as coffee from Laos might conceivably have to await the full release of the last of the political prisoners held in the mountainous eastern provinces since 1975.

An irritant in Laos-United States relations was the United States charge in 1981 that Laos had engaged in aerial spraying with deadly toxins—yellow rain—against Hmong villages. The United States government adopted the position that chemical weapons were used in Laos in the late 1970s through 1983. Such reports lost credibility after 1984, however, when the

United States stationed scientific personnel in Bangkok to test any incoming evidence, which never appeared.

Capitalist Donor States

Laotian leaders have increased their visibility among capitalist nations. A small coterie of dedicated government officials, including President Kaysone, has taken advantage of a sympathetic attitude toward Laos within the key international governmental organizations. Similarly, the UN, Australia, and Japan saw an opportunity in the opening of Laos. The Australian-funded Friendship Bridge over the Mekong River at Nong Khai, Thailand, and the generation of 280 foreign investment ventures from twenty-four countries during 1988–92 testify to creative communication in proper channels. Germany and France each supplied approximately US$6 million of aid in 1990.

Australia, Japan, and Sweden have established significant economic aid relationships with Laos. In 1992 the Laos Roundtable for bilateral aid and pledges recorded approximately US$134.62 million for eight bilateral projects led by Australia, Japan, and Sweden. France has also begun to increase its aid to Laos, beginning with projects worth approximately US$900,000 in 1989 and increasing to approximately US$5.2 million in 1993.

Australia has established itself as a special friend, even though not in a "special relationship" with Laos. The Friendship Bridge, authorized in October 1991 and opened in April 1994, is expected to stimulate trade and stable relations between Laos and its neighbors. Australia has sustained a generosity toward Laos that put it in first place among aid-pledging nations in March 1992, even though Australian political interests in the nation are far from vital. In addition to its pledge of US$45 million in aid in 1992, Australia is hosting more than 100 Laotian university students.

Japan is also responding to the economic needs of Laos, providing almost 12 percent of disbursed bilateral aid in 1990. In 1992 Japan made the third largest pledge of bilateral economic assistance at an aid-pledging conference of the UNDP in Geneva. Among the projects Japanese assistance has provided are buses and a bus terminal in Vientiane and health and food production projects. The somewhat modest Japanese investments in Laos were likely raised by Kaysone and Nouhak dur-

*Man transporting bamboo; posters, removed around 1990, proclaim the
New Economic Mechanism and urge a stop to United States bombing.*
Courtesy Gina Merris

ing their historic state visits to Japan in November 1989 and
January 1992, respectively. Kaysone's trip to Tokyo was his first
to an industrialized capitalist state, and it preceded by a month
a similar visit to France.

Multilateral Donors

The international governmental organizations active in Laos
constitute a distinguished list, and, in a sense, Laos has become
one of their star pupils. The World Bank (see Glossary), IMF,
UNDP, and Asian Development Bank (see Glossary) work
closely with the small coterie of economic planners within Laos
and can point to notable economic progress in the 1990s as a
result of the application of their advice. The national currency,
the kip, has remained stable at its official rate since 1990, foreign reserves have grown, and inflation has fallen dramatically.
The party leadership undertook tough measures such as reducing government employment, encouraging privatization, and
ending special subsidies, in line with advice from international
advisers. The resident IMF representative received private telephone calls from the president in search of economic counsel.
In the early 1990s, an unusual level of satisfaction with the Laotian leadership's willingness to receive economic advice from

experts could be found among international governmental organizations' personnel in Laos.

In 1990 the UNDP coordinated approximately US$12.3 million in economic assistance from various UN financial and development agencies, and thirteen international governmental organizations disbursed approximately US$4.1 million (see Foreign Aid, ch. 3). The most active among these were the UNHCR, the United Nations Children's Fund (UNICEF—see Glossary), the UN Drug Control Program, and the Food and Agriculture Organization. In March 1992, the Laos Roundtable for bilateral aid and pledges recorded approximately US$472 million in project aid from international governmental organizations. In 1992 and 1993, the Asian Development Bank was funding such projects as road construction, hydropower, and water supply.

Nongovernmental organizations have tried to make an impact on Laos, particularly in the lives of villagers outside the privileged Mekong Valley towns adjacent to prospering Thailand. Twenty-two such organizations disbursed approximately US$3.259 million in 1990, with the American Friends Service Committee (Quakers) and the Mennonite Central Committee (Mennonites) contributing approximately 15 percent and 10 percent of the total, respectively, and concentrating on health and agricultural programs. From 1990 to 1993, the American Friends Service Committee budgeted slightly more than US$2.3 million for programs in Laos. These included small-scale irrigation and rice-based integrated farming system projects, women's development and veterinary vaccination programs, and emergency relief projects that include assisting internally-displaced communities. The Mennonite Central Committee contributed approximately US$1.2 million during the 1990–93 period for programs in agriculture and integrated development, emergency assistance, education, health, and social services, economic and technical assistance, and "material resources in kind."

Constraints on foreign policy nonetheless remain in the ideological commitment, pronounced since 1975, to the socialist road to social welfare, mapped out exclusively by the party. This theoretical baggage, however, has not precluded generous foreign aid from Australia, Japan, and Sweden, or Laos's attendance at conferences of the Nonaligned Movement (see Glossary). The country's obtaining of observer status in ASEAN in

1992 also was constructive and points toward possible membership in that organization before the end of the century. But the punitive seminar camps and the unrecorded death of the sequestered former King Savang Vatthana have left a negative impression on democratic nations that Laos cannot afford to disregard or exacerbate as it seeks investors and donors among the capitalist states.

In the early 1990s, the possibility that a domineering neighbor might arise from the competing rivalries of the regional states seemed unlikely, and Laos's policy of encouraging the economic engagement of many states in its economy appeared to suit the circumstances. That Thailand, Vietnam, or China would consider aligning with Laos, thereby creating tension with their neighbors, also seemed unlikely. It was easier to foresee the gradual assimilation of Laos into ASEAN and the regional states continuing to compete for Laos's dormant and modest market.

*   *   *

Few books dealing exclusively with contemporary Laos have been published since the establishment of the LPDR in 1975. Among those with political analyses are MacAlister Brown and Joseph J. Zasloff's *Apprentice Revolutionaries: The Communist Movement in Laos, 1930–1985*, which includes examinations of the LPDR's leadership and ruling party, political institutions and policies, economic policies and political doctrine, social politics, and external relations. A more recent volume is *Laos: Beyond the Revolution*, edited by Zasloff and Leonard Unger, which contains essays on politics, economics, society, external relations, and United States policy toward Laos. Two books written or edited by the Australian scholar Martin Stuart-Fox are also useful: *Contemporary Laos: Studies in the Politics and Society of the Lao People's Democratic Republic* has essays on various subjects by international experts, and *Laos: Politics, Economics and Society* provides a succinct, insightful account of the social, political, and economic systems of the country and its domestic and foreign policies.

For the reader who wishes information in English about politics in Laos since 1975, the following periodicals with occasional articles on Laos are helpful: *Asian Survey, Current History, Southeast Asian Affairs,* and *Indochina Issues.* The best journalistic coverage of Laos is found in the weekly *Far Eastern Economic Review,* and its annual *Asia Yearbook.* The United States government provides two valuable sources of translations from the Lao media: the Foreign Broadcast Information Service's *Daily Report: East Asia,* and the Joint Publications Research Service's *Report: East Asia/Southeast Asia.* Summaries of important items on Laos appearing in these two publications are found in the quarterly *Indochina Chronology.* (For further information and complete citations, see Bibliography.)

Chapter 5. National Security

The Anousavari, on Lan Xang Avenue in Vientiane, built to commemorate those who died in the prerevolutionary wars, was begun in the early 1960s and completed in 1969.

LAOS HAS HISTORICALLY FACED a number of unique problems in national defense and internal security, stemming from its central position in mainland Southeast Asia and its historically stronger neighbors. This continued to be true after the Phak Pasason Pativat Lao (Lao People's Revolutionary Party—LPRP; see Glossary) came to power and proclaimed the Lao People's Democratic Republic (LPDR, or Laos) in December 1975. By mid-1994, however, Laos had succeeded in stabilizing its relations with its neighbors, so it faced no immediate foreign threat and only a small continuing internal threat.

Laos is geopolitically vulnerable, a landlocked nation surrounded by more powerful neighbors. Its closest foreign ally has been Vietnam, with whom it signed a twenty-five-year mutual security treaty in July 1977. Laos is also on close terms with China, whose long-term interest in Laos is to limit Vietnam's ambitions in Southeast Asia while sharing with Hanoi and Vientiane (Viangchan) a common aim in maintaining Marxist-Leninist single-party regimes in power. In view of the strong presence of senior military officers in the top ranks of the party and government, it is not surprising that the country maintains close ties with the military-controlled State Law and Order Restoration Council in Burma. Relations are also close with the royal government of war-torn Cambodia. With Thailand, relations have changed over the years. Prior to 1975, Thailand saw Laos as a buffer against an expansionist Vietnam, but by 1994 Thailand looked upon Laos as the likeliest place for commercial expansion of its own. The country shares with Burma and Thailand possession of the Golden Triangle, the area where a significant portion of the world's heroin traffic originates.

Laos is also vulnerable because its small population—estimated at approximately 4.7 million people as of July 1994—limits its ability to deter foreign intervention in the event of a crisis. Furthermore, the significant population of ethnic minorities—about 50 percent of the total—is always a potential factor for instability. In 1994 ethnic minorities continued to suffer discrimination in terms of their representation in the country's institutions and their access to government services, although to what extent this discrimination feeds political and cultural tension vis-à-vis the government in Vientiane is speculative. The situation is complicated by the fact that although 1.5 million ethnic Lao reside in Laos, ten times that number live in northeastern Thailand. Similarly, Hmong (see Glossary) and Mien (Yao) tribes live in southern China, and Hmong and many tribal mountain Tai reside in northwestern Vietnam.

Other factors contribute to the vulnerability of Laos. The underdeveloped state of the economy and the lack of adequate means of transportation and communication encourage regionalism, which facilitates insurgent movements against the government. Additionally, the mountains and jungles of Laos provide an ideal environment for guerrilla warfare because the terrain and lack of infrastructure inhibit the concentration of military forces to counter guerrilla action. Such forces, moreover, expose themselves to ambush in narrow mountain defiles if guerrillas control the surrounding high ground. There are few places in Laos where a conventional army does not risk a siege such as that of Dien Bien Phu in 1954. If the insurgents have bases outside permeable borders, they are virtually secure from pursuit and are able to mount raids with impunity.

The Armed Forces

The Lao People's Army (LPA—see Glossary), the armed forces of the country, is the product of the successful transition from a guerrilla army in the 1950s and 1960s to a conventional military organization with three branches of service (ground, air, and water). The term "liberation" was dropped from the nomenclature of the Lao People's Liberation Army (LPLA—see Glossary) after the army was restructured in 1976.

Historical Background

Historically, Laos was subject to the will of its stronger neighbors, enforced by military means. By force of circumstances in warding off repeated foreign invasions, Laotians developed battle skills using elephants and compiled a history full of warlike deeds. Lan Xang, or the Kingdom of the Million Elephants, the first state in the recorded history of Laos, maintained a standing army of 150,000 men (see The Founding of Lan Xang, ch. 1). Regiments included cavalry, infantry, and an elephant corps. Prince Fa Ngum, Lan Xang's founder, redeveloped the old Mongol model of an army composed of units of 10,000, which gave rise to the name of the successive reign, Sam Sen Thai, or 10,000 Thai. The army's strength enabled Fa Ngum to expand Lan Xang's borders to the western escarpment of the Khorat Plateau, the crest of the Annamite Chain in the east, and the northern edge of Khmer and Cham civilizations in the south. To the north and east especially, however, mountain tribes resisted absorption and maintained a degree of independence.

Following Fa Ngum's death, struggles with Siamese and Burmese states in which his successors became embroiled sapped the strength of the army and led to the decline and eventual splitting up of Lan Xang. In 1778 the capital of the Vientiane kingdom was attacked and destroyed for the first time by a Siamese army. By the 1820s, Laos had reestablished sovereignty over its own borders, enough so that the king of Vientiane launched a disastrous military expedition against Siam (present-day Thailand). Laotian forces were overwhelmed by the superior firepower and strategy of the Siamese army, which attacked and destroyed Vientiane for a second time in 1828.

The Colonial Era

Following the destruction of Vientiane, Laotian affairs were dominated militarily by Siam, although the Vietnamese also involved themselves over the mountains (see Developments in the Nineteenth Century, ch. 1). It was not until 1884, when France guaranteed Annam the integrity of its territorial domain, that Siamese hegemony over the left bank of the Mekong encountered a new challenge. Using Annam's claims to Laotian territories as a diplomatic pretext, France forced Siam to renounce all claims to territory east of the Mekong and even to islands in the river by successive treaties between 1893 and 1907.

To preserve order in the new administrative structure and to reinforce their security forces, which up to the twentieth century consisted largely of Vietnamese militia, the French formed local Laotian police and military constabulary units and provided them with some modern weapons, equipment, and rudimentary training. The Laotian units, whose salaries were paid for by the royal house of Louangphrabang (Luang Prabang), pledged allegiance to the monarchy, establishing a military tradition that ended only in 1975.

Between 1901 and 1907, France's colonial forces in Laos directed their attention to putting down a group of southern mountain Mon-Khmer rebels who had become angered over France's suppressing their customary slave-trading activities. Bandits from China's Yunnan Province also kept the colonial army occupied in the north between 1914 and 1916. The army's final major action—from 1919 to 1921—was led by Pa Chai against the Hmong, who were conducting raids on the Lao and other groups in Houaphan and Xiangkhoang provinces with the aim of expelling the French and establishing an independent Hmong kingdom.

The first entirely Laotian military unit was formed by the French in 1941 and was known as the First Battalion of Chasseurs Laotiens (light infantry). It was used for internal security and did not see action until after the Japanese *coup de force* of March 9, 1945, when Japan occupied Laos. The unit then went into the mountains, supplied and commanded by Free French agents who had received special jungle training in camps in India and who had parachuted into Laos beginning in December 1944 with the aim of creating a resistance network.

Meanwhile, taking advantage of the temporary absence of French authority in the towns, the Lao Issara (Free Laos—see Glossary) government armed itself to defend the Laotian independence it claimed on behalf of the people (see World War II and After, ch. 1). For the most part, effective components of the Lao Issara armed forces consisted of Vietnamese residents of the towns of Laos, who either had received weapons given them by the surrendering Japanese troops—sold by the Chinese Nationalist soldiers who occupied northern Laos under the 1945 Potsdam Conference agreements—or looted from French arsenals. In the Battle of Thakhek (Khammouan) in March 1946, which decided the issue of sovereignty in Laos in favor of the French, the Lao Issara used mortars and light machine guns against French armored vehicles and planes. One of the main preoccupations of the members of the Lao Issara government exiled in Bangkok between 1946 and 1949 was to procure weapons to fight back against the French.

French efforts to train and expand the Royal Lao Army continued during the First Indochina War (1946–54), by which time Laos had a standing army of 15,000 troops (see The Coming of Independence, ch. 1). The French knew the lightly equipped Royal Lao Army was not in a position to defend Laos against Viet Minh (see Glossary) regular forces formed by General Vo Nguyen Giap. To counter Viet Minh invasions of

Laos in 1953 and 1954, the French Union High Command diverted regular colonial units from the Democratic Republic of Vietnam (North Vietnam) into Laos; Giap exploited this weakness to disperse French Union forces. The French originally picked Dien Bien Phu as the site of a major strong point because it blocked a main invasion route into Laos, which they felt they had to defend at all costs in order to preserve their credibility with the king of Louangphrabang, who sought France's protection. Some of the most effective fighters against the Viet Minh were Hmong from Xiangkhoang whom the French recruited and formed into guerrilla units; one of these units, under a sergeant named Vang Pao, was on the march to Dien Bien Phu when the garrison fell in May 1954.

Under the terms of the armistice signed at the Geneva Conference on Indochina on July 20, 1954, by the French Union High Command and the Viet Minh, all Viet Minh troops had to withdraw from Laos within 120 days. Laos was prohibited from having foreign military bases or personnel on its soil and from joining any military alliance. The agreements provided for the regrouping of Pathet Lao (Lao Nation—see Glossary) guerrillas in the provinces of Houaphan and Phôngsali and their integration into the Royal Lao Army. The Pathet Lao, however, taking advantage of their easy access across the border to North Vietnam, immediately began to expand their guerrilla army, the first unit of which, the Latsavong detachment, had been formed in 1949 by Kaysone Phomvihan.

The Royal Lao Army

With the end of the war, Laos was no longer under the French Union but entirely sovereign. The country was divided into five military regions. The chain of command of the Royal Lao Army was placed under the Ministry of Defense in Vientiane.

To meet the threat represented by the Pathet Lao, the Royal Lao Army depended on a small French military training mission, headed by a general officer, an exceptional arrangement permitted under the Geneva agreement. Military organization and tactical training reflected French traditions. Most of the equipment was of United States origin, however, because early in the First Indochina War, the United States had been supplying the French with war matériel ranging from guns to aircraft. A small United States legation in Vientiane kept Washington informed about the status of the Royal Lao Army. There was real concern that Laotians were not maintaining their equipment properly and that much of it was becoming useless under the tropical sun and rain. The question also arose of who was to pay the salaries of the Royal Lao Army because France was no longer responsible for Laos's finances.

It seemed evident to the legation that only United States personnel in Laos could ensure that the Royal Lao Army was capable of meeting the threat posed by the Pathet Lao backed by North Vietnam. To circumvent the prohibition against foreign military personnel imposed by the 1954 Geneva agreement—which the United States had pledged to honor—the Department of Defense in December 1955 established a disguised military mission in Laos called the Programs Evaluation Office (PEO). The PEO worked under the cover of the civilian aid mission and was staffed by military personnel and headed by a general officer who wore civilian clothes. Over the 1955–61 period, the PEO gradually supplanted the French military mission in providing equipment and training to the Royal Lao Army. With increasing numbers of Laotian officers receiving training in Thailand and at staff schools in the United States, there was a perception that the French military mission in Laos was a relic of colonialism. By 1959 the PEO had more than 100 members on its staff, and the United States was paying the entire cost of the Royal Lao Army's salaries.

The prohibition against joining any military alliance prevented Laos from joining the Southeast Asia Treaty Organization (SEATO—see Glossary), formed by Australia, Britain, France, New Zealand, Pakistan, the Philippines, Thailand, and the United States in September 1954. A protocol to the treaty, however, designated Laos as a country to which its mutual security provisions would apply in the event it became the victim of aggression. When fighting broke out along Laos's border with North Vietnam in July–September 1959 following the collapse of efforts to integrate two battalions of Pathet Lao into the Royal Lao Army, the Royal Lao Government (RLG) wanted to appeal to SEATO for help. The RLG was dissuaded from doing so by the United States, which felt that such an appeal risked involving United States troops in combat in Laos. The nature of the fighting—by guerrillas belonging to ethnic tribes that lived on both sides of the border—made the question of aggression ambiguous. Similarly, in January 1961, when the RLG proposed appealing to SEATO to counter North Viet-

Pathet Lao honor guard at Wat Ong Teu, Vientiane, in November 1974, participating in an annual ceremony during which the ranking officials of Laos pay homage to the king
Courtesy Ernest Kuhn

nam's intervention on behalf of the Pathet Lao and Kong Le, it was discouraged from doing so by the United States.

Kong Le's coup d'état on August 9, 1960, threatened to split the army between Kong Le's Lao Neutralist Revolutionary Organization—known as the Neutralists, whose troops' unofficial name was the Neutralist Armed Forces—and the rest of the army under General Phoumi Nosavan, the former minister of defense (see The Attempt to Restore Neutrality, ch. 1). PEO headquarters in Vientiane became inactive because United States diplomats were instructed to find a way to isolate the rebellious paratrooper. Finally, aid was cut off. Meanwhile, the PEO branch office in Savannakhét—Phoumi's headquarters—continued to supply and pay Phoumi's troops. After Phoumi captured Vientiane, the Neutralists were compelled—for their survival—to enter into an alliance with the Pathet Lao and their North Vietnamese backers, on whom they thereafter depended for supplies.

In April 1961, the PEO was upgraded to a Military Assistance Advisory Group (MAAG), and its members were allowed to wear uniforms. The MAAG was withdrawn in 1962 under the terms of the Geneva Agreement, which was supposed to neutralize Laos (see International Pressure and the Advent of the Second Coalition, ch. 1). Because the North Vietnamese did not respect the withdrawal requirement, however, the United States stepped up military aid to the RLG, but avoided sending ground troops into Laos, which would have violated the agreement.

As part of this effort, United States Central Intelligence Agency (CIA) personnel operating from a base at Udon Thani, Thailand, took over the support of 30,000 to 36,000 irregulars, including Hmong guerrillas who bore the brunt of the fighting in northern Laos. A CIA-chartered airline, Air America, dropped rice and ammunition from its C–46s and C–47s to isolated Hmong outposts, which were sometimes behind enemy lines. A variety of short-takeoff-and-landing aircraft used dirt airstrips carved out of the jungle by the Hmong. The irregulars were instrumental in helping to rescue a large number of United States airmen who were shot down over Laos. By this time, the Hmong leader Vang Pao had risen to the rank of general in the Royal Lao Army and commanded the Second Military Region.

In October 1964, in response to an offensive by the Pathet Lao and North Vietnamese to expel the Neutralists from the Plain of Jars, the United States began providing air support against Pathet Lao positions and North Vietnamese supply lines. However, it was not until March 1966 at Phoukout, northwest of the Plain of Jars, that the Pathet Lao started to win major battles against the Royal Lao Army. In July 1966, the Pathet Lao won another major battle in the Nambak Valley in northern Louangphrabang Province by overrunning a Royal Lao Army base and inflicting heavy casualties. These victories gave the Pathet Lao new momentum in the war for control of Laos.

Meanwhile, in southern Laos, where the North Vietnamese had been working steadily every dry season to expand the Ho Chi Minh Trail network leading into the Republic of Vietnam (South Vietnam), the intensity of the air war also grew. The air war in Laos operated under a complicated command-and-control system that involved the United States embassy in Vientiane, the Military Assistance Command Vietnam in Saigon, Royal Thai air bases in Thailand, the commander in chief, Pacific, in Honolulu, and sometimes even the White House.

The United States ambassador in Vientiane had the final say on target selection, using criteria that included taking into account the distance of targets from civilian habitations and the types of ordnance to be expended. The ambassador also was to keep the RLG informed so as to avoid, or at least minimize, the latter's embarrassment vis-à-vis the British and Soviet embassies in Vientiane and the heads of the Indian, Canadian, and Polish delegations to the International Control Commission, who were jointly responsible for enforcing the 1962 Declaration on the Neutrality of Laos signed in Geneva.

During the June 1969 rainy season, the Pathet Lao and two North Vietnamese battalions, using Soviet tanks, pushed the Royal Lao Army and the Neutralists out of their base at Muang Souy northwest of the Plain of Jars. Fighting continued during the monsoon season. In September 1969, Vang Pao's Hmong, supported by United States bombing, launched a series of surprise attacks against key points on the Plain of Jars. A new North Vietnamese army division joined the battle shortly thereafter and by February 1970 had regained all of the devastated plain.

In 1970, despite eight years of ground offensives by the Royal Lao Army and massive United States air support, the Pathet Lao had grown into an army of 48,000 troops and was prepared to challenge Royal Lao Army forces on their own territory by mounting large offensives in the south, engaging an even greater number of North Vietnamese forces. The introduction of Soviet-made long-range 130-mm artillery pieces onto the battlefield in that year allowed the Pathet Lao and North Vietnamese to neutralize to some extent the Royal Lao Army's advantage of air superiority.

In 1970 the combat elements of the Royal Lao Army were organized into fifty-eight infantry battalions and one artillery regiment of four battalions. The largest tactical unit was the battalion, which was composed of a headquarters, a headquarters company, and three rifle companies. Royal Lao Army units were devoted primarily to static defense and were stationed near population centers, lines of communication, depots, and airfields. These units were complemented by military police and armored, engineer, and communications units. Between 1962 and 1971, the United States provided Laos with an estimated US$500 million in military assistance, not including the cost of equipping and training irregular and paramilitary forces. During the 1971–75 period, it added about seventy-five T–28 light-strike or training aircraft, about twenty C–47s in both transport and gunship configurations, fewer than ten H–34 helicopters, and some small U–1 and U–17 aircraft.

In February 1971, a major offensive by the South Vietnamese army, with United States logistical and air support, sent two divisions into Laos in the vicinity of Xépôn with the objective of cutting North Vietnamese supply lines. However, once inside Laos, South Vietnamese commanders were separated from their resupply bases by long logistics lines, resulting in an early termination of the offensive. By December 1971, the Pathet Lao had taken Paksong on the Bolovens Plateau and had surrounded the main Hmong base at Longtiang. Communist advances continued into 1972 and encircled Thakhek on the Mekong, and Vientiane.

The cease-fire of February 22, 1973, ended United States bombing and temporarily halted ground offensives. The Pathet Lao, however, following their usual practice, used the cessation of military operations to resupply their forces over the long and exposed roads from North Vietnam. In further fighting in the spring of 1975, the Pathet Lao finally broke the resistance of Vang Pao's Hmong, blocking the road junction linking Vientiane, Louangphrabang, and the Plain of Jars. Under the watch of two battalions of Pathet Lao troops, which had been flown into Vientiane and Louangphrabang on Soviet and Chinese planes for neutralizing those towns under the cease-fire agreement, the communists organized demonstrations to support their political and military demands, leading to the final, bloodless seizure of power in the towns held by the RLG up to then.

Structure and Administration of the Armed Forces

As of mid-1994, the most powerful military officer in Laos was Lieutenant General Choummali Saignason, concurrently minister of national defense and commander in chief of the LPA. In addition to his military position, he was also the seventh highest ranking member of the ruling LPRP Political Bureau (Politburo). He took over as chief of the LPA in 1991 when General Khamtai Siphandon was elevated to prime minister (see The Lao People's Revolutionary Party, ch. 4). As a ranking member of the Politburo, Choummali is responsible for formulating both government and military policy. As commander in chief, he has absolute power over all internal and external security matters. All state security personnel, commanders of the air and naval forces, and police officials report to Choummali.

Lao People's Army

The Pathet Lao guerrillas became the LPLA in October 1965; in 1976 it was renamed the LPA. In the beginning, the LPLA consisted of regular forces organized under a central military command, with regionally recruited units and local forces operating on a part-time basis at the village level as a people's militia. These three levels of the armed forces were derived from the wartime structure of the main force units and regional and local guerrillas.

In December 1975, the LPA had a total strength of about 60,000 personnel, including 35,000 Pathet Lao troops and dissident Neutralists (see table 14, Appendix). In a January 20, 1976 broadcast, government authorities outlined five principal tasks for the LPA in defending the nation against Thai reactionaries and exiled Laotian counterrevolutionaries. The first task was to heighten vigilance in preserving peace and public order. The second was to raise political and ideological understanding in the armed forces, improve discipline, and implement government policy. The third and fourth tasks were to reinforce traditions of solidarity with the people and raise the quality of the army through political and military study. Finally, the army was called upon to strengthen its organization and improve internal defense.

By 1976 the LPA was organized along North Vietnamese military lines, with approximately 42,500 troops in sixty-five infantry battalions, divided among four military regions. By 1979 there were as many as 50,000 Vietnamese troops in Laos, advising and working side by side with their Laotian counterparts to suppress the remaining opposition forces. In the mid-1980s, Vietnamese troops began their withdrawal; by late 1988, all operational elements had been withdrawn. It is likely, however, that a few Vietnamese military technical specialists remained in Laos as of mid-1994.

During the late 1970s and early 1980s, the armed forces were reequipped with military hardware, including MiG jet fighters from the Soviet Union. Despite the influx of new equipment, however, the bleak economic situation of the country prevented the allotment of a large enough military budget for a modern fighting force. In the absence of military support from the former Soviet Union and with limited equipment purchases from China and Vietnam, the LPA had embarked on private business ventures to support itself. In the early 1990s, aging equipment and lack of funds precluded further modernization.

Dependence on direct foreign military aid ended with the withdrawal of Vietnamese troops and Soviet and Vietnamese military advisers in the mid- to late 1980s. The mutual security treaty with Vietnam, however, allows Vietnamese troops to reenter Laos in case of need.

By mid-1994, the LPA had approximately 33,000 troops, divided into four military regions. The LPA headquarters in Vientiane controls all four military regions, which in turn are responsible for LPA elements in the provinces. Military Region One is headquartered in Louangphrabang, Louangphrabang Province; Military Region Two, in Muang Phônsavan, Xiangkhoang Province; Military Region Three, in Xénô, Savannakhét Province; and Military Region Four, in Pakxé, Champasak Province.

The LPA ground component consists of five infantry divisions. The First Division is situated in the Vientiane area. The Second Division monitors the Laos-Thailand border and north-central Laos. The Third Division monitors the Laos-China border. The Fourth Division and the Fifth Division patrol southern Laos.

LPA ground equipment generally is of vintage Soviet design, with PT–76s (light tanks); T–34/85s and T–54/55s (main battle tanks); and 122mm and 130mm artillery (see table 15, Appendix). For the most part, United States-made equipment captured from the Royal Lao Army in 1975 has been retired from active service.

By the early 1990s, because of the lack of any real external threats, the armed forces were largely responsible for internal security, support against dissidents, and border patrol against incursions from Thailand-based resistance elements. The LPA also played a significant role in combatting the armed Laotian resistance movement, especially those troops stationed along the Thai border. And, presumably, the LPA is responsible for any further border conflicts such as occurred with Thailand in

1988 (see The Confrontational Relationship with Thailand, this ch.; Bilateral Relations, ch. 4).

Lao People's Air Force

In 1975 the LPA took possession from the Royal Lao Air Force of an inventory of 150 United States-made aircraft ranging from T–28 ground attack to UH–34 helicopters. Without an air force of its own, the LPA had to rebuild the United States-backed and United States-trained Royal Lao Air Force. In order to do so, Laos turned to Vietnam and the Soviet Union.

By the end of 1976, Vietnamese advisers had laid the foundation for the Lao People's Air Force. Vietnamese technicians developed and implemented the training of Laotian cadres for command and operational positions. With the exception of new aircraft, Vietnam also provided the majority of equipment needed by the air force for day-to-day functioning. Laotian air force officers of promise were sent to schools in Vietnam for specialized training. Vietnamese and Soviet technical advisers had withdrawn from Laos by 1990.

In 1977, in order to modernize and make the transition from a United States-supplied counterinsurgency air force into one capable of providing air-to-air intercepts, a high-level Laotian military delegation visited the Soviet Union. Later that year, Laos received ten MiG–21 fighter aircraft, six An–24 transport aircraft, and four Mi–8 helicopters from the Soviet Union, along with in-country technical expertise. In addition, the Soviets funded construction of air bases and radar sites. Together, the Soviets and Vietnamese constructed a large air force base at Muang Phônsavan on the Plain of Jars, 240 kilometers north of Vientiane, and rebuilt the former French air base at Xénô, near Savannakhét. In the late 1970s and early 1980s, the Soviets built early-warning radar systems in northern and western Laos to monitor Vietnamese, Chinese, and Thai aircraft movements.

Over time, the air force inventory measurably decreased. In 1975 there were 150 aircraft. By the mid-1980s, however, the inventory had been reduced to seventy aircraft of predominantly Soviet design. In the 1988–94 period, budgetary problems further reduced the air force inventory to approximately fifty aircraft. Few of the former Royal Lao Air Force's United States-made aircraft are still in use. As of mid-1994, there were approximately twenty-nine MiG–21s armed with AA–2 Anab air-to-air missiles that provided Laos with a credible air defense against its neighbors and principal adversaries, Cambodia and Thailand. However, the MiG–21 force, assessed as moderately capable in the mid-1980s, has deteriorated from age and poor maintenance and is marginal at best. Funds for replacing aircraft are not available. There were approximately 3,500 persons in the air force as of mid-1994.

Lao People's Navy

In 1975 the Lao People's Navy was established with the remnants of the Royal Lao Navy. Composed of approximately twenty United States-made river patrol boats and sixteen amphibious landing craft, the navy in mid-1994 had a personnel strength of around 500. As with the air force, Vietnamese advisers helped organize the Lao People's Navy and trained Laotian cadres in river operations and boat maintenance. The force is responsible for maintaining the security of inland waterways, which includes controlling the movement of resistance forces from their sanctuaries in Thailand, across the Mekong River. In the early 1980s, the navy received six used Soviet Shmel patrol boats and at least twelve more river patrol boats, bringing its total inventory to around thirty-one patrol boats. By mid-1994, the navy had a total of fewer than fifty river patrol boats and continued to provide a marginal level of security for inland waterways.

Other Military Units

The LPA is augmented by provincial forces, numbering 20,000 to 30,000 men and women, and the local militia, or Irregular People's Army, estimated at somewhat more than 100,000 men and women. Provincial forces receive little pay, have few weapons, and are minimally trained. They are under the operational control of provincial authorities for border control and internal security. The militia is lightly armed and receives no pay and little or no military training. The irregular forces are organized in their workplaces and local villages, have a role in local security, and act as a reserve for the regular armed forces. Promising recruits from the provincial forces and militia units frequently advance to regular army duty.

Manpower and Conditions of Service

As of mid-1994, there were approximately 37,000 persons, or slightly more than 4 percent of the labor force of approxi-

New Year's parade in Louangphrabang, 1975; royal elephant and marchers accompanied by Royal Lao Police on left and Royal Lao Army soldier on right
Courtesy Ernest Kuhn

mately 1,574,100 males and females between the ages of thirteen and thirty-two, in the military. There is an eighteen-month minimum military conscription draft for males seventeen to twenty-six years. Most draftees serve the minimum time. The ground forces are the primary destination for draftees. The other, smaller services seem to get sufficient numbers of voluntary recruits to fill their ranks.

Life in the LPA is austere. Pay is low, and there is a shortage of uniforms and equipment, including most basic supplies. Consequently, it is not a popular career path for most young Laotian males. In late 1989, LPRP chairman Kaysone Phomvihan in a major speech to senior LPA officers complained that "Our youths throughout the country have failed to associate with the army and failed to use the army as a school to carry out practices as they were expected to do in the past." Seminars were held in many districts during 1989–90 to discuss requiring local authorities to help enforce compliance with draft laws, which many Laotian youths were actively seeking to avoid.

During the Pathet Lao's struggle against the RLG, women—for the most part voluntarily—played a significant role fighting alongside men in combat units. Women also served in a medical corps and as porters for combat units. Since 1975, however, the role of women in the armed forces has changed significantly. Although not subject to the draft, women are part of the active armed forces but perform only minor administrative functions. Women do, however, serve in police and militia forces.

The Defense Budget

As of mid-1994, Laos had the smallest defense budget in Southeast Asia, but it also is one of the region's poorest countries. Since 1975, Laos has relied heavily on Vietnamese and Soviet military aid; by the early 1990s the loss of this aid had affected military capabilities.

There is little available information on the defense budget (see table 16, Appendix). In the late 1970s and early 1980s, Laos undertook a concerted effort to eliminate internal armed resistance and was preoccupied with a continuous border conflict with Thailand (see The Confrontational Relationship with Thailand, this ch.). In the late 1980s and early 1990s, however, a noticeable improvement in the security situation, marked by better relations with its neighbors and a reduced internal security threat from resistance groups, enabled the leadership to reduce the defense budget. In 1992 military expenditures—which included public security—were approximately US$102.2 million, or 11.7 percent of the gross domestic product (GDP—see Glossary). In 1993 military expenditures had increased slightly to about US$104.9 million, approximately 12.4 percent of the US$1.3 billion estimated GDP.

Threats to National Security

Internal Threats and Resistance Movements

After December 1975, the newly formed LPDR was faced with disarming and neutralizing former rightist soldiers and police, countering armed resistance efforts by those who had fled to Thailand and by their supporters who had remained in Laos, and preventing Thailand from interfering in political developments in Laos. The ease with which the Pathet Lao had managed to neutralize the rightist armed forces and police and form a coalition government reflected how tired the Laotians were of war. The prevailing attitude at the time seemed to be general relief that the civil war was over. Even most middle- and lower-ranking officers in the Royal Lao Army—who had spent their adult lives fighting the insurgents of the Neo Lao Hak Xat (Lao Patriotic Front—LPF; see Glossary)—were prepared to cooperate in building a united and socialist Laos. When opposition to the new regime materialized, it came mainly from across the Mekong River in Thailand. Insurgents found sanctuary across the 1,000-kilometer boundary with Thailand, where, under the new, strongly anticommunist government, the military provided them with supplies and intelligence data.

The armed resistance movement—a shadow force of several thousand persons—never gained enough momentum to become any more than a nuisance to the communist government because the combination of approximately 50,000 Vietnamese troops stationed in Laos and the LPA ensured adequate protection against this relatively minor threat. Broad security measures, including control of the media, were implemented.

The armed resistance was led mainly by individuals who had played a military role during the hostilities of the 1970s. Former members of the Royal Lao Army and the special guerrilla units supported by the CIA intermittently harassed government installations such as police stations and army posts, blasted bridges, ambushed vehicles, and blocked roads. The honeymoon period following the communist takeover ended abruptly when thousands of members of the previous government and military apparatus failed to be released from remote reeducation centers or "seminar camps" (see "Seminar Camps" and the Death of King Savang Vatthana, ch. 1).

In cooperation with Vietnamese forces in Laos, the government launched a military campaign intended to control dissidents, notably the irregular forces—made up of ethnic tribes who had long resisted Vietnamese and Laotian communists from their mountain hideouts. The military campaign, along with deteriorating economic conditions and government attempts to enforce political control, prompted an exodus of lowland Lao and Hmong in the early years of LPDR rule. About 10 percent of the population—approximately 300,000 persons—fled Laos after 1975, passing through refugee camps in Thailand on their way to receiving refugee status and taking up residence in the United States, France, Australia, and other countries. Those who remained in the refugee camps in Thailand provided the recruits for the resistance movements, supported by funds sent from their friends and relatives who had resettled abroad. Resistance forces continued operating from sanctuaries in refugee camps across the border in Thailand— with numerous reports of cross-border resistance actions— much as the Pathet Lao had originally operated from sanctuaries in North Vietnam. Resistance forces are perceived as a stumbling block for the repatriation of individuals in refugee camps in Thailand.

The deteriorating political situation between China and Laos in 1980 worked in favor of the resistance forces. And, following the outbreak of hostilities between China and Vietnam, China took a greater interest in the Laotian resistance movement by providing sanctuary, military training, and equipment to various resistance elements, including Kong Le's Neutralists. China's involvement was intended both to tie up the Vietnamese troops stationed in Laos and to provide China with intelligence on Vietnamese troop movements along the border. China also supported the political activity of Laotian exiles and reportedly established insurgent training camps in Yunnan Province for as many as 3,000 Laotian resistance fighters. Despite training and equipment from China, the newly trained resistance fighters were no match for the LPA and Vietnamese troops. The resistance was relegated to committing acts of sabotage against government facilities and mounting small unit attacks on troops. China cut off support to the resistance when moves toward normalization of relations between Laos and China began in 1986.

In 1985 the resistance movement escalated its military campaign against the government. Laotian resistance groups based in Thailand claimed to have as many as 7,000 to 8,000 members in 1985. These groups were active in mounting limited guerrilla operations, such as harassing LPA transportation routes and sabotaging military supply depots, and reportedly bombed the Wattai Airport in Vientiane in 1985. In April 1985, the guerrillas reportedly downed a helicopter, killing several senior

LPA officers, as well as three Soviet military advisers and two Vietnamese major generals. General Phoumi Nosavan's death in exile in Thailand in November 1985, however, left a significant leadership void and caused a serious setback to the resistance movement.

Although the resistance movement was losing momentum in the early 1990s, and resistance operations did not appear to threaten the stability of the communist government in Vientiane, incidents continued. In March 1992, fighting between resistance forces and Laotian troops took place at Ban Tak Huai Sao. Scores of people on both sides were wounded and killed by artillery and small arms fire. In June 1992, there were reports of 300 Laotian rebels attacking LPDR military positions in Muang Sanakham across the Mekong from Chiang Khan, Thailand. In July 1992, Thai military officials reported sporadic antigovernment activities and skirmishes in different parts of Laos, especially in the remote mountainous border areas with Thailand.

Laos continued to seek Thai action against rebel forces remaining in Thailand, and the decline in resistance activity was attributable both to an improvement in relations between Laos and Thailand and to the once isolationist LPDR's successful negotiations with the United Nations High Commissioner for Refugees (see Glossary) to close refugee camps in Thailand and repatriate the remaining inmates, mostly Hmong tribespeople. Not only did these negotiations cut off the sanctuaries, but they also cut off the traditional sources of new recruits and arms. Further, the Thai government began steps in 1992 to stop anti-LPDR forces from using Thailand as a base to stage attacks into Laos. Also, the United States pressured Thailand to cut back on tacit military assistance to Hmong resistance elements. As a result of these developments, armed resistance was reduced by mid-1994 to isolated incidents of little more than armed banditry—hardly a threat to the stability of Laos.

As of the early 1990s, it remained difficult to garner and confirm information about the strength of the various resistance forces and their activities because of the nature of their operations and the remoteness of their locations. The main resistance forces are the Lao National Liberation Movement (also known as the United Lao National Liberation Front) and the Ethnic Liberation Organization of Laos. The former resistance movement, remnants of the Hmong irregulars led by Vang Pao, is estimated to have approximately 2,000 members in the early 1990s and is a bitter enemy of the latter. The Lao National Liberation Movement continues to work toward replacing the government with a coalition of opposition groups.

The Ethnic Liberation Organization of Laos

The Ethnic Liberation Organization of Laos is the largest opposition group. The organization grew out of a major Hmong resistance group, the Chao Fa (Lords of the Sky, or God's Disciples). The Chao Fa was organized in 1975 by Zhong Zhua Her (Pak Au Her, or Pa Kao Her), a senior resistance fighter who had received aid from the United States in his fight against Pathet Lao and Vietnamese forces.

In the late 1970s, the Chao Fa boasted of having 20,000 members; however, only 2,000 to 4,000 were armed. By the mid-1980s, the number of armed Chao Fa was probably around 2,000. Because it had been subjected to years of attacks by government and Vietnamese forces, the group was split and forced to flee into China, which provided it with assistance.

By late 1984, China had sent Laotian resistance groups back across the border. In 1985 Zhong Zhua Her reorganized the Chao Fa under the banner of the Ethnic Liberation Organization of Laos and set up his base camp in Xaignabouri Province near the border with Thailand. From his base, Zhong Zhua Her attempted to organize resistance elements in the northern provinces of Laos and sought to establish an autonomous region for the Hmong.

In 1990 the Ethnic Liberation Organization of Laos reportedly had 3,000 members in armed units and another 6,000 persons trained but without weapons. Individual weapons reportedly were variants of the AK–47, a few M–79 grenade launchers, RPG–2s, RPG–7s, and a few 60mm mortars. In the early 1990s, the group concentrated on mounting small-unit operations and consolidating support. Beginning in 1992, relations with the other resistance groups were poor to nonexistent. This fact greatly hampered efforts of resistance movements to organize a broader agenda and larger operations, as did closer relations between Laos and Thailand. As of mid-1994, the strength of the Ethnic Liberation Organization of Laos was estimated at approximately 2,000 persons.

Royal Lao Army soldier
standing guard at the
Royal Palace,
Louangphrabang, 1975
Courtesy Ernest Kuhn

The Hmong

The Hmong are one of the principal ethnic minorities inhabiting the higher elevations of Laos, living in mountain villages situated above 1,000 meters where they grow rice and corn using swidden (shifting, or slash-and-burn) agriculture, raise livestock, and grow opium as a cash crop. Several million Hmong also live in Thailand, Vietnam, and China (see Population, ch. 2). The Hmong traditionally have aggressively protected their independent life-style, and their independence has kept them at odds with the central government.

Throughout the twentieth century, the Hmong maintained their tradition of rebellion. In the 1920s, successful Hmong uprisings against the French colonial power in northeastern Laos led to negotiated settlements rather than defeat. The French colonial government later used the Hmong to help subjugate lowland Lao dissidents. In the mid-1960s, the United States, recognizing the Hmong's tenacious fighting ability and superior knowledge of mountainous terrain, employed them as irregular mercenary units against the Pathet Lao (see The "Secret War," ch. 1). Hmong forces, trained and supplied by the United States, fought alongside the Royal Lao Army and were used extensively in many of the most pitched battles of the Indochina wars. As a consequence, a disproportionate number of Hmong were wounded and/or died in combat (see Historical Background, this ch.).

After the disastrous defeat of two major Hmong armies in March and April 1975 at Sala Phou Khoun by North Vietnamese and Pathet Lao forces, the United States evacuated Vang Pao from Longtiang to Thailand on May 14, 1975. Thousands of his followers were left to their fate because the United States evacuation aircraft requested by Vang Pao did not materialize. The vast majority of Hmong who made it safely to Thailand did so on their own. This defeat left the Hmong who had not fled to Thailand in great disarray. One group of Hmong, after a long and dangerous march through hostile countryside, fled to Thailand, where 25,000 persons reached safety. But a larger group of some 60,000 persons retreated to the heights of the Phou Bia Massif south of the Plain of Jars, where they set up defensive positions. Aside from occasional harassing attacks by Pathet Lao forces, no serious attempt was made to interfere with the Hmong for more than a year after the communist takeover.

In 1977 Vietnamese troops backed by Soviet 130mm long-range artillery encircled and attacked the Hmong sanctuary in the Pho Bia Massif. Hmong defenses held and drove off the attackers. Later that same year, however, Vietnamese forces, unable to penetrate the Hmong ground defenses, began to overfly the redoubt, reportedly dropping napalm, gas, and a mycotoxin known as trichothecene, or "yellow rain," on Hmong villages (see Bilateral Relations, ch. 4). An unknown number of Hmong died, while others tried to escape into Thailand.

As a result of decades of warfare, dislocation, and a campaign mounted against them by Vietnamese and RLG forces in the late 1970s and early 1980s, the Hmong population was reduced to approximately 200,000 in Laos and about the same number in Thailand in the early 1990s. From their sanctuary in Thailand, the Hmong continued their armed resistance efforts against the communists throughout the 1980s and into the 1990s. Many thousands of other Hmong, however, had sided with the Pathet Lao and were living peacefully in Laos, particularly in the northeastern provinces; others went to Thailand and on to the United States. Nevertheless, by 1992, cross-border Hmong raids into Laos were reduced to little more than banditry—a casualty of wavering Thai support and apathy among the Hmong themselves.

In 1992 a major Hmong refuge, the Ban Vinai Hmong refugee camp in Thailand, was closed as part of a Thai effort to close all camps holding Laotian refugees. In late 1992, there were an estimated 30,000 Laotian refugees in Thailand and about 1,700 in China. In March 1993, Thailand announced that it was closing two more refugee camps, one in Nakhon Phanom Province, the other in Phayao Province. These two camps held more than 27,000 Laotians, the majority of whom were Hmong. Although the government is making attempts to reintegrate the Hmong, the lack of resources limits these efforts. Continuing participation of Hmong in resistance activities poses no threat to the stability of the government of Laos, but it does complicate the repatriation process.

Foreign Military Presence

Since 1975 Laos has maintained a special relationship with Vietnam, formalized by the Treaty of Friendship and Cooperation signed in July 1977. Article 1 of the treaty states that "the two parties undertake to deploy all of their efforts to safeguard and develop the special relationship between Laos and Vietnam, to reinforce their solidarity and mutual confidence, their long-term cooperation and mutual aid in all domains in a spirit of proletarian internationalism." Article 4 of the treaty stipulates that "the two sides affirm their determination to build the Vietnamese-Lao border into a border of lasting friendship and fraternity."

The treaty is much more than its name implies because it gives Vietnam almost carte blanche in the internal affairs of Laos, especially in the military. Vietnamese military forces have been continuously present in Laos since 1961, if not earlier. The strength of these forces has varied over the years from 30,000 to 50,000 troops in the 1975–83 period, to several hundred advisers in late 1987. In November 1988, the LPDR Ministry of Foreign Affairs formally announced that all Vietnamese troops had been withdrawn from Laos. Although Western intelligence sources initially doubted the claim of total withdrawal, later they reportedly confirmed that it was true. Indeed, there was no Vietnamese presence in the two border conflicts between Laos and Thailand in the late 1980s. Moreover, expatriate employees of international organizations working in

Vientiane had noticed the removal of many Vietnamese technical and advisory personnel from the capital. It is likely that a full withdrawal of Vietnamese forces and a reduction of aid personnel occurred in order to advance economic agreements between Vietnam and China.

Vietnamese troops performed a variety of functions during their long stay in Laos. They fought alongside Pathet Lao insurgents in their struggle to overthrow the RLG. They trained and, along with the Soviets, equipped the military. Vietnamese cadres played a primary role in combatting the insurgency against the LPDR, undertaking security tasks such as guarding access to airport perimeters, controlling important road junctions, and patrolling sensitive areas. They performed border patrol duties and carried out joint military maneuvers with LPA units along the Cambodian, Chinese, and Thai borders to demonstrate strong Laotian-Vietnamese military cooperation. These maneuvers were especially evident during periods of border tension between Vietnam or Laos and their neighbors. The Vietnamese also rendered valuable engineering services such as building roads and improving infrastructure damaged by years of war.

The Confrontational Relationship with Thailand

Despite cultural and linguistic ties between Laos and Thailand, after 1975 relations between these two countries were often marked by severe strains (see Bilateral Relations, ch. 4). Such strains often resulted in exchanges of gunfire followed by border closures.

Relations between Laos and Thailand entered a new phase of tension in the middle of 1984 after a period of relative calm. Thai Army roadbuilding crews encountered three remote villages whose location on available maps they apparently took to favor Thai sovereignty. The LPDR government and army thought otherwise, and a military and diplomatic standoff ensued for several months. Laos took the dispute to the United Nations (UN), where Thailand was striving for election to the Security Council. In keeping with such aspirations, Thailand announced that it would remove its troops from the three villages and seek a peaceful settlement through a resurvey of the watershed border.

Further complicating the border situation, in late 1984 Thailand accused Vietnam of meddling in Laotian affairs by pushing Laos into hostilities with Thailand in order to draw attention away from the situation in Cambodia. Thailand also complained that Laos was harboring Thai communists belonging to a new organization called Green Star, whose cadres numbered 2,000 and who were said to be training in six insurgent camps along the Laos-Thailand border. Little came of Thai accusations because world attention was focused on Vietnam's activity in Cambodia, not on Laos.

Following the mid-1984 incident and until early 1986, relations were tense. However, by mid-1986 tension began to ease as both sides attempted to downplay the various minor border incidents. For example, in mid-July 1986, approximately thirty-five Laotian ethnic minority refugees were killed in Thailand. Thailand alleged that LPA troops had attacked a refugee settlement near the village of Ban Huai Pong, Phayao Province, killing the refugees. The government said Thailand fabricated the accusation. Previously, less significant border incidents had become contentious; this time, however, after Laos and Thailand traded vitriolic charges in both countries' media, the issue died down, foreshadowing an improvement in cross-border relations.

In late 1986, relations between Laos and Thailand moved forward when several delegations were exchanged in order to work out border differences. Of significance were discussions between military and police delegations, who exchanged information on problems with resistance groups, infiltration, smuggling, and bandit gangs. Laos was concerned with the embargo Thailand had placed on strategic goods crossing Thailand for import into the country. As a landlocked country, Laos is dependent upon goods transiting from and through its neighbors. Negotiations ended the embargo on these goods, excluding some military-related items. Laos was also concerned about restrictions on commercial goods.

Between 1986 and 1990, the number of border incidents along the Laos-Thailand border declined significantly. There was, however, a major border dispute in December 1987. A cease-fire was proclaimed in February 1988, ending the fighting that had resulted in 1,000 deaths, and meetings were held to defuse the conflict (see Developments in the Lao People's Democratic Republic, ch. 1).

Other factors helped to soften the confrontational relationship. Thailand's criticism of Laotian-Vietnamese military ties lessened after 1988, when the majority of Vietnamese troops had departed Laos. Commercial trade continued to be a stabilizing force. Diplomatic relations between the two countries were normal but wary. The fact that resistance fighters operated from refugee camps in Thailand, however, remained a constant source of irritation.

In 1991 several high-level Laotian-Thai military delegations were exchanged in hopes of resolving remaining border incidents. These talks resulted in agreements in which both sides agreed to withdraw military forces from disputed areas in Xaignabouri Province. The withdrawals, which took the form of a mutually supervised pullback, created several unpopulated demilitarized zones. Thailand also promised to help curtail the illegal activities of Laotian refugees and exiles residing in Thailand. Specifically, it agreed to cooperate in disarming and arresting any armed individuals apprehended crossing the border. In 1992 Thailand reportedly made good on its promise to arrest border violators, and the brother of General Vang Pao and a group of Hmong were taken into custody in northern Thailand as they were attempting to stage a cross-border incursion.

In August 1992, Laos again called for increased Laotian-Thai cooperation to suppress anti-LPDR activity by ethnic resistance fighters. Cooperation was to include tougher restrictions on exiled Hmong wishing to travel to and within Thailand. Vientiane wanted Bangkok to strengthen its screening procedures of visa applications from exiled and ethnic Lao living in third countries of resettlement. It was also seeking Thai cooperation in patrolling the common border to combat the resistance movement. In 1993 the LPDR's ambassador to Thailand, Bounkeut Sangsomsak, summed up the resistance problem when he noted that the two countries still needed to resolve the problem, that both sides had been consulting each other at government and military levels, but that stringent measures were needed to further disrupt resistance efforts.

Relations with the United States

Since the mid-1980s, relations between the United States and Laos have been largely concerned with accounting for those persons classified as prisoner of war/missing in action (POW/MIA) in Laos from the Indochina wars (1946–75) and on counternarcotics issues (see Narcotics and Counternarcot-

A group of senior Royal Lao Government officials in November 1974. At the center is Prince Saykham Southakakaoumal, then governor of Xiangkhoang Province.
Courtesy Ernest Kuhn

ics Issues, this ch.; The Origins of the Prisoner of War/Missing in Action Question, ch. 1; Bilateral Relations, ch. 4). In February 1985, a Laotian-United States team conducted the first joint excavation of a plane crash site, resulting in the identification of the remains of thirteen missing servicemen. Progress in Laos-United States relations accelerated after 1988, with Laos agreeing to expand POW/MIA activities. The two countries have conducted numerous site surveys and recovery operations since January 1989.

National Police and Paramilitary Forces

One of the first priorities for the LPDR was restructuring defense and security forces and improving effectiveness in these new roles. After the major Mekong River towns were liberated, soldiers were assigned police duties, although they lacked the necessary training. As the pace of political change quickened and the government became increasingly concerned about security, the public expressed dissatisfaction with heavy-handed military controls, Pathet Lao arrogance, and the excesses committed by some guerrillas.

The emphasis on discipline, training, and reorganization reflected the difficulties encountered by the former Pathet Lao cadres in converting from a guerrilla insurgency into a national security force. Men taught to think of urban-dwelling lowland Lao as their bitter enemies found it difficult at first to treat them as liberated brothers (see Lowland Lao Society, ch. 2).

Also, most young Pathet Lao guerrillas brought in to keep order in the Mekong towns were members of upland minorities who had never before been confronted with the temptations of city life (see Upland Lao Society, ch. 2). Consequently, there were reports of abuses such as extortion and robbery by drunken Pathet Lao police officers.

By the end of 1976, an effective police force had been established. Its mission was simple: to maintain basic law and order and strictly enforce government policies, often with little regard for human rights. A police academy was established at the former United States-built police school at Ban Donnoun, ten kilometers east of Vientiane, where Vietnamese and Soviet instructors began teaching Laotian cadres basic police procedures. The crime rate reportedly was very low.

The academy also trained a Laotian secret police organization similar to the Vietnamese internal security apparatus. The secret police were to provide internal security for the party and to look for dissidents within the population, that is, those individuals who disagreed with the LPRP's pro-Vietnamese line and who expressed pro-Chinese or Laotian nationalist sentiments that could be construed as anti-Vietnamese. By late 1978, there were reportedly 800 Vietnamese secret police in Laos engaged in military and civilian surveillance activities. By the late 1980s, their presence had been reduced to a few senior advisers.

The Criminal Justice System

Civil Liberties and Human Rights

The criminal justice system, like every aspect of life in Laos, is controlled by the party and the government. There are few legal restraints on the often arbitrary actions—including arrests—by the government, and dissent is handled by suppressing basic civil rights. Although the constitution provides for the freedoms of worship, speech, and press, as of the early 1990s, citizens did not feel free to exercise these rights fully. There are no legal safeguards, and people are frequently arrested on vague charges. Although a penal code and a constitution that guarantee certain civil liberties have been promulgated, implementation is another matter, particularly where freedom of political expression is concerned. And, the media are state-controlled (see Mass Media, ch. 4).

Nonetheless, there is a system for prosecuting criminal behavior. Common crimes are evaluated at the local village level. More serious cases, especially politically sensitive ones, are referred to higher authorities. People's tribunals operate at district and provincial levels with judges appointed by the government.

Both Laotian journalists and Western officials are critical of the limitations on personal freedoms. In 1987 a Laotian journalist living in Thailand noted that there was little popular support for the government, but that most Laotians accepted its authority because they had little choice. In 1988 a Laotian journalist protested that open criticism of the government was forbidden and noted that one of his friends had been imprisoned after he complained about the continuing lack of a constitution. In 1988 Western diplomats reported that hundreds—perhaps thousands—of individuals were being held in detention centers around the country and that people still were being arrested and held for months without being charged.

In the late 1980s and early 1990s, the government instituted the New Economic Mechanism, a series of sweeping economic reforms geared toward establishing a market-oriented economy. Along with these economic reforms came a slight opening to the West, which provided some opportunity for scrutiny of human rights violations. However, few foreign journalists are allowed to visit Laos, and travel by diplomats and foreign aid workers is restricted. Both domestic and foreign travel by Laotians also is subject to scrutiny and restriction.

The Ministry of Interior is the main instrument of state control and guardianship over the criminal justice system. Ministry of Interior police monitor both Laotians and foreign nationals who live in Laos, and there is a system of informants in workplace committees and in residential areas. According to the United States Department of State's *Country Reports on Human Rights Practices for 1993*, both the party and state monitor various aspects of family and social life through neighborhood and workplace committees. These committees are responsible for maintaining public order and reporting "bad elements" to the police, as well as carrying out political training and disciplining employees.

The criminal justice system is deficient in the area of legal precedent and representation. Trials are not held in public, although trial verdicts are publicly announced. Although there is some provision for appeal, it does not apply to important political cases. Under the constitution, judges and prosecutors are supposed to be independent and their decisions free from outside scrutiny. In practice, however, the courts appear to accept recommendations of other government agencies, especially the Ministry of Interior, in making their decisions. Theoretically, the government provides legal counsel to the accused. In practice, however, defendants represent themselves without outside counsel. The government suspended the bar in late 1992, pending new rules on the activities of private lawyers, thereby paving the way for private lawyers to practice in Laos. Meanwhile, persons accused of crimes have to defend themselves.

In 1992 the government launched a campaign to disseminate the new constitution, adopted by the National Assembly in 1991. The leadership touted its efforts at developing a legal system with a codified body of laws and a penal code. By most Western accounts, however, as of mid-1994, there had been little, if any, progress in implementing the freedoms provided for in the constitution. Although the National Assembly had enacted a criminal code and laws establishing a judiciary in November 1989, as of mid-1994 these codes still had not been implemented. Individuals are still being held without being informed of the charges or their accusers' identities.

Detention Centers

There were four categories of persons held in confinement. Aside from common criminals, there were political, social, and ideological deviants. The crimes of the three latter groups were often vaguely defined, their arrests arbitrary, and their length of confinement ambiguous.

The LPDR established four different types of detention centers: prisons, reeducation centers or seminar camps, rehabilitation camps, and remolding centers. Social deviants or common criminals were considered less threatening to the regime than persons accused of political crimes, who were considered potential counterrevolutionaries. Social deviants were confined in rehabilitation camps. According to MacAlister Brown and Joseph J. Zasloff, prisons were primarily for common criminals, but political prisoners also were held there for short periods, usually six to twelve months. Ideologically suspect persons were sent to remolding centers. Reeducation centers were for those deemed politically risky, usually former RLG officials. Political prisoners usually served three- to five-year terms or longer. As at the prisons, inmates worked hard under rugged conditions and had limited supplies of food. Oddly, there was little political indoctrination. Bribery in order to secure food and medicine was reported.

In 1986 Brown and Zasloff also reported that prisoners were not tried but were incarcerated simply by administrative fiat. Former inmates said that they were arrested, informed by the security officials that they had been charged with crimes, and then sent off to camps for indeterminate periods. Typically, prisoners were told one day prior to their release to prepare for departure.

The status of the detention centers also is vague. In 1984 Vientiane declared that all reeducation centers had been closed. At that time, Amnesty International estimated 6,000 to 7,000 political prisoners were held in these centers. The government acknowledged that there were some former inmates in remote areas but claimed that their confinement was voluntary. In the late 1980s, the government released most of the detainees. As of mid-1994, the exact number of political prisoners was unknown.

In 1989 Laos took steps to reduce the number of political prisoners, many of whom had been held since 1975. Several hundred detainees, including many high-ranking officials and officers from the former United States-backed RLG and Royal Lao Army, were released from reeducation centers in the northeastern province of Houaphan. Released prisoners reported that hundreds of individuals remained in custody in as many as eight camps. Included among those in custody were at least six generals and former high-ranking members of the RLG. These individuals reportedly performed manual labor such as cutting logs, repairing roads, and building irrigation systems. In 1993 Amnesty International reported human rights violations in the continued detention of three "prisoners of conscience"— detained since 1975 but not sentenced until 1992—as well as those held under restrictions or the subjects of unfair trials according to international standards.

As of 1993, reports indicated that some high-ranking officials of the RLG and military remained in state custody. Those accused of hostility to the regime are subject to arrest and confinement for long periods of time. Prison conditions are harsh, and prisoners are routinely denied family visitation and proper medical care. Prisons are not independently monitored.

Narcotics and Counternarcotics Issues

Laos is the world's third largest producer of opium—primarily in the northern provinces. Narcotics trafficking in Laos is difficult to control because of the remoteness of many border areas, their attendant lack of communications, and the scarcity of resources, all of which which make stationing officials at many of the border crossings difficult. Nevertheless, several counternarcotics policy initiatives have been undertaken.

During the late 1980s, narcotics control became an important United States concern because Laos is a major producer of opium and marijuana. In 1987 Laos began to cooperate with the United States in drug control efforts when it requested assistance in providing a viable crop alternative to opium farmers. Increased efforts on counternarcotics cooperation have been evident since January 1990 when a memorandum of understanding on the Bilateral Cooperation of Narcotics Issues was signed. This agreement focused on ways for the United States to provide antinarcotics programs. The United States provided narcotics-related training to a number of Laotian officials in June 1990 and again in August 1991. And, in 1992 United States Customs Service officials held a training session in Vientiane for Laotian customs officers and other officials. Since then, Laotian officials have also traveled to Australia, Japan, and Europe for counternarcotics cooperation training.

In late 1992, as part of the continuing counternarcotics effort, the LPDR Customs Department set up an antismuggling unit in Vientiane. The Council of Ministers approved the formation of this counternarcotics police unit, operationally under the Ministry of Interior but with policy controlled by the Lao National Committee on Drug Control and Supervision. Progress in the configuration of the unit was negligible. As of mid-1993, however, the United States was working with the LPDR to provide support and training for the unit, and the site for the unit was being renovated.

Estimated opium production has declined annually since 1989, largely through successful crop reduction and replacement programs that target specific areas and are funded and initiated by the United States and the UN Drug Control Program. Laos has facilitated these crop substitution programs—

United States landing craft on land along the Mekong River in Vientiane, now used as storage containers
Courtesy Gina Merris

aimed at developing alternative crops and occupations—in Houaphan, Vientiane, and Xiangkhoang provinces. In 1989 there were an estimated 42,130 hectares of land deemed "potentially harvestable" for cultivating opium. By 1993 there were approximately 26,040 hectares. The potential opium yield declined from 380 tons in 1989 to 230 tons in 1992 and to 180 tons in 1993. The United States government estimated that opium production in Laos had declined some 27 percent in 1990 over the previous year, approximately 13 percent from 1991 to 1992, and about 22 percent from 1992 to 1993, the latter mainly as a result of adverse weather because the estimated hectarage under cultivation did not decrease.

Decreased opium cultivation and production are also the result of increased law enforcement efforts, narcotics-related arrests and crop seizures, and a greater effort to disseminate information on the disadvantages of drug trafficking. Although the government tends to deny that it has a domestic drug problem, a public awareness program stressing the dangers of drug use and trafficking has been established, and, as part of the information and education campaign, there has been increased publicity on penalties for offenses.

In April 1993, Laos was certified ("with explanation") for narcotics cooperation in 1992 by the United States Department of State. (Certification is granted for performance in narcotics cooperation in the previous calendar year and is categorized by cooperation or certification, noncooperation or decertification, and national interest waiver.) Certification guarantees Laos increased United States cooperation and funding of counternarcotics programs. Certification (with explanation), however, stipulates that in order to receive full United States support, Laos has to take visible, significant, and continuing action to improve the enforcement of antinarcotics laws, which were first enacted in November 1989. Other reasons for the designation certification with explanation include the slow pace of cooperation with officials from the United States Drug Enforcement Administration and allegations of involvement in drug trafficking by high-level members of the government.

In April 1994, the United States granted Laos a national interest waiver for certification of narcotics cooperation in 1993. It was determined that the waiver was preferable to decertification or certification and was in the United States national interest in order to exact continued cooperation on the POW/MIA issue.

Previous efforts—although modest—to curb the drug trade continue. At the same time, however, corruption among civilian and military personnel and their collusion in narcotics activities reportedly continue as well. In 1993 the prime minister ordered the provinces to organize antidrug committees and cooperate with the Lao National Committee on Drug Control and Supervision. Cooperation is to take the form of publicizing existing laws and regulations and educating the public on the dangers of drugs.

For the foreseeable future, drug production and trafficking will likely remain serious problems. Still, the 27 percent drop in opium cultivation, coupled with the arrests of drug traffickers and the government's stated commitment to take further action on enforcement, are encouraging. Laos has also signed a memorandum of understanding with China and Thailand on strengthening regional cooperation in controlling illicit drugs. In the near term, the United States will probably continue to assist Laos in efforts to decrease opium cultivation and production through crop substitution programs.

This improvement in the narcotics arena is indicative of the overall improvement in the country's national security situation. Since 1988 Laos has experienced a period of relative calm in its turbulent history. It has been at peace with its neighbors, and its internal armed resistance movement has been reduced to a mere annoyance. It is doubtful, however, that the armed forces will modernize much in the 1990s, unless the country's overall economic situation improves or a new political patron emerges. It is more likely that the military will lag farther and farther behind its stronger neighbors.

One of the last holdouts of communist ideology in the world, Laos has slowly opened its doors to the West in order to improve its economic situation. In mid-1994, however, Laos was still a long way from providing its citizens with the basic civil rights fundamental to Western societies: there are few personal freedoms, no freedom of the press or assembly, and harsh prison conditions for citizens who deviate from the party line.

*   *   *

Detailed and current reference material on the military forces and judicial and penal systems is difficult to obtain. Several books written in the mid- to late 1980s are recommended for a good overview of the security situation. These include Martin Stuart-Fox's *Contemporary Laos: Studies in the Politics and Society of the Lao People's Democratic Republic* and MacAlister Brown and Joseph Zasloff's *Apprentice Revolutionaries: The Communist Movement in Laos, 1930–85*. Written information on military training and equipment is sparse. The Institute for Strategic Studies' annual *Military Balance* is the best source of information on the status of military equipment. The *Asia Yearbook* also yields some information on national security issues. The United States Department of State's annual publications, *International Narcotics Control Strategy Report* and *Country Reports on Human Rights Practices*, provide yearly updates on narcotics production, counternarcotics operations, and human rights. (For further information and complete citations, see Bibliography.)

Appendix

Table

Table 1. Metric Conversion Coefficients and Factors

When you know	Multiply by	To find
Millimeters	0.04	inches
Centimeters......................	0.39	inches
Meters..........................	3.3	feet
Kilometers	0.62	miles
Hectares	2.47	acres
Square kilometers	0.39	square miles
Cubic meters	35.3	cubic feet
Liters	0.26	gallons
Kilograms	2.2	pounds
Metric tons	0.98	long tons
....	1.1	short tons
....	2,204	pounds
Degrees Celsius (Centigrade)	1.8 and add 32	degrees Fahrenheit

Table 2. Estimated Population by Province, 1992

Province	Population
Attapu	83,000
Bokeo[1]	104,000
Bolikhamxai	151,000
Champasak	477,000
Houaphan	232,000
Khammouan	258,000
Louang Namtha	125,000
Louangphrabang	355,000
Oudômxai[1]	188,000
Phôngsali	149,000
Saravan	237,000
Savannakhét	673,000
Xaignabouri	195,000
Xekong	59,000
Xiangkhoang	191,000
Vientiane	321,000
Vientiane Municipality	489,000
Special zone[2]	73,000
TOTAL	4,360,000

[1] The populations of Bokeo and Oudômxai provinces have been adjusted to reflect the redistricting of Paktha and Pha Oudom districts from Oudômxai Province to Bokeo Province in 1992.
[2] The special zone consists of Hôngsa and Xianghon districts, formerly of Xaignabouri Province.

Source: Based on information from Laos, State Statistical Centre, Committee for Planning and Cooperation, *Basic Statistics about the Socio-economic Development in the Lao P.D.R*, Vientiane, 1993, 26.

Table 3. Population by Ethnic Group, 1985

Ethnic Group Subgroup	Population
Lao Loum	
Lao	1,804,101
Phu Thai	441,497
Lue	102,760
Total Lao Loum	2,348,358
Lao Theung	
Kammu	389,694
Katang	72,391
Makong	70,382
Suai	49,049
Nyuan	33,240
Loven	28,057
Ta-oi	24,577
Taliang	23,665
Chali	20,902
Phong	18,165
Lavae	16,434
Katu	14,676
Lamet	14,355
Htin	13,977
Alak	13,217
Pako	12,293
Oi	11,194
Ngae	8,917
Chaeng	4,540
Nyaheun	3,960
Yang	3,447
Yae	3,376
Saek	2,459
Sam Tao	2,359
Sing Mun	2,164
Tum	2,042
Mon	2,022
Bit	1,530
Sila	1,518
Nguan	988
Lolo	842
Hayi	727
Lawi	584
Sedang	520
Khmer	169
Kri	110

Table 3. Population by Ethnic Group, 1985

Ethnic Group Subgroup	Population
Numbri	67
Total Lao Theung	868,609
Lao Sung	
Hmong	231,168
Akha	57,500
Phu Noi	23,618
Mien (Yao)	18,091
Lahu	9,200
Kui	6,493
Hô	6,361
Total Lao Sung	352,431
Other	
Vietnamese	12,086
Chinese	2,624
Thai	1,459
Cambodian	274
Burmese	185
Indian	44
French	13
Total Other	16,685
TOTAL	3,586,083

Source: Based on information from Laos, National Committee of Plan, *Population Census of 1985*, Vientiane, 1986.

Table 4. *Production of Major Crops, Selected Years, 1980–90*
(in thousands of tons)

Crop	1980	1985	1987	1989	1990[1]
Cardamom	n.a.[2]	n.a.	0.4	1.7	2.7
Coffee[3]	4.4	6.1	7.0	5.4	5.3
Corn	28.4	33.3	35.7	43.8	81.9
Cotton	4.9	2.9	4.0	4.4	5.0
Fruit	15.2	48.0	32.2	53.0	55.0
Mung beans	1.6	1.5	1.9	3.1	3.2
Peanuts	7.9	5.2	5.8	5.9	8.0
Rice	1,053.1	1,395.2	1,232.5	1,404.0	1,508.4
Soybeans	3.3	2.1	3.4	4.9	4.5
Sugarcane	24.1	73.0	81.8	126.0	111.9
Sweet potatoes	80.3	85.4	103.5	159.2	162.8
Tobacco[4]	16.6	15.7	22.7	33.5	58.4
Vegetables	42.6	39.4	40.6	65.7	60.7

[1] Estimated.
[2] n.a.—not available.
[3] In dried beans.
[4] In green leaves.

Source: Based on information from *Environment, Natural Resources, and the Future Development of Laos and Vietnam: Papers from a Seminar,* Fairfax, Virginia, 1991, 32.

Table 5. Yields of Major Crops, Selected Years, 1980–90
(in tons per hectare)

Crop	1980	1985	1987	1989	1990[1]
Cardamom	n.a.[2]	n.a.[2]	0.21	0.30	0.26
Coffee[3]	0.68	0.49	0.48	0.34	0.31
Corn	1.00	1.24	1.44	1.44	1.70
Cotton	0.70	0.56	0.71	0.61	0.72
Fruit	6.06	6.15	10.49	10.60	10.00
Mung beans	0.56	0.62	0.65	0.63	0.70
Peanuts	0.74	0.78	1.23	0.97	0.95
Rice	1.44	2.10	2.16	2.32	2.30
Soybeans	0.69	0.67	0.60	0.81	0.81
Sugarcane	26.73	27.66	27.73	32.93	27.83
Sweet potatoes	8.80	8.37	7.05	5.81	9.32
Tobacco[4]	4.16	4.30	4.11	4.14	4.86
Vegetables	8.14	5.70	6.79	8.54	7.70

[1] Estimated.
[2] n.a.—not available.
[3] In dried beans.
[4] In green leaves.

Source: Based on information from *Environment, Natural Resources, and the Future Development of Laos and Vietnam: Papers from a Seminar,* Fairfax, Virginia, 1991, 32.

Table 6. Industrial Production, Selected Years, 1980–90

	1980	1983	1985	1987	1989	1990
Wood products (in thousands of cubic meters)						
Timber	54.5	n.a.[1]	141.5	365.0	291.9	309.4
Lumber	11.2	n.a.	41.7	55.0	114.0	78.4
Veneer	n.a.	n.a.	143.0	668.0	1,069.0	1,660.0
Cigarettes (in millions) ...	1,100	1,100	1,125	1,200	n.a.	n.a.
Metal products (in tons) ..	489.2	472.4	138.7	n.a.	n.a.	n.a.
Tin plate (in thousands of sheets)	981	820	664	n.a.	n.a.	n.a.
Food (in tons)	1,037	742[2]	1,255	n.a.	n.a.	n.a.
Beverages (in thousands of hectoliters)	21.9	22.8	19.6	n.a.	n.a.	n.a.
Clothing (in thousands of pieces)	260	363	440	n.a.	n.a.	n.a.
Hydroelectricity (in millions of kilowatt-hours)	930	1,030	1,000	1,050	1,095	n.a.
Mining and quarrying						
Tin (in tons)	400	362	520	450	n.a.	n.a.
Gypsum (in thousands of tons)	30	70	100	70	n.a.	n.a.
Salt (in tons)	n.a.	6.5	9.1	12.8	n.a.	n.a.
Coal (in tons)	n.a.	750	1,000	1,550	n.a.	n.a.

[1] n.a.—not available.
[2] Excludes fish.

Source: Based on information from Edu H. Hassing, "Potential for Private Sector Investments in the Industrial and Mining Sector," in Asian Development Bank and The Thai-Canada Economic Co-operation Foundation, *Thai-Lao Forum on Investment and Trade Opportunities in Lao PDR, 3–4 October 1991, Bangkok, Thailand,* Bangkok, 1991.

Table 7. Value of Major Manufactures, Selected Years, 1980–90 (in millions of kip) [1]

	1980	1986	1988	1990
Wood products (except furniture)	3,246	6,253	8,830	14,692
Tobacco products	2,746	3,224	1,082	5,417
Metal products	2,701	3,965	1,298	4,200
Food and beverages	1,229	2,193	2,117	3,626
Clothing	833	461	1,662	2,468

[1] For value of the kip—see Glossary.

Source: Based on information from Edu H. Hassing, "Potential for Private Sector Investments in the Industrial and Mining Sector," in Asian Development Bank and The Thai-Canada Economic Co-operation Foundation, *Thai-Lao Forum on Investment and Trade Opportunities in Lao PDR, 3–4 October 1991, Bangkok, Thailand*, Bangkok, 1991.

Table 8. Government Budget, Selected Years, 1980–90 (in millions of kip) [1]

	1980	1982	1984	1986	1988	1990
Revenues						
Taxes	98	775	1,669	1,755	21,474	44,270
Nontax revenues	650	1,980	3,278	16,748	7,057	13,975
Total revenues	748	2,755	4,947	18,503	28,531	58,245
Expenditures						
Current	1,028	2,259	4,126	14,803	28,038	65,877
Capital	749	3,216	4,258	11,732	47,006	66,080
Total expenditures .	1,777	5,475	8,384	26,535	75,044	131,957
BALANCE	−1,029	−2,720	−3,437	−8,032	−46,513	−73,712

[1] For value of the kip—see Glossary.

Source: Based on information from Economist Intelligence Unit, *Country Profile: Indochina: Vietnam, Laos, Cambodia, 1991–92*, London, 1991, 54; and United Nations, Economic and Social Commission for Asia and the Pacific, *Statistical Yearbook for Asia and the Pacific, 1991*, Bangkok, 1991, 214.

Table 9. *Balance of Payments, Selected Years, 1985–91*
(in millions of United States dollars)

	1985	1987	1989	1991
Exports	74.9	90.5	93.4	109.2
Imports	–219.3	–233.8	–233.9	–249.5
Trade balance	–144.4	–143.3	–140.5	–140.3
Official transfers and grants (net)	50.6	29.1	25.0	88.5
Current account balance	–93.8	–114.2	–115.5	–51.8
Long-term capital (net)	47.7	56.4	42.8	24.1
Other	50.2	55.0	83.2	17.5
Capital account balance	97.9	111.4	126.0	41.6
Errors and omissions	19.3	–5.3	1.6	–6.7
Balance of payments...................	23.4	–8.1	12.1	–16.9
Foreign exchange reserves (excluding gold) .	25.3	20.6	16.1	n.a.[1]

[1] n.a.—not available.

Source: Based on information from World Bank, *World Tables, 1992,* Baltimore, 1992, 371; and International Monetary Fund, *Balance of Payments Statistics Yearbook, 1992,* Pt. 1, 43, Washington, 1992, 405.

Table 10. *Major Exports, 1985, 1987, and 1989*
(in millions of United States dollars)

Commodity	1985	1987	1989
Hydroelectricity	26	12	15
Timber and wood products	11	33	21
Coffee	9	9	9
Tin concentrates	1	2	2
Gypsum	1	2	n.a.[1]
Other[2]	6	6	n.a.
TOTAL	54	64	47

[1] n.a.—not available.
[2] Includes gemstones, gold, and clothing.

Source: Based on information from *The Asia and Pacific Review, 1991–1992: The Economic and Business Report,* Saffron, Walden, United Kingdom, 1991, 106; Economist Intelligence Unit, *Country Report: Indochina: Vietnam, Laos, Cambodia* [London], No. 1, 1992, 5; and Edu H. Hassing, "Potential for Private Sector Investments in the Industrial and Mining Sector," in Asian Development Bank and The Thai-Canada Economic Co-operation Foundation, *Thai-Lao Forum on Investment and Trade Opportunities in Lao PDR, 3–4 October 1991, Bangkok, Thailand,* Bangkok, 1991.

Table 11. *Balance of Trade in Convertible and Nonconvertible*
Currencies, Selected Years, 1982–91
(in millions of United States dollars)

	1982	1985	1988	1991
Merchandise exports				
Convertible currencies	n.a.[1]	34.6	36.8	75.5
Nonconvertible currencies	n.a.	19.0	21.0	2.4
Total merchandise exports	40.0	53.6	57.8	77.9
Merchandise imports				
Convertible currencies	n.a.	77.6	90.4	188.6
Nonconvertible currencies	n.a.	115.6	97.6	4.2
Total merchandise imports	132.2	193.2	188.0	192.8
Balance of trade	−92.2	−139.6	−130.2	−114.9
Percentage of imports financed by exports ...	20.3	27.7	30.7	40.4

[1] n.a.—not available.

Source: Based on information from World Bank, *World Tables, 1992*, Baltimore, 1992,
371; and International Monetary Fund, *Balance of Payments Statistics Yearbook*,
1992, Pt. 1, 43, Washington, 1992, 405.

Table 12. *Foreign Aid Statistics, Selected Years, 1984–91*
(in millions of United States dollars)

	1984	1985	1988	1990	1991
Long-term loans					
Drawings on loans received					
Convertible currencies	10.1	12.1	23.7	49.2	34.5
Nonconvertible currencies	30.2	50.0	44.2	2.6	0.0
Total drawings on loans received	40.3	62.1	67.9	51.8	34.5
Remaining balance on loans received	10.9	−31.8	43.5	n.a.[1]	n.a.
Total long-term loans	51.2	30.3	111.4	n.a.	n.a.
Grants					
Convertible currencies	26.7	45.4	21.0	22.6	63.9
Nonconvertible currencies	15.4	4.2	4.5	0.8	5.3
Total grants	41.2	49.6	25.5	23.4	69.2
TOTAL	92.4	79.9	136.9	n.a.	n.a.

[1] n.a.—not available.

Source: Based on information from World Bank, *World Tables, 1992*, Baltimore, 1992,
371; and International Monetary Fund, *Balance of Payments Statistics Yearbook*,
1992, Pt. 1, 43, Washington, 1992, 406.

Table 13. External Debt, Selected Years, 1985–91
(in millions of United States dollars)

	1985	1987	1989	1991
External debt				
Convertible currency...................	135.0	190.0	252.0	n.a.[1]
Comecon[2]	342.0	536.0	695.0	n.a.
Total external debt[3]	476.0	726.0	947.0	n.a.
Debt service				
Convertible currency...................	5.0	11.0	12.0	n.a.
Other	4.0	2.0	1.0	n.a.
Total debt service	9.0	13.0	13.0	n.a.
Debt service as a percentage of exports	12.0	14.4	13.9	n.a.

[1] n.a.—not available
[2] Council for Mutual Economic Assistance. Dissolved January 1991.
[3] Figures may not add to totals because of rounding.

Source: Based on information from Paul Marer et al., *Historically Planned Economies*, Washington, 1992, 171.

Table 14. Armed Forces Personnel, Selected Years, 1974–93

Year	Army	Navy	Air Force
1974[1]	60,000	500	2,300
1976[2]	40,000	500	2,000
1980	46,000	550	2,000
1982	46,000	1,700	1,000
1984	50,000	1,700	2,000
1986	50,000	1,000	2,000
1988	52,500	1,000	2,000
1990	52,500	600[3]	2,000
1991	50,000	600[3]	2,000
1992	33,000	500[3]	3,500
1993	33,000	500[3]	3,500

[1] Royal Armed Forces; 35,000 Pathet Lao troops, including dissident Neutralists.
[2] Royal Armed Forces disbanded; figures for Lao People's Army.
[3] Estimated.

Source: Based on information from *The Military Balance* (annuals 1974–1975 through 1993–1994), London, 1974–93.

Table 15. Major Equipment of the Armed Forces, 1994

Type and Description	In Inventory
Ground forces	
Tanks	
Main battle tanks: T–54–55, T–34/85	30
Light tanks: PT–76	25
Armored personnel carriers: BTR–40/–60/–152	70
Artillery	
75mm (towed): M–116 pack	—[1]
105mm (towed): M–101	25
122mm (towed): M–1938 and D–30	40
130mm (towed): M–46	10
155mm (towed): M–114	—[1]
Mortars	
81mm	—[1]
82mm	—[1]
107mm: M–2A1 and M–1938	—[1]
120mm: M–43	—[1]
Recoilless guns	
57mm: M–18/A1	—[1]
75mm: M–20	—[1]
106mm: M–40	—[1]
107mm: B–11	—[1]
Air defense guns	
14.5mm: ZPU–1/–4	—[1]
23mm: ZU–23 and ZSU–23–4 SP	—[1]
37mm: M–1939	—[1]
57mm: S–60	—[1]
Surface-to-air missiles: SA–3, SA–7	—[1]
Naval forces	
Patrol craft	
PCI	12[2]
LCM	4
Boats	40–50
Air forces	
Fighters, ground attack	
MiG–21	29
Transports	
An–24	5
An–26	2
Yak–40	2
Helicopters[3]	
Mi–	2
Mi–8	10

Table 15. Major Equipment of the Armed Forces, 1994

Type and Description	In Inventory
Trainers	
MiG–21U	2[4]
Air-to-air missiles	
AA–2 Atoll	—[1]

[1] Numbers not reported.
[2] Reported as "some."
[3] No armed helicopters.
[4] The *Asian Defence Journal* reports four MiG–21Us. The International Institute for Strategic Studies counts these training craft as combat capable.

Source: Based on information from *The Military Balance, 1994–1995*, London, 1994, 181–82; and *Asian Defence Journal* [Kuala Lumpur], January 1993, 108.

Table 16. Military Expenditures Compared with the Gross National Product, Selected Years, 1974–93
(in millions of United States dollars)

Year	Military Expenditures	GNP
1974	27.0	n.a.[1]
1977	42.0	256
1978	29.0	260[2]
1979	37.9	n.a.
1980	21.0	400
1982–88	n.a.[3]	n.a.
1989	18.9[2]	n.a.
1992	102.2[4]	n.a.
1993	104.9[4]	n.a.

[1] n.a.—not available.
[2] Estimated.
[3] Military assistance estimated at US$125 million in 1983.
[4] Includes public security budget.

Source: Based on information from *The Military Balance* (annuals 1974–1975 through 1993–1994), London, 1974–93.

Bibliography

Chapter 1

Adams, Nina S., and Alfred W. McCoy (eds.). *Laos: War and Revolution*. New York: Harper and Row, 1970.

Boyle, Andrew J. *Senior Officers Oral History Program*. Washington: U.S. Military History Institute, 1971.

Breazeale, Kennon, and Snit Smuckarn. *A Culture in Search of Survival: The Phuan of Thailand and Laos*. (Southeast Asian Studies, Monograph Series, No. 31.) New Haven: Yale University, 1988.

Briggs, Lawrence P. "The Appearance and Historical Usage of the Terms Tai, Thai, Siamese and Lao," *Journal of the American Oriental Society*, 69, No. 2, April–June 1949, 60–73.

Brown, MacAlister, and Joseph J. Zasloff. *Apprentice Revolutionaries: The Communist Movement in Laos, 1930–1985*. Stanford: Hoover Institution Press, 1986.

Bui Quang Tung. "Chao Anou, roi de Vientiane, à travers les documents vietnamiens," *Bulletin de la Société des Études Indochinoises* [Saigon], 33, No. 4, 1958, 401–06.

Caply, Michel. "Le Japon et l'indépendance du Laos (1945)," *Revue d'Histoire de la Deuxième Guerre Mondiale* [Paris], 1971, 67–81.

Castle, Timothy N. *At War in the Shadow of Vietnam: U.S. Military Aid to the Royal Lao Government, 1955–1975*. New York: Columbia University Press, 1993.

Cordell, Helen (comp.). *Laos*. (World Bibliographical Series, No. 133.) Oxford, United Kingdom: Clio Press, 1991.

Dengler, Dieter. *Escape from Laos*. Novato, California: Presidio Press, 1979.

De Pelacot. "Le Tran Ninh historique," *Revue Indochinoise* [Hanoi], Nouvelle Série, Tome IV, 34, May 30, 1906.

Deuve, Jean. *Le Laos 1945–1949: Contribution à l'histoire du mouvement Lao Issala*. Montpellier: Université Paul Valéry, 1992.

Deuve, Jean. *Le Royaume du Laos 1949–1965 (Histoire événementielle de l'indépendance à la guerre américaine)*. Paris: EFEO, 1984.

Dommen, Arthur J. *Conflict in Laos: The Politics of Neutralization.* New York: Praeger, 1971.

Dommen, Arthur J., and George W. Dalley. "The OSS in Laos: The 1945 Raven Mission and American Policy," *Journal of Southeast Asian Studies* [Singapore], 22, No. 2, September 1991, 327–46.

Dore, Amphay. "Aux sources de la civilisation Lao (Contribution ethno-historique à la connaissance de la culture Louang-Phrabanaise)." Paris: Cercle de culture et de recherches laotiennes, 1987. Mimeographed.

Furuta, Motoo. "The Indochina Communist Party's Division into Three Parties: Vietnamese Communist Policy Toward Cambodia and Laos, 1948–1951." Pages 143–63 in Masaya Shiraishi and Motoo Furuta (eds.), *Indochina in the 1940s and 1950s.* Ithaca, New York: Southeast Asia Program, Cornell University, 1992.

Goscha, Christopher E. "Thailand and the Vietnamese Resistance Against the French." (Master's thesis.) Canberra: Australian National University, 1991.

Gunn, Geoffrey C. *Political Struggles in Laos (1930–1954): Vietnamese Communist Power and the Lao Struggle for National Independence.* Bangkok: Editions Duang Kamol, 1988.

Hamilton-Merritt, Jane. *Tragic Mountains: The Hmong, the Americans, and the Secret Wars for Laos, 1942–1992.* Bloomington: Indiana University Press, 1993.

Heintges, John A. *Carlisle Barracks, PA, U.S. Army Military History Institute.* Carlisle Barracks, Pennsylvania: Senior Officers Oral History Program, 1974.

Hirshfield, Claire. "The Struggle for the Mekong Banks, 1892–1896," *Journal of Southeast Asian History* [Singapore], 9, No. 3, March 1968, 25–52.

Jumsai, M.L. Manich. *History of Laos.* Bangkok: Chalermnit, 1971.

Kaysone Phomvihane. *Revolution in Laos: Practice and Prospects.* Moscow: Progress, 1981.

Le Boulanger, Paul. *Histoire du Laos français.* Paris: Plon, 1931.

Levy, Paul. *Histoire du Laos.* (Que Sais-Je? No. 1549.) Paris: Presses universitaires de France, 1974.

Lindell, Kristina, Hakan Lundstrom, Jan-Olof Svantesson, and Damrong Tayanin. *The Kammu Year: Its Lore and Music.* London: Curzon Press, 1982.

Long, Lynellyn D. *Ban Vinai, The Refugee Camp.* New York: Columbia University Press, 1993.

Neo Lao Haksat. *A Quarter Century of Grim and Victorious Struggle.* Sam Neua: Laos: 1970.

Ngaosyvathn, Mayoury, and Pheuiphanh. "Lao Historiography and Historians: Case Study of the War Between Bangkok and the Lao in 1827," *Journal of Southeast Asian Studies* [Singapore], 20, No. 1, March 1989, 55–69.

O'Neill, Thomas. "The Mekong: A Haunted River's Season of Peace," *National Geographic,* 183, No. 2, February 1993, 2–35.

Osborne, Milton E. *River Road to China: The Mekong River Expedition, 1866–73.* New York: Liveright, 1975.

Quincy, Keith. *Hmong: History of a People.* Cheney, Washington: Eastern Washington University Press, 1988.

Randle, Robert F. *Geneva 1954: The Settlement of the Indochinese War.* Princeton: Princeton University Press, 1969.

Sage, William W., and Judith A.N. Henchy (comps.). *Laos: A Bibliography.* (Library Bulletin No. 16.) Singapore: Institute of Southeast Asian Studies, 1986.

Scott, Joanna C. *Indochina's Refugees: Oral Histories from Laos, Cambodia, and Vietnam.* Jefferson, North Carolina: McFarland, 1989.

Shiraishi, Masaya, and Motoo Furuta. "Two Features of Japan's Indochina Policy During the Pacific War." Pages 55–85 in Masaya Shiraishi and Motoo Furuta (eds.), *Indochina in the 1940s and 1950s.* Ithaca, New York: Southeast Asia Program, Cornell University, 1992.

Sila Viravong, Maha. *Phongsavadan Lao* (History of Laos). New York: Paragon Books, 1964.

Sirikrai, Surachai. "Thai-American Relations in the Laotian Crisis of 1960–1962." (Ph.D. dissertation.) Binghamton: State University of New York, 1979.

Stieglitz, Perry. *In a Little Kingdom.* Armonk, New York: M.E. Sharpe, 1990.

Stuart-Fox, Martin. *Laos: Politics, Economics, and Society.* Boulder, Colorado: Lynne Rienner, 1986.

Stuart-Fox, Martin, and Mary Kooyman. *Historical Dictionary of Laos.* Metuchen, New Jersey: Scarecrow Press, 1992.

Tarling, Nicholas (ed.). *The Cambridge History of Southeast Asia, 1: From Early Times to c. 1800.* Cambridge: Cambridge University Press, 1992.

Toye, Hugh. *Laos: Buffer State or Battleground.* London: Oxford University Press, 1968.

United States. Congress. 103d, 1st Session. Senate. Select Committee on POW/MIA Affairs. *POW/MIAs: Report of the Select Committee on POW/MIA Affairs.* Washington: GPO, January 13, 1993.

United States. Department of State. *Foreign Relations of the United States, 1952–54, 13: Indochina, Pt. 1.* Washington: 1982.

United States. Department of State. *Foreign Relations of the United States, 1955–1957, 21: East Asian Security; Cambodia, Laos.* Washington: 1990.

United States. Department of State. *Foreign Relations of the United States, 1958–1960, 16: East Asia-Pacific Regions; Cambodia, Laos.* Washington: 1992.

Wyatt, David K. "Siam and Laos 1767–1827," *Journal of Southeast Asian History* [Singapore], 4, No. 2, 1963, 13–21.

Chapter 2

Archaimbault, Charles. *The New Year Ceremony at Bassac.* (Southeast Asian Studies, Data Paper No. 78.) Ithaca, New York: Cornell University, 1971.

Archaimbault, Charles. "Religious Structures in Laos," *Journal of the Siam Society* [Bangkok], 51, No. 1, April 1964, 57–74.

Barber, Martin John Philip. "Migrants and Modernisation: A Study of Change in Lao Society." (Ph.D. dissertation.) Hull, United Kingdom: University of Hull, 1979.

Barney, George L. "The Meo of Xieng Khouang Province, Laos." Pages 271–94 in Nina S. Adams and Alfred W. McCoy (eds.), *Laos: War and Revolution.* New York: Harper Colophon, 1978.

Bernatzik, Hugo Adolf. *Akha and Miao: Problems of Applied Ethnography in Farther India.* (Trans., Alois Nagler.) New Haven: Human Relations Area Files, 1970.

Chanda, Nayan. "Economic Changes in Laos, 1975–80." Pages 116–28 in Martin Stuart-Fox (ed.), *Contemporary Laos: Studies*

in the Politics and Society of the Lao People's Democratic Republic.
New York: St. Martin's Press, 1982.

Clément-Charpentier, Sophie, and Pierre Clément. *L'habitation Lao: Dans les régions de Vientiane et de Louang Prabang,* 1. Paris: Peeters Press, December 1990.

Condominas, Georges. "Essai sur la société rurale Lao de la région de Vientiane." Vientiane: Commissariat des affaires rurales, 1962. Mimeographed.

Condominas, Georges. "The Lao." Pages 9–28 in Nina S. Adams and Alfred W. McCoy (eds.), *Laos: War and Revolution.* New York: Harper Colophon, 1978.

Condominas, Georges. "Phiban Cults in Rural Laos." Pages 252–77 in G. William Skinner and A. Thomas Kirsch (eds.), *Change and Persistence in Thai Society.* Ithaca, New York: Cornell University Press, 1975.

Conquergood, Dwight, Paja Thao, and Xa Thai. *I Am a Shaman: A Hmong Life Story with Ethnographic Commentary."* (Southeast Asian Refugee Studies, Occasional Papers No. 8.) Minneapolis: Center for Urban and Regional Affairs, University of Minnesota, 1989.

Cooper, Robert G. *Resource Scarcity and the Hmong Response: Patterns of Settlement and Economy in Transition.* Singapore: Singapore University Press, 1984.

Cooper, Robert G. "Sexual Inequality among the Hmong." Pages 174–86 in John McKinnon and Wanat Bhruksasri (eds.), *Highlanders of Thailand.* Kuala Lumpur: Oxford University Press, 1983.

Damrong Tayanin. *Being Kammu: My Village, My Life.* Ithaca, New York: Southeast Asia Program, Cornell University, 1992.

Damrong Tayanin. "Environment and Nature Change in Northern Laos." Pages 131–47 in Ole Broun and Anne Kalland (eds.), *Asian Perceptions of Nature.* (Nordic Proceedings in Asian Studies, No. 3.) Copenhagen: Nordic Institute for Asian Studies, 1992.

Damrong Tayanin and Kristina Lindell. *Hunting and Fishing in a Kammu Village.* London: Curzon Press, 1991.

Evans, Grant. *Agrarian Change in Communist Laos.* (Occasional Paper No. 85.) Singapore: Institute of Southeast Asian Studies, 1988.

Evans, Grant. *Lao Peasants under Socialism.* New Haven: Yale University Press, 1990.

Evans, Grant. "Reform or Revolution in Heaven? Funerals among Upland Tai," *Australian Journal of Anthropology* [Sydney], 2, No. 1, 1991, 81–97.

Evans, Grant. "'Rich Peasants' and Cooperatives in Socialist Laos," *Journal of Anthropological Research,* 44, No. 3, Fall 1988, 229–50.

Geddes, William Robert. *Migrants of the Mountains: The Cultural Ecology of the Blue Mieo (Hmong Njua) of Thailand.* Oxford: Clarendon Press, 1976.

Godley, G. McMurrie, and Jinny St. Goar. "The Chinese Road in Northwest Laos, 1961–73." Pages 285–314 in Joseph J. Zasloff and Leonard Unger (eds.), *Laos: Beyond the Revolution.* New York: St. Martin's Press, 1991.

Gunn, Geoffrey C. *Political Struggles in Laos (1930–1954): Vietnamese Communist Power and the Lao Struggle for National Independence.* Bangkok: Editions Duang Kamol, 1988.

Gunn, Geoffrey C. *Rebellion in Laos: Peasant and Politics in a Colonial Backwater.* Boulder, Colorado: Westview Press, 1990.

Håkangård, Agneta. *Road 13: A Socio-Economic Study of Villagers, Transport and Use of Road 13 S, Lao P.D.R.* Stockholm: Department of Social Anthropology, Stockholm University, 1992.

Halpern, Joel Martin. *Economy and Society of Laos.* (Southeast Asia Studies Monograph No. 4.) New Haven: Yale University, 1964.

International Fund for Agricultural Development. *Bokeo Food Security Project: Beneficiary Needs Assessment.* Rome: 1993.

International Fund for Agricultural Development. "Hmong Farming Systems and Social Organization in Nong Het District, Xieng Khouang." North Caulfield, Australia: International Development Support Services, 1991. Mimeographed.

International Fund for Agricultural Development. "Xieng Khouang Agricultural Development Project: Project Preparation Report." Rome: 1990. Mimeographed.

Ireson, Carol. "Nutrition Survey of Six Lao Villages." Vientiane: International Voluntary Service, 1969. Mimeographed.

Ireson, Carol. "Women's Forest Work in Laos," *Society and Natural Resources,* 4, No. 1, 1989, 23–36.

Ireson, Carol J., and W. Randall Ireson. "Ethnicity and Development in Laos," *Asian Survey*, 31, No. 10, October 1991, 920–37.

Ireson, W. Randall. "Hmong Demographic Changes in Laos: Causes and Ecological Consequences." (Paper presented at annual conference of Northwest Regional Consortium for Southeast Asian Studies, Eugene, Oregon, November 8–10, 1991.)

Ireson, W. Randall. "Laos: Building a Nation under Socialism," *Indochina Issues*, No. 79, February 1988.

Ireson, W. Randall. "Patterns of Agricultural Cooperation in Pre-revolutionary Laos." (Paper presented at annual meeting of Canadian Council for Southeast Asian Studies, Vancouver, British Columbia, October 1989.)

Ireson, W. Randall. "Peasant Farmers and Community Norms: Agricultural Labor Exchange in Laos," *Peasant Studies*, 10, No. 2, 1992, 67–92.

Ireson, W. Randall, and Carol J. Ireson. "Laos: Marxism in a Subsistence Rural Economy," *Bulletin of Concerned Asian Scholars*, 21, Nos. 2–4, April-December 1989, 59–75.

Izikowitz, Karl Gustav. *Lamet: Hill Peasants in French Indochina.* (Ethrografiska Studier No. 17) Goteborg, Sweden: Etnografiska Museet, 1951.

Johns, Brenda, and David Strecker (eds.). *The Hmong World.* (Council on Southeast Asia Studies.) New Haven: Yale Center for International and Area Studies, 1986.

Kacha-ananda, Chob. "Le système de la famille Yao," *Journal of the Siam Society* [Bangkok], 60, No. 1, January 1972, 187–94.

Keen, F.G.B. "Ecological Relationships in a Hmong (Meo) Economy." Pages 210–21 in Peter Kundtedter, E.C. Chapman, and Sanga Sabhasri (eds.), *Farmers in the Forest: Economic Development and Marginal Agriculture in Northern Thailand.* Honolulu: University Press of Hawaii, 1978.

Keyes, Charles F. "Millenialism, Theravada Buddhism and Thai Society," *Journal of Asian Studies*, 36, No. 2, February 1977, 283–302.

Lafont, Pierre-Bernard. "Buddhism in Contemporary Laos." Pages 148–62 in Martin Stuart-Fox (ed.), *Contemporary Laos: Studies in the Politics and Society of the Lao People's Democratic Republic.* New York: St. Martin's Press, 1982.

Laos. Ministry of Agriculture and Forestry. "Development Strategies on Shifting Cultivation Stabilization and Environment Protection." (Ministry of Agriculture and Forestry Symposium on Forestry and Environment.) Vientiane: October 18–23, 1989. Mimeographed.

Laos. Ministry of Agriculture and Forestry. "Lao People's Democratic Republic Tropical Forestry Action Plan (First Phase) Main Report." Vientiane: 1990. Mimeographed.

Laos. National Committee of Plan. *Population Census of 1985.* Vientiane: 1986.

Laos. State Statistical Centre. Committee for Planning and Cooperation. *Basic Statistics about the Socio-economic Development in the Lao P.D.R.* Vientiane: Ministry of Economy, Planning, and Finance, 1992.

Laos. State Statistical Centre. Committee for Planning and Cooperation. *Basic Statistics about the Socio-economic Development in the Lao P.D.R.* Vientiane: Ministry of Economy, Planning, and Finance, 1993.

Laos. Statistical Centre. *Lao People's Democratic Republic Multiround Vital Statistics Survey: Population, Size, Distribution and Growth.* Vientiane: 1991.

Laos. State Statistical Centre. *Lao People's Democratic Republic Multiround Vital Statistics Survey: Preliminary Results July 1987–December 1988.* Vientiane: 1988.

LeBar, Frank M., Gerald C. Hickey, and John K. Musgrave. *Ethnic Groups of Mainland Southeast Asia.* New Haven: Human Relations Area Files, 1964.

Lee, Gary Yia. "Minority Policies and the Hmong." Pages 199–219 in Martin Stuart-Fox (ed.), *Contemporary Laos: Studies in the Politics and Society of the Lao People's Democratic Republic.* New York: St. Martin's Press, 1982.

Lemoine, Jacques. *Un village Hmong vert du Haut Laos.* Paris: Centre national de la recherche scientifique, 1972.

Lewis, Paul, and Elaine Lewis. *Peoples of the Golden Triangle.* London: Thames and Hudson, 1984.

Lindell, Kristina, Rolf Samuelsson, and Damrong Tayanin. "Kinship and Marriage in Northern Kammu Villages: The Kinship Model," *Sociologus* [Berlin], 29, No. 1, 1979, 60–84.

Lindell, Kristina, et al. *The Kammu Year: Its Lore and Music.* (Studies on Asian Topics, No. 4.) London: Curzon Press, 1982.

Moréchand, Guy. "Le Chamanisme des Hmong," *Bulletin de l'École Française d'Extrême Orient* [Paris], 54, 1968, 53–294.

Moréchand, Guy. "Principaux traits du chamanisme Meo Blanc en Indo-chine," *Bulletin de l'École Française d'Extrême Orient* [Paris], 47, 1955.

Murdoch, John B. "The 1901–1902 'Holy Man's' Rebellion," *Journal of the Siam Society* [Bangkok], 62, No. 1, January 1974, 47–66.

O'Neill, Thomas. "The Mekong: A Haunted River's Season of Peace," *National Geographic,* 138, No. 2, February 1993, 2–35.

Ovesen, Jan. "Anthropological Reconnaissance in Central Laos: A Survey of Local Communities in a Hydropower Project Area," *Uppsala Research Reports in Cultural Anthropology* [Uppsala], No. 13, 1993.

Phouy Vongkhamchanh, and Jan van der Heide. "Discussion Paper on Land Use in Forestry." Vientiane: Tropical Forestry Action Plan, 1989. Mimeographed.

Savina, F.M. *Histoire des Miao.* Hong Kong: Société des missions étrangères de Paris, 1930.

Shifting Cultivation Project. *Agriculture Programme 1990–1991 Technical Report.* (Annex 2.) Vientiane: World Conservation Union, 1992.

Southeast Asian Universities Agroecosystem Network. *Swidden Agroecosystems in Sepone District Savannakhet Province, Lao PDR.* Khon Kaen: SUAN Regional Secretariat, 1991.

Stuart-Fox, Martin. "The First Ten Years of Communist Rule in Laos," *Asia Pacific Community* [Tokyo], No. 31, Winter 1986, 55–81.

Stuart-Fox, Martin. "The Initial Failure of Agriculture Collectivization in Laos," *Asia Quarterly* [Brussels], 4, 1980, 273–99.

Stuart-Fox, Martin. *Laos: Politics, Economics, and Society.* London: Frances Pinter, 1986.

Stuart-Fox, Martin. "Marxism and Theravada Buddhism: The Legitimization of Political Authority in Laos," *Pacific Affairs* [Vancouver], 56, No. 3, Fall 1983, 428–54.

Stuart-Fox, Martin (ed.). *Contemporary Laos: Studies in the Politics and Society of the Lao People's Democratic Republic.* New York: St. Martin's Press, 1982.

Stuart-Fox, Martin, and Rod Bucknell. "Politicization of the Buddhist Sangha in Laos," *Journal of Southeast Asian Studies* [Singapore], 13, No. 1, March 1982, 60–80.

Taillard, Christian. "Les berges de la Nam Ngum et du Mekong: Systèmes économiques villageois et organisation de l'espace dans la plaine de Vientiane (Laos)," *Études Rurales* [Montrouge Cedex], 53–56, January–December 1974, 119–68.

Taillard, Christian. "De la campagne à la ville: Le paysage bâti de la région de Vientiane," *Asie du Sud-est et Monde Insulindien* [Paris], 11, Nos. 1–4, 1980, 239–64.

Taillard, Christian. "Le dualisme urbain-rural au Laos et la récupération de l'idéologie traditionnelle," *Asie du Sud-est et Monde Insulindien* [Paris], 10, Nos. 2–4, 1979, 91–108.

Taillard, Christian. "Essai sur la bi-polarisation autour du vat et de l'école des villages Lao de la plaine de Vientiane: Le bouddhisme populaire confronte au développement économique," *Asie du Sud-est et Monde Insulindien* [Paris], 5, No. 3, 1974, 91–104.

Taillard, Christian. *Le Laos: Stratégies d'un état-tampon.* Montpellier: Reclus, 1989.

Taillard, Christian. "Le village Lao de la région de Vientiane: Un pouvoir local face au pouvoir étatique," *L'Homme: Revue française d'anthropologie* [Paris], 17, Nos. 2–3, April-September 1977, 71–100.

Tapp, Nicholas. *Sovereignty and Rebellion: The White Hmong of Northern Thailand.* Singapore: Oxford University Press, 1989.

Thao, T. Christopher. "Hmong Customs on Marriage: Divorce and the Rights of Married Women." Pages 74–98 in Brenda Johns and David Strecker (eds.), *The Hmong World.* (Council of Southeast Asia Studies.) New Haven: Yale Center for International and Area Studies, 1986.

Trankell, Ing-Britt. "On the Road in Laos: An Anthropological Study of Road Construction and Rural Communities," *Uppsala Research Reports in Cultural Anthropology* [Uppsala], No. 12, 1993.

United Nations. Department of Economic and Social Information and Policy Analysis. Statistical Division. *Statistical Yearbook, 1990-91.* New York: 1993.

United Nations Children's Fund. *An Analysis of the Situation of Children and Women in the Lao People's Democratic Republic.* Vientiane: 1992.

United Nations Children's Fund *Children and Women in the Lao People's Democratic Republic.* Vientiane: 1992.

United Nations Development Programme. *Development Cooperation: Lao People's Democratic Republic, 1991 Report.* Vientiane: 1992.

United Nations Development Programme. *The Implications of HIV/AIDS on Social and Economic Development in the Lao People's Democratic Republic.* (Conference Report.) Vientiane: 1992.

United Nations High Commission for Refugees. *Statistics Concerning Indo-Chinese in East and South-East Asia for the Month of December 1992.* Geneva: January 1993.

United Nations High Commission for Refugees. "Voluntary Repatriation to Laos as of 31 December 1992." Vientiane: 1993.

Westermeyer, Joseph. *Poppies, Pipes, and People: Opium and Its Use in Laos.* Berkeley: University of California Press, 1982.

Wyatt, David K. *Thailand: A Short History.* New Haven: Yale University Press, 1982.

Zago, Marcel. *Rites et cérémonies en milieu bouddhiste Lao.* Rome: Università Grĕgoriana Editrice, 1972.

Zasloff, Joseph J., and Leonard Unger (eds.). *Laos: Beyond the Revolution.* New York: St. Martin's Press, 1991.

Chapter 3

Almazan, Alec. "Laos: Government Ready to Privatise 670 State Enterprises," *Business Times* [Singapore], January 31, 1992.

The Asia and Pacific Review 1991–1992: The Economic and Business Report. Saffron Walden, United Kingdom: World of Information, 1991.

Asia Yearbook, 1992. Hong Kong: Far Eastern Economic Review, 1992.

Asian Development Bank. *Asian Development Outlook, 1991.* Manila: 1991.

Asian Development Bank and The Thai-Canada Economic Co-operation Foundation. *Thai-Lao Forum on Investment and Trade Opportunities in Lao PDR, 3-4 October 1991, Bangkok, Thailand.* Bangkok: 1991.

Asian Economic Handbook. London: Euromonitor, 1987.

Ballantyne, Tom. "Indo China: Barriers Still Exist to Prevent Laos and Cambodia from Becoming a Major Air Transport Market," *Airline Business* [London], June 1, 1992, 42.

Baluyut, Elvira A. *A Regional Survey of the Aquaculture Sector in East Asia, including Brunei Darussalam, China, Hong Kong, Japan, the Democratic People's Republic of Korea, the Republic of Korea, Laos, Macau, Mongolia, Philippines, Taiwan Province of China and Viet Nam.* (Aquaculture Development and Coordination Programme, ADCP/REP/88/31.) Rome: United Nations Development Programme, Food and Agriculture Organization of the United Nations, 1989.

Bogdan, Michael. "Legal Aspects of the Re-Introduction of a Market Economy in Laos," *Review of Socialist Law* [Leiden], 17, No. 2, 1991, 101–23.

Boonsong Kositchotethana. "Laos Welcomes Private Power Utility Investment," *Bangkok Post* [Bangkok], November 5, 1992, 22.

Bourdet, Yves. *Laos: Reforming Laos' Economic System.* Stockholm: Swedish International Development Authority, 1991.

Brahm, Laurence J., and Neill T. Macpherson. *Investment in the Lao People's Democratic Republic: A Specially Commissioned Report.* White Plains, New York: The Longman Group, 1991.

Clark, Allen L., James P. Dorian, and Wayne A. Hudders. "Mineral Development Prospects of the Indochina Area: Potential Exceeds Problems," *Natural Resources Forum: A United Nations Journal,* 15, No. 1, February 1991, 26–39.

Cummings, Joe. *Laos: A Travel Survival Kit.* Berkeley: Lonely Planet, 1994.

Economist Intelligence Unit. *Country Profile: Indochina: Vietnam, Laos, Cambodia, 1991-92.* London: 1991.

Environment, Natural Resources, and the Future of Development of Laos and Vietnam: Papers from a Seminar. (Ed., Nguyen Manh Hung.) (Indochina Institute Papers Series.) Fairfax, Virginia: The Indochina Institute, George Mason University, 1991.

Europa. *The Far East and Australasia, 1992.* London: 1992.

Evans, Grant, and Kelvin Rowley. *Red Brotherhood at War: Vietnam, Cambodia and Laos since 1975.* London: Verso, 1990.

Fernando, P.N. "Power Subsector Developments in the Lao PDR and Implication to the Private Sector." In Asian Development Bank and The Thai-Canada Economic Co-operation Foundation, *Thai-Lao Forum on Investment and Trade Opportunities in Lao PDR, 3–4 October 1991, Bangkok, Thailand.* Bangkok: 1991.

"Foreign Aid, Loans in Past 15 Years Cited," Vientiane KPL, September 4, 1990. Foreign Broadcast Information Service, *Daily Report: East Asia.* (FBIS-EAS-90-178.) September 13, 1990, 64.

Fujisaka, Sam. *A Diagnostic Survey of Shifting Cultivation in Northern Laos: Targeting Research to Improve Sustainability and Productivity.* (IRRI Social Science Division Papers, No. 90–42.) Manila: Social Science Division, International Rice Research Institute, 1990.

Germany. Statistisches Bundesamt. *Länderbericht Laos, 1990.* Wiesbaden: Metzler/Poeschel for Statistisches Bundesamt, October 1990.

Gunn, Geoffrey C. "Laos in 1989: Quiet Revolution in the Marketplace," *Asian Survey,* 30, No. 1, January 1990, 81–87.

Hassing, Edu H. "Potential for Private Sector Investments in the Industrial and Mining Sector." In Asian Development Bank and The Thai-Canada Economic Co-operation Foundation, *Thai-Lao Forum on Investment and Trade Opportunities in Lao PDR, 3–4 October 1991, Bangkok, Thailand.* Bangkok: 1991.

International Monetary Fund. *Balance of Payments Statistics Yearbook, 1992,* Pt. 1, 43. Washington: 1992.

Ireson, Carol J., and W. Randall Ireson. "Ethnicity and Development in Laos," *Asian Survey,* 31, No. 10, October 1991, 920–37.

Laos. Ministry of Science and Technology. *Lao People's Democratic Republic National Report to UNCED, 1992: United Nations Conference on Environment and Development.* Vientiane: 1991.

Laos. State Planning Committee. State Statistical Centre. *10 Years of Socio-Economic Development in the Lao People's Democratic Republic.* Vientiane: State Statistical Centre, 1985.

"Laos: New Policy Helps Stimulate Economy," *Bangkok Post* [Bangkok], December 2, 1992, 19.

Leung, Wayne. "Laos: Learning from China," *China Trade Report* [Hong Kong], 28, July 1990, 6–7.

Marer, Paul, Janos Arvay, John O'Connor, Martin Schrenk, and Daniel Swanson. *Historically Planned Economies: A Guide to the Data.* Washington: World Bank, 1992.

Mehta, Harish. "Laos Takes Steps to Boost Investor Confidence," *Business Times* [Singapore], December 16, 1992.

Min Tang. *A Survey of the External Debt Situation in Asian and Pacific Developing Countries 1989–1992.* (Report No. 15.) Manila: Economics and Development Resource Center, Asian Development Bank, June 1991.

Morrison, Charles E., and Robert F. Dernberger (eds.). *Asia-Pacific Report, Focus: China in the Reform Era.* Honolulu: East-West Center, 1989.

Nielsen, Preben. "The Changing Face of the Transport System in Lao PDR and Thailand: Implications for the Private Sector." In Asian Development Bank and The Thai-Canada Economic Co-operation Foundation, *Thai-Lao Forum on Investment and Trade Opportunities in Lao PDR, 3–4 October 1991, Bangkok, Thailand.* Bangkok: 1991.

Organisation for Economic Co-operation and Development. *Geographical Distribution of Financial Flows to Developing Countries: Disbursements, Commitments, Economic Indicators, 1987–1990.* Paris: 1992.

Phiane Philakone. "The Banking Sector in the Lao PDR." In Asian Development Bank and The Thai-Canada Economic Co-operation Foundation, *Thai-Lao Forum on Investment and Trade Opportunities in Lao PDR, 3–4 October 1991, Bangkok, Thailand.* Bangkok: 1991.

Radetzki, Marcus. "From Communism to Capitalism in Laos: The Legal Dimension," *Asian Survey,* 34, No. 9, September 1994, 799–806.

Shinawatra, Thaksin. "Potential Lao PDR/Thailand Joint Telecommunication Development Projects: A Private Industry Perspective." In Asian Development Bank and The Thai-Canada Economic Co-operation Foundation, *Thai-Lao Forum on Investment and Trade Opportunities in Lao PDR, 3–4 October 1991, Bangkok, Thailand.* Bangkok: 1991.

Stuart-Fox, Martin. "Laos 1991: On the Defensive." Pages 174-77 in *Southeast Asian Affairs, 1992.* Singapore: Institute of Southeast Asian Studies, 1992.

"Thailand: Tourism Agreement Signed with Laos," *Business Times* [Singapore], February 25, 1992.

United Nations. Conference on Trade and Development. *The Least Developed Countries, 1990 Report.* New York: 1990.

United Nations. Economic and Social Commission for Asia and the Pacific. *Economic and Social Survey of Asia and the Pacific, 1990.* New York: 1990.

United Nations. Economic and Social Commission for Asia and the Pacific. *Statistical Yearbook for Asia and the Pacific, 1991.* Bangkok: 1991.

United Nations. Economic and Social Commission for Asia and the Pacific. *Traders' Manual for Asia and the Pacific: Lao People's Democratic Republic.* New York: 1991.

United Nations Development Programme. *Report on Development Cooperation: Lao People's Democratic Republic, 1987 Report.* Vientiane: 1988.

United States. Central Intelligence Agency. *Handbook of Economic Statistics, 1990: A Reference Aid.* Washington: 1990.

United States. Central Intelligence Agency. *World Factbook, 1994.* Washington: 1994.

United States. Department of the Interior. Bureau of Mines. *Minerals Yearbook, 1987, 3: Area Reports: International.* Washington: 1987.

United States. Department of State. Bureau of International Narcotics Matters. *International Narcotics Control Strategy Report.* Washington: April 1994.

Vannothone S. Thongsith. "Tourism = The Untapped Potential in Lao PDR." In Asian Development Bank and The Thai-Canada Economic Co-operation Foundation, *Thai-Lao Forum on Investment and Trade Opportunities in Lao PDR, 3-4 October 1991, Bangkok, Thailand.* Bangkok: 1991.

World Bank. *Social Indicators of Development, 1991–92.* Baltimore: Johns Hopkins University Press, 1992.

World Bank. *Trends in Developing Economies, 1991.* Washington: 1991.

World Bank. *World Debt Tables, 1992–93: External Finance for Developing Countries, 2, Country Tables.* Washington: 1993.

World Bank. *World Development Report, 1992: Development and the Environment, World Development Indicators.* New York: Oxford University Press, 1992.

World Bank. *World Tables, 1992.* Baltimore: Johns Hopkins University Press for the World Bank, 1992.

World Resources Institute. *World Resources, 1990–91: A Guide to the Global Environment.* New York: Oxford University Press, 1990.

Zasloff, Joseph J., and MacAlister Brown. "Laos 1990: Socialism Postponed but Leadership Intact." Pages 147–50 in *Southeast Asian Affairs, 1991.* Singapore: Institute of Southeast Asian Studies, 1991.

Zola, Anthony M. "Agribusiness Opportunities in Laos." In Asian Development Bank and The Thai-Canada Economic Cooperation Foundation, *Thai-Lao Forum on Investment and Trade Opportunities in Lao PDR, 3–4 October 1991, Bangkok, Thailand.* Bangkok: 1991.

(Various issues of the following periodicals were also used in the preparation of this chapter: *Asian Survey,* 1991–94; Economist Intelligence Unit; *Country Report: Indochina: Vietnam, Laos, Cambodia* [London], 1991–94; and Foreign Broadcast Information Service, *Daily Report: East Asia,* 1993–94.)

Chapter 4

American Friends Service Committee. *Annual Reports, 1990–93.* Philadelphia: 1990–94.

Amnesty International. *Background Paper on the Democratic People's Republic of Laos Describing Current Amnesty International Concerns.* (AI 26/04/85.) New York: April 1985.

Asia Yearbook, 1990. Hong Kong: Far Eastern Economic Review, 1990.

"Birth Commemorated in Vientiane, Souphanouvong Speech," Foreign Broadcast Information Service, *Daily Report: Asia and Pacific.* January 18, 1977.

Brown, MacAlister. "Anatomy of a Border Dispute: Laos and Thailand," *Pacific Focus* [Inchon], 11 No. 2, 1987, 5–30.

Brown, MacAlister. "Laos: Bottoming Out," *Current History,* 82, No. 483, April 1983, 154–57, 180–82.

Brown, MacAlister. "Laos in 1975: People's Democratic Revolution-Lao Style," *Asian Survey*, 16, No. 2, February 1976, 193–99.

Brown, MacAlister, and Joseph J. Zasloff. *Apprentice Revolutionaries: The Communist Movement in Laos, 1930–85.* Stanford: Hoover Institution Press, 1986.

Brown, MacAlister, and Joseph J. Zasloff. *Communism in Indochina: New Perspectives.* Lexington, Massachusetts: Lexington Books, 1975.

Brown, MacAlister, and Joseph J. Zasloff. "Dependency in Laos," *Current History*, 75, No. 442, December 1978, 202–07, 228.

Brown, MacAlister, and Joseph J. Zasloff. "Laos 1976: Faltering First Steps Towards Socialism," *Asian Survey*, 17, No. 2, February 1977, 107–15.

Brown, MacAlister, and Joseph J. Zasloff. "Laos 1977: The Realities of Independence," *Asian Survey*, 18, No. 2, February 1978, 164–74.

Brown, MacAlister, and Joseph J. Zasloff. "Laos 1978: The Ebb and Flow of Adversity," *Asian Survey*, 19, No. 2, February 1979, 95–103.

Brown, MacAlister, and Joseph J. Zasloff. "New Stages of Revolution in Laos," *Current History*, 71, No. 422, December 1976, 218–21, 228–29.

Butwell, Richard. "From Feudalism to Communism in Laos," *Current History*, 69, No. 411, December 1975, 223–26, 246.

Chanda, Nayan. "An Undisputed Leader with a Taste for Secrecy," *Far Eastern Economic Review* [Hong Kong], May 28, 1982, 24.

Chi Do Pham (ed.). *Economic Reforms in the Laos PDR: Current Trends and Perspectives.* Vientiane: International Monetary Fund, April 1992.

Cordell, Helen (comp.). *Laos.* (World Bibliographical Series, No. 133.) Oxford, United Kingdom: Clio Press, 1991.

Dore, Amphay. "The Three Revolutions in Laos." Pages 101–15 in Martin Stuart-Fox (ed.), *Contemporary Laos: Studies in the Politics and Society of the Lao People's Democratic Republic.* St Lucia: University of Queensland Press, 1982.

Evans, Grant. *Lao Peasants under Socialism.* New Haven: Yale University Press, 1990.

Evans, Grant. "Planning Problems in Peripheral Socialism: The Case of Laos." Pages 84–130 in Joseph J. Zasloff and Leonard Unger (eds.), *Laos: Beyond the Revolution.* New York: St. Martin's Press, 1991.

Evans, Grant, and Kelvin Rowley. "Laos: The Eclipse of 'Neutralist' Communism." Pages 59–80 in *Red Brotherhood at War: Vietnam, Cambodia, and Laos since 1975.* London: Verso, 1990.

Everingham, John. "The Pathet Lao Make it Official," *Far Eastern Economic Review* [Hong Kong], September 5, 1975, 39–40.

Fletcher, Don, and Geoffrey C. Gunn. *Revolution in Laos: The 'Fourth Generation' of People's War?* Townsville, Australia: James Cook University, 1981.

Gunn, Geoffrey C. "Resistance Coalitions in Laos," *Asian Survey,* 23, No 3., March 1983, 316–40.

Halpern, Joel Martin. *Government, Politics, and Social Structure of Laos: A Study in Tradition and Innovation.* Christiansburg, Virginia: Dalley Book Service, 1990.

Hannah, Norman B. *The Key to Failure: Laos and the Vietnam War.* Lanham, Maryland: Madison Books, 1987.

Hiebert, Murray. "Socialist Transformation in Laos," *Current History,* 79, No. 461, December 1980, 175–79, 194–95.

Huxley, Andrew. "The Draft Constitution of the Laotian People's Democratic Republic," *Review of Socialist Law* [Leiden], 17, No. 1, 1991, 75–78.

Johnson, Stephen T. "The Lao People's Democratic Republic at Fifteen." (Paper presented at a conference at Columbia University, May 14, 1990.) New York, Columbia University, 1990.

Johnson, Stephen T. "Laos in 1992: Succession and Consolidation," *Asian Survey,* 33, No. 1, January 1993, 75–82.

Kamm, Henry. "The Greying of Vientiane," *New York Times Magazine,* May 20, 1979, 29, 78, 80, 82, 84, 86.

Kaysone Phomvihan. "Political Report Presented by Mr. Kaysone Phomvihan at the National Congress of the People's Representatives in Laos (December 1, 1975, condensed)," *Journal of Contemporary Asia,* 6, No. 1, 1976, 110–19.

"Kaysone Phomvihan," *Pravda* [Moscow], December 22, 1988.

"Kaysone Phomvihan Addresses 12 October Viengsay Rally," Radio Pathet Lao in Lao, October 1, 1975. Foreign Broadcast Information Service, *Daily Report: Asia and Pacific,* October 15, 1975.

Langer, Paul F., and Joseph J. Zasloff. *North Vietnam and the Pathet Lao: Partners in the Struggle for Laos.* Cambridge: Harvard University Press, 1970.

McBeth, John. "Squeezing the Vietnamese: Dissident Lao Confirm that some Anti-Pathet Lao Forces Are Receiving Arms and Training from the Chinese," *Far Eastern Economic Review* [Hong Kong], December 19, 1980, 9.

Meng, Ng Shui. "Laos in 1986: Into the Second Decade of National Reconstruction," *Southeast Asian Affairs* [Singapore], 1987, 177–93.

Norindr, Chou. "Political Institutions of the Lao People's Democratic Republic." Pages 39–61 in Martin Stuart-Fox (ed.), *Contemporary Laos: Studies in the Politics and Society of the Lao People's Democratic Republic.* St. Lucia: University of Queensland Press, 1982.

"Oudom Katthi-nga Reports Revision of Party Rules," Vientiane Pasason in Lao, March 29, 1991. Foreign Broadcast Information Service. *Daily Report: East Asia.* (FBIS-EAS-91-071-2.) April 12, 1991.

Panaristis, Andrea. "Yellow Rain: A Vanishing Trail?" *Indochina Issues*, No. 47, June 1984.

Pheuiphanh Ngaosyvathn. "Political Report to Fourth Party Congress by Secretary General Kaysone Phomvihan." Foreign Broadcast Information Service, *Foreign Broadcast Information Service Supplement,* January 6, 1987, 37.

Pheuiphanh Ngaosyvathn. "Thai-Lao Relations: A Lao View," *Asian Survey*, 25, No. 12, December 1985, 1242–59.

Quinn-Judge, Paul. "Roundup in Vientiane: Silence Surrounds Reports of a Purge Against Corrupt Government Officials," *Far Eastern Economic Review* [Hong Kong], June 30, 1982, 36.

Quinn-Judge, Paul. "A Soft-Shoe Shuffle: Overlord of the Economy Steps Aside as Laos Brings in the Technocrats," *Far Eastern Economic Review* [Hong Kong], September 24, 1982, 32–34.

Radetzki, Marcus. "From Communism to Capitalism in Laos: The Legal Dimension," *Asian Survey*, 34, No. 9, September 1994, 799–806.

Robinson, Julian, Jeanne Guillemin, and Matthew Meselson. "Yellow Rain: The Story Collapses," *Foreign Policy*, No. 68, Fall 1987, 100–17.

Sarasin Viraphol. "Reflections on Thai-Lao Relations," *Asian Survey*, 25, No. 12, December 1985, 1260–76.

Southeast Asian Affairs, 1974. Singapore: Institute of Southeast Asian Studies, 1974.

Souvannaphouma, Mangkra. *L'agonie du Laos/Prince Mangkra Souvannaphouma.* Paris: Plon, 1976.

Stuart-Fox, Martin. "The Constitution of the Lao People's Democratic Republic," *Review of Socialist Law* [Leiden], 17, No. 4, 1991, 299–317.

Stuart-Fox, Martin. "Lao Foreign Policy: The View from Vientiane," *Journal of Contemporary Asia* [London], 11, No. 3, 1981, 351–66.

Stuart-Fox, Martin. "Laos in 1988: In Pursuit of New Directions," *Asian Survey*, 29, No. 1, January 1989, 81–88.

Stuart-Fox, Martin. *Laos: Politics, Economics, and Society.* London: Frances Pinter, 1986.

Stuart-Fox, Martin. "Politics and Patronage in Laos," *Indochina Issues*, No. 70, October 1986.

Stuart-Fox, Martin. "Reflections on the Lao Revolution," *Contemporary Southeast Asia* [Singapore], 3, No. 1, June 1981, 41–57.

Stuart-Fox, Martin. "Socialist Construction and National Security in Laos," *Bulletin of Concerned Asian Scholars*, 13, No. 1, January-March 1981, 61–71.

Stuart-Fox, Martin (ed.). *Contemporary Laos: Studies in the Politics and Society of the Lao People's Democratic Republic.* New York: St. Martin's Press, 1982.

Toye, Hugh. *Laos: Buffer State or Battleground.* London: Oxford University Press, 1968.

United Nations Development Programme. *Development Cooperation: Lao People's Democratic Republic, 1990 Report.* Vientiane: 1991.

United States. Central Intelligence Agency. *World Factbook, 1994.* Washington: 1994.

United States. Department of State. *Country Reports on Human Rights Practices for 1992.* (Report submitted to United States Congress, 103d, 1st Session, Senate, Committee on Foreign Relations, and House of Representatives, Committee on Foreign Affairs.) Washington: GPO, February 1993.

United States. Department of State. *Country Reports on Human Rights Practices for 1993.* (Report submitted to United States Congress, 103d, 2d Session, House of Representatives, Committee on Foreign Affairs, and Senate, Committee on Foreign Relations.) Washington: GPO, February 1994.

Wain, Barry. "Rulers of Laos Are Absorbing Hard Economic Lessons," *Bangkok Post* [Bangkok], November 26, 1980.

Wurfel, David, and Bruce Barton. *The Political Economy of Foreign Policy in Southeast Asia.* London: Macmillan, 1990.

"Yellow Rain in Laos: New Reports," *Wall Street Journal,* June 13–14, 1990.

Zasloff, Joseph J. "Lao People's Democratic Republic." In Albert P. Blaustein and Gisbert H. Flanz (eds.), *Constitutions of the Countries of the World.* Dobbs Ferry: Oceana, January 1992.

Zasloff, Joseph J. *The Pathet Lao: Leadership and Organization.* Lexington, Massachusetts, Lexington Books, 1973.

Zasloff, Joseph J. "Political Constraints on Development in Laos." Pages 3–39 in Joseph J. Zasloff and Leonard Unger (eds.), *Laos: Beyond the Revolution.* New York: St. Martin's Press, 1991.

Zasloff, Joseph J. *Politics in the New Laos, Pt. 1: Leadership and Change. Pt. 2: The Party, Political 'Re-education' and Vietnamese Influence.* (American Universities Field Staff, Fieldstaff Reports, Asia, Nos. 33–34.) Hanover, New Hampshire: AUFS, 1981.

Zasloff, Joseph J. *Postwar Indochina: Old Enemies and New Allies.* Washington: Center for the Study of Foreign Affairs, 1988.

Zasloff, Joseph J. *The Three-Village Dispute Between Laos and Thailand.* (Universities Field Staff International, UFSI Reports, No. 23.) Indianapolis: 1985.

Zasloff, Joseph J., and MacAlister Brown. *Communist Indochina and U.S. Foreign Policy: Postwar Realities.* Boulder, Colorado: Westview Press, 1978.

Zasloff, Joseph J., and MacAlister Brown. "Laos: Coping with Confinement." Pages 211–28 in *Southeast Asian Affairs, 1982.* Singapore: Institute of Southeast Asian Studies, 1982.

Zasloff, Joseph J., and MacAlister Brown. "Laos 1990: Socialism Postponed but Leadership Intact." Pages 147–50 in *Southeast*

Asian Affairs, 1991. Singapore: Institute of Southeast Asian Studies, 1991.

Zasloff, Joseph J., and MacAlister Brown. "Laos since the Communist Victory." Pages 87–121 in Joseph J. Zasloff and MacAlister Brown (eds.), *Communist Indochina and U.S. Foreign Policy: Postwar Realities.* Boulder, Colorado: Westview-Press, 1978.

Zasloff, Joseph J., and Allan E. Goodman (eds.). *Indochina in Conflict: A Political Assessment.* Lexington, Massachusetts: Lexington Books, 1972.

Zasloff, Joseph J., and Leonard Unger (eds.). *Laos: Beyond the Revolution.* New York: St. Martin's Press, 1991.

(Various issues of the following periodicals were also used in the preparation of this chapter: *Asian Survey,* 1990–94; *Current History,* 1990–94; *Far Eastern Economic Review* [Hong Kong], 1990–94; Foreign Broadcast Information Service, *Daily Report: East Asia,* 1990–94; *Indochina Chronology,* 1990–94; and *Southeast Asian Affairs* [Singapore], 1990–94.)

Chapter 5

Adams, Nina S., and Alfred W. McCoy (eds.). *Laos: War and Revolution.* New York: Harper and Row, 1970.

Amnesty International. *Amnesty International Report, 1993.* New York: 1993.

Amnesty International. *Amnesty International Report, 1994.* New York: 1994.

Amnesty International. *Laos. Freedom of Expression Still Denied. Multi-Party Advocates and Political Prisoners Sentenced after Unfair Trials.* London: Amnesty International Secretariat, July 1993.

Anson, Robert Sam. "Again the Indochina Quagmire Beckons," *New York Times,* October 18, 1989, 1, 29.

Asia Yearbook, 1988. Hong Kong: Far Eastern Economic Review, 1988.

Blaufarb, Douglas S. *Organizing and Managing Unconventional War in Laos.* (R-919-ARPA.) Santa Monica, California: RAND, January 1972.

Brown, MacAlister. "Easing the Burden of Socialist Struggle in Laos," *Current History,* 86, April 1987, 152–55, 177.

Brown, MacAlister, and Joseph J. Zasloff. *Apprentice Revolutionaries: The Communist Movement in Laos, 1930–1985.* Stanford: Hoover Institution Press, 1986.

Castle, Timothy N. *At War in the Shadow of Vietnam: U.S. Military Aid to the Royal Lao Government, 1955–1975.* New York: Columbia University Press, 1993.

"Communist Party Veterans Dropped by Laos Politburo," *New York Times,* March 30, 1991, A9.

Conboy, Kenneth J. *War in Laos, 1954–1975.* Carrollton, Texas: Squadron/Signal, 1994.

"Course on Drug Law Enforcement Held in Vientiane," Vientiane KPL, September 14, 1992. Foreign Broadcast Information Service, *Daily Report: East Asia.* (FBIS-EAS-92-180.) September 16, 1992, 24.

Cumming-Bruce, Nicholas. "Lao Communists Do an About-Face," *U.S. News & World Report,* 107, July 3, 1989, 35–36.

Cummings, Joe. *Vietnam, Laos, and Cambodia.* Berkeley: Lonely Planet, 1991.

Defense and Foreign Affairs Handbook. Washington: Perth, 1988.

Dommen, Arthur J. *Laos: Keystone of Indochina.* Boulder, Colorado: Westview Press, 1985.

"Envoy Calls for Thai Help to Suppress Ethnic Resistance," *Nation* [Bangkok], August 1, 1992, A3. Foreign Broadcast Information Service, *Daily Report: East Asia.* (FBIS-EAS-92-164.) August 3, 1992, 18.

"Ethnic Lao's [sic] with U.S. Passports Arrested," *Bangkok Post* [Bangkok], October 21, 1992, 1. Foreign Broadcast Information Service, *Daily Report: East Asia.* (FBIS-EAS-92-204.) October 21, 1992, 50–51.

"Fighting Between Government Troops, Rebels Noted," *Bangkok Post* [Bangkok], March 4, 1992, 5. Foreign Broadcast Information Service, *Daily Report: East Asia.* (FBIS-EAS-92-044.) March 5, 1992, 28.

Gunn, Geoffrey C. *Rebellion in Laos: Peasant and Politics in a Colonial Backwater.* Boulder, Colorado: Westview, 1990.

Hamilton-Merritt, Jane. *Tragic Mountains: The Hmong, the Americans, and the Secret Wars for Laos, 1942–1992.* Bloomington: Indiana University Press, 1993.

Hiebert, Murray. "Laotian Reforms Help Spur Economic, Social Revival," *Washington Post,* January 2, 1988, 1.

Hiebert, Murray. "The Road to Reform," *Far Eastern Economic Review* [Hong Kong], 34, February 16, 1989, 18–20.

Ireson, W. Randall. "Laos: Building a Nation under Socialism," *Indochina Issues,* No. 79, February 1988.

Kamm, Henry. "Laos Is Courting New Benefactors," *New York Times,* January 11, 1990, A6.

Kamm, Henry. "U.S. and Laos Are Getting Friendlier," *New York Times,* January 31, 1990, A3.

Karniol, Robert. "Laotian Resistance Emerges from Mist," *International Defense Review* [Geneva], 23, No. 3, March 1990, 269-72.

"Lao People's Democratic Republic: Biographic Information on Officials." Joint Publications Research Service, *Southeast Asia Report.* (JPRS-SEA-89-020.) May 17, 1989, 1–121.

Lao People's Democratic Republic. Lao National Commission for Drug Control and Supervision. *Drug Control in 1991.* Vientiane: February 1992.

"Laotian Leader Gains with New Constitution," *New York Times,* August 16, 1991, 37.

Liebchen, Peter A.W. "MAP Aid to Laos 1959–1972," *PACAF: Project CHECO Report.* Reprint. Christiansburg, Virginia: Dalley, 1973.

Loetcharoenchok, Yindi. "Crackdown on Lao Rebels to Foster Vientiane Ties," *Nation* [Bangkok], July 31, 1992, A6. Foreign Broadcast Information Service, *Daily Report: East Asia.* (FBIS-EAS-92-148.) July 31, 1992, 37–38.

Meng, Ng Shui. "Laos in 1986: Into the Second Decade of National Reconstruction," *Southeast Asian Affairs* [Singapore], 1987, 177–93.

The Military Balance (annuals 1974–1975 through 1994–1995). London: International Institute for Strategic Studies, 1974–94.

"Military Courts Set Up in Six Northern Provinces," Vientiane Vitthayou Hengsat Radio Network, November 15, 1992. Foreign Broadcast Information Service, *Daily Report: East Asia.* (FBIS-EAS-92-221.) November 16, 1992, 36.

"Police Concerned about Heroin Traffic from Laos," *Bangkok Post,* October 8, 1989, 1.

Pratt, John C. "The Royal Laotian Air Force 1954–1970," *PACAF: Project CHECO Report.* Reprint. Christiansburg, Virginia: Dalley, 1970.

Ratnam, Perala. *Laos and the Superpowers.* New Delhi: Tulsi, 1980.

Sananikone, Oudone. *The Royal Lao Army and U.S. Army Advice and Support.* (Indochina Monographs.) Washington: U.S. Army Center of Military History, 1981.

Sesser, S. "Forgotten Country," *The New Yorker,* 66, August 20, 1990, 39–42.

Stuart-Fox, Martin. "Politics and Patronage in Laos," *Indochina Issues,* No. 70, October 1986.

Stuart-Fox, Martin (ed.). *Contemporary Laos: Studies in the Politics and Society of the Lao People's Democratic Republic.* New York: St. Martin's Press, 1982.

"Two More Refugee Camps to Close in 1994," Bangkok Radio Thailand Network, March 20, 1993. Foreign Broadcast Information Service, *Daily Report: East Asia.* (FBIS-EAS-93-054.) March 23, 1993, 62.

United States. Central Intelligence Agency. *World Factbook, 1992,* Washington: 1992.

United States. Central Intelligence Agency. *World Factbook, 1993.* Washington: 1993.

United States. Central Intelligence Agency. *World Factbook, 1994.* Washington: 1994.

United States. Department of State. Bureau of International Narcotics Matters. *International Narcotics Control Strategy Report.* Washington: March 1992.

United States. Department of State. Bureau of International Narcotics Matters. *International Narcotics Control Strategy Report.* Washington: April 1993.

United States. Department of State. Bureau of International Narcotics Matters. *International Narcotics Control Strategy Report.* Washington: April 1994.

United States. Department of State. Bureau of Public Affairs. *Background Notes: Laos.* (Department of State Publication No. 8874.) Washington: GPO, March 1991.

United States. Department of State. Bureau of Public Affairs. "U.S.-Lao POW/MIA Technical Meeting Concludes," *Department of State Bulletin,* January 1988, 9.

United States. Department of State. *Country Reports on Human Rights Practices for 1992.* (Report submitted to United States Congress, 103d, 1st Session, Senate, Committee on Foreign Relations, and House of Representatives, Committee on Foreign Affairs.) Washington: GPO, 1993.

United States. Department of State. *Country Reports on Human Rights Practices for 1993.* (Report submitted to United States Congress, 103d, 2d Session, House of Representatives, Committee on Foreign Affairs, and Senate, Committee on Foreign Relations.) Washington: GPO, 1994.

United States. Embassy in Vientiane. *Briefing Paper on Lao Narcotics Issues.* Washington: February 1993.

United States. Embassy in Vientiane. *Laos: 1993 World Refugee Report,* 3. Washington: February 1993.

United States. Embassy in Vientiane. *Soldiers Guide: Laos.* Washington: February 5, 1993.

Vongsavanh, Soutchay. *RLG Military Operations and Activities in the Laotian Panhandle.* (Indochina Monographs.) Washington: U.S. Army Center of Military History, 1981.

White, Peter T. "Laos," *National Geographic,* 171, No. 6, June 1987, 772–95.

Willwerth, J. "Excavating the Recent Past: Search for MIAs," *Time,* March 4, 1985, 32.

Wing, Roswell B., et al. *Case Study of U.S. Counterinsurgency Operations in Laos, 1955–1962.* McLean, Virginia: Research Analysis, 1964.

Zasloff, Joseph J. *The Three-Village Dispute Between Laos and Thailand.* (Universities Field Staff International, UFSI Reports, No. 23.) Indianapolis: 1985.

Zasloff, Joseph J. *Vietnam, Laos, and Cambodia: Implications for U.S. Policy in Southeast Asia.* (Universities Field Staff International, UFSI Reports, No. 1.) Indianapolis: 1987.

(Various issues of the following periodicals were also used in the preparation of this chapter: *Asian Defence Journal* [Kuala Lumpur], 1990–94; *Asian Survey,* 1978–94; Economist Intelligence Unit, *Country Report: Indochina: Vietnam, Laos, Cambodia* [London], 1990–94; Foreign Broadcast Information Service, *Daily Report: East Asia,* 1990–94; *Indochina Chronology,* 1982–94; *Indochina Digest,* 1991–93.)

Glossary

Asian Development Bank—Established in 1967, the bank assists in economic development and promotes growth and cooperation in developing member countries. The bank is owned by its forty-seven member governments, which include both developed and developing countries in Asia and developed countries in the West.

Association of Southeast Asian Nations (ASEAN)—Founded in 1967 primarily for economic cooperation and consisting of Brunei (since 1984), Indonesia, Malaysia, the Philippines, Singapore, and Thailand. Laos has had observer status since 1992 and applied for membership in July 1994.

ban—Village; grouped administratively into *tasseng* (*q.v.*) and *muang* (*q.v.*).

dharma—Buddhist teaching or moral law; laws of nature, all that exists, real or imaginary.

fiscal year (FY)—October 1 to September 30.

gross domestic product (GDP)—A value measure of the flow of domestic goods and services produced by an economy over a period of time, such as a year. Only output values of goods for final consumption and intermediate production are assumed to be included in the final prices. GDP is sometimes aggregated and shown at market prices, meaning that indirect taxes and subsidies are included; when these indirect taxes and subsidies have been eliminated, the result is GDP at factor cost. The word *gross* indicates that deductions for depreciation of physical assets have not been made. Income arising from investments and possessions owned abroad is not included, only domestic production. Hence, the use of the word *domestic* to distinguish GDP from gross national product (*q.v.*).

gross national product (GNP)—The gross domestic product (GDP—*q.v.*) plus net income or loss stemming from transactions with foreign countries, including income received from abroad by residents and subtracting payments remitted abroad to nonresidents. GNP is the broadest measurement of the output of goods and services by an economy. It can be calculated at market prices, which include indirect taxes and subsidies. Because indirect taxes and subsidies are only transfer payments, GNP is often calculated at

339

factor cost by removing indirect taxes and subsidies.

Hmong—Largest Lao Sung (*q.v.*) ethnic group of northern Laos. This tribal group dwells at higher elevations than other ethnic groups. During the period of the Royal Lao Government (RLG—*q.v.*), the Hmong were referred to as Meo.

International Monetary Fund (IMF)—Established on July 22, 1944, the IMF began operating along with the World Bank (*q.v.*) on December 27, 1945. The IMF is a specialized agency affiliated with the United Nations that takes responsibility for stabilizing international exchange rates and payments. The IMF's main business is the provision of loans to its members when they experience balance of payments difficulties. These loans often carry conditions that require substantial internal economic adjustments by the recipients. In 1994 the IMF had 179 members.

karma—Buddhist concept of the sum of one's past actions, which affect one's current life and future reincarnations.

khoueng—Province; first-order administrative division.

kip(K)—Lao currency. In June 1994, US$1=K721.

Lao Issara (Free Laos)—Movement formed in 1945 to resist any attempt to return to French colonial status.

Lao Loum—Literally translated as the valley Laotian. Inclusive term for people of Tai stock living in Laos, including lowland Lao and upland Tai. Group of lowland peoples comprising the majority population of Laos; generally used to refer to ethnic Lao, the country's dominant ethnic group (approximately 66 percent of the population according to the 1985 census), and speaking Tai-Kadai languages, including Lao, Lue, Tai Dam (Black Tai), and Tai Deng (Red Tai).

Lao Patriotic Front (LPF) (Neo Lao Hak Xat)—Successor to Neo Lao Issara (*q.v.*), the political arm of the Pathet Lao (*q.v.*) during the Indochina Wars (1946–75). The Lao People's Liberation Army (*q.v.*) is its military arm.

Lao People's Army—Formed in 1976 when the Lao People's Liberation Army (LPLA—*q.v.*) was restructured after the establishment of the Lao People's Democratic Republic in December 1975.

Lao People's Liberation Army (LPLA)—Official title of Pathet Lao armed forces, more commonly known as the communist revolutionaries, or guerrilla forces. The LPLA originated with the Latsavong detachment, formed in January

1949 by Kaysone Phomvihan, and steadily increased in number to an estimated 8,000 guerrillas in 1960 and an estimated 48,000 troops between 1962 and 1970.

Lao People's Revolutionary Party (LPRP) (Phak Pasason Pati-vat Lao)—Founded secretly in 1955 as the Phak Pasason Lao (Lao People's Party—LPP); name changed in 1972. Seized full power and became the ruling party of Laos in 1975. The LPRP Central Committee formulates party policy; it is dominated by the Political Bureau (Politburo) and the Secretariat and maintains control by placing its members in key institutions throughout the government and the army.

Lao Sung—Literally translated as the Laotian of the mountain top—those who traditionally live in the high altitudes in northern Laos. In official use, term denotes a category of ethnic groups that speak Tibeto-Burmese, Miao-Yao languages; chiefly the Hmong (*q.v.*) group of highland or upland minorities but also the Mien (Yao) and Akha. According to the 1985 census, these groups make up approximately 10 percent of the population.

Lao Theung—Literally, Laotian of the mountain slopes; group—including Kammu, Loven, and Lamet—that traditionally lives in medium altitudes, practices swidden, or slash-and-burn agriculture, and speaks Mon-Khmer languages and dialects. According to the 1985 census, approximately 24 percent of the population. Regarded as original inhabitants of Laos, formally referred to by ethnic Lao as *kha*, or slave.

mandala—Indian geopolitical term referring to a variable circle of power centered on a ruler, his palace, and the religious center from which he drew his legitimacy.

muang (*muong*)—Administrative district; also an independent principality; comprises several *tasseng* (*q.v.*), second-order administrative divisions.

Neo Lao Issara (Free Laos Front)—Organization established by former Lao Issara (Free Laos) (*q.v.*) to continue anti-French resistance movement with the Viet Minh (*q.v.*); succeeded by Neo Lao Hak Xat (Lao Patriotic Front—LPF) (*q.v.*) in 1956.

net material product—Gross material output minus depreciation on capital and excluding "unproductive services." According to the World Bank (*q.v.*), net material product is "a socialist concept of national accounts."

Nonaligned Movement—Established in September 1961 with the aim of promoting political and military cooperation apart from the traditional East and West blocs. As of 1994, there were 107 members (plus the Palestine Liberation Organization), twenty-one observers, and twenty-one "guests."

Pathet Lao (Lao Nation)—Literally, land of the Lao. Until October 1965, the name for the Lao People's Liberation Army (*q.v.*), the military arm of the Lao Patriotic Front (*q.v.*).

Royal Lao Government (RLG)—The ruling authority in Laos from 1947 until the communist seizure of power in December 1975 and the proclamation of the Lao People's Democratic Republic.

Sipsong Panna—Region in southern Yunnan Province, China, from which migrated many groups that now inhabit Laos.

Southeast Asia Treaty Organization (SEATO)—Established in September 1954 as a result of the 1954 Geneva Agreements to stop the spread of communism in Southeast Asia. SEATO never had an active military role and was ultimately disbanded in June 1977 following the success of the communist movements in Cambodia, Laos, and Vietnam in 1975. Original signatories to SEATO were Australia, Britain, France, New Zealand, Pakistan, the Philippines, Thailand, and the United States.

tasseng—Administrative unit; territorial subdivision of *muang* (*q.v.*), subdistrict grouping of ten to twenty villages.

That Luang—Most sacred Buddhist stupa in Vientiane and site of annual festival on the full moon of the twelfth month.

Theravada Buddhism—Predominant branch of Buddhism practiced in Laos, Cambodia, Sri Lanka, and Thailand.

United Nations Children's Fund (UNICEF)—Acronym retained from predecessor organization, United Nations International Children's Emergency Fund, established in December 1946. Provides funds for establishing child health and welfare services.

United Nations Development Programme (UNDP)—Created by the United Nations in 1965, the UNDP is the world's largest channel for multilateral technical and preinvestment assistance to low-income countries. It functions as an overall programming, financing, and monitoring agency. The actual fieldwork is done by other United Nations agencies.

United Nations High Commissioner for Refugees (UNHCR)—
Established by the United Nations in 1949, it did not
become effective until 1951. The first world institution to
aid refugees, the UNHCR seeks to ensure the humanitarian treatment of refugees and find a permanent solution
to refugee problems. The agency deals with the international protection of refugees and problems arising from
mass movements of people forced to seek refuge.

Viet Minh—Coalition of Vietnamese national elements formed
in May 1941 and dominated by the communists in their
movement calling for an uprising against the French colonial government.

World Bank—Informal name used to designate a group of four
affiliated international institutions: the International Bank
for Reconstruction and Development (IBRD), the International Development Association (IDA), the International
Finance Corporation (IFC), and the Multilateral Investment Guarantee Agency (MIGA). The IBRD, established
in 1945, has as its primary purpose the provision of loans
at market-related rates of interest to developing countries
at more advanced stages of development. The IDA, a
legally separate loan fund but administered by the staff of
the IBRD, was set up in 1960 to furnish credits to the poorest developing countries on much easier terms than those
of conventional IBRD loans. The IFC, founded in 1956,
supplements the activities of the IBRD through loans and
assistance designed specifically to encourage the growth of
productive private enterprises in the less developed countries. The MIGA, founded in 1988, insures private foreign
investment in developing countries against various noncommercial risk. The president and certain senior officers
of the IBRD hold the same positions in the IFC. The four
institutions are owned by the governments of the countries
that subscribe their capital. To participate in the World
Bank group, member states must first belong to the Inten-
tional Monetary Fund (IMF—*q.v.*).

Index

50; popular support for, 48, 110; power seized by, 3, 66–67, 270; propaganda by, 58; publications of, 238; religion under, 128–29; in Royal Lao Army, 38, 39, 42–43, 266; schools, 133; villages controlled by, 48, 55–56, 67, 105, 270

Patriotic Neutralists, 57

Pavie, Auguste, 3, 16

Paxa Sangkhom. *See* Social Party

Peace Convention Between France and Thailand (1941), 20

Peace Party (Santiphab), 40

PEO. *See* United States Programs Evaluation Office

People's Committee, 27

Phak Pasason Lao. *See* Lao People's Party

Phak Seli. *See* Independent Party

Phak Xat Kao Na. *See* National Progressive Party

Pham Van Dong, 36

pharmaceuticals, xli, 142

Phaya Khammao. *See* Xieng Mao

Pheng Phongsavan, 54, 61, 69

Phetsarath, Prince, 21, 22, 23, 24–26, 31, 39, 44

phi. See spirits

Phone Chantaraj, 63

Phôngsali Province: economy of, 151; Pathet Lao in, xxx

Phoui Sananikone: in elections of 1951, 34; at Geneva Conference (1954), 34, 56; government of, 42

Phoumi Nosavan, 26, 44–45, 46, 47, 59; anticommunist offensive under, xxxi, 50, 54; death of, 279; in elections of 1951, 34; in elections of 1960, 44–45; lack of support for, 49–51, 56; military support for, 267; in Phoui government, 42

Phoumi Vongvichit, 27, 51, 61; arrested, 43; in coalition government, 40; death of, xli; at Geneva Conference (1961–62), 56; in Pathet Lao government, 32; retirement of, 211

Phoun Sipaseut, xli, 43, 211, 218

Phu Noi people, 110

Phu Tai people, 95

Pibul Songkram, 20

PIP. *See* Public Investment Programme

Plain of Jars, 82

Po, Prince, 14

Poland: in International Control Commission, 35, 269; trade with, 189

police, national, xl, 263, 287–88; anti-smuggling unit, 292; counternarcotics unit, 113; informants, 289

Politburo (Political Bureau), xxxvi; decision making in, 211; Khamtai in, 218; members of, 68, 207, 211, 224

Political Bureau. *See* Politburo

political demonstrations: after coup of 1960, 45–46; procommunist, 66–67, 270

political reeducation. *See* seminar camps

political unrest: under French rule, 19, 21, 24

polygyny, 98, 108, 116

population, xxxii, 86–94, 153, 213, 261; density, xxxiii, 79, 86–87; displacement of, 60, 121; ethnic distribution in, 87, 88, 95; of Hmong, 110, 111, 282; of Hô, 110; of Kammu, 104; of Lao Loum, 87, 95; of Lao Sung, 88; of Lao Theung, 104; of Louangphrabang, 93, 121; of Pakxé, 93, 121; rural, xxxiii, 93–94; of Savannakhét, 93, 121; urban, 93, 94, 121; of Vientiane, 93, 120; in villages, xxxiii, 93

population statistics: birth rate, 86, 87; child mortality rate, xxxiii, 81, 87, 137–38; death rate, 86; fertility rate, 86; growth rate, xxxii–xxxiii, 81, 86, 121; infant mortality rate, xxxiii, 81, 87, 137–38; life expectancy, xxxiii, 81, 137

postal service, 173

POW/MIA issues, xxxix, 253, 286, 287, 294; origins of, 63–65

POWs. *See* prisoners of war

Praxathipatay. *See* Democratic Party

president (*see also* executive branch), 228–29

press (*See* media; newspapers)

prices, 162, 184–86, 187

prime minister (*see also* executive branch), 229

prison camps: conditions in, 63, 290, 291–92

prisoners, political, xxxvii, 233, 290–91

prisoners of war (POWs) (*see also* POW/MIA issues), xxxix, 286–87, 294; demands for release of, 64; schedule for release of, 63, 64

Contributors

Nicholas C. Auclair is a senior Asian military/political analyst with the Department of Defense, Washington, D.C.

MacAlister Brown is Fairleigh S. Dickinson, Jr., Professor of Political Science, Williams College, Williamstown, Massachusetts.

Arthur J. Dommen is Senior Associate, the Indochina Institute, George Mason University, Fairfax, Virginia.

Joel M. Halpern is Professor Emeritus of Anthropology at the University of Massachusetts, Amherst.

Susannah Hopkins is a development consultant based in Vietnam, who works for multinational and nongovernmental organizations.

W. Randall Ireson is a rural sociologist and independent development consultant based in Salem, Oregon.

Andrea Matles Savada is Supervisor, Asia/West Europe Unit, Federal Research Division, Library of Congress, Washington, D.C.

Joseph J. Zasloff is Professor of Political Science at the University of Pittsburgh, Pittsburgh, Pennsylvania.

Published Country Studies

(Area Handbook Series)

550–65	Afghanistan	550–52	Ecuador
550–98	Albania	550–43	Egypt
550–44	Algeria	550–150	El Salvador
550–59	Angola	550–28	Ethiopia
550–73	Argentina	550–167	Finland
550–111	Armenia, Azerbaijan, and Georgia	550–173	Germany, East
550–169	Australia	550–155	Germany, Fed. Rep. of
550–176	Austria	550–153	Ghana
550–175	Bangladesh	550–87	Greece
550–170	Belgium	550–78	Guatemala
550–66	Bolivia	550–174	Guinea
550–20	Brazil	550–82	Guyana and Belize
550–168	Bulgaria	550–151	Honduras
550–61	Burma	550–165	Hungary
550–50	Cambodia	550–21	India
550–166	Cameroon	550–154	Indian Ocean
550–159	Chad	550–39	Indonesia
550–77	Chile	550–68	Iran
550–60	China	550–31	Iraq
550–26	Colombia	550–25	Israel
550–33	Commonwealth Caribbean, Islands of the	550–182	Italy
550–91	Congo	550–30	Japan
550–90	Costa Rica	550–34	Jordan
550–69	Côte d'Ivoire (Ivory Coast)	550–56	Kenya
550–152	Cuba	550–81	Korea, North
550–22	Cyprus	550–41	Korea, South
550–158	Czechoslovakia	550–58	Laos
550–36	Dominican Republic and Haiti	550–24	Lebanon

550–38	Liberia	550–180	Sierra Leone
550–85	Libya	550–184	Singapore
550–172	Malawi	550–86	Somalia
550–45	Malaysia	550–93	South Africa
550–161	Mauritania	550–95	Soviet Union
550–79	Mexico	550–179	Spain
550–76	Mongolia	550–96	Sri Lanka
550–49	Morocco	550–27	Sudan
550–64	Mozambique	550–47	Syria
550–35	Nepal and Bhutan	550–62	Tanzania
550–88	Nicaragua	550–53	Thailand
550–157	Nigeria	550–89	Tunisia
550–94	Oceania	550–80	Turkey
550–48	Pakistan	550–74	Uganda
550–46	Panama	550–97	Uruguay
550–156	Paraguay	550–71	Venezuela
550–185	Persian Gulf States	550–32	Vietnam
550–42	Peru	550–183	Yemens, The
550–72	Philippines	550–99	Yugoslavia
550–162	Poland	550–67	Zaire
550–181	Portugal	550–75	Zambia
550–160	Romania	550–171	Zimbabwe
550–37	Rwanda and Burundi		
550–51	Saudi Arabia		
550–70	Senegal